Immigrants and Boomers

Immigrants and Boomers

Forging a New Social Contract
for the Future of America

Dowell Myers

Russell Sage Foundation, New York

The Russell Sage Foundation

The Russell Sage Foundation, one of the oldest of America's general purpose foundations, was established in 1907 by Mrs. Margaret Olivia Sage for "the improvement of social and living conditions in the United States." The Foundation seeks to fulfill this mandate by fostering the development and dissemination of knowledge about the country's political, social, and economic problems. While the Foundation endeavors to assure the accuracy and objectivity of each book it publishes, the conclusions and interpretations in Russell Sage Foundation publications are those of the authors and not of the Foundation, its Trustees, or its staff. Publication by Russell Sage, therefore, does not imply Foundation endorsement.

Library of Congress Cataloging-in-Publication Data
Myers, Dowell.
   Immigrants and boomers : forging a new social contract for the future of America /
   Dowell Myers.
     p. cm.
   Includes bibliographical references and index.
   ISBN-13: 978-0-87154-636-4
   ISBN-10: 0-87154-636-1
   1. United States—Emigration and immigration—Economic aspects. 2. United
States—Emigration and immigration—Social aspects. 3. Immigrants—Government policy—United States. 4. Demographic transition—Economic aspects—United States. 5.
United States—Population—Economic aspects. 6. Age distribution
(Demography)—Economic aspects—United States. I. Title.
   JV6471.M94 2007
   304.8'73—dc22   2006033289

The paper used in this publication meets the minimum requirements of American National Standard for Information Sciences—Permanence of Paper for Printed Library Materials. ANSI Z39.48-1992.

Text design by Genna Patacsil.

RUSSELL SAGE FOUNDATION
112 East 64th Street, New York, New York 10021
10 9 8 7 6 5 4 3 2

For my mother, Ruth Dowell Myers,
and my sons, Ben and Jesse

Contents

About the Author

Dowell Myers is professor in the School of Policy, Planning, and Development at the University of Southern California.

Preface and Acknowledgments

THIS BOOK is a river of discovery formed of many tributaries, each of which began in response to different contexts and motivations, and all later merging together far down course. My research on immigration first flourished in the early 1990s as so many of us tried to make sense of the new changes appearing in California and the United States. Never an advocate for or against immigrants, I merely sought to describe and explain the enormous changes facing urban planners and policymakers in the Los Angeles region. What was this new dynamic of change and where was it leading?

That question is not a casual curiosity for planners and demographers. Members of these professions to which I belong are fascinated by the rich dynamics of change, and we are very serious about tracking those trajectories so that we can plan ahead to make the best life possible for all the residents. And, in the American way, we compete to see who understands the situation earliest and who can explain it best. It is a difficult game when the final score will not be known until long in the future. But such acute attention to foresight is crucial if we are to guide a more effective outcome.

It rapidly became apparent that my reading of the data led to a very different story than was read by many of my peers, certainly different from what was commonly heard in public debates. It may have been obvious to all that abrupt changes were underway, but did this foretell a grim and desperate story of doomed fortunes, either for the newcomer immigrants themselves or the host society that was severely strained by permanent new disadvantages? The hazards of change are not to be discounted, and there is ample justification for deep concern, but why would we want to overlook the evidence showing positive signs of dramatic upward mobility hidden amid the seeming chaos of change? The age-old choice between a problem viewed as a glass half empty or half full may have merely found its newest expression. Certainly, if problems like poverty and declining homeownership were increasing in severity, it could make sense to describe the problem as a glass growing ever emptier. On the other hand, the newfound evidence of movement into homeownership and rising economic fortunes was beginning to reveal great promise among the immigrants: the glass half full was growing ever fuller. Nonetheless, most scholars and commentators remained locked in the old perspective and focused on the rapid increase in deficiencies that, if extrapolated forward, foretold our ruin. Only a handful of other scholars and commentators seemed to voice the more optimistic interpretation.

Of good fortune for the outcome in this book, some of the observers in the majority who so emphasized the negative outlook were my own good friends and learned colleagues. As a result I was never so sheltered as to believe the kinds of blunt explanations often used to characterize opposing viewpoints in our current political discourse, namely the accusations of moral failings, devious conspiracy, profiteering or plain stupidity. A large majority of those with opposing viewpoints I knew to be good people and highly intelligent. It may be surprising to some that in our society it is valid to find just a plain difference of opinion. In fact, that difference should be embraced, not rejected or ignored. Of some irony, the very fact of the differences in outlook holds the key to understanding our commonality. Taking this seriously forced me to discover what it was that led so many observers to choose what I considered the wrong interpretation or, alternatively, as I also feared, why it was that I was so naïve and gullible. Surely the resolution between these competing viewpoints of hope and despair would shed considerable light, if only we had the temerity and patience for the endeavor.

Long before I entered the fray over immigration, I had begun my career with a focus on the baby boom generation. Prior to the resurgence of immigration, the baby boom was the largest and most dramatic demographic event in America. As this generation of more than 70 million passed through the life cycle, their arrival at new life stages was a rolling tsunami that first rocked the schools, then flooded the labor market, and next drove up house prices and triggered waves of gentrification. For my whole life, urban planners and their kin have been scrambling to keep ahead of this onslaught. I knew all this too well because I am myself a card-carrying member of the giant generation. I got past the double-sessioned grade school with all the portable classrooms, and I managed to survive the crises of employment competition and the housing squeeze in my early adult years. For me these became professional concerns as well as private endeavors. Never, however, had I enjoyed thinking too far ahead about the future elderly of the baby boom generation. Not only was that much aging difficult for a young man to comprehend, but it was also a little frightening to contemplate the mass impacts when the baby boom tsunami finally swept out of this long middle period of life to which our economy and institutions had grown so attuned. The departure from one stage and arrival at another so very different would surely be shocking once again. And this time was nearly upon us.

Only a handful of years ago did these two great currents of discovery—the future of the new immigration and the future of the baby boomers—come together in my mind. Time was passing, and more than just immigrant history was evolving. All the present-day voters and workers were surely growing older and in twenty years would occupy such different life stations. It was a key step in this book's creation when I began to imagine who would help fill the void behind our aging adults and how the boomers and immigrants might share a rendezvous with destiny.

At about this time yet another tributary to this work sprung forth, this time formed out of personal disgust for the polarization and growing social and political fragmentation that was tearing fissures in America: "Enough of this stuff!" We deserve so much better for one another and ourselves. Although I am hardly the sort to ever be labeled a political activist—I am a committed voter who scrutinizes a ballot and that's about it—it was strange to feel this new tingling that must be what they call a political awakening.

If this book has any political agenda it is simply this: rather than charge to the defense of one of the many different factions, staking a firm position on the left or the right, I felt compelled to rush to the middle, planting my flag in the place of commonality where it seemed many neglected interests overlapped. My awakening was to reassert the common bonds so ignored and belittled by the harshest advocates. Suddenly it appeared: we really are tied together by common values, common needs—things long taken for granted and now failing for our lack of nourishment. And, in one of the great ironies of this age, the lessons about this rediscovered commonality flow from our responses to the immigrant newcomers. Americans are being challenged to reflect anew on what it means to be an American, what it means to be a taxpayer, and why any of us should be a beneficiary of the public sector. This is a story about seniority and respect for all generations of Americans, about rewards for past contributions, and about responsibilities to the future that lies just over the horizon, barely several years away.

The momentum behind this book began with a study of several specific issues but it took on impetus when I discovered my audience. We met face to face in university lecture halls, public meeting rooms, conferences, and community workshops. A new phase of my learning commenced once I began to convey my research before public audiences. I suspect there are two stages of becoming an expert. The first is when you conduct a study of the facts in some topic area and simply present yourself as an expert. But the major stage of expertness begins after appearance before the public. People start tossing all sorts of surprising ideas at this person who declares him or herself the expert. Audience members are unrestrained in their curiosity, often posing very reasonable questions and challenges that were not part of the expert's original research design. So much for science, and welcome to common sense. If you listen enough to the public's ideas, and absorb them, you become much more of an expert. Reporters have the same effect. I cannot count the number of times that a supposed interview about what I knew on a subject would cause me to put two and two together in new ways. It is quite humbling to agree to answer a few questions and upon hanging up the phone realize that I had learned more than I knew before the interview. Some news writers were quite demanding and would not settle for soft, fuzzy, or polite answers. I had to figure out better ways of explaining complex changes in society, distilling the core themes in a more meaningful and direct articulation. So great is my debt to this public interaction, that my first acknowledgment and expression of gratitude must be to all those who pressed me to put together the larger story that has finally emerged in this book.

Throughout my investigations of the last decade, I have been honored to hold a position as professor and research group director in the School of Policy, Planning, and Development at the University of Southern California. Los Angeles has certainly provided an unparalleled laboratory for observing immigration at work, surrounding me with colleagues and neighbors of all ethnicities, and allowing me to hear immigrant sagas and see diverse communities first hand. Perhaps I was destined for this investigation, because I was born in Miami before Castro spurred the great wave of Cuban immigration. And before my time in California, I spent another decade living and working in New York and Texas, two other centers of immigration in America. That is history. This book is about a detailed future with many parts played by those already living here and some new ones yet to arrive. Should anyone wonder where the strong future orientation of this book stems from, I would only note my background in theory of urban planning. That field's interest in long-range planning has converged in this book with the demographer's emphasis on generational progression that I have also adopted. The two fields, fertile unto themselves, create a rich interplay that emphasizes how society changes over time and how it can be made better through the application of foresight and explanation shared with the public.

The concentrated attention needed to write this book was afforded by a faculty sabbatical generously provided by the University of Southern California. That writing drew upon numerous research projects completed over the last decade. Among the most important was a project only dreamed and not completed. As part of an Urban Initiative launched at USC after 2001, a number of faculty members met to discuss and design a project on Wellbeing 2025, a multifaceted study that would link many disciplines in pursuit of a common goal. Ultimately, this project grew too large in scope and failed of its own weight, but a number of preliminary investigations were initiated. In particular, the important study of the California turnaround was supported through the Urban Initiative. Overall, the inspirations from this dialogue at USC have not been lost and many are embedded in chapters that follow.

The ideas in the book are most deeply rooted in a series of studies funded by the major research foundation in Los Angeles, the John Randolph Haynes and Dora Haynes Foundation. Founded eighty years ago, the Haynes Foundation's mission is to fund social science research related to public problems emerging in the Los Angeles context. Thankfully, early on the foundation's trustees saw that immigrant advancement was an important topic worthy of support. I am especially grateful for this problem-initiated support that later fostered a number of scientific innovations and achievements.

The Fannie Mae Foundation of Washington, D.C., was also instrumental in providing support for my series of studies on homeownership. James Carr, Patrick Simmons, and others at the Foundation know well the importance of homeownership to immigrants as part of the American Dream. Fannie Mae also has supported my public outreach and speaking as part of the California Housing Futures project. More recently, a grant from the National Institute of Child Health and Human Development (RO1 HD048910) has enabled me to concentrate intensely on the measurement of immigrant assimilation across many different outcome indicators.

Also expressed in the present book is an application of the California Demographic Futures database that was developed with funding from the USC Urban Initiative, through a transdisciplinary tobacco research project, headed by C. Anderson Johnson, that was supported by the National Cancer Institute, and other sources. These unique projections were prepared under the leadership of John Pitkin, a senior research associate at USC, and also president of Analysis and Forecasting, Inc., in Cambridge, Massachusetts. John is a longtime research collaborator who combines the skills of an economist, demographer, and forecaster in ways unmatched in the United States. His development of the California Demographic Futures projection model over the last decade is a key innovation that enables more informed planning for a rapidly evolving population composed of immigrants, their children, and many other groups. The insights to be gained by drawing on these data are hopefully made apparent in various sections of this book. John's advice on broader issues of immigrant behavior and political reactions were also invaluable in the course of developing the book. John read the full manuscript, and the book gained immensely from his criticism of both technical issues and general exposition.

My effort to squeeze insights about the future from present observations relied heavily on a number of data sets of reliably high quality. Crucial to my work were the demographic forecasts prepared by the Demographic Research Unit of the California Department of Finance. And most of us take for granted the enormous wealth of data supplied by the U.S. Census Bureau—the censuses, monthly or annual surveys, and periodic projections. The gold standard against which most other data investigations are benchmarked, the Census Bureau's offerings are truly the foundation for the current study. Gratitude is expressed to the taxpayers for supporting this beacon of intelligence in an otherwise uncertain world. Also indispensable were the Statewide Survey opinion polls conducted by the Public Policy Institute of California (PPIC) under Mark Baldasarre's leadership. These surveys on selected focus topics afford an unusually rich resource for understanding the interplay of demographics and political opinion. Thanks go to PPIC and their principal partners—the James Irvine Foundation, Hewlett Foundation and others—for making these surveys freely available to researchers.

Much of the background research relied upon in writing the book was carried out by the capable staff in the Population Dynamics Research Group that I head at USC. Their assistance was essential in helping me pursue the writing of this book in and amongst our many other tasks. Julie Park, associate director of the group, was an indispensable leader, serving both as sounding board at numerous points in the research and writing, and also holding the fort while I retreated during my sabbatical. Without her stabilizing force and broad-minded judgment, I could not have sustained such an extensive writing process.

I have benefited also from assistance by a remarkable group of graduate students, each of whom has contributed a mark on this book. Xin Gao and Cathy Liu helped substantially with my analysis of the demographic transition. Sung Ho Ryu was my principal assistant in the housing analysis and helped in many other ways. Seong Hee Min executed the data analysis of the opinion polls and assisted with labor force and political projections. Stephanie Nawyn was instrumental in the early research related to the social contract, and Pria Hidisyan assisted with key indicators research.

The scope of this book has required advice from a wide array of experts. I have benefited from the insightful reviews by the anonymous reviewers recruited by the press, as well as from the thorough readings of my manuscript provided by Shelley Lapkoff, Peter Morrison, and John Pitkin. Each of them helped forge the separate chapters into a more coherent overall story. Commenting on particular chapters were Steve Levy, Estela Bensimon, Patricia Gandara, Larry Picus, Janelle Wong, Harry Pachon, Julie Park, Kevin Starr, Phil Ethington, David Sloane, Michael Moody, Vern Bengston, Walter Zelman, Richard Little, Bill Baer, Patrick Simmons, Hans Johnson, Richard Alba, Clara Irazabal, Tamar Jacoby, Zhou Yu, Dan Mazmanian, and Niraj Verma. I truly appreciate these readings, the insights offered, and their encouragement. I would be remiss in not acknowledging also the special influence of Jim Throgmorton in helping me to tell the story.

Suzanne Nichols at the Russell Sage Foundation was especially helpful and encouraging in bringing this book to life. I also appreciate the assistance of David Haproff and Genna Patacsil in guiding the book to its final form and successful launch.

I have no more important supporter in this project than my wife, Sue. Always a source of counsel, on countless occasions she provided helpful responses to the anxious question, "How does this sound?" She has shown great patience—more than I should have ever dared to expect—despite the constant intrusion of my writing into our private time together. But for her understanding and encouragement in this great endeavor, this work would have failed long before completion. Sharing this project with her has meant a deeper satisfaction than I can express.

It is only fitting that this book is dedicated to my mother and two sons. My mom is of the generation that brought forth the baby boomers and she is emblematic of the strong women in the World War II generation. What I owe her is a personal gratitude for all that she has done and for which I can never fully repay. My two sons, Ben and Jesse, will inherit this future we are creating, and their mother and I can only strive to prepare them for the tall task ahead. If this book could help make their future a more livable one, I would feel a great satisfaction. This is my hope.

Dowell Myers

Chapter 1

Introduction

THE DEBATE over immigration has generated much more political heat than light. That should not be surprising, given the sensitive issues and deep commitments at play. Even though a few advocates are very sure of their clear-cut positions, most Americans are in a quandary over immigration because they see it as a complex and conflicting subject. On the one hand, most citizens revere the nation's immigrant roots—after all, most of us are descendants of immigrants. Yet, on the other hand, most citizens also value social order and think that access to our nation should not be granted without limit. In addition, both businesses and consumers have economic reasons to welcome hardworking cheap labor, but at the same time many citizens fear a growing poor population that is dependent on taxpayer-funded services.

Our greatest worry about immigration is what it means for the future of the nation and our local communities. Will admitting so many immigrant newcomers put us in danger of losing our country as we know it? How rapidly will new immigrants fit into our culture and economy? This is a key question for our future, especially as it concerns Latinos, most of whom are extremely disadvantaged when they first arrive. Most pointedly, many of us worry about whether the pace of immigrant incorporation into our society can keep up with the surging numbers of new arrivals. Could the nation be swamped by a rising tide that it cannot absorb? And how does this all square with our other problems like a rapidly aging population and our mounting budget deficits?

In the face of accelerating immigration, it is understandable that many Americans would express despair for the future, which can look overwhelming. At the same time, other voices claim that all will be fine and advise citizens not to worry. Some immigrant advocates, more aggressively, accuse the worriers of being selfish and even racist for expressing such concerns about the future.

What is a citizen to do? Surely anyone should be allowed to voice some fear about the impact of immigration on the future of the country he or she loves without categorically being labeled a racist. And certainly there must be some grounds for hope about that future—but what are those grounds, and how much can they be believed? What makes this difficult to know is that immigration trends have been changing rapidly in recent decades, and some effects are much delayed from the past. Lacking good information, we all have a tendency to exaggerate our perceptions and portray the extremes. In both public and private discourse, there seems to be no in-between. Indeed, the observant comedian Jerry Seinfeld has a routine that highlights how simplistically our many judgments of the world are divided into "it sucks, it's great!" Some of our exaggerated views are based on old information blown up into a perceived future of despair. But other information can be newly crafted into a future of greater promise and hope. In this book, I treat both versions of the future seriously, detailing them for public consideration in the hope that, armed with better information, citizens can decide more thoughtfully which view better expresses their own stand on the immigration issue.

This book is for the citizen-voters and taxpayers of the United States, who have a right to demand usable information that provides a realistic guide to the future of their country. It is crucial that America have an enlightened citizenry because—let's be direct—we are the ones who hold the power to remake our society. Not only are we the voters who are the ultimate decision-makers, but we are also the taxpayers who will be asked to fund any necessary improvements. Only citizens can bring about a better future, but there is some strategic information that must be made part of the solutions we put in place.

The citizens' current knowledge may not be sufficient for the wise leadership they desire, but it is an essential starting point. Much of what citizens know is popular knowledge, drawn from impressions, expectations, local stories, and political claims. Even if much of this knowledge is received wisdom from the past, and thus inherently outdated by new trends, it remains a relevant benchmark. For enhanced credibility among the citizenry, my responsibility is to show how the new knowledge shared in this book relates to existing citizen beliefs.

The future has suffered particular neglect at the hands of scholars because it lies outside their data, which are necessarily historical. Yet the future is what citizens care most about, and for lack of much expert assistance they have merely filled in the blanks to the best of their colorful imaginations. In chapters to follow I show how existing and new forecasts of a few key details can be interwoven with other facts to create much more useful descriptions of the future. Some clear alternatives can be laid out for citizen consideration. Within this future-oriented framework, my aim is to share my evidence and that of other experts in an open fashion that can aid citizen decisionmaking. The ultimate goal is to bridge between the popular and expert bodies of knowledge about immigration and immigrant advancement so that we might increase the wisdom of both the public and the experts.

More than just immigrants are changing in the future, and a broader context is needed for a realistic assessment. Most surprising to the public could be new knowledge about the coming partnership of immigrants and baby boomers. The progress of the giant baby boom generation through its life cycle has long held our interest. Although it is not surprising that much of the future is about that aging population, how many have yet considered that the boomers' future could be intimately tied to the immigrant population? Some basic demographic insights provide a startling picture of new connections unfolding in the future. In short, when the baby boomers retire, who will replace them? Who will pay the taxes to support their much deserved retirement benefits? And who will pay them a good price for their homes? New knowledge of these coming events should command all our attention.

Viewing the Future Through the California Window

For those seeking foresight, it helps to explore early prototypes of the coming future. Providing such a window on the future of an American nation composed of immigrants and the U.S.-born is the state of California, which represents the vanguard of demographic changes in America and, in some respects, the world. The takeoff of immigration after 1965 was concentrated at first in California, where the foreign-born share of the population leaped from 8.8 percent to 21.7 percent between 1970 and 1990 before beginning to grow more slowly. In comparison, the nation's foreign-born share remained at 7.9 percent in 1990, only accelerating thereafter. Much can be gained by examining how California's immigrants fared in this early period and the improvement in their circumstances after they had been settled there for two decades. In turn, this analysis of the dynamics of change can be used to project immigrant circumstances forward to 2010 and 2030 and shed new light on the implications for the nation's future. In other words, through the window of California we can gain an early look into the future and see the changes experienced by both long-settled immigrants and their fellow citizens.

Today in California the central questions in the immigration issue have shifted. Back in 1990 immigration was on the upsurge, and California was home to an estimated 45 percent of all unauthorized immigrants in the nation. (Today it is estimated that 24 percent or fewer live in California.) The presence of this large unauthorized immigrant population led California voters in 1994 to pass Proposition 187, which would have restricted access to public services by unauthorized immigrants if it had not been overturned in the courts. Today, however, the debate in California is less about blocking illegal immigration and controlling the border; instead, it has moved on to a new question: what is to be done about the challenges posed by the state's increasingly large population of settled immigrants? Is California doomed to rising poverty, a deskilling of its workforce, and social decline? The balance of evidence is now tipping in a more favorable direction, although the fate of the state still teeters. Slowly and grudgingly, the state's citizens and leaders are recognizing that this new population will play a key role in shaping the quality of the future of all Californians. Indeed, California has arrived at a newer and unproven stage in its incorporation of immigrants. How the state weathers its new challenges is an early test of the nation's eventual social and economic success in the twenty-first century.

Other states and even many nations are moving along similar paths toward an increasingly diverse ethnic mix and a growing immigrant population. For some states this is a new phenomenon, and they have much to learn from viewing the struggle of the conflicted citizenry in California. An earlier generation—predominantly white and now aging—is being replaced by a new generation comprising immigrants and their children, who are a mix of U.S.-born young of all ethnicities. A destabilizing factor in this transformation is the substantial electoral gap that has opened up as demographic change races ahead of political participation. The white non-Hispanic population has fallen below 45 percent of the state's residents (and is nearing 30 percent of public school children) but retains a two-thirds majority at the polls. A projection offered here suggests that this electoral dominance by a minority will continue for many years, at least through 2024 or 2031.[1] In the meantime, California voters are making many decisions that will determine the quality of life and apportion economic burdens in a future that will be inherited largely by members of other ethnic groups who are not white.

Throughout the developed world, especially in Europe and North America but also in Australia and East Asia, the unfolding of a historic demographic transition is bringing many nations to a similar crossroads. This transition features surging international migration that injects greater cultural diversity into societies with falling birthrates, shrinking pools of young workers, and the growing burden of an aging population. Europe may lead the world in falling birthrates and aging populations, but the United States has its own urgent problems looming from the retirement of the giant baby boom generation. Meanwhile, California leads all other states with its 27 percent foreign-born share in the population, a share that is higher than in any nation in the world of comparable or larger size. The history of California and the United States is replete with the friction of racial and ethnic strife, but through it all, Americans have demonstrated a remarkable ability to incorporate immigrants of diverse origins. How many other nations can boast of homeownership being achieved by more than 50 percent of their poorest immigrants after just twenty years of residence?[2] Yet all is not well in California, and the state's unfinished transformation holds crucial lessons about what works in incorporating immigrants and what does not, and about how other states and nations can negotiate their own path through the difficult transitions brought about by major immigrant movements.

How Much Should We Welcome Immigrants?

Many residents of California and the United States have mixed feelings about whether immigrants are a benefit or a burden, and when asked to make a choice, they are almost evenly divided. A 2005 Gallup poll found that 44 percent of U.S. adults feel that immigrants cost taxpayers too much by using government services rather than eventually becoming productive citizens and paying their fair share of taxes.[3] A more detailed survey in 2004 by the Public Policy Institute of California found that a substantial share of California's majority-white voters feel that immigrants are more of a burden than a benefit, with opinions varying by political leaning: 61.9 percent of conservatives share this sentiment, as do 45.3 percent of moderates, but only 28.5 percent of liberals.[4]

Complex values and assumptions are wrapped up in this assessment of burden and benefit. At root lie some basic questions: Do we owe immigrants anything? Do they owe us? What is the price of their inclusion? The answers reached in this book to these rather blunt questions are multifaceted, but they can be reduced to the following. The nation needs immigrants to fill our needs, not simply in today's world, where most citizens and experts have looked for their answers, but especially in tomorrow's. They are an integral part of our demographic transition because the trend of lower fertility is pulling down our labor force growth at the same time that we are about to face a tidal wave of increase in our retired senior population. Supporting our retirees is widely expected to place tremendous strain on the budgets of federal and state governments, and larger contributions will be required from an invigorated new corps of middle-class taxpayers, many of whom today are still only schoolchildren.

The urgent need to invest in this next generation has not yet been recognized by a majority of today's voters and taxpayers from the old majority group, even though there are grave doubts about the preparedness of the rising new generation, which is substantially Latino, to assume the new duties. Questions regarding this demographic challenge are being raised nationwide, especially in states like California and Texas that have prominent and growing Latino populations.[5] Most recently, the National Research Council (NRC) completed a major study, "Hispanics and the American Future," which reached the following conclusion:

> That Hispanics are coming of age in an aging society has important implications for the nation's future. As the youngest segment of the U.S. population, second- and third-generation Hispanics could play a vital role in shouldering the burden of a graying society. Yet realizing this potential productivity boost

will depend on whether the necessary educational investments are made. . . . An emphasis in this report, then, is on the potential costs of underinvesting in the young Hispanic population.[6]

Here is the drawback to the emphasis of the National Research Council report: as much as we may want, *in the future*, to have better-prepared workers and taxpayers who can support the growing costs of an aging society, the expanded educational preparation needed for the future rests on tax consequences *today*. The rub is that reducing tax burdens has been a major concern of many voters, and it is a central issue linking voters to the future. Whether cutting taxes is an act of hope or despair is a judgment for each voter to make. However, in the past decade tax reductions have been accompanied by record budget deficits that were covered by new government borrowing. Such an approach simply transfers the tax burden to the next generation of workers (pencil in "despair"). New projections by the U.S. Government Accountability Office (GAO) foresee a quadrupling of annual debt payments, first doubling from 9.3 percent of total federal revenue in 2006 to 18.8 percent by 2020, and then doubling again to 39.2 percent in 2030. The key problem is that public expenditures are bound to soar when Social Security and Medicare outlays skyrocket following the retirement of the giant baby boom generation. To cover the debt and the growing costs of entitlements, the next generation, according to academic studies of generational accounting, will see a roughly 80 percent increase in lifetime tax payments.[7] Despite the potential for despair in these budget figures, we can *hope* that the next generation of taxpayers will be prepared to accept this burden. In fact, the great majority of the next generation wants to achieve a level of earning that would make this possible, and the rest of the nation needs to help them succeed (pencil in "hope").

Of even keener personal interest to most voters is the security of their house values. A new threat to be recognized is that California and the nation face the threat of a generational housing bubble that could have deeper and more prolonged impacts than the "little" price bubble currently faced in many areas (more despair). For many older citizens, a major portion of their assets is wrapped up in home values that have doubled or even tripled in just the past decade. When the baby boomers decide to sell their overpriced houses, prices may be forced down to a lower level to bring them within the reach of the less-advantaged next generation. This great transfer of real estate assets will join the two generations in mutual dependency, matching older sellers with younger buyers, many of whom are likely to be of a different ethnicity. Fortunately, these exchanges will not begin for a decade or more, and so there might be just enough time to grow the next generation of home buyers (hope again).

Rebuilding the Social Contract of a Divided Society

Immigration is not the only source of division in our fractious society. Yet this issue changes the terms of debate used to sustain more familiar divisions, and it may force us out of old political ruts. Through the lens of immigration we can get a better look at ourselves as Americans, at our concept of citizenship, and at our commonality and interdependency.

As mentioned earlier, the demographic majority has diverged from the voting majority, and the challenge to democracy is the projected electoral dominance of this minority for many years, at least through 2024 or 2031. The imbalance between voting and population in California would take on tragic proportions if the outgoing group, today's voting majority, reacted at the polls out of despair against unwanted changes, instead of voting out of hope for the incoming group, a population that is crucial to the future. However, why should we assume that the outgoing majority would vote for future-oriented investments—such as education and infrastructure—that would require higher taxes today if they did not benefit personally from these investments?

What is needed to mediate these relations is an agreed-upon *social contract* that mobilizes divergent self-interests to achieve a common good—that is, a workable consensus across generations. Of course, it is a highly contentious issue whether the social contract should be in the spirit of the New Deal, offering social support for those in need, or along the lines of former congressman Newt Gingrich's "Contract with America," which expressed a middle-class vision of self-sufficiency and limited government. Of the many options, there is yet another basis for the social contract, one that seems most relevant for both the current and coming eras in America.

It is time to rejuvenate the *intergenerational* social contract as a primary guide to solving our current problems. The new pressures of an aging society, the need to enlist support from an ethnically different younger generation, and the importance of generational investment all recommend this version of the social contract. The intergenerational social contract may also help us mend a society polarized along party lines, cultural beliefs, race, and immigrant roots. Seemingly deep-seated and insurmountable, these divisions may only intensify if Americans continue battling along the same lines of entrenched opposition. A wholly different tack is needed if we are to build the necessary foundation for an enduring intergenerational consensus. A new emphasis on intergenerational bonds could have strategic importance because those bonds span not only age groups but also racial-ethnic groups, as well as the native-born and immigrant populations that are concentrated in the different generations. Perhaps most important, intergenerational bonds call attention to the crucial but neglected linkages between present and future, and between individual self-interest and the public good.

bond

The key step in breaking the current impasse is to see ourselves in a longer time perspective. The time frame adopted for our purposes covers 1970 to 2030, roughly the lifetime of the baby boom generation from its youth to its retirement. Looking at immigration and aging issues within this length of time, we rediscover the interdependence of the nation's residents, because over the course of sixty years everyone changes roles. Today's workers, taxpayers, and voters will become tomorrow's retirees, who will be replaced by other workers and supported by a new set of taxpayers. In turn, today's children, who are the beneficiaries of today's taxpayers and voters, will become those valued replacements. Rather than see all these parties as separate interest groups locked into isolated roles, many of them despairing over the competition for scarce resources, instead we could see the interchangeability of their roles over time. That view gives us hope that the generations can be mutually supportive.

Pursuing a Future of Hope or Despair?

Solutions to the problems of an aging society and immigrant incorporation require cooperation that spans seemingly unrelated groups. However, the willingness to work on those partnerships may depend most of all on how the public perceives the prospects for the future. In times of fear or despair, most of us grow more defensive and self-centered and less open to newcomers. In contrast, in times of hope and promise we are more likely to be willing to build an inclusive coalition for mutual progress. The question is this:

what kind of time are we living in now—a time of hope or a time of despair?

In the chapters that follow, I address two competing "stories," or realistic scenarios of the future that are centered on immigration and the relative advancement and integration of immigrants. An older story, rooted most strongly in the trends of 1970 to 1990, is contrasted to a newer story based on more recent trends and more recent assessments. Each scenario describes how past trends will unfold in the future, but the two stories adopt very different stances. The older story is the most widely accepted because it is rooted in earlier experience that has been adopted as common knowledge by the public. Extrapolating into the future some of the most negative trends from the recent past, and adding some crucial assumptions about immigrants, the older story presents a pessimistic view and encourages policies motivated by despair.

The alternative scenario of the immigrant future draws on more current trends and formulates a more optimistic view and a different policy conclusion. The future of hope emphasizes the newfound record of recent immigrant advancement and focuses on the benefits to follow in subsequent decades. Obviously, neither story of the future can be proven correct before that future unfolds. For now, the older story carries more weight simply because it is more widely believed, being so strongly anchored in recent popular experience. The newer story of the future, on the other hand, is tied to data and trends that are just beginning to be brought into common knowledge. In this book, I share the new evidence that highlights the story of hope and endeavor to explain this evidence in a forthright, commonsense fashion.

When choosing between the two scenarios for the immigrant future, citizens need to consider the effects of newness of immigration. More than numbers alone, *when immigration is a new event, all the immigrants are new.* Many observers have misestimated the future prospects of immigrants by overlooking this simple fact. Indeed, the effect of newness was crucial in shaping the older, pessimistic view of the future. The sudden upsurge in immigration to California was shocking to many of the state's residents in the 1970s and 1980s, just as the current upsurge is shocking to residents of other states who have encountered immigration only recently. As new arrivals, immigrants have very different characteristics than will be typical of them twenty years later, after they have settled in. If nothing else, twenty years later they will all be twenty years older, and clearly better off in many ways. As is now plainly visible in California, immigrants do in fact make significant advances after twenty years of settling in. The evidence I present shows convincingly that most gain proficiency with English, work their way out of poverty, and realize the American Dream of homeownership. Indeed, by 2005 the top five surnames of California home buyers were Garcia, Hernandez, Rodriguez, Lopez, and Martinez, and nationwide four of the top ten names were Latino, compared to only two in 2000.[8]

This record of successful immigrant advancement is not widely recognized, partly because people have simply assumed that adult immigrants make no improvements and that only their children can advance. The evidence of the progress of immigrants who were earlier arrivals has also been obscured by the much larger numbers of newcomers in later decades. The National Research Council study also notes that with the acceleration of immigration in recent decades, the characteristics of newcomers overshadow and mask the upward advancement of previous arrivals. Citizens have simply extrapolated past conditions into the future, ignoring the fact that settled immigrants grow older, assimilate, and make economic gains. The naive assumption is that *immigrants are like Peter Pan*, frozen in time, never changing and always remaining just like new immigrants, rather than becoming older, more settled, and more successful citizens. California has the most experience with the post-1965 immigration, and the lessons about immigrant advancement visible there deserve to be shared more broadly.

Once revealed, the benefits of immigrant advancement create much greater hope about the potential success of immigrants and their contributions to society. Seen from this perspective, immigrant advancement after settlement deserves to be nourished so that even greater levels of achievement might be attained by both adult immigrants and their children. That is the message of the story of hope for the new immigrant future.

Early in the twenty-first century, we stand on a dramatic threshold of change. Our opportunity as citizens—indeed, our responsibility—is to seize this moment to create a better future for the average resident and for society as a whole. The great tragedy is that many of us fail to recognize how dependent we are on the rising new majority who will supply the workers, the taxpayers, and the home buyers. When we vote to undercut this group, how much are we undercutting our own future? Adding to the tragedy is the fact that the dismal view of the future is almost completely unwarranted by present conditions, and yet that pessimism supports policies that undermine our otherwise hopeful future.

The Drama Unfolding

In the chapters that follow, our time horizon will sweep forward a generation to the year 2030, but first we go backward, to 1970, to remind ourselves of whence we came and of why we hold the attitudes that shape our current opinions. This is the beginning of a story about the future upon which we have already embarked—and upon which we can improve if we can first make out which direction is better and how the parts connect. The great immigrant transition is playing out over an even longer time period and probably will not be completed in much of the developed world until later in the twenty-first century. But it is already well under way in California, and an examination of these six decades is sufficient for us to grasp its dynamics and impacts.

The scope of this work is uncommonly broad because the topic of immigration and immigrant settlement touches on so many facets of life. Even if I have left out many of these facets, it is still necessary to delve into the domains of many different specialists, from demographers to sociologists, economists, geographers, and political scientists. Our focus on a sixty-year span of time also necessitates that we visit two very different groups of experts, social historians and forecasters drawn from business or urban planning. In addition, two topical foci draw us into dialogue with the education profession and with housing and real estate analysts. Certainly the problem at hand deserves deeper investigation in all of these realms. Lest the scope of this effort seem sheer madness, I should note that I am guided by the insights of Ernest Boyer, who urged both a scholarship of integration that links disciplines and isolated facts and a scholarship of application that addresses the most important problems of the day.[9] My aim throughout is to make coherent a broad picture that will illuminate the understanding of citizens—the ultimate decisionmakers who will guide our collective future.

My aim is to take the reader on a journey of enlightenment as together we seek answers to certain guiding questions: How did we get here? Where are we going? What should we now do differently to reach a better end result? Many conflicting attitudes and values are competing in this saga: this is a struggle between hope and despair, between rejection and inclusion, and between individualism and interdependency. The story is told with primary reference to California, but always in comparison to parallel or supporting trends in the United States. I begin with a discussion of how we go about knowing the future, emphasizing the interplay between popular and expert knowledge and exploring some of the simple devices we use to make sense of the future, including extrapolated expectations, stories spun from facts, and assumptions. My emphasis is on our use of stories as self-fulfilling prophecies. I believe that citizens face a choice between two broadly different stories, one pessimistic and the other hopeful. I prefer the hopeful story, which is constructed with newer information, over the older story of despair.

I present the key demographic facts in chapter 3, focusing on three key issues: the aging of the baby boomers, growing racial and ethnic diversity, and growing populations of immigrants and their children. These three dimensions are intertwined in a new demographic transition that is sweeping the industrialized nations in the twenty-first century, driven by an age structure that is top-heavy with retirees and by a relative shortage of workers and taxpayers.[10] When immigration is induced to fill these needs, the result is not only ethnic diversity but new challenges of social, economic, and political incorporation. There is much that can be done to make immigration a more beneficial outcome by the time the baby boomers complete their retirement years. Thus the analysis offered here looks well beyond current policy debates focused on border control and issues of illegal immigration, as important as those matters may be.

The account is loosely organized as a chronology, beginning with the early phase of the new transition, which is already concluded in California, and then focusing on the present, middle phase of voter opinion and perceptions of the social contract. Chapter 4 explains how the dismal view of the future evolved in the 1980s and 1990s. Evidence on the surprising and favorable turnaround in trends is then presented in chapters 5 and 6. These trends, especially concerning immigrant advancement, are not widely recognized in either their facts or their positive implications for the future.

A middle set of chapters addresses the present challenges to governance. Chapter 7 examines how much political participation lags behind population change and shows how it is that a white and mostly native-born minority can dominate the electorate. Analysis of opinion on some key political issues shows that the white electorate's preferences are substantially different from those of the population majority, and often less mindful of the future. Some say the problem we face in America today is a total breakdown of consensus regarding the social contract. In chapter 8, I conduct a broad review of how the social contract has evolved over the last century and find numerous strands that have competed for prominence, each with a different premise and social understanding. Each strand emerged in a particular historical context to address urgent problems of the day, and most have remained as part of a package of accumulated expectations. Today, in response to new crises, the neglected intergenerational strand of the social contract is becoming prominent again. Chapter 9 addresses the fiscal crisis stemming from the baby boom's retirement and outlines a new strategy based on mutual self-interest that links the generations, spans ethnic groups, and helps tie together an otherwise fragmented society. This new spirit of interdependency and mutual aid corrects some of the excesses of the past, but its promise cannot be borne out without some proof of its benefits for the majority of voters.

The final set of chapters addresses the future benefits to be gained from investing in the new generation, cast from the perspective of the retiring baby boomers. Older voters may well find substantial benefits in supporting the younger generation, including the development of skilled replacements for the large number of retiring baby boom workers and a new base of middle-class taxpayers (addressed in chapter 10). Also important to older homeowners is protecting the value of their homes as assets either to draw upon for retirement income support or to sell outright. It is in the interest of homeowners that future home buyers be well educated and have sufficient income to make the price bids desired by home sellers. The risk is that the next generation will be so economically disadvantaged that baby boomer home sellers will outnumber their buyers and face the massive collapse of a generational housing bubble (addressed in chapter 11). These fundamental fiscal and economic relationships tie together interests, span the ethnic divisions, and bridge the generations.

The final chapter draws conclusions and lessons about how these findings inform starkly different policy choices. The great advantage for other states and nations is that California is preceding them through the great demographic transition. The drama is not a natural event unfolding without human intervention. Every inch along the way is guided by the choices of voters and decisionmakers. Much can be gained by other states and nations from seeing how these issues have played out in the Golden State. If they can absorb the lessons at hand there, they should have an easier time of it. And indeed, all of us can learn how to turn the demographic transition from a problem leading to a future of despair into a promising advantage that becomes the foundation for building a future of hope.

PART I

IMMIGRATION AND
THE GREAT TRANSITION

Chapter 2

Knowing and Making the Future

THE FUTURE is not predictable, but we know it anyway. People act with reference to the future that they envision, however impressionistic or shortsighted their knowledge may be. In times of great stability, a straightforward vision may suffice; in times of calamity and upheaval, the only knowledge that may be relevant is how to survive one day at a time. Our current era lies between these extremes, and thus we face a particular challenge of knowing what changes lie ahead and how best to proceed.

Rapid changes in immigration, race, and aging are all combining with a changing global economy to create a very uncertain future. Global restructuring may be beyond the citizen's reach, but surely population changes at home can be controlled, he or she might think. Some of the voters and taxpayers observing these trends may foresee extreme changes in the future and judge those outcomes to be highly undesirable. Such "knowledge" of the future can have real consequences in the current political arena, leading to bold decisions expressed in referenda or elections.

Guiding the public's expectations is an older, pessimistic story of the immigrant future that often dominates the public debate, for reasons to be explained. Meanwhile, a newer, more optimistic scenario is beginning to take root, one with very different policy implications. Certainly, our citizens and leaders require the most complete information to make the best choices for the future. Simply presenting a mass of naked facts, however, is not helpful, since there are so many of those already in our complex world. Here I describe a number of simplifying and organizing devices that citizens often use to select out key facts. Despite their faults, these devices often guide citizens in forming the common knowledge that is so influential in shaping the future.

Who Knows the Future and Leads Us into It?
Politicians, Experts, or Citizens?

We need to rethink our expectations about the future and about who should lead the way. My belief is that far more respect should be accorded the voters and taxpayers. Not only are these citizens the people who will provide the political and financial support for any solutions regarding the future, but they already possess relevant and necessary knowledge. The common knowledge that makes sense to citizens is an important starting point. Certainly this knowledge can and must be improved, but it should not be rejected. Because facts about the future can never be proven, only believed, any understanding of the future that we hope to see adopted by others should be agreed upon through a process of shared discovery. If it does not make sense to the citizen voters, then the knowledge is not effective.

Our elected leaders are chronically slow to address the future so rapidly approaching. No matter the seriousness of the issues, this reluctance is understandable if we think about the short horizons of their political lives. Because they are at the mercy of election cycles of two or four years, politicians seek rapid rewards to ensure their popularity and electability. A basic rule followed by all politicians is to never acknowledge a problem without having a solution ready at hand to propose. Even farsighted leaders run afoul of the harsh reality that future improvements often require short-term pain. But however severely negative the consequences ten or twenty years ahead may be, politicians can ill afford to propose solutions for the long run that would generate displeasure among voters and campaign contributors in the short run. Thus, it is the short-term bias of our political system that discourages leaders from looking ahead and knowing anything about the future. Only if the voters demand it and provide short-term support can a political leader afford to emphasize benefits beyond his or her term of office.

We often count on experts to help us judge problems and solutions, although they just as often disagree with one another, making the best course of action difficult to ascertain. Expectations about the future are especially difficult for the experts because they cannot be verified by the basic rules of evidence and proof. There are no facts that exist in the future, and there is no way to measure and verify conditions at a future date in advance. All that is available is a record of past trends, which can be interpreted for future consequences by using various theoretical models. Even when a great majority of experts come to agree on what the trends mean for the future—such as has now been achieved about the problem of global warming—the conclusions can prove so inconvenient that they are resisted as unproven. Thus, the inherent unpredictability of the future leaves experts in a weakened position that they would rather avoid. Not surprisingly, they often avoid predictions of the future and instead keep their focus on the present, much like politicians. And again, the citizens are left to their own devices.

The citizens already know a lot, even if it is based only on folk wisdom or local experience. Their expectations are deeply engrained and make them resistant to any findings from experts that seem counterintuitive. Too often experts assume that their conclusions will automatically be accepted as authoritative, a misconception soundly challenged by both political scientists and psychologists. Charles Lindblom and David Cohen emphasize that professional social inquiry can modify only slightly the popular beliefs that form a "mountain of ordinary knowledge."[1] Indeed, if the experts refrain from taking a leadership role on the future because it is unpredictable, all that exists for guidance is this ordinary knowledge. Even when experts do provide a rich array of facts related to the future, these products of reason and research are usually insufficient to change people's minds. Instead, according to the psychologist Howard Gardner, people's minds are set more in line with stories that feel right and that bear out theories they have held from early in life.[2] In a democracy, the chief decisionmakers are the voters, and with or without expert information on which to base their expectations, they have plenty to go on.

Surely, however, the knowledge base of citizen voters can be brought more up to date. When matters of the future are at stake, the currency of our knowledge should be especially valued. So many different types of information about the future need to be considered. Later chapters introduce detailed facts about future demographics that are grounded in the inexorable process of aging. I tie these facts to coming changes in educational attainment, the workforce, and home buyers and analyze differences in political opinion about changing demographics and actions for changing the future.

Presented here is an assessment of the ordinary knowledge with which people form judgments about the future of immigration and a comparison of that common knowledge with the knowledge set brought by demographers who study the future numbers of immigrants. Although the experts' information is fraught with uncertainty, it is set in a historical record of past immigration and anchored by better-known dimensions of demographic change. However, it is limited by a lack of attention to the characteristics of immigrants in the future, a deficiency at least partly redressed in later chapters. The popular view, in contrast, is not hampered by lack of evidence, and it animates a portrait of future immigrants that can be imagined in rich detail. As mentioned earlier, common knowledge is often based on simple extrapolations of past trends, with the implications of those trends colored in by exaggerated hopes and fears. In addition, such knowledge is susceptible to tunnel vision focused on a single dimension. The resulting view often amounts to a distorted caricature of future possibilities. We can do better, and we must.

Simple Devices for Organizing Facts

> Prediction is very difficult, especially if it's about the future.
> —Niels Bohr, physicist

Tunnel Vision

Often it is the experts, working in different agencies and motivated by distinct organizational mandates—occupying "separate silos"—who are faulted for having tunnel vision. Or they are faulted for viewing the world with blinders on, owing to their disciplinary training in economics instead of law, for example, or the paradigm restrictions within a particular science. Ordinary citizens, on the other hand, are assumed to have a broader view, being freer to integrate a range of experiences into their outlook. But when it comes to the future, citizens are also prone to tunnel vision.

Sound expectations about the future are very difficult to construct, whether by experts or citizens, and so it is always necessary to simplify. Not only is the future difficult to predict, but it is also vast. How do we account for so many interconnected facets of change? Understandably, we must concentrate on particular aspects of the future, tunneling ahead by focusing on highly selective dimensions of change. Later we flesh out what we think about these changes with broad generalizations and leaps to conclusions. While simplification may be necessary, oversimplification is the rule.

When projecting themselves into an imagined future world, most people are myopic about how much will really change. Typically we assume that we ourselves will stay basically the same and that the future will happen only in *the world around us.* Furthermore, when we imagine that future world through our tunnel vision, we tend to focus on only one or two chosen elements and assume that the rest will remain as it is in the present.

For example, a young boy in 1935 might have looked forward to the fantastic personal mobility of cruising anywhere he would want to go on newly paved highways in a speedy new roadster of streamlined design, but he probably never foresaw the congestion that would result many decades later when everyone obtained such vehicles. When he imagined himself speeding home from the workplace to an isolated country cottage, his individualistic vision of the future overlooked the suburban sprawl realized as a product of his dreams multiplied. More telling, the young boy might have assumed that he would rush home to a waiting wife carrying out domestic chores, like his mom in 1935, and probably could not have imagined greeting the executive career woman of the future instead. His futuristic fantasy, viewed through the tunnel, foresaw individual satisfaction with only one aspect of technology, not its mass consequences or the many other social patterns that were likely to be changed by it.

Expectations and Extrapolations

Fantasies of future life are one thing, but in imagining even just the coming decade, the average citizen is a very poor forecaster. People merely hope for or fear more of the same. For example, real estate economists have marveled at the irrational expectations of home buyers in different housing markets. A 2003 survey by the noted economists Karl Case and Robert Shiller found that in San Francisco and Boston, where prices have increased at record rates, home buyers typically stated an expectation that the recent trend would continue for the next ten years.[3] An earlier survey conducted by the same researchers in 1988 at the peak of the previous housing boom found the same expectation, even though prices subsequently fell in those cities. No matter that ups and downs in home prices have been the typical pattern over the past decades—home buyers expect the extreme recent trend to continue well into the future. This illustrates the strong human propensity for *extrapolated ex-*

pectations—that is, the assumption that recent trends will continue apace indefinitely.

Perceptions of crime trends illustrate a further aspect of the principle, showing how even *current* perceptions can be influenced by expectations extrapolated from the *past*. Because they are based even further back in time, these current perceptions lead to an even more outdated expectation of the future. The discrepancy in perceptions is a puzzle, and the sociologist Barry Glassner uses it to introduce his thesis that America is afflicted with a culture of fear: "Why, as crime rates plunged throughout the 1990s, did two-thirds of Americans believe they were soaring? How did it come about that by mid-decade 62 percent of us described ourselves as 'truly desperate' about crime—almost twice as many as in the late 1980s, when crime rates were higher?"[4]

Fear may well lie at the root of all crime perceptions, but crime fell precipitously after 1992. Violent crime in the United States fell from 758 incidents per 100,000 population in 1992 to 611 in 1997 and 495 in 2002. Although the rate was higher in California, it fell by an even greater proportion, as shown in figure 2.1. The question that Glassner raises about why citizens failed to recognize this pronounced and sustained decrease in crime may have other explanations than simply fear. It is important to note that the long and highly publicized run-up in crime rates during the 1970s and 1980s surely led people to expect and fear a *continued* escalation in crime (figure 2.1). With escalating crime rates now part of their common knowledge, citizens may have simply assumed that the upsurge was continuing—that is, they may have extrapolated a continued upward trend. For example, given the previous decade's rise, by 1997 the violent crime rate could have been assumed to have risen to 817 per 100,000 in the United States, and to 1,313 in California, more than one-third higher than the actual crime rate, which had in fact declined.

If this extrapolation seems capricious or at least unlikely, we might ask what evidence would indicate to citizens that the crime trend had changed? Surely the expert reports on the declining crime rate were reported by the news media and would have been noticed. Maybe not, since that news would hardly have been as attention-getting or memorable as a rise in the crime rate. Such a report would also have been inconsistent with other, more salient news reports, such as a feature on the latest gruesome murder (usually in a distant city). Thus, another reason why citizens failed to recognize the declining crime rate in the 1990s was that their extrapolated high expectations of violent crime were affirmed and underscored by the continued *news publicity given to indi-*

Figure 2.1   Extrapolated Versus Actual Rates of Violent Crime,
California and the United States, from a 1992
Vantage Point

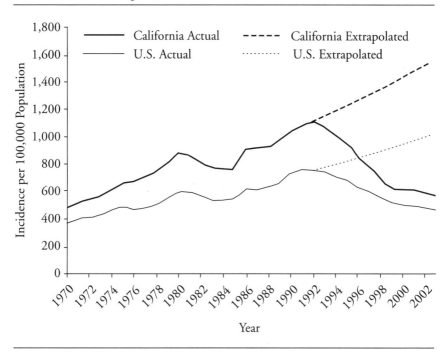

Source: Uniform Crime Reports, 1970 to 2003.

vidual crime events. No matter that these events may become increasingly rare—newspaper and television accounts feature enough examples of the kind of crime people most fear that their extrapolated expectations are never challenged and reversed. Thus, the most astute observers of crime trends may have caught on to the trend reversal, but for the majority who pay more attention to daily crime stories, the assumed trend from the past continues to prevail.

House prices and crime rates illustrate two aspects of extrapolated expectations: our outlook for the future is often a mere extension of past trends, and our perceptions of even the present can be colored by extrapolations from the past. Once our expectations have been set and they are entrenched in our common knowledge, they can be sustained by a relatively small amount of confirmatory information. We simply filter out discordant information because it does not fit with what we believe.

As a result of these extrapolations from the past, our view of the future is often an old view, and we are slow to replace this "old future" with a more contemporary view that represents the "new future." This book seeks to provide a window on that new future and discusses the changes in public policy required to take advantage of new opportunities. For this new future to become the operating guide to decisionmaking, however, the well-established old future first needs to be confronted and dislodged, a task taken up in later chapters.

Future Immigrants

Most citizens ask three questions when they think of immigrants and the future: How many will there be? What will they be like? What will it mean for me to have these people around? In the absence of information about the future, the increase in foreign-born residents is fertile ground for the formation of extrapolated expectations. That is because the growth of immigration has been dramatic and well publicized, and because citizens' fears of negative consequences can be attached to these trends. These citizen perceptions are strongly rooted, and they can be compared to the body of knowledge developed by professional forecasters.

Extrapolated Expectations About the Number of Future Foreign-Born Residents

The foreign-born consist of all immigrants living in the United States, an accumulation of new arrivals in addition to previous arrivals. Expressed as a percentage of total residents, the foreign-born share can grow only from additions of new arrivals; when immigration speeds up, the foreign-born share rises more rapidly. In 1990, 7.9 percent of the U.S. population was foreign-born, only moderately higher than the 6.2 percent recorded ten years earlier. At that rate of growth, the foreign-born share in the nation would be extrapolated to reach 10.1 percent in 2000, but in fact the 2000 census recorded a foreign-born share in the United States that had increased even faster, reaching 11.1 percent instead (figure 2.2). This accelerated growth in the foreign-born share during the 1990s would lead to much higher extrapolated expectations for 2030 than had been previously suggested by the slower rate of increase during the 1980s.[5] Nonetheless, either extrapolation is far higher than the foreign-born share estimated by professional forecasters (16.2 percent).[6]

Figure 2.2   Extrapolated Increase in the Foreign-Born Share of Residents in California and the United States, Comparing 1990 and 2000 Vantage Points

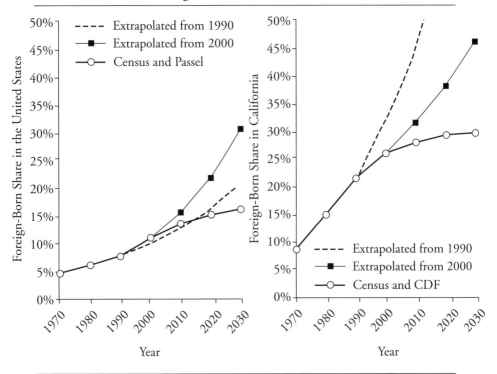

Source: Censuses of 1970, 1980, 1990 and 2000; USC California Demographic Futures; Jeffrey Passel (projections for United States); and extrapolations by author.

Even more exaggerated trends were experienced in California. Already by 1990, 21.7 percent of the population was foreign-born, up from 15.1 percent ten years earlier. At that rate of growth, the foreign-born share might have been extrapolated to reach 31.1 percent in 2000 and 92.2 percent by 2030, a preposterously high level (see figure 2.2). In fact, at the time of the 2000 census it was discovered that the foreign-born share in California was substantially lower than most had expected, only 26.2 percent. This reflected a substantial slowdown in the rate of immigration to California (discussed in chapter 5). If the 1990 to 2000 decade of growth became the new basis for extrapolation, the foreign-born share in 2030 (46.2 percent) would be far lower than the extrapolation from the earlier period (figure 2.2). In either case, professional projections of the foreign-born share in the state in 2030 amount to only 29.8 percent, well below either set of extrapolated expectations.[7] Meanwhile, despite the slowdown of immigrant growth in California, which is now dwarfed by the number of babies born in the state, a majority of the state's residents in 2005 still believed that this was the biggest factor in the state's growth.[8]

Here is the point: most citizens know nothing of the professional forecasts and perceive only the trends of the past. These simple extrapolations create a very different set of expectations, and the outlooks are very different in the United States as a whole than in California. Although California's foreign-born share may be higher, its growth has been *decelerating*, and thus the long-term outlook has been moderating. In contrast, in the United States as a whole the outlook for a growing foreign-born share has been *accelerating*, much as it was in California a decade or two ago. Even if the numbers are much lower than in California, the perceived rate of change is much greater. The novelty of the upturn has also precipitated a proliferation of new stories regarding the spread of the immigrant population. Thus, the rising trend and the news publicity combine to promote a consistent body of knowledge that reaffirms the average citizen's extrapolated expectations. Increasing news coverage of immigration in other states even affects Californians, whose own expectations about immigrant growth in California are thus slower to adjust downward. Under these circumstances, many U.S. citizens, including Californians, might fear that the takeoff of foreign-born population will continue without limit until there is an immigrant "takeover."

Expert Projections of Future Immigrant Numbers

The common knowledge of citizens has immense power, and as discussed earlier, political scientists have shown that its conclusions are not easily dislodged by contributions from experts. When it comes to the future, no numbers can be proven, so they can only be accepted as a matter of faith. Nonetheless, the outlook of professional forecasters calls for the foreign-born share of California's population to stop growing and then level off around 2030. Expert projections take account of many trends in the population, including the rate of new immigrant arrivals, the growth and behavior of current residents, and the rate at which immigrants have native-born children and thus make their own contribution to balancing the foreign-born share.

For their part, demographers agree that projecting the number of future immigrant arrivals is more difficult than most factors.[9] Unlike fertility and mortality, which have been quite stable for the last twenty years or longer in the United States, or aging, which is a constant, migration is more volatile— it ebbs and flows with economic opportunity. International migration (immigration) is especially uncertain because it is subject to changes in policy regarding admissions criteria and border enforcement. Immigration is also affected by changes in other countries, including war or economic catastrophe, that could drive more people to flee toward the United States. Over a thirty-year time horizon, much could change. Accordingly, demographers approach their key assumptions conservatively, averaging the input factors of recent years and preserving these into the future unless there are clear grounds for increase or decrease. With respect to annual immigrant arrivals, the major professional forecasters generally have assumed that the average flow of annual arrivals, both legal and unauthorized, will remain near its peak level from 1995 through 2005. That assumption implies that the accelerating growth of immigration to the United States will cease, as it already has in California. Indeed, two highly regarded demographers have already proclaimed that the nation's recent wave of immigration has crested.[10] The latest projections by the Census Bureau, prepared in 2000, foresee net immigration declining from 964,000 per year in 2000 to 872,000 in 2005 and 751,000 in 2020.[11] A similar schedule of leveling immigration to the United States was adopted for the projections series of the California Demographic Futures (CDF) project at the University of Southern California. Since that time, growing political debate in Congress makes it even more likely that future increases in immigration will be restrained, and a decline in the numbers of new arrivals is now more plausible than an increase. California today foreshadows how this decrease will alter the characteristics of the foreign-born living in the United States.

Questions About Characteristics and Consequences

Aside from the *number* of immigrants, citizens also harbor questions about *what immigrants will be like* in the future and what the *consequences* will be for themselves. Questions about future characteristics are much more complex and must be deferred to later chapters. There I discuss the Peter Pan fallacy— the assumption that immigrants never grow older or advance in any way— and also the impact on citizens' perceptions about all immigrants that is created when accelerated immigration yields an unusual concentration of newcomers. Further, the evidence may be surprising on the degree of advancement achieved by Latino immigrants when their length of settlement in the United States grows to two or three decades.

Answers to questions about what this all means for current residents are developed over the book. But first we need to address the dynamics of aging by the baby boomers and consider these issues: projecting future replacements for retirees in the workforce; future middle-class taxpayers; and increasing the purchasing power of future home buyers, without whom prices will decline. These are just three of the many different factors at play in the future we are building. How can they all be remembered? In practice, there is a simple way: it is all about the story.

A Story About the Future

Some people are optimists by nature, and others are pessimists. Fortunately, most people are relatively equal-minded and can sway either way, depending on the facts they face. As I have argued, however, it is difficult for people to keep track of many different factors at once, especially those that pertain to the future. That is why people resort to the simplifying devices of tunnel vision and extrapolated expectations. Of course, either technique yields an outlook that is devoid of much human detail. These stripped-down futures do not take place in the kind of environment we could see ourselves living in. To be adopted as believable scenarios, they must be fleshed out. Therefore, one more crucial device for knowing the future is an organizing *story*.

A story told about current trends and the future is not crafted as a bland, numerical account but instead is made captivating, filled with subjective commentary, and given a compelling point. Necessarily exaggerated in order to hold our attention, stories about the future are either stories of disaster, complete with villains, victims, and incompetents, or, less commonly, stories of a glorious promised land, featuring heroes and deserving beneficiaries. These stories matter because they are the primary means of mobilizing political support for a point of view on the future.[12] They also matter because they comprise scripts for creating the future. We might begin to act the parts we are given, myth might be turned into action, and through concerted effort we might make the story come true.

Competing Stories to Make Sense of Future Immigration

Business strategists and planning theorists have come to emphasize the power of stories as ways of preparing for the future and organizing attention. Stories written as scenarios of the future have the advantage that they explain the significance of past trends and, according to the story, are likely to occur. They tie together different facts and make the scenario believable, a place where the listener can view himself or herself residing, whether for better or worse. According to Peter Schwartz, "Stories have a psychological impact that graphs and equations lack. Stories are about meaning; they can help explain why things could happen in a certain way. They give order and meaning to events—a crucial aspect of understanding future possibilities."[13]

Stories often come in pairs—one hopeful and the other pessimistic. Even though several different combinations of assumptions could of course lead to the construction of multiple stories, nonetheless, it is often just two that we hear. There is good reason to consider a pessimistic story if it generates a healthy skepticism and helps prepare us to avoid events such as a terrorist attack. In other cases, the pessimistic story can be disempowering if the despair it invokes leads to inaction. When it comes to demographic matters, there is a natural basis for crafting two stories. Both are about the passage of time, which is inevitable, but in the pessimistic version time leads to aging and ultimately death.[14] Never a popular thought. In the alternative, optimistic view, the passage of time leads to birth, a replacement of older forms with new forms, a regeneration, and a continuity through generational succession. The hopeful story of life and our passing time is about more than just a difference in attitude: it reminds us of the necessity of investing in others. The pessimistic story is more introverted and describes a future that is more short-sighted.

Investment and foresight are fundamental to two broadly different stories told in the United States about immigration and the future. Both of these stories are told from the perspective of the majority-white, native-born population, the citizens who make up the great bulk of voters. (Different stories obviously could be told from the vantage point of particular immigrant groups or other groups.) The most prevalent story relies heavily on evidence from the recent past and presents a pessimistic view and a particular policy conclusion. The alternative story, pointing not only to evidence from the distant past but to some new trends as well, leads to a more optimistic view and a different policy conclusion. Here I offer only very brief, stylized renditions of the two; in future chapters, the facts and assumptions in the stories are dissected in more detail.

The most widely accepted story is that immigration is increasing dramatically and producing a rapidly growing population of unassimilated foreigners in our midst. Many of the newcomers have used illegal means to gain residence in the United States, despite the wishes of the citizenry to maintain order and restrict access. As a result, many unfavorable trends are worsening, the story goes, with dire consequences for the future: English is losing its status as the nation's language, and in places like Miami and Los Angeles, Spanish has already become dominant, at least in many neighborhoods. Now that immigrants are spreading across America, more places will lose their traditional English orientation and poverty will grow, placing even greater pressure on already overburdened taxpayers. Citizens need to guard against these growing economic burdens, according to this story, and government needs to respond by clamping down on these new arrivals, calling a halt to the illegality, and stopping the negative changes.

How accurate is this story? The facts selected by this story, although exaggerated, are not completely untrue, but the emphasis and interpretation reflect a mood of despair.

A different and newer story of the future is beginning to spread, also told from the perspective of the native-born majority. After its initial acceleration, immigration has begun to level off and is becoming a more permanent, continuing part of our society. This story holds that these waves of workers have arrived to fill low-skilled jobs that Americans do not want. Some arrivals are also scientists and engineers who help us maintain global leadership in high-technology sectors. We especially need these new immigrants and their children because so many baby boomers will retire soon, leaving our economy with a shortage of skilled workers and taxpayers. The newcomers have now settled in and are rapidly learning English and working their way up the economic ladder. According to this story, after a period of time they will eventually become as assimilated as the early-twentieth-century European immigrants. We need to encourage all these new residents to become citizens and voters so that they can participate in our democracy, and we should make sure the immigrant children are well educated so that they can help us with their best efforts as well.

The facts of this story are also true, but the interpretation and emphasis are based in hope, and perhaps because of that hopefulness, the mood is more invested in the future than is the pessimistic story of the immigrant future.

Both stories have implications for the future. The story of despair is anchored to the negative trends of the last twenty years. It magnifies them and rolls them forward into the future. The alternative story of hope interprets current trends differently—foreseeing less growth in immigration, and more assimilation—and it emphasizes the positive benefits to follow in the next twenty years. Neither story can be proven to be true, but the pessimistic story is probably more widely believable because it is more strongly anchored in recent popular experience. Unfortunately, this pessimistic story leads to a more pessimistic future. The newer story of the future, on the other hand, is tied to data and trends that are more recent, and if it were to become more widely believed and acted upon, it would be likely to lead to a more optimistic outcome.

The Circularity of Expectations and Results

These mental constructions of the future have begun to shape reality, blurring the distinction between imagination and reality. The future can be shaped by minds when people begin to act in concert based on knowledge held in their imagination. It may seem a paradox, but "hard" facts can be generated by "soft" imagination. At least, that is the conclusion of experts who have philosophized about the practice of forecasting.[15]

Unlike a weather forecast, the knowledge of which cannot alter whether it rains or shines, forecasts of human activity have substantial opportunity to influence outcomes. The very reason we want to make forecasts or projections is so that we can adjust our behavior accordingly, either to accommodate the expected trends or, more pointedly, to take advantage of favorable opportunities or avoid undesirable outcomes. With any of these decisions, there is the distinct probability that we will alter the outcomes that would have occurred in the absence of the forecast. Some forecasts become self-fulfilling prophecies if they are widely believed and everyone acts in accordance with them. Others may be self-defeating forecasts: they describe such unpleasant consequences that everyone seeks to act in opposite ways.

Simply stated, there is a circular connection between the expectations created by a forecast and the results that unfold. The two competing stories of future immigration could certainly have that effect. Both stories describe future trends that will flow from their interpretations of the present, and both invite responses that will reinforce their premises. The forecast of despair calls upon the citizenry to withhold financial support from immigrant arrivals, inviting a response that chokes off their settlement and integration into society. The presumed benefit would be to reduce the immigrant burden on society. In contrast, the forecast of hope invites the opposite stance, calling for a nurturance of immigrant arrivals and their more rapid incorporation. The alleged benefit in this case would be to increase immigrant contributions to society by filling vacancies in the skilled workforce and enlarging tax revenues by expanding the capacities of the future taxpayer base.

Given the stark differences between these two stories, one wonders which is the more plausible or more likely to occur. There is no confident answer to that question. Alternatively, we might consider which story better describes a society in which we would prefer to live. Preferences aside, plausibility is not entirely a matter of choice, because there are factual trends that make the realization of one story or the other more feasible. The principal factual differences between the two stories center on just two issues—how fast immigration will increase in the future, and how rapidly immigrants will assimilate. Evidence already presented in this chapter—and there will be more in later chapters—indicates why it is that many citizens believe the story of despair, but much of that evidence is dated from the early 1990s or before and reflects an older view of the future.

The newer evidence I present describes a much more positive future. In later chapters, I take great care to explain why there has been this shift in understanding and why it is that many citizens still hold on to the older view. I argue that it is time to embrace this new information that is consistent with the story of hope and the new future that is within our grasp. When a new future lies ahead that is so promising, why hold on to the old?

Making, Not Predicting, a Future We Know Is Possible

Ultimately, the future of our society is not about prediction. Forecasts are merely guides to the plausibility of one outcome or another. By themselves, they are only sterile quantitative indicators and cannot describe the environments we will actually inhabit. Rather, the society of the future is something *we make* out of our collective choices, the combined result of many different people pushing toward a shared goal or following a common vision. Once each of us chooses between the two basic scenarios, based on the plausibility of the new data presented here and on how well the alternative stories fit our understanding, our actions will begin to generate the future we believe.

In the next chapter, as a first step, I introduce the powerful insights from demographic analysis of immigration and the future. Demographics describe the building blocks of society in ways that anyone can readily appreciate. All of us have experienced the process of growing up, into young adulthood or beyond, and we all have family members in different generations. So no matter what technical measurement demographers use, such analysis is well grounded in the ordinary knowledge of citizens. What may be new is to think of so many lives aggregated together, all moving forward in time, but each at a different stage in the life course. Some generations, like the baby boomers, are larger than others; when they reach certain age thresholds, such as retirement, their aggregate behavior places a major strain on society. Immigrant arrivals represent a different generation: most of the strains they put on society occur at the beginning of their U.S. residence, and the benefits of their presence come later.

Better understanding of the broad demographic transition now reshaping our nation is vital to understanding the future, including how immigration fits together with the other major aspects of change. With only a few key insights, citizens can be empowered to become leaders in forming a future they have consciously chosen.

Chapter 3

Demographic Transition in California and the United States

WHEN DID IT become most clear to Americans that the nation was undergoing dramatic demographic change? Was it the day early in 2001 when the *Washington Post* declared that, for the first time in centuries, the African American population was no longer the nation's largest minority group? Blacks, the *Post* reported, had been outnumbered by the Hispanic population, which had reached 12.5 percent of the total U.S. population.[1] Latinos had been projected to grow more numerous, but the speed with which they surpassed blacks in population surprised demographers. In the large states of Texas and California, Latinos now make up over one-third of the population.

Certainly, many also noticed the steady stream of announcements in the 1990s regarding the contentious issue of immigration. Immigration surged upward each year from 1993 into the new century, and the rapid increase in illegal immigrants became a lightning rod for attention in Congress in 2006. The total number of new foreign-born residents surpassed even the level of the great migration wave before World War I, and the newcomers spread out to states not previously known as immigrant gateways. Immigration was said to now account for 50 percent of all population growth and a comparably large share of newly filled jobs.[2] Americans have been divided about the various implications of so many new immigrants, as reflected in the Gallup poll. A June 2005 poll showed that immigration was judged as more of a good thing (61 percent) than a bad thing (34 percent), but 46 percent wished the flow was decreased (only 16 percent wanted it increased).[3]

Perhaps for some Americans the realization that the nation's demographic change was getting personal and that little could be done to stop it dawned on December 12, 2005, when the Census Bureau press headline screamed, "Oldest Baby Boomers Turn 60!" Not that any of the boomers needed to be reminded of this prospect: as fully 7,918 of their peers turned sixty every single day during 2006, the Census Bureau kindly reminded all of us: "Among the Americans celebrating their 60th will be our two most recent presidents, George W. Bush and Bill Clinton. Other well-known celebrities reaching this milestone include Cher, Donald Trump, Sylvester Stallone and Dolly Parton." Those baby boomers used to be rambunctious youths—and now they were sixty? Still vigorously shaping our world, the baby boomers are not going anywhere soon. The Census Bureau added that in 2030, 57.8 million baby boomers, age sixty-six to eighty-four, will still be with us.[4]

Less apparent to most observers is that these separate developments form parts of a larger demographic puzzle. The many details of demographics often obscure the big picture. The aging of the population, the growth of minority groups, more immigrants and foreign cultures, poverty rates, educational attainments—all are newsworthy factoids that are readily formed from tides of data, instantly analyzed, and broadcast in so many reports. A flood of information on changing demographics fills the front pages, the business section, and even the sports news—just look, for instance, at the dominance of Latin American players in major league baseball, or consider how many of the top NBA basketball players are from France, Germany, and China. The wide differences of opinion on what it all means provide steady fodder for the editorial page. With so many competing ideas and bits of facts, it is no wonder that most people have little grasp of what is really up with demographics.

In this chapter, I provide an overview of the big picture on these trends, unveiling their basic dynamics and showing how it all fits together. Once comprehended, all the indicators point to an epic transformation in America, a reshaping of the nation's mainstream over the span of just a generation or two. The story of this transformation is simply this: A lot of Americans are growing older because of the baby boom long ago. Meanwhile, newcomers— in ever-increasing numbers—are arriving as immigrants, and because of their racial and ethnic differences, the reception they are receiving from the well-established older generation is less than welcoming. Nonetheless, the new-comers are filling vital roles in an undersized younger generation that cannot otherwise replace the retiring baby boomers.

The implications of demographic trends are hard to grasp at any given moment. In the short term, it is hard to even *perceive* the trends. For example, does aging occur? Not this year, I might try to argue, but after a decade or two the facts do become more apparent. *Evaluating* the trends takes even more distance and a longer view of the subject. Most of us are prone to react to the immediate change we perceive, but our evaluations would be more accurate if we saw the broader and longer context.

Although immigration is a central focus of this study, it is best understood as one change among many in society, albeit an integral one. The most fundamental change is the ongoing aging of the population within which immigrants settle. The best way to grasp these dynamics is through the life course of the baby boom generation, the large group born from 1946 to 1964. Over the entire course of the nation's transition, from 1970 to 2030, the baby boom generation will pass from youth (age six to twenty-four) to retirement (age sixty-six to eighty-four). By the latter age, the baby boomers will have largely surrendered their economic role to a new generation that is ethnically very different. As we shall see, the need to replace workers and productive tax-payers will be massive in this later period. In parallel to the aging of the baby boom, we have the cumulating numbers of immigrants and their children, accompanied by rapid racial change in the population. The rising generation must attempt to fill the shoes of its predecessors and support their health and pension benefits in their retirement years. With a better grasp of the overall transition, we might be able to plan ahead and make the transition proceed more smoothly and with greater reward for all concerned.

California: The Leading Edge

Many of the trends associated with this transition have advanced further in the state of California than elsewhere in the United States, or even in the rest of the world. Already 27 percent of California's population is foreign-born, and nearly 50 percent is made up of the foreign-born and their children. The long-established majority population of non-Hispanic white residents has now fallen to minority status, accounting for barely 45 percent of the state's population. As a result, California is now a state composed entirely of minorities. In the nation as a whole, one-third of the population has grown to be minority, the Census Bureau announced in May 2006.

The "new demographics" of California that pertained in 1990 no longer describe its population. And what is "new" today will not describe tomorrow. We need to think of demographics as a process of transition passing through important phases. The transition described here can be divided into three twenty-year phases:

- *Early phase:* 1970 to 1990 or 1995
- *Middle phase:* 1990 or 1995 to 2010
- *Mature phase:* 2010 to 2030

The demographic story differs between California and the United States. For California, the first phase of the demographic transition, from 1970 to 1990, witnessed tremendous growth in immigrant population, including the arrival in great numbers of unauthorized or illegal immigrants. In the subsequent phase, from 1990 to 2010, immigration leveled off in California, ceasing its upward acceleration. In contrast, in the nation as a whole, immigration was slower to grow before 1990 but increased rapidly in the 1990s and early 2000s; more of these later immigrants were unauthorized, and more of them settled outside of California. Thus, the rest of the nation is now experiencing the demographic changes from immigration that California experienced twenty years earlier. This recent acceleration of immigration will not continue forever. As discussed in chapter 2, the flow of new immigrants has already leveled off; although abrupt policy shifts or catastrophes in other countries could change that trend, forecasters say that the most likely scenario is a slow decline in the annual volume of newcomers over the next twenty years. That forecasted scenario makes it more likely that the nation will enter the phase of a settled immigrant population that now characterizes California.

The lessons from California spill beyond the borders of the United States. With 27 percent of its 37 million residents being foreign-born in 2005, California had a larger foreign-born population than did any of the leading nations in the world, including its only rivals in immigration experience: 18.8 percent of Canada's 30 million residents were foreign-born, and Australia numbered 23.6 percent foreign-born among its 20 million residents. The eminent historian Kevin Starr frequently has observed that California has always tested the nation's future. Similarly, the political observer Peter Schrag recently called California "America's high-stakes experiment."[5] Today, in fact, California may be one of the *world's* major laboratories for successful settlement and incorporation of immigrant residents.

The Long View on the Great Transition

The social reality of America or any nation is composed of millions of individual biographies. The way people are passing through their life cycles and the relative growth of some groups over others add up to the total demographic change. In the playing out of these two dynamics—the changing mix of the population and the changes within individuals' lives as they grow older—are the molecules of changes that reshape our society. The demographer's advantage lies in the societal picture that forms from collecting these statistical molecules of change across several decades. Only from this perspective can we see where we are today, imagine clearly where we are headed, and understand what it all might mean.

The time frame at the heart of this study, 1970 to 2030, is a crucial period in the transition of California and the United States. In 1970 the resurgence of immigration in America was just beginning, newly authorized by the landmark Immigration Act of 1965. In that year the foreign-born population of the United States was at its lowest level in history, representing only 4.7 percent of the nation's residents, but that was about to drastically change. The year 1970 was also important because the bulk of the giant baby boom generation were still pre-adults, and their parents were immersed in the heavy duties of caring for their children's many needs.

Looking ahead, current population projections shine a beam of light that extends out to the middle of the century, 2050, but we need not look that far ahead to draw our conclusions. Most of the crucial events shaping the coming change will play out in just twenty years' time. The future horizon for our range of investigation is 2030, a year when all the former baby boom children will be of retirement age. The current swell of immigration will also have been substantially absorbed by that time, and a new "second generation," the children of these first-generation residents who were foreign-born, will have matured into adulthood.

This sixty-year sweep of time marks a complete demographic transition in California, and to some extent the nation. Our youth-based society will transition into a senior-oriented one, as well as from white-dominated to racially pluralistic, and from new immigrant arrivals to long-settled foreign-born and their children. Today we stand midway in this transition, and we can better understand our current stresses and strains, and pending policy decisions, by seeing ourselves in this manner.

Certainly, there have been other eras of sweeping change in the history of America. The nation experienced major economic transformations during the successive industrial revolutions of the eighteenth and nineteenth centuries, as well as in the midst of the emerging postindustrial economy and now our restructured global economy (1970 to the present). Living conditions also have undergone major transitions, marked most acutely by the shift of the nation's population from rural to urban areas. As recently as 1900, 62.7 percent of Americans lived in rural areas, but that proportion had fallen to 26.5 percent by 1970. Of no small consequence to the quality of life was the spread of electricity to operate lights and appliances, advancing in just fifty years from coverage of virtually no American structures to 98.4 percent of all dwellings in America by 1955.[6] These historic transitions surely were profoundly important.

The Classical Demographic Transition

A demographic transition describes not so much an increase in material standard of living as an intimate transformation of the population: the families and households into which that population is grouped, the trajectories of assimilation by newcomers, and the population's racial and ethnic makeup. The classic theory of demographic transition was developed to explain the population explosion that began in western and northern Europe around 1800 and thereafter spread to other countries around the world. Improvements in nutrition and public health broke the long-standing balance of high fertility and high mortality. When mortality declined, other social customs that sustained high fertility persisted, fueling nearly a century of rapid population growth until childbearing norms finally adjusted and a prolonged decline in fertility rates ensued. Thus, the nations of western and northern Europe transitioned from a regime of many deaths offset by even more newborns to one with low mortality balanced by low fertility. The United States and other nations around the globe have followed a similar transition path, although the least developed nations are only just beginning to reduce fertility to a new level that balances their reduced mortality.

Close to home, Mexico has experienced this change so rapidly that few

Americans have yet realized it. As recently as 1970, the Mexican total fertility rate was 6.8 births per woman, but by 2000 that had declined to 2.4, just above the replacement level of 2.1 lifetime births per woman. Of considerable consequence to the United States, this decline in Mexico's fertility rate means that many fewer young adults will be available to migrate from Mexico to the United States in future decades than would have been expected before.

A Second Demographic Transition

A second demographic transition began to emerge in Europe and the United States in the 1960s. First identified by the Dutch demographers Ron Lesthaeghe and Dirk J. van de Kaa, the theory of this transition describes a bundle of changes in family formation behavior, sexuality, and economic roles for women.[7] Accompanying the economic transformation to a post-industrial economy, this transition was grounded in new attitudes about intimate behaviors, gender equality, and individual self-fulfillment, as indicated in sharp changes in public opinion after 1965.[8] If the first demographic transition entailed a rebalancing of fertility and mortality, under the second transition reproduction has become underemphasized and fertility has fallen so low as to create a growing "birth dearth." As of 2005, not a single European nation had a replacement level of fertility: most nations were near the level of Italy and Germany, which have a total fertility rate of 1.3.[9] The countries of East Asia have joined in the fertility plunge: also registering only 1.2 or 1.3 births per woman are Japan, Taiwan, and South Korea. The mega-countries of China and India have fertility rates of 1.6 and 3.0, respectively, but throughout Africa fertility rates are 5 or 6 births per woman. The imbalance in fertility between the developed and developing nations poses a grave problem, with some countries brimming with young people while others are aging and suffer a lack of workers.[10]

The (Emerging) Third Demographic Transition

Today a new demographic transition is materializing in the developed world. In many ways this is a continuation of, or at least a chain reaction to, the first two, but there is a different character to this transition. Building for some time, this transition is the result of the convergence of several forces.[11] For the first time in history, we are learning to accommodate an aging society, a transition common in much of the industrialized world.[12] In many ways this aging is a direct consequence of the lowered mortality and sharply reduced fertility of the first two demographic transitions. An aging society creates many challenges, one of which is the slowdown in labor force growth. The easiest remedy for an emerging shortage of workers is an increase in immigration, particularly from countries that produce more babies than jobs. Although there has been some debate about the effectiveness of immigration as a replacement for fertility, it is clear that immigrants and their children help balance an otherwise top-heavy age structure.[13] In addition, as international migration has accelerated across Europe and in Canada and Australia, as in the United States, we are witnessing a reshaping of the population across age and racial groups and between native and foreign-born populations.[14] Prior waves of immigration to the United States did not have this character of racial transformation.[15] More importantly, the prior waves of immigration did not coincide with an era when the age structure of the U.S. population had become top-heavy with seniors.

The new, third demographic transition that now characterizes the twenty-first century takes its unique importance from the political, social, and economic interactions at its core: masses of stakeholders, sharply differentiated along demographic lines, are embroiled in this transition. In essence, the older generation is the established majority group, thus reflecting the past, while the incoming younger generation, made up in sizable part of immigrants, differs by race or culture. These distinctions between the generations—racial, immigrant, and size—are straining the political relations that enable consensus in democratic societies. The new demographic transition embodies this overt political dimension. Despite their racial and cultural differences, the older and incoming generations need to negotiate a new relationship suited to handling the burdens on society that will emerge in the near future. Thus, the new demographic transition, unlike the prior transitions, entails the forging of a new social contract that spans racial and generational divisions.

European nations continue to lead the world in fertility decline and aging. However, the immigration and ethnic dimensions of the transition have been more slowly recognized and accepted in Europe. A recent United Nations report concludes that, in comparison to the United States and Canada, which accept immigration as a permanent feature of their populations and encourage settlement, most European countries do not consider themselves immigration countries and so follow ad hoc and control-oriented policies. . . . Pursuing a deliberate and systematic immigration policy, which balances human rights, human capital requirements and integration concerns, is the best option to ensure that future migration is beneficial for both individual migrants and their children as well as for their receiving and sending countries. . . . [Also,] immigration brings diversity and the necessity to manage increasing cultural pluralism and multiethnicity.[16]

Population Growth and Aging

The population's growth and the net effects of its members' aging lie at the heart of demographic change. Both California and the United States are experiencing substantial growth in population. From a base of 20 million in 1970, California's population is expected to rise to 38.1 million by 2010 and 46.4 million by 2030.[17] The U.S. population was 203.3 million in 1970—almost exactly ten times the size of California—but it has risen more slowly, with 308.9 million projected in 2010 and 363.3 million in 2030.

The Graying of the Population

The distribution of population growth by age group has particular impacts. For example, the growth of a pre-adult population increases educational expenditures, while the growth of an elderly population drives up health care expenditures. In between these extremes, growth in the number of young adults boosts the entry levels of the workforce and the housing market, while increasing ranks of the late-middle-aged magnify the number of residents in their peak earning years. These changes in the character of population growth are quite substantial in both California and the United States owing to the large concentration of baby boomers who, like the proverbial bulge of the pig in a python, are rippling through the successive age groups decade by decade. Between 1970 and 1990, the proportion of the population under age twenty dropped from 38 percent to 29 percent in both California and the United States. Instead, in the same period, the share of residents age twenty to thirty-nine bulged, while from 1990 to 2010 it is the forty- to fifty-nine age group that is experiencing a growing share. Finally, in the mature phase of the transition, from 2010 to 2030, the share of those over age sixty will grow from 16 percent to 23 percent in California and from 18 percent to 25 percent in the United States.

Figure 3.1   Share of Total U.S. Population Growth by Age Group

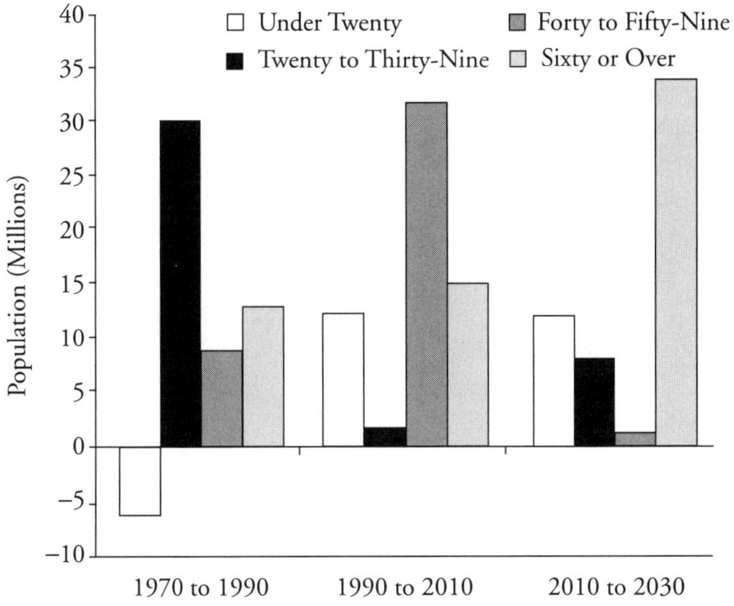

Source: U.S. Census Bureau decennial censuses and projections.

These shifts in shares have major impacts: consider that 1 percent of the U.S. population in 2010 will amount to 3 million people, or that 1 percent of the California population will amount to 380,000 people. These impacts are highly leveraged, because a shift of 1 percent from one category to another means a loss of 3 million here and a gain of 3 million there. Just how great a shift this represents is shown in figure 3.1 for the United States as a whole. Over 30 million people were added in the age range of twenty to thirty-nine in the first period, from 1970 to 1990, but population growth shifted to the next older age ranges in successive time periods. In the coming time period, growth above age sixty will dwarf all other age ranges, accounting for 62.6 percent of expected growth. As is often said, a squeaky wheel gets the grease, and the age groups that are growing and making new demands are the ones that get the most attention. This certainly has been the case for the baby boomers throughout their lives.[18]

Looking ahead, the principal impact of aging is going to be the growing weight of the elderly population compared to smaller numbers of working-age residents. Demographers have a measure termed the old-age dependency ratio, which is simply the ratio of all people age sixty-five and older to those of working age, here defined as twenty-five to sixty-four to exclude those in late adolescence and the transitional stage of the early twenties. Granted that some of those over age sixty-five are still working, while some of those who are younger are not, but this is a useful overall benchmark for describing age balance over time. Early in the twentieth century, at the time of the last great immigration wave, the dependency ratio in California and the United States was very low, around 100 seniors for every 1,000 working-age residents (see figure 3.2). From 1970 to 2010, the dependency ratio was about twice as high, but remained fairly constant. However, from 2010 to 2030, during the later phase of the demographic transition, the ratio in California is expected to climb from 214 seniors for every 1,000 workers to 350, and in the United States as a whole from 246 to 411. In a dramatic upward shift, the old-age dependency ratio will have increased by more than half in just twenty years. Meanwhile, the ratio of children under age twenty will hold fairly constant during this period at around 500 per 1,000 working-age adults in both California and the United States. Working-age adults, our principal taxpayers, are going to be burdened from both ends.

The climate of social, political, and economic behavior will look very different in a society dominated by the elderly compared to one dominated by youth and their parents. Institutions that serve this age group will need to be greatly expanded to accommodate its growing needs. One topic receiving widespread attention is the expected burden of numerous seniors on the Social Security system and the Medicare program. Between 1980 and 2015, the elderly share of all expenditures in the federal budget is projected to increase from 31 percent to 48 percent.[19] It goes without saying that, in a time of fiscal austerity, every percentage-point share of the budget is hotly contested, because an increase of even one percentage point, let alone seventeen, must come from some other program. Moreover, the preferences of elderly voters cannot be dismissed, because they are politically more active and register and turn out to vote at much higher rates than younger adults. We return to the coming intergenerational conflicts in chapter 9.

The Impact on the Labor Force and Economy

More than government services or politics are affected by the shifting age structure. One realm in which the consequences will be particularly broad is

Figure 3.2   Ratio of Seniors per 1,000 Working-Age (Twenty-Five to
Sixty-Four) Residents, California and the United States

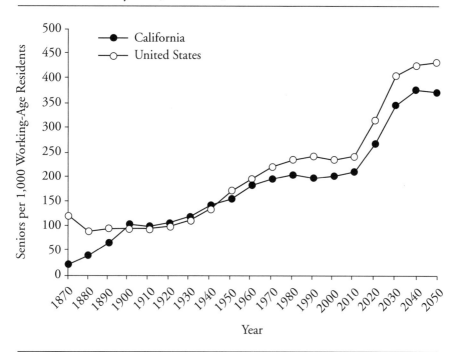

Source: U.S. Census Bureau decennial censuses and projections; California Department of Finance Demographic Research Unit projections.

employment. The economy depends on there being workers who can hold jobs; filling those jobs is a matter of finding enough people who are old enough to have acquired suitable training and who have not retired from the labor force. Without these workers, the economy cannot grow and may in fact shrink in certain sectors. Over recent decades we have witnessed dramatic changes in the labor force, but the first half of the twenty-first century is likely to see equally dramatic changes from the last half of the twentieth.

A recent study by the U.S. Bureau of Labor Statistics offers fascinating insights.[20] Two major trends characterized previous decades, one of which was the increase in labor force participation among women. The percentage of women age sixteen and older who were employed or looking for work rose from 43.3 percent in 1970 to 57.5 percent in 1990; a period of slower growth is projected to follow, with the rate rising to 62.2 percent in 2010 and then declining to 57.4 percent in 2030. Meanwhile, men's participation has been *falling steadily*, from 79.7 percent in 1970 to 76.1 percent in 1990; further decline is projected for the twenty-first century, from 73.2 percent in 2010 to 67.6 percent in 2030. Thus, the difference between men's and women's participation is narrowing to a ten-point differential, compared to the thirty-six-point differential that prevailed in 1970. This convergence of the roles of men and women is a hallmark of the recent social change that is remaking life in America.[21]

The baby boom is the second dominant factor shaping labor force trends in recent and future decades: "Just as the entry of the baby boomers swelled the ranks of the labor force in the last three decades, their exit will have a profound effect on the level and composition of the U.S. labor force in the next two decades. The baby-boom generation will remain a generator of change even at its retirement."[22] Indeed, so important is the baby boom generation that employers will be reluctant to let these older workers go, and employers will probably offer inducements (part-time work, flexible hours, higher pay) to forestall their retirement. Already there is evidence that a growing share of older workers are delaying their retirement or continuing with part-time employment. In fact, compared to past generations, baby boomers over the age of sixty-five are projected to continue working at substantially higher rates in the decades up to 2020, when the highest number of baby boomers will be retiring.[23]

California and the nation are headed for a drastic slowdown in workforce and employment growth, owing to the falling population growth in prime working-age adults, a point heavily emphasized by demographers.[24] California's workforce will continue to grow at a faster rate than the nation's, but its growth is also expected to slow markedly (see figure 3.3).[25] The rate of annual labor force growth in the 1970 to 1990 period was remarkably high in California, even exceeding 3 percent per year. A sharp drop-off followed in the recession of the early 1990s, with a bounce back in the latter half of the decade. But in this middle period of 1990 to 2010, California's labor force growth is much slower and fairly similar to the nation's. Thereafter, from 2010 to 2030, the nation's labor force growth will slow even more dramatically, falling below California's, even as California labor force growth sinks to its lowest level sustained across multiple years since the Great Depression.

The three phases of the demographic transition are clearly evident in the slowdown of labor force growth—the boom in labor force growth as young baby boomers flooded the employment market, a stable phase marked by their mature middle age, and then the sharp slowdown that will accompany

Figure 3.3   Annual Percentage Growth in the Labor Force During Each Phase of the Demographic Transition, California and the United States

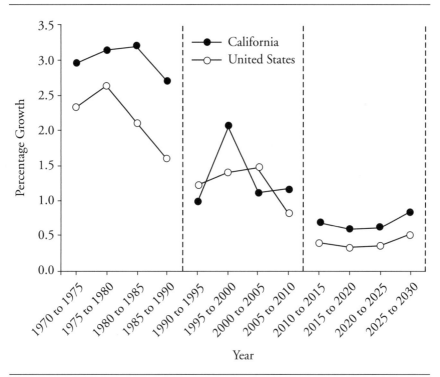

Source: Data by Toossi (2002); California data from Current Population Survey (1970 to 2000) and projections by author (2005 to 2030).

their eventual retirement. These phases are clearly marked by the changes in the generational composition of the growth. Between 1970 and 1990, the high growth in labor force participation was sustained primarily by workers under the age of forty-five (85 percent of the total growth in California and 90 percent in the United States). These young workers were more recently educated and carried many of the newer skills demanded in the evolving economy, leading to enhanced labor force productivity. In the current period, 1990 to 2010, the growth in the younger labor force has slowed to a small fraction of its prior level, amounting to only 20 percent in California and 18 percent in the United States of a much-diminished total increase in the labor force. Instead, the great bulk of labor force growth consists of adults over age forty-five, who are not truly new workers but the formerly young adults who have now aged into a more senior labor force position. Finally, in the coming period, 2010 to 2030, the growth of this experienced labor force will subside to a level similar to that seen in the pre-1990 period. Instead, the burden of labor force growth will then be carried by a new younger generation.

Changing Racial and Ethnic Composition

One of the most often cited aspects of demographic change involves race and ethnicity. A difference in color is what is most visible to many people, although this factor by itself may be less important than age, skill level, or immigrant status. Many people simply assume that racial-ethnic identification is a surrogate for all these other factors.

In the racial and ethnic aspects of the great transition, California is well advanced beyond the nation as a whole. An overview of changes from 1970 to 2030 is provided in figure 3.4, which shows the portion of the total population in a given year that is composed of the white non-Hispanic population (the shrinking white portion at the top of the figure) and the portion that comprises people who are African American, Asian and Pacific Islander, or Hispanic (the growing bottom portion of the figure). Also included is the small percentage of American Indians and other races, including multiracial residents, a category first introduced by the Census Bureau in 2000.[26] Census respondents self-select into one of these historical racial-ethnic categorizations of the population, but professional analysis, and some politics, interjects itself into this choice by having determined in the first place what the categories will be.[27] The tabulation of results is also a matter of professional, not individual, choice, particularly with regard to sorting out people who are both Hispanic and of some race. We have followed the convention of the California Department of Finance and others of treating Hispanics as equivalent to a racial category and subtracting their numbers from all other racial groups. For example, a respondent who describes his or her racial and ethnic identity as white and Hispanic, or as black and Hispanic, is counted only in the Hispanic category, not in the white or black category. It bears emphasis that the projections do not pretend to describe the future self-identification of residents of California or the United States. Rather, the projections are best understood as representing the predominant racial and Hispanic *heritage* of residents as population groups were defined in 2000.

In 1970 California already had a population with a substantial Hispanic

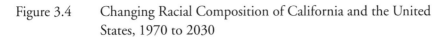

Figure 3.4   Changing Racial Composition of California and the United States, 1970 to 2030

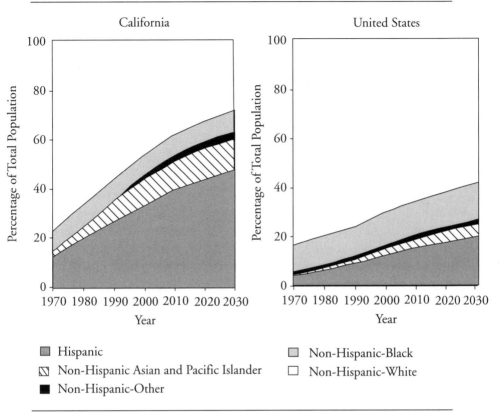

Source: U.S. Census Bureau decennial censuses and projections; California Department of Finance Demographic Research Unit projections.

presence, 12.1 percent, and in total 22.7 percent of the state's population was identified in some group other than white non-Hispanic.[28] In comparison, in the United States as a whole Latinos were a much smaller share of the population at that time, 4.7 percent, and instead African Americans were the largest minority group, at 11.1 percent of the total.[29] The overall share of the national population formed by groups other than white non-Hispanic was 16.8 percent, somewhat less than in California.

Over the decades, the racial makeup of California and the United States has shifted rapidly. The pace of change has been especially abrupt in California, where the Latino share of the population had surged to 26.0 percent by 1990 and is projected to be 38.7 percent in 2010 and 46.8 percent in 2030.[30] The Asian and Pacific Islander portion of the California population also has grown rapidly, from 3.3 percent in 1970 to 9.2 percent in 1990, but this group is expected to grow more slowly, reaching 12.4 percent in 2010 and leveling off at 13.2 percent in 2030. Meanwhile, the white non-Hispanic portion of California's population is expected to continue its decline: falling from 77.3 percent in 1970 to 57.1 percent in 1990, it is projected to decrease to 39.2 percent by 2010 and to reach 29.5 percent in 2030. The steepness of that decline can be seen in a comparison with other major immigrant receiving states (figure 3.5). The white share is decreasing much more rapidly in California than in Texas, New York, New Jersey, Florida, or Illinois.[31]

The racial shifts in the United States are proceeding in the same direction, although they are less abrupt than in California, and so the dynamics have not yet revealed themselves as clearly.[32] Even though white decline is slower in the United States as a whole than in California, by about 2010 the white share in the United States will have fallen to about the level witnessed in California thirty years earlier. African Americans constitute a much larger and continuing presence in the nation as a whole than they do in California; however, in the nation African Americans have already been surpassed in number by Latinos and are now the third largest racial-ethnic group. Of course, the population is not evenly mixed across the entire United States. African Americans constitute a much larger share of the population in most southern states and in certain midwestern and northeastern states. Conversely, Latinos are most heavily concentrated in the West, from California through Texas, and in New York and Florida, but their ranks are growing throughout much of the South and Midwest as well.[33]

The various racial-ethnic groups are distributed unevenly across age groups, a fact of some consequence. This is well illustrated in California as it evolves toward a multiethnic society. In 1990 over half of the state's population under twenty years of age already comprised Latinos and others who were not white non-Hispanic (see figure 3.6). Whites were a majority, however, of all other age groups, and the white majority was successively greater in older age groups, reaching 76.7 percent white among those age sixty and older. By 2010 we anticipate that the white shares will have decreased in all age groups, falling under 30 percent among those under age twenty and declining to 60 percent among those age sixty and older. Looking ahead to 2030, we see that the white

Figure 3.5   The Declining White, Non-Hispanic Population Share in California, Texas, New York, New Jersey, Illinois, and the United States, 1970 to 2030

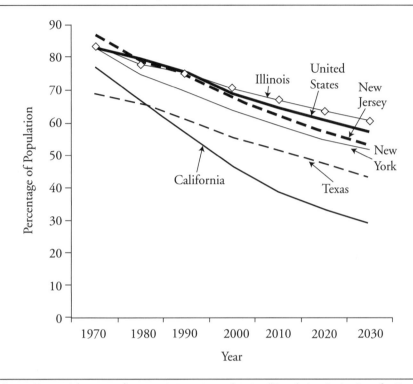

Source: Decennial census of 1970, 1980, 1990, and 2000; "Population Projections for States by Age, Sex, Race, and Hispanic Origin: 1995 to 2025," PPL 47 (Washington: U.S. Census Bureau); extrapolations by author from 2025 to 2030.

population will have lost its majority in the older age group, and its share among the other age groups will range only from 29.0 percent at ages forty to fifty-nine down to 21.3 percent among those under age twenty.

This is a dramatic change from the picture before 1990. Whereas whites were once the majority in California, or at least the largest group at every age, by 2010 they will be outnumbered by Latinos in the younger two age groups, and by 2030 they will be outnumbered by Latinos in all age groups save the oldest. Indeed, in the prime age range of twenty to fifty-nine, white residents will amount to little more than one-quarter of the state's population, while Latinos

Figure 3.6   Racial Transition of Age Groups in California

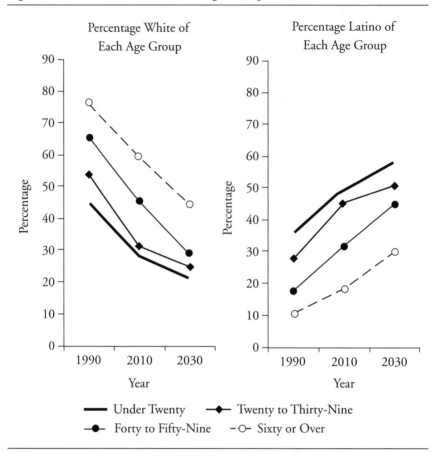

Source: Demographic Research Unit, California Department of Finance, population projections issued in 2004.

will amount to one-half. This shift underscores the previous findings about the greatly slowed growth in labor force participation in the later phase of the demographic transition. Not only will the group age sixty and older, largely retired from the labor force, be predominantly white, but the prime working ages in California will be filling with Latinos and, to a smaller degree, Asians.

Two of the most crucial questions in California are whether this future generation of workers will be able to replace the highly skilled baby boomers who are retiring and whether they will be able to carry the tax burdens required to support services for this large population of retirees. Similar questions regarding the demographic challenge of labor force preparation have been raised in other states, most notably in Texas.

Immigration and a Growing Foreign-Born Population

To make any sense of the changes wrought by the most recent great wave of immigration, we first need to understand how many foreign-born people have immigrated to the United States and the timing of their arrival.

Our Immigration History

The current wave of immigration is the latest of four great waves of immigration to the United States.[34] The earliest waves gave rise to our traditional identity as a nation of immigrants. The first was the wave of colonization before 1820, when immigrants came largely from the British Isles but also from western Europe. A second wave of immigrants arrived between 1820 and 1860, and the third wave ran from 1880 to the onset of World War I. During this third wave, immigrant origins were diversified: many of them were southern and eastern Europeans, such as Italians and Poles, and Japanese arrived in the western states. Following a long pause, the fourth and current wave of immigration began after 1965.

From the perspective of Americans alive today, the twentieth century was dominated by two great immigration events. Although annual arrivals of immigrants had been slowly increasing since 1950, the Immigration Act of 1965 revamped the old national quota system and opened the door to greatly expanded numbers of new arrivals from Asian and Latin American countries. This led to rapid increases in new immigrants, with the pace of arrival accelerating from the 1970s to the 1980s; annual flows continued to increase from the 1990s into the 2000s. This great resurgence in immigration, the fourth great wave, is the only immigration that most Americans have known.

Yet there was a prior immigration event that was at least as important as this resurgence: the *withdrawal* of immigration in the middle of the twentieth century. During the 1920s a series of immigration acts brought to a close the great wave of immigration that had been flowing from southern and eastern Europe. Whereas immigration from 1920 to 1924 was running at the annual level of 555,000 per year, by 1928 the annual flow had been cut to only 279,678.[35] During the Great Depression and World War II years, immigration plunged to very low levels, averaging 43,000 each year between 1932 and 1945, and even the slow growth in the 1950s did not reach an annual in-flow greater than 250,000 per year. In essence, between 1925 and 1965 the United States sustained a forty-year lull in immigration. This long reduction in new immigrant arrivals was unusual in American history, and coming on the heels of the massive immigration from 1903 through 1914, which aver-aged nearly one million arrivals every year, shutting off the flow of new resi-dents had major impacts on American cities, leading to the problems of urban decay that plagued the 1950s and 1960s.[36] During the immigration lull, previous immigrants incorporated themselves into American society and the economy, and their children—the second generation—came of age. After World War II, and aided by the new public programs of the New Deal, enor-mous progress was achieved in the context of a booming postwar economy by past immigrants and their children.[37] This is richly demonstrated, for exam-ple, in Richard Alba's study of the Italian American population, which shows that Italian Americans had largely closed the gap with the native-born popu-lation of Anglo-Saxon heritage by 1980.[38] The major story of much of the twentieth century thus was one of immigrant incorporation into a growing native-born population.

The Trend in Foreign-Born Share

The rise and fall of the foreign-born presence in the American population is startling in its magnitude. What is most remarkable in viewing this trend over 150 years, from 1880 to 2030, is the steep decline followed by a sharp rebound in the percentage of foreign-born residents of both California and the United States (figure 3.7).[39] In the nation as a whole, a steady-state percentage of for-eign-born of just under 15 percent was achieved in the latter half of the nine-teenth century through 1910. The percentage of foreign-born increased after each wave of renewed immigration, but the figure was moderated by the grow-ing bulk of the native-born population, including the children of the new im-migrants who were born in the United States. Moreover, immigration had been running so long that the deaths of immigrants who had arrived decades earlier also offset the numbers of new arrivals. After 1910 the percentage of foreign-born began its long decline to a low point of 4.7 percent recorded in the nation in 1970. At that time many of the foreign-born were concentrated in older age groups because they had aged since their arrival many decades earlier.[40]

Immigration has always been more prominent in California than the na-tion as a whole, both because its geographic position on the Pacific and bor-

Figure 3.7   Long-Term Trend in Percentage of Foreign-Born Residents of California and the United States, 1880 to 2030

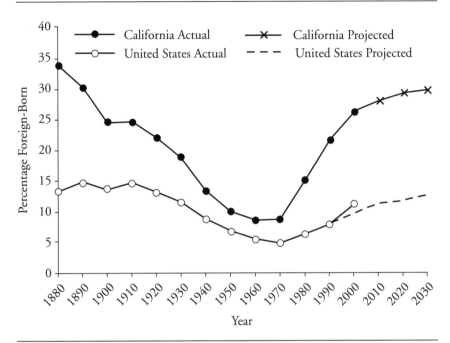

Source: 1850 to 1990: Campbell J. Gibson and Emily Lennon, "Historical Census Statistics on the Foreign-Born Population of the United States, 1850–1990," Population Division working paper 29 (Washington: U.S. Census Bureau, 1999); U.S. Census Bureau, 2000 census PUMS 5 percent data; 2010 to 2020 California Demographic Futures projections by John Pitkin, verson 5.0; final projections consistent with the 1990 census (NP-T5), "Projections of the Resident Population by Race, Hispanic Origin, and Nativity: Middle Series, 1999 to 2100" (Washington: U.S. Census Bureau, Population Division, 2000).

dering Mexico makes it a natural port of entry and because the storied attractions of California have drawn many over the years to settle in the state. In California the foreign-born percentage reached a high of 38.6 percent in 1860 following the Gold Rush, which brought new settlers from around the world. Thereafter, the percentage of foreign-born steadily declined for one hundred years, reaching its low point of 8.5 percent in 1960. From 1970 to 1990, with the resurgence of immigration in the first phase of the demographic transition, the percentage of foreign-born rocketed upward to 21.7 percent. It should not be surprising that some Californians found this sudden rise in the foreign-born population startling and unsettling. No matter that this percentage was well below the level of a century before—recent memory extended only to 1950, when the foreign-born percentage had been less than 10 percent. The relative change within a generation was truly striking.

After 1990 the percentage of foreign-born continued to rise in California, but more slowly, reaching 26.2 percent in 2000, and this proportion is expected to level off at about 30 percent in 2030, according to projections developed by the California Demographic Futures project at the University of Southern California (USC).[41] The surprising absence of information on future foreign-born residents in the United States from most projections creates even more uncertainty than needs to exist. In California substantially more detailed information has been demanded in light of the greater prevalence of the foreign-born population in that state, and the USC information on the foreign-born and their children has been readily adopted for its utility by other forecasters in the state.[42] Similar forecast details have not yet been produced for any other state in the United States,[43] although the Census Bureau has produced somewhat similar information for the nation as a whole. Unfortunately, those projections were last updated before the 2000 census, and they already underestimated the percentage of foreign-born at that time, calling into question their projections for future decades as well.[44] Nonetheless, it appears that the U.S. percentage of foreign-born is headed back to the vicinity of the 15 percent level that was the long-term average in the nineteenth century.[45] This level is about half of what is likely to be reached in California and possibly in some other large states shown by the 2000 census to already have unusually high foreign-born percentages, most notably New York (20.4 percent), New Jersey (17.5 percent), Florida (16.7 percent), and Texas (13.9 percent).[46]

The Annual Arrival of Legal and Unauthorized Immigrants

The demographic story differs between California and the United States. For California, the first phase of the demographic transition, from 1970 to 1990, witnessed tremendous growth in immigrant population, including the unauthorized. In the subsequent phase, from 1990 to 2010, immigration leveled off in California, ceasing its upward acceleration. In contrast, in the nation as a whole immigration continued to rise rapidly in the 1990 to 2010 period, with more of it unauthorized, and with much more of it outside California. Thus, the rest of the nation is now experiencing the demographic changes from immigration that California experienced twenty years earlier. At some point, probably in the near term, immigration will begin to level off in the United States as a whole and possibly decline.[47] At that time the nation will enter the phase of a more settled immigrant population that now characterizes California.

The size of the foreign-born population is increased by the annual flow of new immigrant arrivals, which has steadily escalated since 1965. In the discussion that follows, and throughout the book, I follow the common practice of employing the terms "immigrants" and "foreign-born" interchangeably. Both groups are defined as persons living in the United States who were not born as American citizens. As a practical matter, surveys and censuses of the foreign-born in the United States do not record people's visa status but ask solely about place of birth and whether the person is a citizen. Thus, it is not possible to distinguish in the population data between permanent resident aliens, unauthorized immigrants, and residents on temporary or visitor status.[48]

The inflow of immigrants is difficult to measure accurately because in recent years a sizable portion of them have been undocumented owing to the unauthorized or illegal nature of their entry. Nonetheless, we can observe the annual trend in officially authorized immigrants that is reported by the federal government and supplement that with the numbers of total foreign-born that are reported in Census Bureau surveys of the population at large. The census count or the CPS provide a more complete representation of total immigration than legal admissions because a large sample of all residents of America, regardless of their legal status, are asked their place of birth and, if foreign-born, their year of arrival in the United States.[49]

We can see the story told by these data for California and the United States in figure 3.8. Note that the California graph is scaled at half the size of the U.S. graph because for a time California drew nearly half of the immigrants in America. Authorized immigration in the United States has increased steadily from a level of around 250,000 per year before 1965 to 500,000 per year in the latter 1970s, topping one million after 2000. The total immigrant flow expanded at an even greater pace, reaching an average of 1.6 million for several years from 1998 to 2003. The flow to California accelerated even more rapidly than in the United States through about 1990 and then ceased its growth. During the 1980s California was drawing 38 percent of total immigrant arrivals in the United States, but after 1990 this attraction declined steeply; the figure has been around 22 percent in recent years. The reasons for this reduced immigrant attraction and the impact it has had in California are addressed in chapter 5.

Figure 3.8   Annual Immigration, Total and Legal, to California and the United States, 1960 to 2000

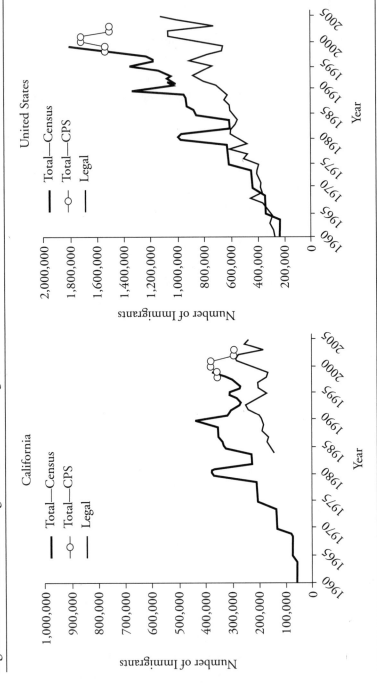

Source: Office of Immigration Statistics, *Yearbook of Immigration Statistics 2004* (Washington: U.S. Department of Homeland Security), available at: http://uscis.gov/graphics/shared/statistics/yearbook/Yearbook2004.pdf; Current Population Survey; PUMS data, 1970, 1980, 1990, and 2000 census.

The surge in unauthorized or illegal immigration is roughly indicated by the gap between the total immigrant flow and what is officially authorized.[50] In the United States, the total and authorized immigrant numbers were fairly similar before 1975 (see figure 3.8). Thereafter, they began to diverge, with a large gap observed in the late 1980s and an especially wide gap opening in the 1990s. This variance between authorized immigrants and census-recorded arrivals has led one of the most respected experts on the subject, Jeffrey Passel, to conclude that unauthorized immigration has grown at an exceptional rate, rising from an annual arrival number of 140,000 in the 1980s to 450,000 per year during the early 1990s, and reaching over 700,000 per year from 1995 through 2004.[51] In the latter period, the number of unauthorized arrivals actually exceeded those who were authorized. These effects were buffered for California. Where California once was the home to roughly half of the unauthorized immigrants in America, that share fell to only 24 percent by the early 2000s.[52] And California's share of the annual inflow of new unauthorized immigrants may have fallen as low as 13 percent in the early 2000s.[53] Meanwhile, the unauthorized population has been spreading across America. Where once it was concentrated in the six major states for immigrant settlement, more of the unauthorized have spread to other states, increasing the other states' share from 12 percent to 39 percent of total illegal immigration between 1990 and the period 2002 to 2004.[54] Thus, the rest of the nation is now experiencing the same kind of demographic changes from immigration that California experienced twenty years earlier. This spreading out greatly broadens the base of interest in Congress on immigration issues from what it was when only five or six states were affected.

The Growth of a Longer-Settled Immigrant Population

During the initial ramp-up of immigration, many of the foreign-born were necessarily newcomers, but in the more mature phase, after immigrant arrivals have accumulated for two or three decades, many more of the foreign-born are long settled. The foreign-born population is built by the layering of new arrivals on top of previous arrivals. In fact, after a generation, many immigrants have children who were born in America, creating a native-born second generation.

In 1970, when immigration was just beginning its resurgence, California had a low percentage of foreign-born (8.8 percent) and a slightly larger second generation (11.5 percent). By 1990, when the foreign-born share had soared to 22.7 percent, half of those foreign-born had lived less than ten years in the United States, and half were longer settled here. By 2010 more of the foreign-born will be longer settled, and the second generation will have expanded (as discussed in detail in chapter 5). The maturing settlement of the immigrant population is expected to progress even further as we reach the mature phase of the demographic transition, from 2010 to 2030. The share of the population made up of new arrivals will continue to decline even as the cumulating waves of long-settled residents pushes the foreign-born share to the highest level seen in the state or nation, respectively, since 1910 or before.

In California we can already discern the contours of a more maturely settled immigrant population, in sharp contrast to the concentrations of newcomers elsewhere. All told, just over half of all residents of California are expected to be immigrant parents and children (the so-called immigrant stock) by 2030. They will be very different people at that time from the newcomers who dominated the images we had in 1990 about what it means to be an immigrant. One of the primary differences will be their experience of being long settled in the United States, a characteristic that holds major implications, including advantages for the future that have not yet been generally recognized.

Conclusion

The demographic change that is sweeping the United States has advanced furthest in California. Like the rest of the United States, California has its share of aging baby boomers, but it differs in that it received concentrated international migration earlier than the rest of the country. Further, the decline of California's white non-Hispanic population has progressed much more rapidly than in any other state. Just as Florida may provide the nation with a preview of its aging future, so California provides an early example of a more diverse society and one with a large component of foreign-born residents.

The changes in California are also representative of a global demographic transition, the third in a series of transitions that began around 1800. The extreme decline in birthrates following the first and second transitions is leading to population aging throughout the developed world. For lack of an adequate number of young people coming of age, the slowdown in workforce growth in developed nations coincides with the growing weight of a senior population. As a result, immigration is on the upsurge worldwide to fill those gaps in the workforce. But immigration brings with it racial and cultural changes that may cause social discomfort or resentment in the long-established, older population that retains political power. As a result, the new demographic transition generates political friction that ignites local firestorms (see chapter 7). Simply bringing a longer perspective to bear is a good beginning for helping citizens and leaders understand how local incidents should be framed and addressed. Thus, the lessons of California may hold global importance for helping us adjust more smoothly to the major transition in which we are all engaged.

Chapter 4

A Dismal Future? The Outlook in the Early Transition Period

IN THIS CHAPTER, we review the background to the rather discouraged outlook on demographic change that arose after 1970. The demographic transition is hardly just a dry set of scientific facts. Race, immigration, and aging are social issues with deep meaning for most people, often invoking highly emotional responses. The demographic transition also has economic consequences for the workforce, the number of home buyers and taxpayers, and the relative burdens shared by the generations. Those economic concerns matter greatly to the average citizen, as well as to the leaders of government and business. Combine these with the social issues of race, immigration, and aging, provide an opportunity for voters to express their opinion, and we have the makings of a highly volatile political mix.

No one has reacted more viscerally to the demographic transition than the established majority population in California, and for good reason. The transition began earlier in California than in most of the United States, and it has proceeded more rapidly, setting up a more abrupt contrast of social regimes. The long-established population has reacted more negatively than others because those residents may feel they have the most to lose, and they compare the ongoing changes to a time in the past they remember as being better.

From the standpoint of many white observers, California and America are in a steep, unlimited social decline. The great demographic transition has been poorly received because the majority population resists accepting the decline of its dominant position. Yet, as I argue here, this group rejected this future even more strenuously than it would have otherwise because it unfolded at such an inopportune time. The general economic gloom in the nation during the 1980s and early 1990s and the sense of violated entitlements made the public both more fearful of the future and less generous toward newcomers. One historical analysis of past eras of change emphasizes this crucial point:

> When their living standards are rising, people do not view themselves, their fellow citizens, and their society as a whole the way they do when those standards are stagnant or falling. They are more trusting, more inclusive, and more open to change *when they view their future prospects and their children's with confidence rather than anxiety or fear.* Economic growth is not merely the enabler of higher consumption; it is in many ways the wellspring from which democracy and civil society flow.[1]

California was once the land of optimism, but something happened to puncture those rosy expectations. As the political journalist Peter Schrag has observed: "California seemed to have an optimism about its population, possibilities, and future whose largest flaw was the very excess of *expectations* on which it rested."[2] But all that unraveled from the mid-1970s through the early 1990s. First a property tax revolt and then growing disaffection undermined political will in the state. Immigration and demographic change play a major role in this discouraged outlook, as Schrag observes, but whether these factors are the cause of the negativism or merely its scapegoat, or whether they might even be the victim of the malaise, is not easily deciphered.[3]

These social and political reactions should not be lightly dismissed, and in fact they require our understanding. Even if these reactions are shortsighted and self-defeating, they are a powerful force to be addressed. By virtue of their majority status among voters, long-established residents have the power to shape public policy in ways that will make the outcomes of long-term trends either turn for the better or grow worse. In a democracy, the voting majority always deserves respectful consideration.

Amid political volatility and historical turmoil, how likely is it that most people will be able to see clearly or that there will be any agreement? If a consensus were to be reached, most likely it would be built on common denominators of recent experience and the most popularly held explanations for that experience. Commonly shared experiences are key to the popular mood and also feed into the mood of a story that is widely agreed upon, even if they are tangential or unrelated to the demographic transition.

This chapter explores the roots of one story about immigration and the future, the story of despair. The future is unpredictable, but it is knowable to the citizens through means described in chapter 2. Unfortunately, such popular knowledge amounts to a mere extrapolation of recent trends, compounded by a visceral assessment of the trends' desirability. Images of the future thus depend greatly on the fortunes of the current day: in a time of prosperity and minimal conflict, people project much more favorable future conditions than they do if recent conditions have been trending unfavorably. Among the key background influences are economic trends, political scandal, crime, and even natural disasters. Many of these national issues have played out most dramatically in California. A review of this crucial background context may help us understand how it led to the dismal outlook on the future held by many California residents, and whether or not that outlook will persist.

A confluence of calamities in the early 1990s may have made the future that was "known" at that time the bleakest possible. Not only had immigration in California (both legal and illegal) accelerated to its greatest increase during that time, but it coincided with recession, natural disaster, and collapsing house prices. With unfortunate timing, California's rise in immigration peaked at a time when despair was rampant, and as a result, immigrants became a symbol of what was wrong in California. Once established, the belief in this version of the future became stubbornly entrenched, even if the supporting evidence may have faded (as demonstrated in chapter 5). What gave rise to this dismal story about the future?

The Roots of Pessimism

The 1990s were a very rocky time for consensus in America, and the fragmentation that took hold then has spilled over into the new century. A number of widely shared perceptions underlie the breakdown in consensus, breeding, ironically, an alternative consensus for dissension.

Perceptions of demographic scenarios are filtered through memories of recent economic and social experience. The sense of decline and dissatisfaction that pervaded the United States in the 1990s was rooted in some well-known historical events. The strife over the Vietnam War and the political trauma of the Watergate scandal had left a legacy of lasting disillusionment with and loss of trust in government.[4] This cynicism was compounded by the economic and social changes that soon followed.

The political events of the late 1960s and early 1970s coincided with a major economic shift that ended a remarkable quarter-century of prosperity and ushered in a quarter-century of stagnation. The shift was so complete that it underlies much of our outlook today. This is best indicated by the trends in family income and government spending.

Family incomes soared during the 1950s by 43 percent in real dollars, and the rising standard of living was met by a rapid increase in consumer goods.[5] Televisions, automobiles, and suburban homes became staples of middle-class life, and life became far more luxurious than had been possible during the hardships of the 1930s and the war years. Even the specter of the cold war and nuclear attack could not dampen the national spirit or suppress the burgeoning family and consumer lifestyles.[6] This sense of prosperity continued through the 1960s. Family incomes continued to rise by 41 percent, and the middle class (together with the more comfortable classes) grew to become a dominant majority, approaching two-thirds (65 percent) of all households by 1970, an extraordinary increase from the 12 percent estimated among the 1940 population.[7] The post–World War II era was one of enormous economic progress and a growing sense of entitlement.

The social protests of the day did not touch most families. The civil rights protests, the emergence of the hippie longhairs, and growing antiwar activism were no more a factor for most families or most cities than were the cold war threats. Life remained good in California and the nation, with continued growth in employment opportunities and rising incomes, an expanding middle class, and record levels of homeownership. Indeed, the nation appeared intently focused on family life: the baby boom children born from 1946 to 1964 were absorbing attention whether as newborns, preschoolers, or high school students.

All began to change rapidly after 1970, however. The oldest cohorts of the baby boomers reached their twenties and began to assume independent adult lives, moving into their own apartments and seeking jobs. At the same time, a set of social changes more profound than civil rights or political protest began to intrude into every family. A sexual revolution was calling into question the gender roles of wives and daughters, as well as those of the husbands and sons with whom they lived. Social normalcy was being increasingly questioned.[8]

On the political front, trust in leadership also came under scrutiny. Never in doubt during the cold war years, trust in leadership was severely challenged during the protests over the Vietnam War. Then the Watergate scandal erupted on the national stage in 1973, causing Richard Nixon finally to resign the presidency on August 9, 1974, under threat of impeachment. Confidence in presidential leadership had kept the nation at ease in the face of cold war missiles, even during the stresses of domestic protest, the civil rights movement, and the war on poverty, but now that confidence was shredded. The legacy of Vietnam and Watergate is widely regarded as one of lasting disillusionment and loss of trust in government.

Economic changes played an equally important role in the developing story of disillusionment. With the OPEC-driven recession of 1972 and 1973, the dramatic postwar income growth enjoyed by U.S. consumers came to an abrupt halt. In the next quarter-century, the average family would struggle to achieve any income growth.[9] Nonetheless, government expenditures continued to grow. During the 1950s and 1960s, per capita government expenditures had increased substantially, by 50 percent and 53 percent per decade, respectively, but this growth was bearable relative to the large increase in family incomes.[10] From 1973 to 1984, however, median family income *fell* by 6.2 percent—Frank Levy has labeled this period the "Quiet Depression"—but government expenditures continued to rise by 16 percent.[11] In fact, over the quarter-century following 1973, family incomes rose only 6.9 percent in real terms, but per capita government expenditures increased 51.9 percent, drawing on increases in both debt and taxes.[12]

Thus was laid a solid basis for the taxpayer revolt. The growing tax burden was simply perceived as excessive relative to taxpayers' incomes.[13] Despite the growing tax resistance, Americans had grown accustomed to ever-increasing government services and were reluctant to scale those back. Spending in excess of tax receipts led to a rapid increase in debt at all levels of government. Californians played a central role in this budding tax revolt. Their passage of Proposition 13 in 1978 led to severe property tax restrictions. This was the first real salvo in the national movement of fiscal discontent that carried former California governor Ronald Reagan into national office.

If ever there was a recipe for loss of confidence in government and American society, surely this was it: political scandal and an unpopular war, followed by faltering income growth, heavier tax burdens, and growing debt. Above all was the failure of the expectations formed in a time of great prosperity. The end of the postwar boom in prosperity created a great sense of violation for both young and old, according to Robert Samuelson, because decades of prosperity—including a triumph over the Great Depression and the challenges of the war years—had led Americans to feel entitled to both ever-increasing personal material comfort and ever-expanding government services and protections.[14] The abrupt cessation of growing prosperity in the 1970s created profound disillusionment and disgruntlement; frustration became so evident and widespread among the middle class that a growing number of authors had begun to address it by the mid-1990s.[15]

This violation of Americans' expectations for the good life fanned dissension by encouraging the search for various scapegoats, as Robert Samuelson observes:

> What upsets us . . . is that we have inherited a country and world different from those that we felt were our due. The disillusion is not simply that we have problems; it is that these problems confound *expectations* that were widespread and were considered realistic. We felt and feel entitled, and so someone must be held accountable for our disappointments. . . . Someone or something has sabotaged the American Dream, and the villains deserve to be pilloried and punished.[16]

Immigrants were a convenient set of outsiders who could be blamed for the unfortunate turn of events because they had arrived on the scene at about the time all the other misfortunes began.

All of these forces played out more acutely in California because prosperity, decline, and immigration were all more exaggerated in that state. California long was viewed as the great exception, a place where even the working man could enjoy the good life on a small rancho or in a bungalow with gardens.[17] Many people had migrated over the years from around the globe and from the depressed farms of the middle United States and the congested cities of the Northeast because the Golden State was seen as a land of opportunity, a place where dreams were made and the future was brighter than elsewhere.

After 1990, for reasons to be explained, California's fortunes staged a dramatic reversal. If the state once was the locus for the best of the nation's hopes and dreams, it now represented the worst of disappointments and the depths of despair. After the economic reversals, political uprisings, dramatic demographic changes, and social breakdowns of this period, a great pessimism about life in the Golden State began to prevail.

The dismal future perceived by so many is a projection of this pessimism onto the unknown decades ahead. Is this failure of disappointed expectations really a permanent feature to be suffered in the future? Might it only be a passing perception, a disillusionment that can be corrected? Before we can answer these questions and begin to rebuild the prospects for a more hopeful future, we must first uncover additional roots of the future of despair.

Concentrated Calamity in California

Despair has many sources, including indirect ones. Two leading chroniclers of California, Kevin Starr and Mike Davis—one proudly boosterish and the other darkly critical—have highlighted the discouraging effects of a concentrated series of calamities commencing around 1990.[18] The public may not realize how much the effects of that discouraging period still linger and haunt their outlook on the future even today. In the next chapter, I will document how much conditions have changed since 1995, but first we must revisit the old memories so that we can expunge their effects—remembering them so that we might finally forget and move on to planning the new future.[19]

In a period of five short years, late 1989 through 1994, California residents lived through enough collective tragedy to last half a century. The calamities were all the more painful because they came at the very peak of popularity and success for the state, including both economic boom and extraordinary dominance of its sports teams in contests with other cities. The sudden turn of events ended a glorious decade when California had prospered while much of the nation rusted, and by startling contrast, the newfound setbacks plunged the collective mood into protracted despair. Immigrants who had been drawn to the state by this very surge of prosperity became intertwined in the public imagination with the ensuing disasters.

The Fall from Glory

The onset of sustained calamity for California came very suddenly and on a very public stage. The downfall began during a sporting event, the third game of the 1989 World Series between the Oakland A's and the San Francisco Giants, an all-California championship that signified the domination of California in the sports world and on the national stage.[20] Just before the lineups were introduced at the beginning of the game, broadcast live on ABC, a violent earthquake shook the stadium and the press box for fifteen seconds. What became known as the Loma Prieta quake registered a 6.9 on the Richter scale, took sixty-seven lives, flattened portions of two freeways (traffic was snarled for months afterwards), and caused $7 billion in property damage. The World Series was postponed for ten days before play could be resumed. The ill-fated third game is now regarded as one of the most memorable World Series games ever, even though not a single pitch was thrown.

No one knew at the time that this October 1989 tragedy would—in an instant—mark the beginning of California's plunge into a period of doom and despair. The series of calamities that followed—natural disasters, economic collapse, and social upheaval—was unprecedented. As Mike Davis puts it: "The virtually biblical conjugation of disaster, which coincided with the worst regional recession in 50 years, is unique in American history."[21] Even if none of these individual events was unveiled as dramatically on the public stage as the Loma Prieta quake at the 1989 World Series, all were duly reported as photogenically as possible by the world press. California was to become the sad story of the 1990s that many delighted in telling. It certainly was not the basis for the golden future of before.

Natural Disaster

Calamity befell California in multiple ways and in rapid sequence. The Loma Prieta quake initiated a cluster of five strong earthquakes in five years' time, including the 1994 Northridge quake that devastated portions of the Los Angeles region. This flurry of earthquakes across the state was in sharp contrast to the relative quiet of the three preceding decades, during which only one earthquake had been recorded in excess of 6.7.[22] Unpredictable and yet a hallmark of California, the devastating series of earthquakes heightened uncertainty about the future.

To these earthquakes were added a series of fires that persisted over days and provided more opportunity for colorful television news footage. The Santa Barbara County fire that broke out on June 27, 1990, consumed 4,900 acres but paled in contrast to the terrible Oakland Hills "Tunnel" fire of October 20, 1991, said to be "the worst fire involving loss of life and property since the Great San Francisco Earthquake and Fire of 1906."[23] The Tunnel fire consumed 1,500 acres in a residential area, destroyed 3,100 structures, took 25 lives, and led to over $2 billion in damages. Two years later, in October

1993, the Los Angeles region was hit with a series of 14 fires that burned simultaneously across several counties, consuming 137,000 acres and destroying 554 homes. Much less devastating than the Oakland Hills fire, the Los Angeles series nevertheless took several days to quell and proved more worrisome because the numerous sites resembled a plague of fire, often arson-initiated, that reflected fears of social breakdown.[24] Capping off these natural disasters was a series of floods and mudslides, some a result of the fires that had destabilized hillsides by destroying vegetation.

Economic Depression

Californians might have absorbed the impacts of quake, fire, and flood as part of the price of living on the edge of nature. However, these natural disasters were accompanied by a major economic collapse. The California economy peaked in 1990 and thereafter plunged into the worst recession to befall the state since the Great Depression. Coincident with a national recession, the downturn was magnified in California by military downsizing and aerospace cutbacks in the southern California region that followed the end of the cold war. Poverty and unemployment nearly doubled between 1990 and 1993 and did not return to former levels until 1999.[25] State and local governments were hit hard by the recession as tax revenues shrank but service needs remained high. Budget managers were pressured by the extended length of the recession into ever more dire and creative means of financing to make ends meet. Finally, in December 1994, the Orange County government succumbed to mounting debt in the largest municipal bankruptcy in U.S. history.[26] Times were tough for residents, and government could not bail them out.

House prices, which fell steeply in the early 1990s (a sharp reversal from the boom of the late 1980s), were another focal point for the gloom of California residents. From 1984 to 1989, the median home price in California had increased an inflation-adjusted 44.1 percent, compared to only a small increase (3.8 percent) in the United States as a whole. Subsequently, prices in California reversed and fell by 21.3 percent from 1989 to 1994, while no such change occurred in the U.S. housing market. So protracted was this slump that California prices did not recover to their 1989 level until 2002.[27] The striking impact of this reversal on consumer psychology was palpable. In the five years before 1989, the average homeowner (and voter) experienced the comfort and security of rising home values and personal wealth and felt inclined to make plans based on those increases, and so the subsequent plunge in home equity was deeply deflating.

Population out-migration underlay this price decline: potential middle-class home buyers were migrating to other states with more promising opportunities. California had always before been the chosen destination for migrants from elsewhere in the United States, but now the state had become an inferior choice. This net out-migration of population was unprecedented in the state's history.[28] Current California homeowners may have wished to join the exodus but were trapped by their fallen home values. Unable to sell their homes without great financial loss, many decided to stay put and fight against the trends that were driving down the state's fortunes.

Social Breakdown and Illegal Immigration

Along with natural disaster and economic depression during this period of calamity, evidence of mounting social breakdown began to emerge, particularly in the Los Angeles region. Here was where the immigration trends became intertwined with the other calamities in an already depressed public consciousness. Gang violence was on the upswing in the early 1990s, and a record number of deaths by firearms—1,554—were recorded in Los Angeles County in 1991. Local news media added to the sense of danger and loss of control by providing daily chronicles of the rising body count. Then, on April 29, 1992, following the announcement of a surprising not-guilty verdict in the videotaped police beating of the motorist Rodney King, three days of intense civil unrest commenced. The Los Angeles riots led to fifty-two deaths, created nearly $1 billion in property damage from fires and looting, and led to the arrest of sixteen thousand people.[29] Television images broadcast the mayhem into homes all across the state and the country, and the southwesterly breeze carried the smell of smoke throughout the Los Angeles basin, even as far as Pasadena. The Rodney King incident and its aftermath signified total social breakdown: loss of control over the streets, the neighborhoods, the justice system, and the police.

Immigration loomed large in Californians' sense of imminent social breakdown. The growing numbers of unauthorized immigrants became an important symbol of what was perceived as a loss of control in the early 1990s period of calamity. Exact numbers of illegal immigrants in the United States or

California are difficult to know, because they are undocumented, but careful estimates prepared by Hans Johnson of the Public Policy Institute of California indicate that the net annual increase in undocumented California residents jumped from virtually zero in the early 1980s to 294,000 in 1988–89 and peaked at 424,000 in 1989–90 before abruptly dropping to 84,000 per year (1992–93) during the recession that followed.[30] This upsurge was heavily publicized in news accounts, and new warning signs on freeways depicted silhouettes of adults and children dashing across roadways like deer. Many citizens probably assumed that this new fact of life in California was a trend continuing upward, even if the inflow of unauthorized immigrants had fallen off sharply (see figure 4.1). As discussed later in this chapter, the perception of undocumented immigrants assumed an importance out of all proportion to their numbers in reality.

A major referendum on immigration in California soon followed on the ballot in 1994: Proposition 187, a citizen-initiated ballot proposition also known as the Save Our State (SOS) initiative. Intended to ban illegal immigrants from using government services but serving as a measure of disapproval of all immigration, the proposition drew majority support from a wide range of voters, passing 59 percent to 41 percent, even though not a single major newspaper endorsed the measure. Exit polls revealed that white voters were the strongest supporters (64 percent), but a majority of Asian American (56 percent) and African American voters (56 percent) were also supporters. Only among Latinos was there minority support (31 percent).[31] A variety of motivations have been ascribed to the majority voters, including racism, anti-immigrant sentiment, and cost-consciousness during a time of recession. All of these may well have been factors. What is noteworthy is that this initiative did not come to ballot until 1994, well after the inflow of illegal immigrants had peaked and subsided, and yet it was still strongly supported. The proposition might be characterized as a delayed effect of the late 1980s escalation in illegal immigration. However, any prior resentment was surely magnified by the gloomy mind-set and sense of lost control that prevailed in the early 1990s. And of course, people's extrapolated expectations about the continued growth of illegal immigration were reaffirmed as "fact" by campaign rhetoric. Indeed, with no verifiable data or even credible estimates of the amount of illegal immigration until the Johnson study was reported in 1996, people's imaginations had free rein.

Figure 4.1   Extrapolated Versus Actual Annual Increase in Unauthorized Immigrants in California

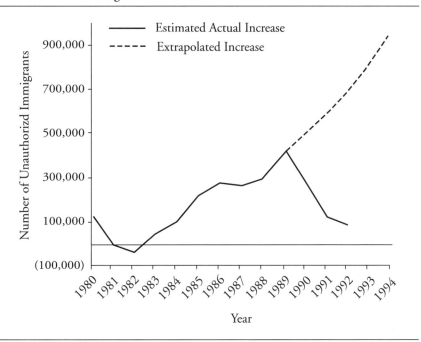

Source: Johnson (1996), series D in table 6.3, and extrapolations by author.

Perceived Trends and Opinions on Immigration

What is the meaning of illegal immigration in the perception of calamity or lost control? Immigration is hardly as damaging as an earthquake or great fire that takes many lives and costs billions in reconstruction. Yet the process of illegal immigration may, in the eyes of some citizens, be considered more threatening to the soul of the nation. Illegal immigration violates the presumption of human control even more than an earthquake or great fire, even though natural disasters cannot be prevented or made enforceable by the police and punishable by the law. Indeed, the very use of the commonly used expression "illegal immigration" emphasizes that violation of legality, even though undocumented immigrants violate no state or local police ordinances. They are termed "illegal" because their entry into the United States is unauthorized by the federal government. Because such immigration involves human actors who defy government authority and evade social control, as an expression of social breakdown it more closely resembles a riot than a fire or earthquake. Even if the simple act of unauthorized immigration involves no property damage or violence against persons, it is damaging to citizens' sense of social order. And as we have emphasized, in times of economic stress citizens are much less comfortable absorbing such a loss.

The "Takeoff" and "Takeover" by Foreign-Born Residents

What are local residents to make of the rapidly growing number of foreign-born residents? I have argued that the practice of extrapolated expectations, following the sharp takeoff in immigrant presence after 1970, probably led the average citizen to assume that this growth in the number of foreign-born would continue its upward trend. The takeoff occurred first in California, where the foreign-born rose from 8.8 percent of the state's population in 1970 to 21.7 percent by 1990. In contrast, in the nation as a whole the rise in foreign-born share has been much slower. By 1990 only 7.9 percent of the nation's population was foreign-born, a figure only moderately higher than the 4.7 percent recorded twenty years before. Many California citizens in this era may well have feared that the takeoff in the foreign-born population would be unlimited and that the previously established majority population would be driven out, the end result being an immigrant "takeover." The popular bumper sticker of the early 1990s read, "Would the last person leaving please turn out the lights?"

Expert evidence shows that this popular perception of immigration, especially illegal immigration was far out of proportion to reality. Even as recently as 2005 a public policy opinion poll in California found that a majority (53 percent) of all residents believed that immigration from other countries was the biggest factor in the state's population growth. In addition, nearly half (49 percent) of all residents felt that *illegal* immigration was contributing "a lot" to the population growth, compared to 26 percent who emphasized the contribution of legal immigration and 27 percent who emphasized births to residents as the source of growth.[32] These perceptions do not square with the demographic facts in the 2001 to 2004 period (or earlier, for that matter). It is the number of babies born to residents in the state each year that is the biggest factor in growth (536,116), followed by net foreign immigration (248,059).[33] Of that immigration, my estimate is that fewer than 100,000 immigrants each year are illegal or unauthorized.[34] Certainly, in the late 1980s, illegal immigration was a much larger factor—300,000 to 400,000 unauthorized immigrants arrived each year, according to the Johnson estimates—but the impression lingers on.

Public Opinion on Immigration

Public opinion about immigration has fluctuated over recent decades, but rarely has it encouraged an increase in immigration. This is reflected in responses to the Gallup Organization's question: "In your view, should immigration be kept at its present level, increased, or decreased?"[35] First asked in 1965, the question was initially repeated only in 1977 and 1986, and as many as 20 percent of respondents expressed no opinion. That reflects the low intensity of interest nationwide about immigration in those years. Thereafter, with rising public interest, Gallup repeated the survey more often, and the number with no opinion dropped under 5 percent. In general, approximately half of all Americans have called for a decrease in immigration in these surveys, while around 10 percent have expressed a desire for an increase. However, this response pattern has varied over the decades. In the early years, fewer than 50 percent of adults said that immigration should be decreased, but during the early to mid-1990s three consecutive surveys found that 62 to 65 percent wanted a decrease. Thereafter, from 1999 through June 2001, the reported preference for decreased immigration dropped back below 45 percent. Following the events of 9/11, the desire for decreased immigration bounced back up to 58 percent in an October 2001 survey. Since that time, opinions have settled again, with the desire for decreased immigration falling in the range of 46 to 49 percent from 2003 through 2005.[36]

Explaining why opinions about immigration fluctuate is not a simple matter, although in general opinions change in response to the changing context of the times. First, it appears that immigration opinions *do not* change in proportion to the growing foreign-born share or increasing racial diversity of the population. In fact, a number of studies have shown that opinion responses to growing diversity do not reflect any increase in racism; to the contrary, measures of racial tolerance in America are rising at the same time that diversity is growing.[37] Moreover, residents in areas with relatively few immigrants appear to be more apprehensive than those in areas with longer-established immigrant populations. Perhaps there are offsetting trends here: rising immigration might cause people to wish for a decrease, but increased exposure to immigrants leads to more acceptance.[38] Thus, the long-term trend is no change.

What does seem to affect fluctuations in opinions on immigration is the context of current events. The most accepted wisdom has it that attitudes toward immigration vary in relation to perceptions of the economy. Thus, the upsurge in preference for *decreased* immigration in the early 1990s probably reflected the sharp national recession at that point. However, the weaker recession of the early 2000s did not engender as clear a response. The weaker upturn in 2002 and 2003 was at least partly attributable to a continuing response to the attacks of 9/11 and fear of terrorism. Nonetheless, survey evidence shows that citizens who perceive the economy as doing well are more open to immigration than those who think that jobs are in short supply.[39] In fact, because immigration has not decreased substantially in years of economic recession, a large share of net job growth in those years was absorbed by foreign-born workers.[40]

Even more influential on immigration opinions may be the media coverage given to political debates. Graphic evidence of this effect was provided in the spring of 2006 when Congress began heated debate over legislation for immigration reform. This debate was not led by Californians but by senators and representatives from other states. In January a California poll had found that 11 percent of Californians believed that immigration was the single most important issue for the governor and state legislature to work on in 2006. However, by April, after sustained publicity of the debate in Congress, 27 percent of Californians now thought that immigration was the most important topic for the governor and state legislature.[41] Immigration had advanced from the third to the first most cited priority and now exceeded in importance both education and the economy, even though no significant immigration-related events in California had received substantial publicity.[42]

Seniority Position and Fears of Social Decline

Citizens have much more than economic impacts and politics on their minds when they contemplate the desirability of immigration. In fact, economic and political issues may constitute a publicly acceptable means of defending more deep-felt interests. We should not overlook the fact that the immigration trend is threatening to the social identity of the white population, which has been the majority for so long. In the past such sentiments of the majority population have been dismissed as unworthy of respect. That political position is unwise.

The social concerns of white residents are extremely important because this group will retain its voting majority for decades to come, and they are the majority of taxpayers who will be helping to finance needed solutions. Respecting their opinions will help to reduce their resistance, and it may encourage their participation in a more willing partnership. Greater sensitivity to these matters is needed if we are to reduce unnecessary friction during the demographic transition.

Voting power aside, Americans share a deep respect for *the value of seniority*, and longer-established residents can claim some moral authority on this basis. More important, to ignore their seniority is to show disrespect, to offend them, and to risk losing their sympathy. As an example of how dismissing the matter of seniority helps win support for anti-immigrationists, Peter Brimelow opens his preface to *Alien Nation* with the following exchange recorded on the television show *This Week with David Brinkley*:

> SAM DONALDSON, ABC NEWS: [Native-born Americans] don't have any more right to this country, in my view, than people who came here yesterday.
>
> COKIE ROBERTS, NATIONAL PUBLIC RADIO: That's right.[43]

With these opening lines, Brimelow wins a sympathetic ear from his readers, the great majority of whom are native-born. The United States may be a nation of immigrants, as is so often said, but the forty-year lull between the 1920s and 1960s has made that a distant memory. In the interim, the shared struggles of the Great Depression, World War II, and the cold war forged a common American identity and shared memory that are held by a long-settled population. Those struggles were strongly assisted by people who had been immigrants, or who were at least the children of immigrants, but these were all people who had lived in America for decades. Having "paid their dues," they too would probably claim seniority in America, and they too might look askance at newcomers today.[44] Providing opportunity for new immigrants simply was not a broadly discussed goal for most of the twentieth century. Instead, the attention of recent generations has been riveted on the impact on established citizens of major social movements—significant causes such as civil rights for African Americans and other underrepresented groups, women's equality, and protection of the environment. None of these movements was argued on the basis of newcomers; rather, claims were made based on long-standing heritage, equal rights for those whose rights had been long suppressed, and protection of an inherited environment.

The sharp escalation of immigration since 1970 was truly a shock to established views of seniority and the ethnic order in America. The recent trends in immigration have fed a popular perception in some quarters of social decline and a dismal outlook for the future in California and America. Drawing upon our common propensity for extrapolated expectations, the fears of social decline weave a particular narrative and vision of the future from the facts at hand. Even if those fears are exaggerated and unjustified, we should not dismiss several factors intertwined in the popular reaction to those trends—race, culture, and political allegiance. Underlying all of this have been the accelerating pace of immigration and the uncertain future path of assimilation for the newcomers—two key factors supporting the future of despair.

Race and the Future "Foreignness" of American Society

The fact that recent immigrants come from different countries than early-twentieth-century immigrants came from and that they do not bear the appearance of white race might not be especially troubling. Americans have grown ever more racially tolerant over recent decades, as expressed by attitudes toward the separation of whites and blacks. The proportion of whites who believe that blacks should have equal opportunity in employment increased from less than 60 percent in 1950 to nearly 100 percent by 1970; closer to home, the proportion who believe that blacks should be free to live in any neighborhood increased from less than 40 percent in 1963 to more than 80 percent thirty years later.[45]

Yet there is a key difference between the case of African Americans and the new immigrants, who are largely of Asian or Hispanic origin—namely, the relative size and stability of the population. Residents who are African American constituted roughly 12.3 percent of the U.S. population in 2000, a proportion that has remained relatively constant over time, rising only from 11.1 percent in 1970. In contrast, Asian and Pacific Islanders increased from only 0.8 percent to 3.9 percent in this time period, while Hispanics increased from 4.5 percent to 12.5 percent, finally surpassing blacks as the largest minority group. Indeed, by 2030 Latinos are projected to make up 20.1 percent of all Americans, while blacks will amount to 13.9 percent.[46]

Such dramatic reshaping of the racial makeup of the American people represents a great departure from the nation that was founded by English colonists centuries ago. For some, the departure has been deeply alarming. The rapid decline in the white share of the population has been projected as a doomsday scenario in works such as Peter Brimelow's *Alien Nation: Common Sense About America's Immigration Disaster* and Samuel Huntington's *Who Are We? Challenges to America's Identity.* What has been termed "Anglo declinism" leads to whites "pouting" over the future.[47] Underlying the fears of racial transition is an accompanying assumption about immigrants taking over America. The national bestseller *Alien Nation* made this racial change a central dramatic thesis, warning about "the unprecedented demographic mutation [America] is inflicting on itself."[48] An entire early chapter of that work is devoted to "The Pincers," emphasizing how being constricted between growing shares of the population that are Hispanic or of a nonwhite race will ultimately reduce whites to a minority.

What is it that makes this projected racial change in the population such a cause for alarm? Surely it has a lot to do with fear of lost majority advantage. In addition, the threat in the forecast numbers may stem from a fear that all the growth in Hispanic and Asian numbers will come from immigration, that is, from the addition of foreigners. That is the emphasis of "alien" rather than "minority" nation. In this interpretation, "white" stands for the established native-borns, even though a great many are the children or grandchildren of immigrants. After two generations, they are visually indistinguishable from the longer-established white population, but the descendants of Asian and Latino immigrants may always look different; indeed, in some people's eyes, they can never be fully American.[49] What is worse, the implied fear is that members of the growing groups will maintain the same characteristics in the future that newcomers in these groups have today; this fear is based on the fallacy that all persons of Asian or Hispanic descent are forever like new immigrants. Simply stated, the story about the dismal future is that America is being taken over by foreigners whose racial difference is the sign of their foreignness. Unchallenged, that assumption festers in the pessimistic outlook of many Americans.

Culture and Allegiance

Immigration critics have expressed additional fears about the cultures and political allegiance of immigrants. Newcomers arrive still immersed in a foreign culture, speaking a non-English mother tongue, and bearing fond allegiance to their country of birth. In a series of famous incidents, Mexican immigrants have waved the flag of Mexico and booed the American national anthem at soccer matches, and they have even been faulted for simply failing to support the "home" team while strongly backing Mexico.[50] As jarring as this might seem, we have to ask: how is this different from the fierce intercity rivalries experienced in American sports, such as when ex-New Yorkers flaunt their allegiance to the Yankees in opposition to the fans of the local team? However, warring sports fans have other attributes that bond them—the same culture and language and an allegiance to the political symbols of American government. Immigrants' pride in their homeland is more likely to take on the appearance of disrespect for the new land that nurtures them.

The rapid increases in foreign-born presence and racial change are viewed by much of the public as markers of a potential cleavage of cultural and political allegiance. The key doubt is about assimilation, the integration of newcomers into the mainstream of America, a process that many observers believe worked so admirably in the middle of the twentieth century.[51] Some writers fear that recent newcomers are *incapable* of assimilation, a fear also expressed about many of the newcomer groups early in the twentieth century (such as the Irish or Italians), but a fear long since proven groundless. Other critics worry that—unlike the twentieth-century experience—many of the newcomers *may not want* to assimilate and that the new multicultural tolerance among our nation's political and intellectual leadership *may not encourage* assimilation as readily as before. These doubts contribute to the growing angst over immigration.

The highest-profile recent statement of concerns about the immigrant threat is Samuel Huntington's *Who Are We? The Challenges to America's National Identity*. A highly regarded Harvard political scientist and author of the acclaimed *Clash of Civilizations*, Huntington argues that immigration is undermining the unity of America. Whereas assimilation previously supported the continuity of the Anglo-Protestant culture at the core of the nation's identity, more recent trends are threatening to undermine that core and divide the nation. Huntington's thesis rests heavily on what he calls the Mexican/Hispanic challenge: "The driving force behind the trend toward cultural bifurcation, however, has been immigration from Latin America and especially from Mexico."[52] In essence, he fears that the use of the Spanish language is challenging English as a binding force in our society and that a large swath of the

United States from Texas to California is in danger of becoming our own Quebec.

Huntington cites several reasons for alarm about Mexican immigration (as opposed to earlier waves of immigration from other countries): the close proximity of Mexico (immigrants never really spatially separate from their homeland); their spatial concentration in the Southwest region of the United States; the dominant share of Mexican-origin immigrants among all the foreign-born in the United States; the long persistence of immigration from Mexico; and Mexicans' historical claim to sovereignty in the Southwest. But it is the character of Mexican culture that disturbs Huntington most—the fact that Mexicans hold on to Spanish as their preferred language, challenging the hegemony of English.

Are Huntington's fears justified? Or is he remarking on a temporary condition created when many just-arrived newcomers have not had time yet to acquire a greater understanding of English? The fundamental dynamic he fears is that "the Spanish-speaking population is being continually replenished by newcomers faster than that population is being assimilated."[53] This reflects the key premise of the old view of the future, namely, that accelerating immigration is outrunning the pace of assimilation. We return to this question later and evaluate Huntington's conclusions through a direct test of his evidence. The new outlook twenty years ahead is surely different from the present.

Conclusion: Extrapolations of Lost Control

The dismal outlook on the future that prevailed during the 1990s can now be better understood. Events were running out of control, and it was human nature to extrapolate the recent trends into the future. The recent picture and recent trend is *how it looks* to most observers, regardless of true behavior or the most likely future outcome. I have argued that the dismal outlook on the future stems from an extrapolation of a series of abrupt changes that unfolded in the 1980s and early 1990s. First came general economic disappointment— the halt to postwar income growth—and political disillusionment. Next came the rapid upsurge in immigration, first in California and later in the rest of the nation, combined with the racial and cultural changes that accompanied the new arrivals. Separately, the great calamities of the early 1990s in California magnified despair in the popular mood and spawned the search for scapegoats. Illegal immigration became commingled in the imagination with riots and earthquakes. Social change was proceeding out of control. Little wonder that there was such pessimism about the future.

This pessimistic view is a product of both objective trends and subjective evaluations. Evaluation of those trends depends on the outlook of different groups. A recent survey showed that whites are substantially more pessimistic about the future than are members of racial minority groups.[54] The extrapolated expectations of unfavorable trends only aggravated this uncharitable mood. The white majority surely was not inclined to support or accelerate its own demise, nor to encourage the social declines it feared. However, no single outlook can last forever; each is particular to a time and context. Surely some basis can now be found for turning around this collective mood—and must be if a more hopeful future is to be constructed. With any luck, future historians will describe the dismal outlook on the future as only a passing phase.

Chapter 5

California Turnaround:
A Renewed Basis for Optimism

CALIFORNIANS' DISMAL outlook on the future reached its peak in the early 1990s. Decades of economic disappointment and demographic fears came to a head in a short period, capped by the remarkable barrage of calamities in the state. In hindsight, we can see that this pessimism reflected what was only a temporary episode. The early 1990s served, in fact, as the divide between one era and the next. Rather than foretelling a continuously ebbing quality of life, as many Californians feared, the early 1990s marked the low point for Golden State residents, a unique time when the pessimistic view had its greatest basis of support. Then the tide turned. Beginning in about 1995, objective support for the dismal outlook rapidly eroded, as measured by many different indicators of life experience. As this chapter shows, California has been witnessing a great turnaround of the trends that once had been perceived so negatively.

Not that all Californians have noticed the changes afoot, in part because the improvements have been gradual and lacking in the drama that marked the negative period. Equally important is that those residents who have grown accustomed to the dismal outlook are slow to revise their worldview. Extrapolated expectations based on the negatives of the past have prolonged their pessimism long after it might have been warranted. As observed earlier, people are often resistant to new evidence that is inconsistent with their established views, and so evidence of the turnaround has been simply overlooked or disregarded by many Californians. Only slowly has the gloomy weight of the dismal outlook been lifting from their shoulders.

It is time to take a fresh and comprehensive look at the trends shaping the outlook for California. Continued pessimism is damaging because it discourages needed investments and commitments. Now that we are more than a full decade into the recovery process, we should survey the evidence and see how much the true outlook for California has turned around. Many observers will be truly surprised at how consistently the trends now point in a favorable direction. With this new evidence, fears for the future may be quelled and new hopes kindled. Make no mistake: this is not to say that California is going back to its prior condition. Population continues to grow and, along with it, traffic congestion and ethnic change. As discussed later, many Californians dislike those changes. Nonetheless, the economic gloom and negative extrapolations have sharply improved from what they were.

Immigration and demographic change are surely central to many people's assessments of California. As I argued in chapter 4, however, those assessments are embedded in a broader-based experience of misfortunes in the state. Our first order of business, therefore, is to address as many of the trends in these natural disasters, crime, air pollution, and other events as can be documented. Then we review how much the economy rebounded in the 1990s and early twentieth-first century. Those trends are easily summarized: The tide has turned in all respects, and Californians are in much better shape than they once feared. Nonetheless, because the calamitous events of the 1990s were coincident with the demographic trends that were so negatively perceived, the general despondency that resulted could still permeate the public's reactions to the new demographics.

I say "new demographics" because they have also shifted to a new phase—one with more favorable consequences than previously feared. With worries about unrelated events cleared away, whether natural disasters or recession, perhaps Californians can absorb the meaning of the new demographics more comfortably. Immigration trends, which previously seemed to skyrocket out of control, have abated and are likely to remain more stable. Most importantly, the future pathway of immigrant upward mobility and incorporation has begun to reveal itself in much more positive terms than could have been previously imagined. Yet the old legacy of extrapolated expectations continues to dominate public perceptions.

The new demographics deserve our special attention because they are so little understood in this middle phase of the great transition and because their effects are likely to be so long-lasting. The deep California recession of the early 1990s triggered a cutback in immigration; after the economic recovery in the late 1990s, the number of new arrivals remained at a stabilized level. This slowdown in the number of newcomers gives added prominence to the longer-settled immigrants in the state who are making rapid strides. Far from constituting a simple continuation of the past, the new demographics are already bearing favorable outcomes for California. Equally important, through the California example we can see the possible consequences for the nation as a whole when the national rate of immigration also begins to level off and longer-settled immigrants become more prevalent.

The Turnaround of Background Trends
The Quality of Life
The public mood was soured by a host of trends "gone bad." Now a great many of those unfavorable trends have reversed themselves in ways that should support a turnaround in Californians' collective outlook. Where to begin this reconstruction of California's future outlook? Since the calamities and downfall began at a World Series game, it might be appropriate to first note the improved fortunes of California sports teams. The 1990s saw a drought of championships, but after 2000 the Lakers and other California teams resumed their championship ways. This included an all-California World Series in 2002, the first since 1989, when San Francisco was shaken by the earthquake that started the run of misfortune.[1] Winning returned as a tradition in the state of California.

Sporting victories might lift the spirits, but limiting the fear of undesired threats is surely more important. Natural disasters, smog, and crime are all quality-of-life features that have given California a bad rap and been shown to discourage middle-class migrants from settling in California.[2] Fortunately, the string of natural disasters abated after 1995. It turns out that the series of earthquakes in the early 1990s was an unusual cluster that was both preceded and followed by years of relative quiet. And there have been no substantial fires in urban areas in the last decade. The maelstrom of the early 1990s is fading into the past.

Even the famed air pollution from smog in the Los Angeles basin has made steady improvement, counter to prior public perception. In just the decade following 1990, the number of days when ozone exceeded federal standards plummeted to less than one-third of its former prevalence.[3] Equally surprising may be the trend in the crime rate, which peaked in 1992 when Los Angeles earned the title of homicide capital of America. Since that time, crime has been cut dramatically: as shown in chapter 2, it fell by more than half by the end of decade. Crime and air pollution are surely unrelated to each other, and largely unrelated to economic and demographic changes, but both contribute to the mood of residents, who integrate all these experiences. Nonetheless, despite the lessening worry, most people still assume that smog is bad and crime is high in Los Angeles and in California as a whole. In this, extrapolated expectations from the past haunt us once again.

The Economic Turnaround

For most of us the economy can have profound effects on our lives, and in California the economy's gyrations have taken all the state's residents on a roller-coaster ride. In appendix A, I track four economic indicators for the United States and California from 1980 to 2005. Economic ups and downs, booms and busts, are surely commonplace, but since the late 1980s the heights of prosperity and the depths of struggle have gone to new extremes in California. Longtime residents had their morale severely deflated in the unusually deep recession of the early 1990s, said to be the worst in California since the Great Depression. The steep plunge in house values, after the giddy boom of the late 1980s, was especially damaging to the collective psyche. Immigrants, for their part, had been drawn to California by the booming opportunities in the state, but they were badly affected by rising unemployment and poverty in the deep recession of the early 1990s. As argued here, the California economic jolt was a major cause in the immigrant dispersal across America.

After 2000, California's roller-coaster ride on the economy once again rose to new peaks of prosperity. Whereas the depressing seven-year decline of the 1990s surely contributed to the dismal outlook of residents in the state, the subsequent turnaround has yielded much brighter prospects (see appendix A). But what happened to immigrants after the economic recovery? Why did they not return to California in greater numbers? And why have longtime residents, in spite of the tremendous surge in housing prices, not absorbed the message that the depressed days of the early 1990s are over?

The Immigration Turnaround

No matter that natural disasters had retreated into the background, or that crime rates had shown great improvement, or that the economy had turned for the better—Californians' outlook remained gloomy at the turn of the new century. Or at least the outlook of white residents, who are the majority of voters, remained gloomy. Asked in a poll if California in 2025 would be a better or worse place to live, 57 percent of whites and 49 percent of blacks said it would be worse, compared to 34 percent of Asians and 39 percent of Latinos.[4] It is noteworthy that the two population groups with the most immigrants were the least pessimistic, while those composed most fully of native-born Americans were most pessimistic.

These contrasting outlooks between long-established residents and others are not coincidental. Immigration and its racial or ethnic markers remain a central feature of the dismal outlook and cannot be sidestepped. Although there is much else about the future that residents might fear, continued population growth made up of new immigrants and a decline in their own population groups are surely part of the package.

Three unrecognized realities are intertwined in the immigrant turnaround and our perceptions of it. One is the challenge of seeing immigration rather than race or ethnicity. A second is that California's attraction for immigrants has declined, and we need to explain why that occurred and determine whether it will continue in the future. A third neglected reality lies in the implications of having fewer new immigrants relative to a larger population of longer-settled foreign-born residents.

Growing Immigration or Growing Ethnicity?

Perceptions are often so much more powerful than facts. How would a California resident even know that immigration to the state had radically slowed after 1995? The beliefs of a resident who fears the impacts of growing immigration would be grounded in the accelerating trends of the 1980s and the dismal outlook of the early 1990s. After all, that was the context in which California voters in 1994 approved Proposition 187, the ballot measure that sought to restrict public services for illegal immigrants.

Certainly, anyone viewing a growing presence of Latinos and Asians on the streets would not find their beliefs about rising immigration dispelled. From that information alone, most observers would simply assume that immigration is continuing its upward trajectory of the 1980s. However, a larger share of the Latino and Asian population today is U.S.-born than ten years ago, and as ever more children are born to today's young adults, an even larger share of these groups will be U.S.-born a decade from now. Most casual observers would assume not only that the greater number of Latino or Asian faces signifies more foreign-born but that this growth all comes from *new* immigration. A much larger share, however, have in fact been long settled in the United States. The growing numbers of Latino and Asian faces belong to long-settled residents and their U.S.-born children more than to newcomers. How would observers on the street know that a sharp deceleration in immigration and a radical shift among the foreign-born are already under way?

Government reliance on racial-ethnic data, as opposed to immigrant data, casts the spotlight only on race and ethnicity. Nor are standard government-issued population projections of any help, because they also report data exclusively by race and Hispanic origin, without any details on U.S. or foreign birth. The standard projections are silent on matters of immigrant arrival, settlement, and the size of the growing second generation of U.S.-born within each race group. Instead, the transformation within ethnic groups is left solely to the imagination and anecdotes of citizens, elected officials, or experts. Without real information on these changes, the steady decline in white share and rapid growth in the number of Latinos and Asians can only spur a continued assumption about the prominence of new immigration and reaffirm the pessimistic outlook held by those who dislike new immigrants.

California's Declining Attraction for New Immigrants

Not widely known is that, after decades of rising attractiveness to immigrants, California's share of new immigrants to America began to decline sharply in the 1990s. At one time California was the most preferred destination for new arrivals in America. The state's share of the nation's new immigrants rose steeply from 22 percent in the late 1960s to a high plateau of about 38 percent during the 1980s (figure 5.1). This growing attraction to California occurred at a time when new immigrants to the nation were mushrooming in total number; hence, California's rising share of a growing U.S. total equated to an upward trend in the absolute number of newcomers attracted to Cali-

Figure 5.1   California Share of Annual Immigrant Arrivals

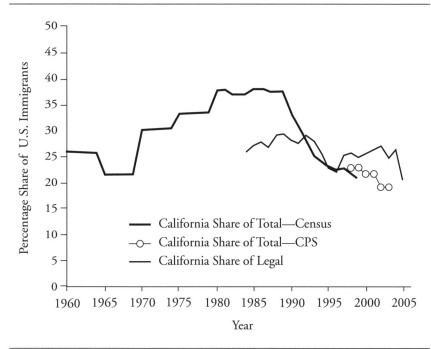

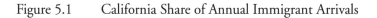

Source: Censuses of 1970, 1980, 1990 and 2000; Current Population Survey of 2000 through 2004; and Office of Homeland Security, Yearbook of Immigration Statistics 2005.

fornia (as shown in figure 3.8). After 1990, however, this attraction rate fell steeply, no doubt because of the relative absence of job opportunities during California's severe recession from 1991 to 1993. The fact that fewer immigrants chose California as their destination during those years should not be surprising.

The puzzle is why California's immigration trends did not rebound after the economic turnaround took hold and employment opportunities improved. We might have expected that immigration would resume its prior course after the recession. Remarkably, however, California's attraction instead continued to decline even after the economy recovered. The share of the nation's total immigrants choosing California as their destination fell to about 23 percent in the depths of the recession, but declined further to around 21 percent in 1999, and then further still to about 20 percent in 2003 (see figure 5.1).

What can account for why California continued to decline in immigrant attraction even after its economic recovery? Several factors seem to be at work, including differences between legal and illegal immigrants, the dynamics of job-seeking networks, and the discouraging effect of high housing prices in California.

One of the major concerns of new immigrants is finding a place to live, and the crucial importance of this issue may provide a possible explanation for California's falling attraction. A newly arrived immigrant needs either to be taken in by a friend or relative or to rent or purchase independent accommodations. The extreme cost of housing in most parts of California, and its dramatic rise from 1998 through 2005, is surely a deterrent to immigration. In fact, we should also be asking how California managed to attract so many new arrivals in the 1980s, when housing prices were also booming. Somehow, back then, new arrivals were able and willing to overcome the obstacles to finding housing—so why not in the 1990s as well?

The network theory of migration provides some clues to California's past attractions as well as to its future.[5] Newly arrived migrants are sustained by a network of kin and friends who direct them to shelter opportunities and introduce them to employers with vacancies. The flow of information extends from individual communities in America to villages and neighborhoods in the home country. Favorable reports of experiences by preceding immigrants help to guide subsequent migrants to destinations where opportunities await. The crucial limitation on the operations of this migration network is that new migrants' range of information depends on the range of destinations already explored by their precursors. Thus, within the network, migration is self-reinforcing and follows the beaten path to destinations chosen by other migrants even when other, lesser-known destinations might offer superior opportunities.

The network theory could explain why it was that during the late 1980s, when the cost of housing in California should have been so prohibitive, streams of migrants poured into well-known California destinations. Arriving in the spotlighted destination, immigrants met their housing needs by renting smaller units, even garages, to house entire families. As a result, California's incidence of overcrowded rental housing soared between 1980 and 1990. Statewide, overcrowding increased from 11 to 20 percent of rental units, but in Los Angeles County it rose to 28 percent, and in the key gateway cities for Mexican immigrants, such as Santa Ana, rental overcrowding reached nearly 50 percent of units.[6] Immigrants may have simply reached a limit on how crowded they were willing to be in their living conditions, even though further increases in crowding certainly were possible; in addition, authorities were clamping down on the most egregious cases of substandard housing.[7]

Much of the decline may be concentrated among unauthorized immigrants. Because their entry into the United States is undocumented, it is difficult to obtain solid numbers; the most authoritative estimates are generally recognized as those of the respected demographer Jeffrey Passel. A total of 10.3 million unauthorized immigrants were estimated to reside in the United States in 2004, an increase of 212 percent since 1990.[8] Of those, 2.4 million resided in California, but the rate at which the state attracted illegal immigrants had slowed sharply from the 1980s. (Recall from chapter 4 that the number of annual unauthorized immigrant arrivals in California increased sharply from 1980 to 1990, followed by its diminution in the early 1990s.) According to Passel, as of 1990 California was home to 45 percent of all the unauthorized immigrants living in America, but that share had fallen to only 24 percent by 2004. Many of those immigrants are now long settled in California, and so this declining share reflects an even lower share of attraction for the most recent unauthorized arrivals, perhaps, I estimate, in the vicinity of 12 to 15 percent.

Unauthorized immigrants make up only one component of total immigration to California, as compared with the United States as a whole. Our best information is the number of immigrant arrivals recorded as permanent residents (legal immigrants) by the federal Office of Immigration Statistics, as shown in figure 5.1. Observe that, except for the dip in the early 1990s, the attraction rate among legal immigrants appears relatively constant over the period for which we have data, hovering between 25 and 29 percent. However, among *total* immigrants, including both legal and unauthorized, the sharp decline in attraction of the early 1990s has continued downward to the present. Given that the trend for legal immigrants remains fairly constant, the downward trend in attraction for immigrants in total must be driven by changes in destination among unauthorized immigrants. Clearly, the attraction of legal immigrants rebounded after the recession, but the attraction of total immigrants, including the unauthorized, fell.

What can explain this abrupt departure of the two trends, one for legal immigrants and the other for unauthorized immigrants? The shift in 1996 suggests that tightened border controls and publicity related to Proposition 187, which was aimed at illegal immigrants in California, may have had a deterrent effect in that time period. Border controls were tightened even further after the events of 9/11. In fact, the immigration scholar Douglas Massey and his colleagues have suggested that the tightening of border controls in the San Diego sector had perverse consequences, one of which was diverting migrants away from California.[9] In addition, the total number of unauthorized immigrants has grown because, instead of moving back and forth across the border, they now are piling up on the American side. Meanwhile, we can see that legal immigrants were better able to continue a steady rate of arrival in California, either by satisfying skills-based admissions criteria or more often by being sponsored for family reunification by previous legal immigrants already settled in California.

A second and complementary explanation for the decreased immigrants' attraction to California, suggested by the UCLA sociologist Ivan Light and others, is that immigrants had saturated their networks of opportunity in California.[10] Unauthorized immigrants are particularly limited to certain job opportunities and certain niches in society, and Light argues that local enforcement activities have curtailed the substandard housing and employment opportunities that were most open to poor immigrants. The large number of previous arrivals may have already filled the great majority of such opportunities. Further, the size of the total immigrant flow in the nation as a whole, both legal and unauthorized, expanded substantially after 1990, as shown earlier. California's flow of new arrivals did not keep up with this expansion but simply leveled off in a manner that is consistent with the notion of saturated opportunities.

The Dispersal of Immigrants Nationwide

A by-product of California's lagging attraction—one with major national political implications—is that immigrants have now dispersed to more states than they did before. The key factor in the expansion of immigrant settlement nationwide may not be the attractions of the newly discovered communities but rather the disruption in the prior destination of choice, namely, California. What we now recognize is that the severe recession of the early 1990s in California had many effects on various trends. What has not been appreciated is the effect on new immigrants of California's skyrocketing unemployment rate, which reached a level far above the nation's in the early

1990s (see figure A.1 in appendix A). That abrupt shift jolted the established migration networks off their beaten paths. No matter that housing became cheaper in California during the 1990s; the shrinkage of employment opportunities in California, particularly in southern California, which had been the major focus of immigration streams, forced new immigrants (and some settled immigrants) to disperse elsewhere.[11]

The dispersal of immigrants has been widely reported in both news media and scholarly accounts of the novel transformation of many small communities across the Midwest and the South.[12] Table 5.1 gives us a systematic view of the extent of dispersal, documenting as it does the change in selected states'

Table 5.1   Change in States' Immigrant Attraction Rates for Total U.S. New Arrivals, 1990, 2000, and 2005

	1990	2000	Change 1990 to 2000	2005	Change 2000 to 2005
California	37.6%	24.8%	−12.8%	20.9%	−3.9%
New York	13.7	11.8	−1.9	8.7	−3.1
Texas	8.3	10.1	1.9	10.6	0.5
Florida	7.6	7.8	0.2	9.2	1.3
Illinois	4.3	5.2	0.9	4.4	−0.8
New Jersey	4.4	4.7	0.2	4.4	−0.3
Georgia	1.0	2.6	1.6	3.2	0.6
Arizona	1.4	2.4	1.1	3.0	0.6
Massachusetts	2.6	2.4	−0.2	2.7	0.3
Washington	1.5	2.2	0.7	2.5	0.3
Virginia	1.8	2.0	0.2	2.3	0.3
North Carolina	0.6	2.0	1.4	2.5	0.4
All other states and D.C.	15.2	21.9	6.7	25.6	3.8
Total United States	100.0	100.0	0.0	100.0	0.0

Source: 1990 and 2000: PUMS; 2005: American Community Survey.
Notes: "New arrivals" are defined as those who arrived in the ten years prior to 1990 and 2000 or in the five years prior to 2005. The twelve states identified are all those that had a 2.0 percent or larger share of the U.S. immigrant arrivals in the 1990s.

attraction of new immigrant arrivals arriving before 1990, 2000, or 2005. Whereas California's share of new immigrants fell steeply, by seventeen percentage points (from 37.6 percent in 1990 to 20.9 percent in 2005), no other state's attraction increased by more than two and a half percentage points. Arizona was the big gainer in the West: its share of new immigrants increased from 1.4 percent to 3.0 percent. In the Midwest, Illinois held the largest share, but the rate there increased very little. In the South, four states exceeded a one-percentage-point increase in their share of the nation's new immigrants—Texas (2.3 percentage points), Georgia (2.2 percentage points), North Carolina (1.9 percentage points), and Florida (1.6 percentage points). Finally, in the Northeast, New Jersey showed no gain in its share of new immigrant arrivals, while New York's share plunged five percentage points— nearly one-third as large a decline as experienced in California.

The overall picture is that California's (and New York's) lost share of new immigrants was split up and spread more evenly across much of the nation. The share going to smaller states not reported in the table grew from 15.2 percent in 1990 to 25.6 percent in 2005. Even if the new host communities received only a small increase in share, the numbers often appeared huge to them. For instance, Iowa increased its share of the nation's new immigrants during the 1990s only to 0.40 percent, but that amounted to an increase from 19,278 to 52,335 new immigrants, or growth of 171 percent in just a decade. Moreover, the new arrivals tended to concentrate in a selected number of communities, such as the meatpacking towns of Lenox and Marshalltown.[13] Local schools, public services, and retail stores were all pressured to respond to the needs of these new immigrants. All change is relative, and it bears emphasis that an extra 100,000 immigrants in California would be scarcely noticed. But one-tenth that number of immigrants draws tremendous attention when they are arriving in a state that has little experience with them, and the political heat generated is not surprising.

The reasons cited by experts for the dispersal of immigrants across the nation have almost always been expressed in terms of the *pull* of local advantages for immigrants—the cheaper housing, safer neighborhoods, and plentiful jobs. However, this dispersal starts and ends with the *push* away from California.[14] California was possibly approaching saturation in its job and housing opportunities, as Ivan Light suggests, but it was the deep recession in California that spurred immigrants to explore new opportunities in unknown destinations across the nation.[15]

This may be the answer to our puzzle: California's share of new arrivals did not rebound to prerecession levels and in fact continued dropping because new networks of information were providing better destination alternatives. Unauthorized immigrants, who made up much of the increased flow in the 1990s, may have been more responsive to the ready opportunities elsewhere, and they were certainly less likely to be sponsored by legal immigrants who were already resident in California. Hence, unauthorized immigrants dispersed even more rapidly across the nation than did all immigrants combined.

How is the future informed by this explanation of past trends? Overall, it does not seem likely that California and New York will reclaim their disproportionate attraction for new immigrants. Given the opening up of immigrant opportunities across America, we have witnessed a relatively permanent shift in the immigration flow. That dispersal, in turn, has long-term consequences for California immigration. Now that immigration networks have tapped into such a wide array of dispersed destinations, future immigrants have access to much better information about relative opportunities, including unfilled job niches and cheaper housing. To their great advantage, immigrants need no longer concentrate in California so reflexively.

In addition, we should recognize a certain political and policy advantage to the dispersal of immigrants across so many states: the broadening attention to immigration among political leaders. Illustrating this most clearly is the fact that back in 1990 only ten senators might have been said to care about the well-being of immigrants or the management of immigration, because immigration was focused largely in only five major states. Now that immigration is growing across the midwestern and southern states, it has the potential to gain that much more broadly shared policy attention in Washington. This increase in the attention of policymakers, for better or worse, was a principal spur to the major rethinking of immigration policy that was debated in Congress in the spring of 2006.

A Preponderance of Longer-Settled Immigrants

The stabilized flow of new arrivals has transformed California's foreign-born population. No longer is it composed so heavily of newcomers, with the total doubling each decade. During the 1970s and 1980s, the number of foreign-born grew from 1.8 million in 1970 to 3.6 million in 1980 and 6.8 million in 1990. That doubling in size each decade meant that about half the foreign-born population was made up of newcomers each decade. In the

1990s, however, when inflows of new immigrants to California leveled off, immigration slowed its increase and the total foreign-born increased only to 8.9 million.

This deceleration in the number of new arrivals has major consequences. One result, as we saw in chapter 2, is the leveling-off of the foreign-born percentage of the total population in the state at around 30 percent. More important than the total numbers of foreign-born, however, may be the changes that are likely to occur *within* the foreign-born population. Longer-settled immigrants have had more time to improve their own living situations, and the greater numbers of settled immigrants also supply a deeper resource of assistance to new arrivals. A summary of the changing makeup of the foreign-born population is provided in figure 5.2, which draws on the California Demographic Futures projections. The figure depicts the total California population each decade from 1970 to 2030. Shown at the bottom is the shrinking share made up of new arrivals, and above that is the share of longer-settled immigrants. Also shown is the share of the state's population that is second-generation (the U.S.-born children of immigrants).[16] The remaining portion of the state's population (filling the top of the figure to 100 percent) is made up of third- or higher-generation U.S. residents.

Reflecting the slowdown in new arrivals, the key finding is that the share of the California population made up of immigrant newcomers (arrivals in the preceding ten years) has begun to decline. From 3.5 percent of the state's population in 1970, the new immigrant share soared to 10.9 percent in 1990. At that time an extraordinarily high ratio of all California residents—one in nine—were recently arrived immigrants. Thereafter, the new immigrant share declined to 9.7 percent in 2000 and 8.3 percent in 2005, and it is anticipated to decline to 6.9 percent in 2030, according to the California Demographic Futures projections. Immigrants may still be arriving in large numbers, but those numbers are balanced by increases in the total California population, including earlier immigrant arrivals and the native-born children of immigrants. A comparison with the other forty-nine states shows that California in the 1990s was alone in experiencing this decline in the share of its population that was made up of newcomers.[17]

In place of population growth from rising numbers of new immigrants, the total foreign-born population in California has continued to grow because of the *accumulation of previous new arrivals* in earlier immigration waves who settled in the state. Accordingly, the share of the state's population made up of longer-settled residents is rising markedly. Whereas in 1990 only half

Figure 5.2   Immigrant Generation and Length of U.S. Residence,
California, 1970 to 2030

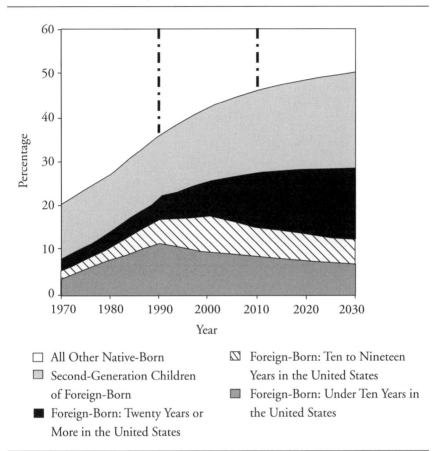

□ All Other Native-Born
▨ Second-Generation Children
of Foreign-Born
■ Foreign-Born: Twenty Years or
More in the United States

▨ Foreign-Born: Ten to Nineteen
Years in the United States
▨ Foreign-Born: Under Ten Years in
the United States

Source: California Demographic Futures database (version 5.0).

the foreign-born had lived more than ten years in the United States, by 2010 that share is expected to increase to 70 percent. In fact, the share of the foreign-born that is growing the most is the group that has resided in California longer than twenty years (figure 5.2). By 2030 the majority of all foreign-born are expected to have lived in California at least that long. Added to these longtime residents will be the sizable numbers of children of immigrants, amounting to more than 20 percent by 2030. At that time it is expected that just over half of all California residents will be immigrant parents and their children—the so-called immigrant stock or foreign stock. They will be very different at that time from the newcomers who dominated our images in 1990 about what it means to be an immigrant.

In California we can already discern the contours of a more deeply settled immigrant population, in sharp contrast to the concentrations of newcomers elsewhere. This settled quality holds major implications, including advantages for the future that have not yet been generally recognized. In essence, California's incorporation of settled immigrants provides an early insight into the unfolding after 2010 of the mature stage of the great transition for which we must begin to prepare.

The importance of this transformation cannot be overemphasized, because longer-resident immigrants take on very different characteristics from those of newcomers. As discussed in detail in the next chapter, longer-settled immigrants have greater facility with the English language, they are much less likely to be living in poverty, and many have purchased homes of their own. This transformation may be surprising to the many observers who assume that there can be no such change—once a new immigrant, always like a new immigrant. What they fail to grasp is that newcomers, who may once have been burdens on the state, are now becoming assets who will bring great advantages to the future, if they are treated as such. Far from constituting a simple continuation of the past, the new demographics are already bearing more favorable outcomes for California. This turnaround of fortunes is proceeding earliest in this state, but it may foretell changes to come in the nation as a whole.

Conclusion: The End of an Unsettled Era

The 1990s are over. Although the dismay of many longtime residents may have lingered into the twenty-first century, it is time to recognize that the bad period has ended, the tide has turned, and a new era has begun. California's passage out of the early phase of the demographic transition was especially traumatic. The period from 1985 to 1995 may have been the most unsettling period in California in a century or longer. Not only did the economy plunge from prosperity into deep recession, but fears about the worsening economy were compounded for some long-established white residents by worrisome racial changes. And unlike the Great Depression, this was a time when Californians could feel singled out for special abuse: their recession was so much worse than the rest of the country endured, their demographic changes were deeper and more rapid, and their natural disasters were unparalleled.

Fortunately, the depths of this dismal period marked the turning point for California. Yes, economic conditions could only improve, but miraculously the string of natural disasters came to a close and, unnoticed, the pattern of immigration shifted. Migration networks had shifted to other destinations with more affordable housing and better job opportunities. In turn, the stabilization of the immigrant inflow to California enabled the state to enter the middle phase of the demographic transition. Now, for the first time, the number of long-settled immigrants outweighs the number of newcomers. A similar pattern of longer-settled immigrants will also develop in other parts of the United States after the recent acceleration of new arrivals in those places begins to stabilize, even at a high level, and the local experience with immigration grows longer.

The new period of long-settled immigrants promises to be very different from the era of escalating numbers of newcomers. The immigrant communities are more established and can offer better help to newcomers. In addition, the average status achievement of foreign-born residents is likely to rise. Exactly how much of an improvement can be expected is addressed in the next chapter. But the prospect of stabilized immigration, on top of all the other improvements, suggests that longtime residents need no longer feel so unsettled themselves. My argument is that, in the middle and later phases of the demographic transition, the benefits of prior immigration will begin to be felt, but only if we shift our outlook. Indeed, the unsettled era with the dismal outlook has ended in California, and a more stabilized period is at hand. But how much hope will actually replace the former despair remains to be discovered.

Chapter 6

Immigrant Upward Mobility:
Support for a More Hopeful Future

RISING ACHIEVEMENT that accompanies a growing length of U.S. residence for immigrants is a major feature of the demographic transition, and it promises significant long-term benefits. An appreciation of this positive force has been slow in coming, perhaps because the key evidence is not known, but also because commonly held old knowledge may bias current perception. Fundamental misconceptions date from the 1970s and 1980s, the period of early transition when so many new immigrants began to arrive in the United States. That old knowledge is often coupled with an unspoken assumption, widely held among residents who are non-immigrants, that the growing foreign-born population retains the same characteristics as first observed when they were newly arrived, that is, that immigrants do not change that much over time.

The aim of this chapter is to present a summary of some of the clear-cut evidence on the changes observed when immigrants reside a longer time in the United States. Focusing on changes among the Latino foreign-born because that group is the subject of greatest concern for its presumably low achievements, I examine a series of indicators, including English use, poverty, homeownership, education, citizenship and voting participation. On some of these, Latino immigrants make substantial progress in the first twenty years of U.S. residence; on others, such as education, advancement occurs largely between immigrants and their children's generation. Although substantial gaps remain with regard to the standard set by native-born white residents, the degree of Latino immigrant progress is so substantial that it is likely to be surprising—because the facts are so at odds with key beliefs and assumptions.

To fully absorb the evidence, one needs a clear vision uncluttered by previous misconceptions. Accordingly, I first try to clear those out of the way, showing how they might have been understandable in the past but today no longer apply. The foremost obstacle is the illusion created during the period of rapid acceleration of immigration. The growing numbers of newcomers have simply made it seem that fewer immigrants are progressing upward in status. This simple observation is so powerful that the *New York Times* featured the following as its quote of the day: "Everybody's going up the escalator but there's a big queue at the bottom and the queue's getting bigger, so the average number of steps people have gotten up has slipped."[1] When more of the immigrants are longer settled instead of recently arrived, progress up the escalator will be more evident. The only serious question is this: *how much* progress do immigrants make as their residence grows longer?

The Illusion of Immigrant Non-Advancement

Our outlook on the future is heavily biased by the recent past. Once again, the specter of extrapolated expectations clouds our vision of current events and likely futures. Simply stated, when immigration is a new event, all the immigrants are new. But once immigration has continued for two or three decades, important changes are destined to happen: the former newcomers become old-timers, and the share of all the foreign-born who are recent arrivals falls. Meanwhile, as their average length of residence increases, the social, economic, and political advancement of immigrants becomes ever more apparent. Why have these changes escaped attention? Two key misconceptions obstruct our understanding.

Blinded by the Concentration of Newcomers

When immigration is a recent event, most immigrants are newly arrived and have the characteristics of newcomers. In cities of burgeoning immigrant settlement, such as Atlanta, Georgia, Charlotte, North Carolina, and cities across the Midwest, the foreign-born share of the population is fairly low (for example, 10.3 percent in Atlanta), but the newcomers account for a large share of all the foreign-born (60.9 percent in Atlanta and even higher in North Carolina cities).[2] In contrast, in areas that have long-established foreign-born populations, such as Los Angeles, 36.2 percent of the residents are foreign-born and barely one-third of these, 34.8 percent, are recent arrivals. Back in 1990, Los Angeles had a somewhat smaller proportion of foreign-born (32.7 percent), but a much larger share of them were newcomers (52.7 percent).[3] Because of the deceleration of immigration to California after 1990, as explained in chapter 5, a much longer-settled foreign-born population now predominates in the state.

Commentators on immigration are simply blinded by the concentration of newcomers at the time when the rise in immigration has recently begun. This masking of the true rate of acculturation and socioeconomic progress was highlighted by the recent National Research Council study of the future of Hispanics in America.[4] Observers at a single moment in time are simply oblivious to the transformations that are likely to occur for that moment's immigrants as time passes. Not only does the share of all foreign-born who are newcomers decline, but the inexorable transition of individuals who have settled from newcomer to old-timer status has very real consequences. Data examined in this chapter show that some features are very slow to change, such as the education level of adult immigrants, while other characteristics, such as poverty and homeownership rates, can improve dramatically.

The Peter Pan Fallacy

Not all foreign-born are the same: long-settled immigrants have characteristics very different from the characteristics they had when they were newly arrived. If nothing else, people who have lived twenty years in the United States are twenty years older than when they arrived, and with that added experience come many other changes as well. But many observers, consciously or not, embrace a second misconception: that immigrants never change and they retain all the characteristics they possessed when they first arrived as newcomers in the United States. Many of us assume, unwittingly, that *immigrants are like Peter Pan*—forever frozen in their status as newcomers, never aging, never advancing economically, and never assimilating. Like Peter Pan, they are consigned in our imagination to a life in Neverland, unlike real humans who follow a life cycle of change. In this naive view, the mounting numbers of foreign-born residents imply that our nation is becoming dominated by growing numbers of people who perpetually resemble newcomers. What may be worse is that many people ascribe the characteristics of newcomers *to Latinos and Asians who have grown up in the United States* (to the consternation of these long-settled and second-generation immigrants). Both racist and self-deluding, this unchallenged assumption must make those who hold it very fearful about the growing numbers of Latinos, even those born and raised in the United States, because that increase must signify to them all the drawbacks of an ever-mounting number of new immigrants. In fact, the newcomers form only a small portion of the growing Latino population, and over time the newcomers transform dramatically.

In the early phase of the demographic transition, most of the immigrants were in fact new. This is still true in portions of the United States where the rise of immigration is a recent phenomenon. In California, however, the middle phase of the transition has been reached, and immigrant communities have become firmly settled. In this state, now is the time when the Peter Pan fallacy is revealed. The overwhelming evidence shows that the old-timers do not retain the characteristics of newcomers. Ignorance of true progress is self-defeating and discouraging because it prevents us from realizing how much more optimistic we should be about the future.

Samuel Huntington's Misconclusion

These two misconceptions—being blinded by concentrations of newcomers and the Peter Pan fallacy—might seem obviously wrong, but they underlie the beliefs of political leaders and even experts. The well-known case of Samuel Huntington's misconclusion illustrates how misleading the results can be. In the spring of 2004, the journal *Foreign Policy* published an essay on the threat of the growing Mexican population in the United States. A storm of controversy blew up over "The Hispanic Challenge," written by the influential Harvard political scientist Samuel Huntington.[5] The essence of Huntington's argument is that the United States risks becoming balkanized because a large section of the nation could be cleaved off by a Spanish-speaking culture—in essence, a new Quebec.

Language is the key marker of cultural division on which Huntington focuses. Whether or not this challenge to the hegemony of English is truly a threat can be debated on value grounds, but the evidence for any takeover by the Spanish language is both fleeting and highly localized. Huntington emphasizes the case of Miami, a worst case that has already happened (from his point of view), but his fears for the future are focused on the rapid immigration of Mexicans and the consequent surge in Spanish-language prevalence in California and the Southwest. Does this recent trend in our reliance on the Spanish language really foretell the future, or might it be another example of extrapolated expectations that, as we have learned before, can so misrepresent the true future?

Huntington's views depend heavily on an assessment of changes in the 1980s and 1990s, and thus most of his assessments were formed at a time when newcomers were most prominent among the Latino population. A closer examination of the underlying dynamics is necessary to reach a reasonable long-term conclusion. According to the long-established three-generation model of language acquisition and use, in the first generation immigrants hold fast to their mother tongue and use it at home and in the community.[6] In the second generation, children become fluent English speakers with little or no accent, but they may retain a bilingual knowledge of their parents' mother tongue, principally for use in the home. Finally, by the third generation English use may be so dominant that the family's historic tongue has been reduced to only a few words and expressions.[7]

A test of Huntington's projection for the future can easily be made. Set in California, where Mexican immigration has been highly concentrated, this is not only a test of future language preferences but also a test of the potential cultural divide that language signifies. In addition, this test may illustrate our claim that extrapolated expectations have misled current observers about the future. Accordingly, there is a lot to learn from looking closely at Huntington's conclusion. Our test is carried out for Latinos age twenty-five to thirty-four living in California, a group expected to grow from 39.3 percent of the state's population in that age group in 2000 to 51.3 percent in 2030.[8] If Huntington is right that Spanish is taking over, surely it should occur among this group.

Our first major piece of evidence is the length of settlement in the United States that is projected for these Latinos in 2000 and 2030, as estimated by the USC California Demographic Futures project. These estimates, summarized in table 6.1, follow some indisputable logic. By 2030 the number of Latino young adults who are second- or third-generation U.S.-born will grow markedly because they are the children and grandchildren of immigrants already living here today. Even while newcomers continue their steady rate of arrival, their share of all Latinos will have fallen by half. Instead, a large por-

Table 6.1   Length of Settlement in California of Latino Residents Age
Twenty-Five to Thirty-Four, 2000 and 2030

	Under Ten Years	Ten to Nineteen Years	Twenty Years or More	Second-Generation	Third-Generation
2000	28.2%	29.1%	8.8%	17.9%	16%
2030	15.4	13.5	9.1	35.7	26.3
Change	−12.8	−15.6	0.3	17.8	10.3

Source: USC California Demographic Futures, 2005.

tion of these young adults will be part of the long-settled population. In contrast, Huntington's implicit projections assume that the length of residency profile in the future will look just like the past.

What constitutes the identity of "Latinos" or their language preferences in 2030 will shift from what Huntington observed in 1990 or 2000 to a very different profile. How might their language use be different? Our second piece of evidence is provided by recent survey data on the current state of the three-generation model of linguistic transition. The Pew Hispanic Survey inquired in a national study about a range of different language uses, asking not only about proficiency with the English language and language use at home, the two foci of census questions on language, but also about people's comfort with and preference for using English in different tasks. The survey results were used to code respondents into three groupings— those who were Spanish-dominant, those who were bilingual with equal preferences, and those who were English-dominant. Huntington fears that a Spanish-dominant culture will emerge, and so I focus on those data here. The Pew study found that 72 percent of foreign-born Latinos were Spanish-dominant, but that this fell to 7 percent in the second generation and to 0 percent in the third. The startling shift in language use between immigrant parents and their children is attributable to the children's lifelong immersion in U.S. culture and schools. Regardless of state policies that may or may not promote bilingual education, parents themselves are strongly encouraging their children to learn English. A 2000 California poll asking parents about language instruction for their children found that 90 percent of foreign-born Latinos agreed "very strongly" that all children should learn English in school.[9]

Now that we know that the length of settlement will be much longer in the future than in the past, and knowing that language use shifts over time, we realize that the future is not simply an extrapolation of trends magnified from the past. A Latin Miami whose elders are all first-generation will be Spanish-dominant, as will Mexican sections of Los Angeles. But what will be the likely outcome when the second and third generations begin to prevail? We can project this likely future by combining all our available information—the growing Latino share of the population, the changing generational mix among Latinos, and the different language preferences in successive generations.

The analysis shows that, rather than growing, as it did during the upturn in immigration during the 1970s and 1980s, the likelihood of Spanish dominance for the future in California is now receding. To be sure, in 2000 nearly half of all Latinos age twenty-five to thirty-four were Spanish-dominant by our estimate (49.6 percent). But Latinos made up only 39.3 percent of the age group, and so a total of 19.5 percent of all residents in the age group were Spanish-dominant. Huntington imagines Spanish dominance growing mightily in the future because Latinos are increasing in number and making up a larger share of the population. The fundamental dynamic he fears is that "the Spanish-speaking population is being continually replenished by newcomers faster than that population is being assimilated."[10] For lack of any future-oriented data, and subject to the Peter Pan fallacy, Huntington presumes that Latinos will retain the same language preference thirty years hence as he observes today. And when Latinos become a larger share of the total population, he assumes that Spanish-dominance will grow proportionally. In essence, Huntington's conceptual model assumes no lengthening of settlement and no language assimilation at all. In other words, he would believe that Spanish-dominance will grow from 19.5 percent of the entire age group in 2000 to 25.4 percent in 2030. In contrast, a projection by the generational method takes account of the changing generational mix and the language assimilation associated with it. By that method, we find that, even with a growing Latino population, the share of the entire age group that is Spanish-dominant will *decline* from 19.5 percent in 2000 to 14.9 percent in 2030.

Following a period of increased Spanish use, the future looks very different.[11] Indeed, the National Research Council study of the future of Hispanics reached a similar conclusion: "The seeming ubiquity of Spanish in these neighborhoods is, in reality, a transitory phenomenon reflecting the large number of recent immigrants."[12] That language use changes with increasing length of settlement cannot be denied.

Upward Mobility over Time

In how many other ways besides language use do immigrants adapt themselves to life in America? There are many different dimensions of socioeconomic advancement. Proficiency with the English language is one, but also important are educational attainment, poverty rates, homeownership, and measures of civic participation, such as naturalization and voting.[13] I examine all these indicators here, beginning with an overview that compares them and then delving more deeply into two particular realms, poverty and homeownership.

Selected Indicators of Immigrant Advancement and Incorporation

What impact might the lengthening settlement of the immigrant population have on broad dimensions of social, political, and economic life in California? The lengthening settlement of the foreign-born and their children has yet to be appreciated for its important effects. When the foreign-born are no longer dominated by newcomers, what are the implications for improvements on various dimensions? Using a varied set of indicators, we can compare how much achievements and participation vary between recent arrivals and longer-settled immigrants or between these foreign-born and their second-generation children. To facilitate this summary comparison, I present a snapshot comparison of relative achievements that were observed mostly in 2004 and 2005.[14] Although this does not actually follow immigrants through their lives, we can compare groups that have reached different lengths of residence.[15] To reduce any biases stemming from the changing mix of people who may have arrived in each decade, I focus only on Latinos living in California. The results are summarized in figure 6.1.

High school completion is a minimal threshold for labor force preparation, yet many Latinos have not attained this level of education. Within the first generation, this achievement differs only moderately by length of residence in the United States, ranging only from 35.3 percent to 42.5 percent. This varies so little because educational achievement is not a status that steadily grows over a lifetime but is largely fixed after age twenty-five for most people. Among immigrants, unless they arrive as young children, it is very unlikely

Figure 6.1   Latino Immigrant Status Attainment by Length of Residence and Generation, California

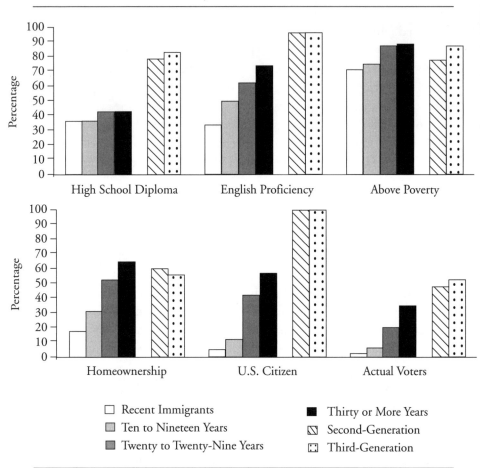

Source: 2005 Current Population Survey Demographic (March) Supplement; 2004 CPS Voting and Registration (November) Supplement; 2000 Census Public Use Microdata Sample.

that they will return to school for more education.[16] They are too busy earning an income and raising families. A far higher level of high school completion is attained by second-generation (77.8 percent) or third-generation Latinos (82.5 percent) because they have lived their lives in the United States and have passed through the U.S. education system from first grade. Based on these data, we would expect to see a rising average level of education among Latinos when a greater share are native-born. Nonetheless, this level of high school completion will hardly be satisfactory for the future and deserves our most urgent attention, as addressed in chapter 10.

English proficiency is measured by the percentage of people who say they speak English well or very well (or who only speak English). This ability is held by essentially 100 percent of the native-born, while among the foreign-born English proficiency more than doubles between newcomers and those who have lived in the United States for a long time. Among residents of less than ten years, barely one-third (33.4 percent) claim proficiency in speaking the English language, but that rises to 73.5 percent among residents of thirty years or more. English proficiency is a job skill that has been shown to increase earnings, and it surely helps in other civic activities outside the home.[17] In contrast to the cultural interpretation of English use, such as in the Huntington analysis, the emphasis on proficiency emphasizes English as a skill useful for economic incorporation. The same people may or may not prefer to use another language at home.

Income above the poverty level indicates the percentage of the population who live in families with income above the federally designated poverty line. This indicator thus measures escape from poverty as the percentage rises for longer-settled groups. Although the great majority of immigrants are living above the poverty level, that does not imply that they are well off. Nonetheless, the number below the poverty line reflects an especially needy population, and I examine those more closely later.

Homeownership attainment is often regarded as a key indicator of entry into the middle class, and this achievement exhibits exceptionally large gains within the first generation, rising from 16.4 percent of householders who arrived in the last ten years to 64.6 percent of householders who have lived here for thirty years or more.[18] There is no statistically significant further increase between the foreign-born and the second or third generations, indicating that advancement into homeownership is an achievement largely attained within the first generation. It is apparent that as the average length of settlement increases for the Latino foreign-born, average levels of homeownership would be expected to rise. I also examine this more closely later.

Citizenship and *voting* are key indicators of civic incorporation of immigrants, and there is clear evidence that civic incorporation increases both within the first generation and between the first and second generations.[19] Becoming a naturalized U.S. citizen and voting both increase markedly with length of residence in the United States, respectively from 4.4 percent to 56.7

percent, and from 2.0 percent to 35.1 percent. In the second generation, citizenship leaps to 100 percent (by virtue of birth in the United States), and voting also climbs to 48.4 percent in the second generation. By way of comparison, average voting participation in the United States in the fall 2004 election was 63.8 percent for citizens of all ages and ethnicities, but this participation was lower among adult citizens under age thirty-five, 51.8 percent, and this is the group most likely to include the second generation.[20] Based on these data, we would expect Latinos to become much more integrated as civic participants in America once the settled immigrants outnumber the recent arrivals, the second or third generations have grown in size, and all have matured in age. The topic of voting participation and differences between Latinos and whites is discussed more thoroughly in chapter 7.

The above snapshots of immigrant advancement, taken at a single moment in time, suggest that a Latino population dominated by newcomers is likely to have much lower status and different behavior than one that is longer settled. This simple conclusion has escaped the attention of Samuel Huntington, among others. Skeptics might ask what really happens over time as each wave of immigrant arrivals increase their length of residence in the United States. Next I present evidence on the trajectories of progress across the decades, focusing on two key indicators, poverty and homeownership.

The Surprising Turnaround in Poverty Rates

The greatest fears about immigration have been expressed with regard to poverty. The poverty rate of the foreign-born is taken as a key barometer of not only immigrant well-being but also the risk of growing a dependent class that will be a burden on society. Bluntly stated, if the newcomers are ill equipped to become productive citizens, could immigration simply be importing poverty?[21] Indeed, the outlook for poverty was very grim in California prior to 2000. That this has now turned around may be so surprising, and so inconsistent with prior expectations, that it has been ignored as an aberration.

For this reason, immigrant experience in escaping poverty deserves especially close examination. Rather than rely solely on the earlier snapshot comparison, we ought to trace actual progress across the decades as immigrants reside longer in the United States. Prior to 2000, poverty was trending rather badly for immigrants. Measured in the census of each decade, foreign-born poverty steadily worsened in California, rising from 14.7 percent in 1970 to 19.8 percent in 1990. However, the 2000 census revealed that the foreign-born poverty rate had declined slightly, to 19.1 percent.[22] Could this small improvement represent a change in immigrant fortunes, or might it just be a small aberration reflecting a measurement error or a momentary upturn in the economy? Alternatively, perhaps the improvement reflected a shift in the mix of immigrants that could have given more weight to Asians than to Latinos, who have higher poverty rates on average. There is more than one possible explanation that needs to be considered. Furthermore, what is the significance of such a small shift in any event? Most observers would argue that such a small decrease could hardly be taken as evidence of substantial immigrant progress. In fact, this small shift is truly the tip of the iceberg, a small indicator of much larger and more dramatic advances in status that lie just below the surface of what is visible.

Evidence is clear-cut that this small decline in foreign-born poverty was no accident. First, the decline was not due to a changing mix of immigrants who had more favorable origins. In fact, poverty decreased among both Latinos and Asians, the two groups that make up more than 80 percent of California's foreign-born.[23] Further, the possible explanation of a temporary upturn in the economy also can be dismissed. Detailed analysis has shown that this decline in immigrant poverty, also observed nationwide, is not the result of the economic cycle but represents a long-term trend.[24] Economic conditions were very comparable in the income year preceding the 1990 and 2000 censuses (see appendix figure A.1), and accordingly, that leaves the possibility that the small improvement in poverty indicates a real change in immigrant poverty.[25] Small as the improvement might have been, it was important because it stemmed the steady deterioration of the previous two decades. More importantly, it was a harbinger of larger improvements ahead.

We now know that, in fact, the poverty reversal was an important sign of a turnaround of immigrant fortunes in California. The poverty reversal was no fluke but directly attributable to the maturing residence of California's immigrant population. Longer-residing immigrants generally experience substantial improvements in poverty, but in the past those gains were outweighed by the ever-increasing numbers of newcomers.[26] Now that longer-settled immigrants are beginning to outweigh the newcomers in number, the force of upward mobility is no longer being offset by the relatively high poverty of newcomers, and the total poverty rate of the foreign-born has turned around.

Projecting the Immigrant Escape from Poverty

So strong and predictable is the effect of longer residence that it can form the basis for projections of future poverty, as demonstrated in a test conducted before the 2000 census. The evidence on poverty is extremely heartening. Aligning the poverty data for censuses in several decades, we can track the steady progress as each wave of newcomers settles in and climbs the economic ladder. Latino immigrants are singled out for special attention, because they have been the source of particular concern. In fact, a series of studies shows that poverty improvement has been even more rapid among Asian immigrants, especially the Vietnamese from 1980 to 1990.[27] Accordingly, the evidence assembled for the changing poverty rates of Latino immigrants in California and the United States offers an understated portrait of the upward mobility occurring among all immigrants.

How much have these Latino immigrants been able to escape from poverty? Here I focus on the percentage living in poverty, that is, with incomes *below* the federally defined poverty line (in contrast to our earlier examination of those living above poverty). Longtime immigrant residents who arrived before 1970 can be observed across more decades, and their trajectories of declining poverty can be used to gauge the average progress of upward mobility.[28] Among those who arrived between 1960 and 1970, for example, the poverty rate declined from an initial level of 23.9 percent in 1970 to 16.8 percent in 1980 and 12.6 percent in 1990 (figure 6.2). More recent arrivals have commenced their U.S. careers with higher levels of poverty, but they too have experienced proportional declines in subsequent poverty. The consistency of the poverty improvement over time for each arrival wave is remarkable, suggesting great regularity in the pace of improvement with regard to poverty as immigrants lengthen their residence further in the future.

As a public test of these expectations of future improvement, my colleague John Pitkin and I prepared projections and presented them for public scrutiny. Prior to data being released from the 2000 census, we projected trajectories of poverty improvement to future decades under the assumption that future improvements with lengthened residence will mirror those of the past. Using 1990 as the launch point, we projected trends in the 1970 to 1990 period to 2000 before the Census 2000 results for poverty and immigration were released. Prepared in January 2001, these results were posted to the project website and published on the front page of the *Los Angeles Times*.[29] Having made the projection public, the project team awaited the detailed results from the new census that would be necessary to test the accuracy of the expected poverty improvement. Those data ultimately appeared in June 2003. The actual poverty level of each arrival cohort recorded in the 2000

Figure 6.2   Trajectories of Poverty Decrease for Latino Immigrants by Decade of Arrival and Lengthening
              Settlement, 1970 to 2020

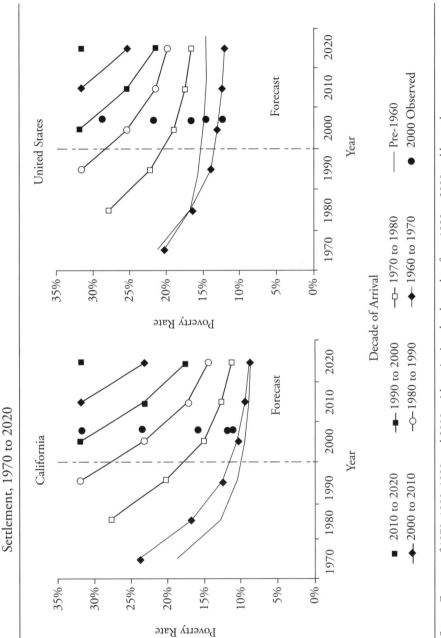

Source: Censuses of 1970, 1980, 1990, and 2000, with projections by the author from 1990 to 2000 and beyond.

census is reported in figure 6.2 as a black dot. The similarities to the projected values are remarkably close for California Latinos, underscoring the consistency of upward mobility and the usefulness of these trajectories for projecting future immigrant progress.[30] A more recently prepared companion projection of Latino immigrant poverty in the United States as a whole is also shown in figure 6.2. Poverty in the nation fell even more than would have been expected based on projections prior to the 2000 census, and thus Latino upward mobility in the nation would have been underestimated by this method. Nonetheless, the test of projected poverty decline is a strong validation of our method for measuring expected improvements with growing length of U.S. residence.

Given this understanding of how much poverty levels improve with the lengthening residence of immigrants, the turnaround in foreign-born poverty in the 2000 census can be better evaluated. The improving poverty levels of immigrants are not an unexplainable aberration. In fact, the force of upward mobility has proceeded as predicted, or even more rapidly in the case of the United States as a whole. What creates the overall turnaround in foreign-born poverty is the lowering of the average poverty rate by the growing numbers of longer-settled immigrants. For lack of understanding of these dynamics, and misled by extrapolated expectations from the dismal period, most observers have been blind to the turnaround in fortunes already under way.

Immigrant Entry into Homeownership

Escape from poverty may be one thing, but access to homeownership, the putative American Dream, may be another. Upward mobility into the middle class may be best indicated by entry into homeownership.[31] This upward mobility can be traced in the same fashion we traced poverty: linking census data observations in 1970, 1980, 1990, and 2000. Again we focus on Latino immigrants because they have been perceived as most at risk for socioeconomic failure. Indeed, Latino immigrants are generally much less advantaged than other new arrivals. However, what we find from the analysis of immigrant trajectories into homeownership is quite striking. In their first census after arriving in California, immigrant households exhibit a homeownership rate in the range of 10 to 16 percent (figure 6.3). This is true for newcomers in all four decades of observation. In their subsequent full decade of residence, their homeownership rate rises roughly twenty percentage points. For example, the Latino immigrant cohort that arrived in the 1970s in California was reported

Figure 6.3   Progress into Homeownership of Native-Born and Foreign-Born Households, by Decade of Arrival, Hispanic Only

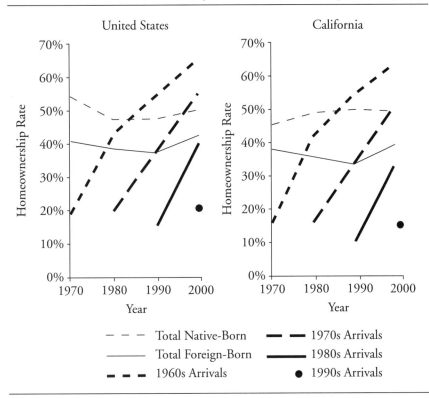

Source: Decennial census, public microdata files.

to have a 16.3 percent homeownership rate in 1980, which rose to 33.6 percent in 1990 and then climbed still further to 51.9 percent in 2000.[32] Very similar steep upward trajectories have been found for all the major immigrant receiving states.[33] There are some notable differences between Latinos and other immigrants: Asians experience initially steeper upward trajectories, and Latinos have more sustained upward trajectories from lower starting points.[34]

How is it possible for all groups of immigrants to improve their status so much and yet have the average decline? An apparent paradox is that the rapidity of immigrant progress into homeownership stands in sharp contrast to the downward trend for homeownership among Latino foreign-born as a whole. That trend drifted downward in California from 1970 (38.4 percent) to 1990 (33.9 percent), before finally moving up to 40.3 percent in 2000. Most observers have judged the progress of immigrants by this overall trend, and it offers a much more pessimistic view of immigrant success. According to the overall trend in homeownership among all foreign-born, immigrants were losing ground in California until 1990 and barely made any progress after that. How is the discrepancy to be explained between these upward cohort trends and the flatter foreign-born trend, and which is a more accurate depiction of immigrant fortunes?

The explanation for the seeming paradox is actually quite simple. The overall foreign-born homeownership rate is nothing more than a *weighted average* of the homeownership rates pertaining to each separate group of immigrant arrivals. The earlier arrivals have had time to reach high levels of homeownership, but they are heavily outnumbered by the more recent arrivals. For example, in the United States in 2000, the number of immigrants who had arrived in the 1970s amounted to 4.7 million, while 13.2 million arrived in the 1990s—nearly three times as many.[35] Thus, the low homeownership rates of the newcomers carry much greater weight in the overall foreign-born total. As a result, the strong upward progress of immigrants has been disguised amid the large number of immigrants beginning their U.S. careers with very low homeownership. As I have described, immigration has slowed its increase in California, and so the newcomers in the 1990s are only twice as numerous as the immigrants who settled in the 1970s. The result is that the weight of newcomers is not as great as in the United States as a whole, and thus their low homeownership rate did not drag down the average homeownership rate as much among the foreign-born in California.[36] Now that immigration to California has ceased its acceleration, the progress of longer-settled immigrants is beginning to characterize the overall status of the foreign-born, and thus their overall rate of homeownership has begun to rise (figure 6.3).[37]

Conclusion: The Basis for a More Hopeful Outlook

We now have a well-rounded picture of how rapidly immigrants make progress after arriving in this county, specifically Latinos, who traditionally have been among the least advantaged of immigrants. This so sharply contradicts widely held assumptions that the difference must be explained. Much of the misconception is due to the newness of immigration early in the demographic transition, which creates a concentration of newcomers. It is the generally low status of immigrants at first arrival that has led many observers to a negative impression of subsequent trends. Combined with the Peter Pan fallacy of assuming people are frozen in time, it is understandable how a very pessimistic view of the future could be generated from this impression. In fact, we now see that the evidence leads to a very different conclusion. When immigrants have resided longer in the United States, their upward mobility is dramatic, as witnessed by their reductions in poverty and increases in homeownership. In addition, their English use, voting participation, and other factors also improve markedly after the early years of immigrant arrival.

The nation is now beginning to turn a corner and enter the middle phase of the demographic transition. A longer-settled immigrant population has taken root in California, soon to be followed by a similar development in other states, and upward mobility is carrying Latino and other immigrants to unimagined success. Although many of these immigrants continue to lag behind the achievements of native-born white residents and more needs to be done to cultivate their advancement, their revealed progress is much greater than we have been led to expect. Surely their progress is an unexpected boost to the fortunes of California and the nation and should help to finally dispel the visions of a dismal future that emerged during the early phase of the transition.

Today much has changed from what we expected in the past. We now know that immigrant settlement is maturing in our nation, and we can begin to see its benefits. As the average characteristics of residents change, so do the trends that prevailed in the past. Nevertheless, the positive outlook may not be fulfilled automatically. Despite the apparent facts, the knowledge underlying a more positive outlook is not widely shared, and pessimism still reigns in many sectors of the electorate. The real challenge is to capitalize on this newfound potential for immigrant progress so we can build a more hopeful future. In part II, I examine these political attitudes and the challenge to democratic governance that is posed in the midst of the great demographic transition.

PART II

SELF-INTEREST AND GOVERNANCE

Chapter 7

The Political Lag During the Demographic Transition

WHEN THE Census Bureau declared in 1999 that California was no longer a majority-white state, many assumed that an important balance had been tipped. In fact, in terms of political power, little has changed in subsequent years. The white share of the population has slowly declined and in some sectors even dwindled. White non-Hispanic children have fallen to only 32 percent of the public school enrollment in California. Yet, where it counts—among the voters—non-Hispanic whites still hold a dominant majority, in some recent elections as high as 71 percent. Despite the demographic forces of change, political power sharing is not proceeding at the pace that some might assume.

The transition of political power is an important dimension of the demographic transition in America. Where once political power was consolidated in the hands of the broad white majority, today we see a broader sharing among voters and leaders of different major racial-ethnic groups, and there is every reason to believe this will continue into the future. Of course, whites themselves are divided between Democrats and Republicans, or alternatively, they vote as liberals, moderates, or conservatives. Already the vanguard state of California is being heralded as a majority-minority state where politicians know that electoral success requires building broad-based multiethnic support.[1] However, even in California, where minority groups have grown to be a majority, white voters' continued dominance suggests that, until they tackle the problems of guiding the state through the demographic transition, the future well-being of the state is very much in doubt.

Much can be learned about the dynamics of political lag and transition by examining the experience of California, the leading edge of the demographic transition in the United States. Some say a turning point in the transition came when Loretta Sanchez ousted the flamboyant and conservative Robert K. Dornan from his longtime seat in the Forty-sixth Congressional District in suburban Orange County. Some observers believed that Sanchez's victory in November 1996 was due to thousands of newly energized Latino supporters, but in fact Dornan was ousted primarily by the white voters who formed the great majority of the electorate. In coalition with Latinos, it was primarily white moderates and liberals who turned Dornan out of office. Such coalitions among ethnic groups and political factions have already come to dominate big-city politics nationwide, and as whites gradually become a smaller share of the electorate, such coalitions will become ever more widespread, appearing even in the suburbs, as illustrated by Orange County.[2] The white majority of voters is so large, however, that even California's politics continue to revolve around this one group and its various factions.

This chapter explores the pace of political change that follows behind the demographic transition. We need to better understand what causes this imbalance between growing population size and lagging electoral influence. How long this lag will persist is another question. Using the example of California, the question of persistence is encapsulated by a more specific question: how long will white voters remain a majority of the electorate now that whites have fallen to a minority of the population? And most important, what difference does it make if whites retain majority electoral power? To better understand the consequences of electoral majority, we delve here into differences of opinion on a number of public policy issues, including immigration and population change, actions for planning a better quality of life in the state, and willingness to increase taxes for more public spending.

Seniority, Time Perspective, and Voting Power

The temporal perspective produces new insights on political process and consequences. It does not focus solely on pursuing current self-interest and garnering a majority of votes, but rather asks: how are these decisions positioned on a time path, and what do today's voting patterns mean for the future? Given that all voters have their own individual pasts and futures, how do their expressions of perceived self-interest add up for the good of the community in the future? This question takes on salience in the face of rapid demographic transition, which carries the potential for a disconnect between past and future. White and African American voters, especially older ones, may lean toward the interests of a time gone past, while Latino and Asian voters, in contrast, represent the incoming majority and have a burgeoning stake in the future. For several decades, voters of different heritages will need to work together to plan a better future desired by all.

The current imbalance only creates the *potential* for a disconnect. Certainly, white and African American voters are often the ones with the greatest life experience and longest tenure in California, and their seniority counts for something. Nonetheless, consider the danger for the long-term well-being of the state if the majority group is focused on short-term benefits, or if the majority voters represent interests remembered from a lost past and not those foreseen in the future. How likely is it in this case that the majority voters are responding to the old fears of a dismal future, a vision that still lingers despite the positive turnaround? Voters who are unnecessarily pessimistic may not make constructive and responsible decisions about the future. Unwittingly, a misguided perception of self-interest could undercut the promise of a more optimistic future.

Close examination of voter opinions allows us to test how much such divergent visions characterize the electorate. As a first step, we must address the imbalance in the numbers of voters relative to new population majorities. Long-established populations have a seniority that allows them to wield disproportionate political influence.

Seniority and Minority Dominance in Compton

A dramatic illustration of seniority effects on political transition is found in the case of Compton, California, a close-in suburb south of Los Angeles made famous by its contributions to African American popular culture ("gangsta rap") and to the courts of Wimbledon (the Williams sisters, Venus and Serena).[3] Compton experienced a series of racial transitions, from white to black in the 1960s and 1970s, and then from black to Latino after 1985.[4] Despite presumptions, the city was never composed of solely one group or another, and even in 1960 there was a noticeable presence of Latinos as well as a large number of African Americans. The majority white, non-Hispanic population declined from 50.9 percent to 15.1 percent of the Compton population from 1960 to 1970, a steep decline spurred by the white exodus after the Watts riots of 1965. Nonetheless, whites retained disproportionate electoral power because they retained a majority in the older age groups that are the most active voters.[5]

Transition was also impeded because the city council and mayor are elected "at large," not by district. From 1960 forward, distinctly black or Latino neighborhoods took form in Compton, and even Latinos, who were a small minority overall, formed a majority of residents in these districts.[6] However, with citywide voting for the mayor and each council seat, localized majorities had little effect on these elections.

Nonetheless, the pace of racial change in the 1960s was so abrupt that the African American population soon consolidated its population gains into political positions. Among the five major elected officials in the city, including the mayor and four council members, the first black was elected in 1963; by 1964 there were two black seat holders, then three in 1967, and then four from 1969 through 1994.[7] The last white council member, Jane Robbins, a relic of the past without any significant white constituency, did not surrender her seat until 1994; since that time, all five officials have been African American. None of these officials has ever been Latino.

The African American population reached an apogee in 1980 when whites had declined to 2.6 percent and the black population share had grown to 73.9 percent. At that time, the Latino population was beginning to grow, amounting to nearly 21.1 percent and subsequently expanding to 43.7 percent by 1990. Meanwhile, during the 1980s the black population began to decline sharply; it had fallen to 52.7 percent of the Compton total by 1990. Even in 2000, when the Latino population in Compton had increased to 57.2 percent of the total and the share of African Americans had declined to 40.0 percent, black voters still ruled the city. That was because the African American minority accounted for 65.6 percent of all persons eligible to vote, that is, those who were citizens and age eighteen or older.[8] The higher rates of citizenship and registration for blacks than Latinos combine with the older age of black registrants to suggest that the African American voter turnout will continue to be much larger than it is for Latinos. Thus, in the coming decade, even if the black share of Compton's population decreases to 30 percent,

African Americans are still likely to retain a voting majority in the city, thus dominating all the at-large elections. In a demographic twist of voting power, the African American residents of Compton who had been dominated earlier by a white minority of the local population were now a minority themselves, and in similar fashion, they were dominating the rising Latino majority. As of 2005, the mayor and all the city council members in Compton were still drawn from the minority African American population.

Explaining the Imbalance of Population and Voting in At-Large Elections

The imbalance displayed in Compton is also played out in many cities and states across the United States. More often white than black, the longer-established population holds on to its electoral majority even when minority groups are rapidly expanding. This has significance in any at-large election but is especially important for shaping major policies in statewide elections to choose governors and members of the U.S. Senate. A growing feature of statewide policymaking is the presence on the ballot of voter initiatives and referenda, which have become increasingly important in this era of direct democracy.[9] Growing reliance on such ballot initiatives enhances the political power of whatever groups hold the largest share of the statewide electorate.

The difference between at-large and district-based elections is starkly portrayed by veteran political observers:

> Legislative districts are drawn on the basis of population, not citizenship or even legal residency. Thus, immigrants who cannot vote provide additional legislative seats for certain geographic areas. Since these immigrants often cluster in ethnic "enclaves," representation in the California legislature is weighted toward Democrats and minorities with liberal policy attitudes. On the other hand, the statewide electorate, which decides the gubernatorial race and ballot initiatives, is whiter, older, and wealthier than the population as a whole. Accordingly, outcomes in these contests tend to be more heavily influenced by Republican and conservative voters.[10]

In the case of California, statewide ballots delay the decline in electoral power of the white voters, despite their shrinking proportion of the California population (about 45 percent in 2005). The actual share of white non-Hispanic voters varies somewhat between elections, with higher percentages in less publicized elections and lower percentages in presidential elections, which draw a stronger turnout from other groups. For example, the spring 2004 primary election, which included a major statewide bond issue for education, drew a turnout of whom 74 percent were white, whereas the fall 2004 presidential election in California drew a record high turnout of whom 67 percent were estimated to be white.[11]

It is fair to ask how exactly larger populations garner so many fewer voters. To better understand the translation of population into voters, we can compare each group's share of population with its share of the total in the key stages necessary for voting: adult-age population, citizens, and registered voters. For this assessment of relative voting strength, the most reliable gauge is the federal government's Current Population Survey, with its November voting supplement conducted in even numbered years.[12]

The size of the voter representation gap is clearly shown in table 7.1. Of the total California population in 2000, 46.6 percent were non-Hispanic white and 32.3 percent were Hispanic; other groups were much less numerous. California was the first large state in the nation to become majority-minority, meaning that whites now number less than 50 percent of the total and the population is a composite of minority groups. Nonetheless, despite its minority status, the white population in California accounts for 71.3 percent of the regular voters in these data.[13]

In contrast, Latinos numbered only 13.8 percent of regular voters even though they held a 32.3 percent share of the California population. Given that many Latinos are children or noncitizens, fewer are eligible to vote. Table 7.1 shows how the Latino share shrinks, first to 28.0 percent among adults, and then more drastically to 17.7 percent among adults who are citizens. Conversely, whites' share steadily rises as a percentage of each of these categories. A similar imbalance is observed in the United States as a whole, although, compared to California, whites begin with a far larger share of the population and Latinos a far smaller share. Comparisons by other scholars show that the political overrepresentation of whites in California is substantially greater than in other large, immigrant-receiving states.[14]

What underlies each group's share of a jurisdiction's voters is not only the relative size of the group but also its per capita rate of voting participation. Some groups may have a large share of their population who are under age eighteen or noncitizens, and hence ineligible to vote. Other groups may have a low percentage of their eligibles registered to vote, or it may be that a low

Table 7.1   Shares of Total Population, Eligible Citizens, and Voters in California and the United States

	Total	Age Eighteen or Over	Citizens Age Eighteen or Over	Registered Voters	Voted
California					
All	100.0%	100.0%	100.0%	100.0%	100.0%
White	46.6	51.0	64.1	69.1	71.3
Black	6.4	6.2	7.8	7.5	7.1
Asian	11.1	11.6	9.3	7.5	7.0
Hispanic	32.3	28.0	17.7	14.8	13.8
United States					
All	100.0	100.0	100.0	100.0	100.0
White	68.2	71.0	77.6	80.3	81.3
Black	11.8	11.0	11.9	11.4	11.2
Asian	3.7	3.7	2.5	1.9	1.8
Hispanic	13.7	12.1	7.1	5.8	5.1

Source: Current Population Survey, November 1998, 2000, and 2002, adjusted to 2000 census population base.
Note: All percentages are ethnic shares of the specific category.

percentage of those registered turn out on election day. The hurdles to voting for those not born in the United States are substantial and have been described as "a three-step process—naturalization, registration and turning out—that involves, at each turn, a set of costs"; as a consequence, there can be substantial delays in achieving full voting participation.[15] It bears emphasis that populations with predominantly older adults typically vote much more heavily than those composed only of young adults. Both sets of adults are of voting age, but the older citizens are much more active.

Seniority and Political Participation

Political participation involves other forms of activism besides voting, and seniority emerges as a major factor here as well. It takes time for a group to build up a sufficient number of political organizers to be competitive in local politics. In the context of demographic transition, the longer-established group holds a key advantage over the more numerous newcomers. One study in Los Angeles County found that the majority of both Democratic and Republican Party activists were longtime residents.[16] Despite rapid population growth and migration flux in the area, the average length of residence in California exceeded thirty years among activists of both parties and among all ethnic groups, and the average years at the same address exceeded twelve years.

Political scientists have long recognized that this seniority effect—length of residence plus age—is among the strongest predictors of political participation among the general population of the United States.[17] A recent study by Karthick Ramakrishnan of immigrant voting and political participation in America also found that length of time at the same address—in addition to the effects of older age and length of time in America—led to higher rates of active voting. Ramakrishnan's explanation is that the longer-settled citizens are more vested in their community and have more stable networks of friends and neighbors.[18] Thus, the time it takes to grow a committed cadre of local political players gives an added advantage to the declining former majority group because of its seniority.

A Challenge to Democracy?

What are we to make of the imbalance between population and voting? Indeed, whose fault is it that whites are overrepresented? In our democracy, we encourage all residents to participate politically. We can hardly ask whites or African Americans, as in Compton, to register and vote less. Rather, the challenge is to raise the participation of others, beginning with enhanced efforts to promote citizenship, the necessary step prior to voting registration.[19] Older whites could well be justified if they complain, "If these people aren't vested enough in their future in this country to become citizens and vote, why should others worry that they are underrepresented?"

Nonetheless, the public policy problem is that large blocs of the population do not have a proportional number of voters who share their race or ethnicity. Whether interests really are that different just because of ethnicity is addressed in the remainder of this chapter. But first I would ask: who is looking out for the next generation? Children under age eighteen are ineligible to vote, whatever their ethnic group, but many more children in California are Latino than white. Children can usually count on their parents to represent their interests at the polls, but many parents either are ineligible to vote or have failed to register and vote. Clearly, it would benefit the next generation and yield more proportional representation if more parents who are not voters registered their preferences.

Disparities Between the Voting Preferences of Whites and Others

The imbalance between population and voting takes on important consequences for public policy only if the preferences of the voter majority diverge from those of the population majority. What is most worrisome is that the dynamics of the demographic transition have implications for more than simple minority-majority relations in the present: they may create a systematic bias against the future. Some groups are rapidly growing and constitute the incoming majority that represents the future, while the older majority of white non-Hispanics may reflect interests that are relatively more oriented toward the present or even the past.

This is a structural problem of the demographic transition that is likely to occur in almost every instance. The self-interest of members of the incoming and outgoing majority groups differ because they have different orientations toward the future. One group knows that the greater part of their lives will be played out in the coming years in a particular locale and that a large portion of that locale's future residents will be members from their own group. The other group knows that a relatively smaller part of their lives remains in the coming years and that only a small portion of future residents will be from their group. Thus, the self-interest of the incoming group is more likely to be invested in the future than that of the outgoing group.

There are other systematic differences between incoming and outgoing groups, and they loom as major divisions of public opinion in California. The outgoing group, by virtue of longer residence, is growing older and has relatively fewer children to raise. Long settled in California, the outgoing majority also remembers a time when life was easier in the state: traffic congestion was not so bad, housing prices were far lower, and more of the residents shared the same cultural background and general racial appearance. As we will see, this experience has shaped their political views about trends in quality of life and the like. In contrast, incoming residents are very likely to be much younger and to have a fresher perspective on new opportunities in California. Latino residents, whose numbers are increasing in California and elsewhere in the nation, will constitute the bulk of future increases in workers, while the outgoing majority will dominate the ranks of retirees. In short, one group is on the way in and will carry more of the workload, while the other is on the way out and may be seeking rewards for a life's hard work.

In prior chapters, I have argued that California residents' extrapolation of perceived negative trends in the past has created their dismal view of the future. Pessimism about future living conditions, in turn, could undermine their willingness to invest in the future. However, there is another possibility: the expectation of future deterioration could have the opposite effect, namely, it could inspire support for greater public investments to forestall the anticipated deterioration. Which outlook is supported by the survey evidence? We can use the opinions expressed by voters on several questions in opinion polls to shed light on differences in outlook among the various segments of the electorate.[20]

The analysis will emphasize differences in opinion between groups, but it bears emphasis that not all members of a group think alike. White voters are subdivided into liberals and conservatives, and even among white liberals, for example, there is no unanimous opinion on any issue. What can be shown is how much the *balance of opinion* differs between groups. Even a 10 percent greater preference by one group rather than another can be very significant, especially in matters subject to voting, where the difference between 45 percent and 55 percent is night and day.

A Feared Decline in the Quality of Life

Earlier we observed that an important feature of California's demographic transition is the relatively greater pessimism of whites, representing the older majority, compared to other groups that are expanding their presence. A special survey on voter attitudes about the future of California, conducted in May and June 2004, provides a rare opportunity to peer into this issue, which the survey casts as an outlook on quality of life. Respondents were asked: "Overall, do you think that in 2025 your part of California will be a better place to live than it is now or a worse place to live than it is now, or will there be no change?" Results showed that the white residents were much more likely to foresee a decline in living conditions. Among all adults, 52 percent of whites and 45 percent of blacks thought that their part of California would be a worse place to live in twenty years. This compares to 41 percent of Latinos and 30 percent of Asians who are this pessimistic.[21]

The reasons for this ethnic distinction in outlook deserve some scrutiny. Perhaps whites and blacks are more educated and just better informed about the ongoing trends. Alternatively, we might suspect that whites and blacks have lived longer in California on average and thus have greater experience from which to judge the trends.[22] Respondents were asked about a series of specific problem areas, each of which might affect one's overall outlook on quality of life. They were asked if population will grow rapidly or not, and if a series of living conditions would improve or grow worse: the public education system, air quality, job opportunities and economic conditions, traffic conditions, and the availability of affordable housing. Taking all the evidence together, we can ascertain each factor's weight in raising or lowering respondents' perceptions of quality of life. After accounting for these many factors, are there still overall differences in outlook between voters of different races?[23]

In fact, large racial differences in pessimism still prevail about the quality of life in the future even after accounting for all these other factors. After controlling for age and education differences, among other things, Latinos are not appreciably different from whites in their outlook, but Asian and black voters express views that are 13.7 percent and 16.9 percent less pessimistic than whites, respectively. We also find that very young adults are 16.0 percent less pessimistic than the middle-aged, and that women are 4.9 percent less pessimistic than men. What appears to have no appreciable effect in shaping a pessimistic outlook are income, education, and foreign birth. However, we observe that homeowners are 6.9 percent less pessimistic than renters, probably because owners have profited from the recent surge in house values while renters are discouraged about their prospects of ever buying a home.

What is especially interesting are the ways in which pessimism about quality of life are rooted in fears of specific changes in living conditions. For example, if people expect rapid population growth, that expectation increases pessimism about future living conditions by 16.4 percent. Similarly, an expectation that conditions will grow worse in the following aspects of community life leads to these expected declines in overall quality of life: education system (20.6 percent), air quality (18.3 percent), jobs and economic conditions (16.2 percent), traffic conditions (9.5 percent), and availability of affordable housing (9.1 percent). Perhaps the most surprising finding, finally, is that political leaning—whether one is liberal or conservative—has no effect on pessimism about future living conditions. Apparently these sentiments cut across residents of all political persuasions.

Trust in Government and Confidence in Planning Effectiveness

Part of people's pessimistic outlook on the future is a sense that government is incapable of arresting the negative trends or that government could even make things worse. An overarching theme in the political landscape of California and the United States has been declining trust in government.[24] In California, trust in state government has fallen to a very low level among both liberals and conservatives, and this feeling cuts across other major segments of voters as well. When asked, "How much of the time do you think you can trust the government in Sacramento to do what is right—just about always, most of the time, or only some of the time?" only 31.7 percent of regular voters expressed trust most of the time or just about always.[25] Whites expressed about the same amount of confidence (31.6 percent) as the average voter, but this was much higher than among blacks (12.9 percent) and lower than among Latinos (38.0 percent). Overall, the low degree of confidence is fairly uniform across segments of the electorate. Even trust in government among liberals (39.3 percent), who usually express more confidence in government than conservatives, was not much higher than among conservatives (25.5 percent).

Dislike of Population Growth

Attitudes toward population growth and the changes that accompany it provide particular insight into the demographic transition. Indeed, as we saw earlier, the expectation of rapid population growth is among the strongest of factors shaping pessimism about future quality of life. An expectation of growth is one thing; whether growth is feared as a bad thing may be another. Taking a closer look at the dislike of population growth, we can draw again on the 2004 special survey on the future, which asked: "Between now and 2025, California's population is estimated to increase by 10 million people from 35 to 45 million. On balance, do you think this population growth is a good thing or a bad thing or does it make no difference to you and your family?"[26] Fully 59.2 percent of all residents judged this population growth to be "a bad thing," including an even larger share of 67.4 percent of white voters.

How much of the dislike of population growth is due to its physical and economic impacts, and how much is due to its social consequences? Most Californians are well aware that population growth is being driven by immigration, and they see from their daily life how much of the growth stems from the rapid increase in the numbers of Latinos and Asians. We might expect that white residents, on balance, would view this population growth with less favor than would Latinos and Asians. It remains to be seen whether this supposition is true, once we account for factors such as age, education, and political leaning and for voters' fears about specific features of declining quality of life. If we control for the declining physical and economic conditions feared by voters, we might find that this fear accounts for much of the dislike they have about population growth. The remaining dislike might then represent the unmeasured social content of population growth—content that is probably viewed differently by members of different racial-ethnic groups.

After accounting for all factors, Latino voters are 8.0 percent *less* likely than white non-Hispanic voters to think population growth is a bad thing (see table B.2 for results of the detailed analysis). Black voters are even less likely to think growth is a bad thing. We also find that young adults are generally 10 percent less likely than middle-aged adults to judge population growth unfavorably, perhaps because they have less experience witnessing its impacts over time. After all, their period of comparison is very brief and very recent, amounting to the short time since they were teenagers.

Of greatest surprise, the rate of population growth expected by voters has no effect on their dislike of population growth. People seem to dislike the simple *idea* of population growth, no matter how rapidly it happens or not. In this sense, population *growth* could well stand for population *change*. Also surprising is that no significant difference is found in opinions about population growth between liberals and conservatives or among those with different degrees of confidence in state and local planners' ability to reduce the ill effects of growth. None of these governmental and political attitudes seem to interact with opinions about population growth.

What *does* increase dislike of population growth, other than race and age, is fear of declining quality of life: citizens who think life will grow worse in their part of California are 20 percent more likely to feel that growth is a bad thing. This result could be puzzling because the effect of this fear is felt even after we have accounted for the rate of population growth and trends in education, jobs, traffic, housing, and air quality. By explicitly addressing those trends, we should have already accounted for the components of declining quality of life that are due to physical and economic deterioration. Thus, there is still some powerful aspect of quality of life that remains unaccounted for and unexplained. It must be something fairly major—probably social—that voters do not like about the anticipated future.

Are Immigrants a Burden or a Benefit?

The most prominent part of population growth in many people's eyes is immigration, something presumably subject to governmental control. In fact, just over half of the residents in California in 2005 thought that immigration from other countries was the biggest factor causing the state's population to grow.[27] Given the widespread dislike of population growth, it surely is no surprise that immigration would be disliked as well. But immigrants have been singled out with special criticism for the burdens they impose. Next to the matter of illegality, concern about the burdens they create has become the central feature of debates about immigration.[28]

The feelings of California voters were revealed in their November 1994 vote to pass Proposition 187, which would have denied services to illegal immigrants, as discussed in chapter 4. The changes in voter opinion since then are of considerable interest. I have argued that the 1980s and early 1990s were a time of maximum turmoil and discontent over the demographic transition in California. Comparison of the available survey data could reveal how much the discontent with regard to immigration might have moderated in recent years. Here we examine opinion polls conducted in 1998 and 2004 that asked voters an identical question.[29] Voters were asked to choose one of the following statements as the one closest to their views: "Immigrants today are a benefit to California because of their hard work and job skills; or immigrants today are a burden to California because they use public services."[30] These opinions were collected in April 1998, just three and a half years following the vote for Proposition 187, and it is instructive to compare them to opinions collected six years later in February 2004. Did voter opinion become more or less sympathetic toward immigrants in the interim? What factors were most important for explaining which voters were more likely to consider immigrants a burden, and did those factors remain the same over the period? The answers found to these questions are quite striking.

Among all adult residents, the proportion of those who judged immigrants to be a burden fell in six years from 41.5 percent to 34.8 percent, a reduction of 6.7 percentage points. However, among *voters* the proportion fell only 2.5 points, and among white voters only 1.5 percentage points. Here we find another instance where the attitudes of voters are lagging behind changing opinions in the population as a whole. Nonetheless, the opinion of some segments of white voters is moving much closer to that of the population majority.

How large is the difference in opinion between white and other voters? And how much of the difference can be accounted for by other factors, such as education, income, or general political leaning? In 2004 Latino and Asian voters were at least 21 percent less likely than whites to believe that immigrants posed a burden, a difference sustained after accounting for all other factors (for details of this analysis, see table B.3). Surprisingly in fact, voters' income and education have virtually no effect on their view of immigrants as a burden.[31] The one factor that carries much weight, other than race and ethnicity, is political leaning. Conservatives are 30.7 percentage points more likely than liberals to think that immigrants are a burden.

These opinions have polarized substantially since 1998, when the differences between liberals and conservatives were half as great, only 13.7 percent. We might wonder what has widened the gap: is it liberals who grew more tolerant of immigrants, or conservatives who grew less tolerant? Closer examination of the original survey data collected from white voters shows that liberals' view that immigrants pose a burden decreased from 40.1 percent to 28.5 percent. Meanwhile, there was no change among political moderates, but we find that the assessment that immigrants pose a burden *increased* from 53.9 percent to 61.9 percent among conservatives. Thus, while liberals grew 12 percent more likely to be tolerant of immigrants, conservatives grew 8 percent less tolerant over the six years, and the resulting gap widened by twenty percentage points between the two political groups of white voters.[32] The clear conclusion is that there has been a growing polarization in the California electorate with regard to immigration, as has happened in the United States as a whole. While most groups have grown more tolerant, white conservatives have gone the other way.

Preferences for Public Spending and Taxing

Decisions about public spending and taxing constitute the very heart of government. Our perspective may shed some new light on how this crucial matter should be considered. Rather than emphasize the tug-of-war between various groups of taxpayers and beneficiaries, a battle fought over current budgets and current legislation, we seek a perspective that emphasizes future consequences. Simply stated, the bulk of state spending, roughly 70 percent, is allocated to education, health, and human services. Although these services are consumed in a current budget period, the spending on them amounts to an *investment* in the future well-being and productivity of the state's population. On a pragmatic level, early care today leads to lower costs and greater benefits tomorrow, as demonstrated in a wide range of policy research.

Not only does current fiscal policy decide investments in the future, but it also passes debt on to future residents. It is one thing for debt to be incurred to cover the costs of infrastructure improvements that will last for many years. However, debt can also be incurred to support current lifestyles at the expense of future taxpayers, As shown later, Californians are loath to cut back public services, even if they also resist tax collections. As a result, since 2000 the State of California has mortgaged the future by issuing $20 billion in bond issues just to cover current operating deficits.[33]

We should examine the budget preferences of California voters from the perspective of the demographic transition. Who wants to pay, and who will benefit? And what impact do the decisions of today's voters have on the future to be inhabited by a different majority group? I first spotlight the voters' lack of desire to cut any services and then turn to the crucial trade-off between maintaining services or cutting taxes.

Resistance to Budget Cuts in Services

Two-thirds of the voting population in June 2003 believed that "the state government could spend less and still provide the same level of services."[34] At the same time, the voters retained a very high level of expectation about government services. No matter how ready they are to discipline government, curbing its wasteful ways and cutting spending, Californians have not appeared eager to reduce the level of services offered. In fact, even though the citizens think the state can cut spending without loss of services, when asked directly, they are opposed to cutting spending in any of the major expenditure areas of the state budget. The share of surveyed voters who expressed opposition to budget cuts in the K-12 education sector was 80 percent, 67 percent in the college sector, 77 percent in health and human services, 63 percent in transportation, and 39 percent in prisons.[35] Thus, a strong majority opposed cuts in every budget sector except prisons. A subsequent survey in January 2006, using different question wording, found even stronger opposition to budget cuts in these program areas.[36]

The breadth of opposition to spending cuts was remarkable. Closer examination shows that the opposition to spending cuts in most sectors was very similar between whites and other racial-ethnic groups. Even ideological opponents joined together in resistance to budget cuts. Surprisingly, among those who did not trust state government to do the right thing and who might be assumed to be more skeptical of spending, resistance to budget cuts was only one to four percentage points lower in every budget sector than among those who did trust government. Among the greatest differentials, not surprisingly, was that between liberals and conservatives. Remarkably, however, even among conservatives at least 57.9 percent were opposed to spending cuts in every sector save prisons.

These findings may show a strong consensus to resist budget cuts, but are voters willing to pay the necessary taxes?

The Preferred Balance of Spending and Taxing

California voters are deeply ambivalent about spending and taxing, expressing a strong desire to "have their cake and eat it too." Survey data show that they want to pay less in taxes, but even conservatives also want to avoid any spending cuts in services. In fact, this tendency is commonplace among voters and is widely recognized.[37] Of particular interest are the findings of voter experiments showing that people will support budget cuts in the abstract but *not* on a program-by-program basis, perhaps because the benefits are more easily imagined in specific program areas.[38]

The only realistic way to understand the true choices that voters are willing to make is to pose a trade-off between how much they prefer receiving services and how much they prefer cutting taxes. Here is where we might detect a substantial difference in priorities among different segments of the voters. The June 2003 survey presented the following choice: "In general, which of the following statements do you agree with more—I'd rather pay higher taxes to support a larger government that provides more services, or I'd rather pay lower taxes and have a smaller government that provides fewer services?" Unlike the responses to the unconstrained questions summarized earlier, this question uncovers greater acceptance of spending cuts by some, but not all, important segments of the electorate. Meanwhile, other segments demonstrate greater preference for increased services accompanied by higher taxes.

A strong racial and ethnic difference of opinion is revealed. In particular, Latino voters (68.0 percent) were far more likely than white voters (38.6 percent) to prefer higher taxes and more services over lower taxes and fewer services. Of course, this raw difference could be related to income and other differences, and in fact, several sets of factors might explain a willingness to support higher taxes and spending. Demographic characteristics such as race, age, gender, and nativity could prove important. Economic factors are also important, measured here by income, education level, and homeownership. In addition, political leaning and trust in government could prove to be significant. All of these factors deserve to be considered and weighed against one another.[39]

Our primary interest is in examining the differences in willingness to tax and spend between voters of different racial-ethnic groups and observing how much those differences persist once we account for other effects of demographics, economics, and political opinions. The key findings are summarized in table 7.2 (the underlying analysis is reported in appendix B). In general, the racial differences in degree of support for taxing and spending are moderated somewhat by the addition of other explanatory factors. For example, unadjusted for any other factors, Latino voters are 29.4 percent more likely than whites to support higher taxes and spending. However, after adjusting for demographic and economic factors, this gap in preferences is reduced to 18.3 percent. And when we factor in degree of trust in government, the perception that taxes are wasted, and political leaning, the preference gap between Latinos and whites declines further, to 13.7 percent. The gap between blacks and whites is even greater than for Latinos, but the gap with Asians is substantially smaller (table 7.2). The fact that the large preference differences between whites and other racial-ethnic groups are only moderately altered by adding all these explanatory factors shows that there is a very firm base of difference in preferences for taxing and spending.

Among the strongest explanations of willingness to pay higher taxes are political attitudes. Voters who feel that taxes are wasted a lot are 16.6 percent less likely, not surprisingly, to support higher taxes and spending (see table B.4). But the largest single explanatory factor, also not surprisingly, is that conservatives are 37.9 percent less willing than liberals to tax and spend, even after taking account of the perception of tax wasting. What is most notable is that the racial and ethnic differences persist even after adjusting for these powerful political factors.

Also important are the demographic and economic differences in willingness to tax and spend, after accounting for differences in political attitudes. Consistent with our generational argument, we find that young voters are much more supportive of raising taxes than are the elderly. Compared to middle-aged voters, eighteen- to twenty-four-year-olds are 18.3 percent more supportive of higher taxes and spending, and those age twenty-five to thirty-four are 8.6 percent more supportive. We also find that foreign-born citizens are 9.4 percent more supportive of raising taxes than are the native-born. In general, women are 6.6 percent more supportive of increasing taxes and spending than are men. Surprisingly, education and income have no significant effect. Homeowners are 11.1 percent *less* supportive of increasing taxes

Table 7.2 Race Gap in Willingness to Support Higher Taxes and More
Services: Differences Between Other Groups' and Whites'
Percentage Preference

	Latinos	Blacks	Asians	Whites
Total survey response	29.4	27.5	19.4	—
Adjusted for demographic and economic differences	18.3	20.6	11.0[a]	—
Adjusted in addition for political attitudes	13.7	18.5	10.0[a]	—

Source: Data pertain to regular voters and are drawn from the PPIC Statewide Survey (June 2003).
Notes: Entries are each group's level of support minus the white level of support. Adjustment for multiple factors is achieved through a linear probability multiple regression, as reported in table B.4.
a. Unlike all other entries, not statistically significant.

and spending, perhaps because they fear that the burden will fall on their property taxes, but that effect dissipates once we account for perceived tax wasting and other political opinions.

All of this underscores the sharp divisions in preference between voters who are white, older, and native-born and those who are part of the rising new generation—younger, foreign-born, and Latino. Homeowners may be especially disinclined to support higher taxes and spending, but as we shall see in later chapters, they have much at stake in cultivating investment in the rising new generation.

The Impact of the Perceived Immigrant Burden

What is it that makes white voters so much less supportive of higher taxes and spending? Controlling for all other demographic and economic differences, and even controlling for political attitudes, we have found that white voters are more resistant than others to raising taxes and increasing public spending. Previously, we also have found that white voters are at least 20 percent more likely than Asians and Latinos to judge immigrants as a burden. A central theme in the demographic transition I have emphasized is that the established white population dislikes the ongoing demographic transition and is disinvested in the incoming population majority. The strong suspicion shared by many political observers is that white voters are restraining public spending because they do not want to support immigrants whom they consider a burden.[40]

Here is a way we can directly test the suspicion that perceived immigrant burden is curbing the public willingness to tax and spend. Fortunately, the February 2004 survey that asked if immigrants were a burden or benefit also asked about voter support for major education spending, a $12.3 billion bond issue known as Proposition 55.[41] Conducted roughly three weeks before the election, the survey found support by 50.2 percent of likely voters, a result that was very close to the eventual outcome: passage at the polls on March 2, 2004, by a slim margin of 50.9 percent.

There was a broad base of support for this school bond issue, reflecting considerable generosity among the voters. Barely one-third of voters have children in their home, suggesting that most voters do not have a direct self-interest in educational quality. Not surprisingly, a higher percentage of those who had children at home supported the bonds (55.7 percent) than did those without children (47.1 percent). However, the fact that so many voters without children also supported the school bonds reflects a broad-based generosity of social support that should not be overlooked.

Weighing all these factors together, several groups of likely voters offered distinctly lower support: men, voters without children in the home, voters with income in the middle range of $60,000 to $80,000, voters who thought a lot of tax money is wasted, and conservative voters (for details, see table B.5). The effect of perceived immigrant burden is discernible when that one factor is added after accounting for all these background factors. We find that those voters who consider immigrants a burden were 8.5 percent less likely to support Proposition 55, all other things being equal. Even though many more children than those of immigrants would benefit from these school bonds, voters who believed immigrants are a burden were disinclined to make school investments.

The perception of immigrant burden is clearly important in depressing the popular willingness to increase public spending. The magnitude of the effect is quite substantial and could easily sway election outcomes that waver near 50 percent majority. All things being equal, and based on the experience of Proposition 55, which was fairly popular as spending measures go, if only one-third of voters feel that immigrants are a burden, that would depress the overall vote in support of a spending measure by about three percentage points. Proposition 55 barely passed despite that negative factor, but had 10 percent more of the voters felt that immigrants are a burden, all else being equal, the proposition would have failed.

The Future Trajectory of the Electorate

The foregoing evidence is clear that white voters express very different preferences than do Latinos and others. In particular, on matters of immigration or public taxation and spending, a sizable bloc of conservative voters, most of whom are white, express views that are highly divergent from the rest. Over time, it is possible that conservative whites may become less numerous than liberal whites, and it is certainly likely that Latinos will significantly increase their share of the electorate. However, neither change is likely to occur in the next few years. The demographic transition is a gradual process playing out over decades. We need to assess its likely trajectory in the electorate so that we can better judge the political landscape and how it might change in the coming years. The debate has been focused primarily on whites and Latinos, as is the following discussion, because those two groups are so much larger than the others, but African Americans and Asian Americans also are important contributors to electoral coalitions.

Projections of Continued White Dominance in the Electorate

Given their current two-thirds majority among voters, how many years might it take for white residents in California to fall below 50 percent of all voters? Or conversely, how many years might it take for Latino voters to exceed 50 percent of the total? These questions are often speculated on, but usually without enough careful attention to the facts. Here I offer a reasonably well-grounded projection. The conclusion I reach may sound a little extreme, but it is comparable in magnitude to an independent projection prepared by respected political scientists. My approach to projecting future voting shares combines long-term population projections with recently observed rates of voting participation in each detailed population subgroup. My conclusion incorporates many of the factors of seniority that have already been discussed.

First, by way of contrast, let us consider the simple extrapolations often used by local commentators, a method that expands on the shifts recently observed at the polls but is prone to unreliable results over the long term. For example, some would extrapolate the recent change in ethnic participation observed between the presidential elections of 2000 and 2004, as reported in the exit polls conducted at the voting place.[42] In just four years' time, the white share reported in exit polls declined by four percentage points, while the Latino share increased by four percentage points. Meanwhile, the black share declined by one point and the Asian share increased by one point. If we extrapolate these short-term changes over twenty or thirty years, we might arrive at a crude projection of future voting strength. According to this, the African American voting share will fall to nearly zero, which is inconsistent with population projections that show African Americans still holding a 6 percent or better share of the population. Extrapolations of short-term shifts for other groups are also distorted up or down in exaggerated ways.

A more stable means of estimating future voting shares is to tie future voting shares to what we know about the changing composition of the population. The extrapolation method treats the voters in an aggregate manner and does not refine the expected level of voting due to aging of the population group, length of immigrant residence, and other factors. We need to account for significant differences. For example, among Californians who are non-Hispanic white, the likelihood of voting increases from 46.0 percent at ages twenty-five to thirty-four and to 73.7 percent at ages sixty-five to seventy-four. Similarly, Latino voting increases from 15.0 percent of those ages twenty-five to thirty-four to 45.6 percent at ages sixty-five to seventy-four. Of course, voting also depends on nativity: Latinos who are native-born are all citizens and consequently have much higher voting rates—for example, 39.8 percent at ages twenty-five to thirty-four—although their voting rates are still below those of whites.

The preferred, compositional method of projection directly accounts for these differences among different segments of each racial-ethnic group. Detailed voting rates per capita are defined for each population subgroup in the base year, say 2000, and then applied to the future population composition as we have projected it to evolve over the decades. The one clear drawback to this approach—sure to be emphasized by political activists—is that voting rates for each age and nativity group are assumed to hold constant for decades. There is no allowance for increases in registration or turnout in future elections by residents of a given group, such as Latino immigrants ages twenty-five to twenty-nine. Political organizers would protest, quite fairly, that their mission to increase registration and voter turnout is totally ignored if we assume that rates will simply hold constant in the future. I seek to accommodate these valid concerns later in the chapter. Nonetheless, the compositional method captures the enormous effects on the likelihood of voting as the population of each ethnic group shifts into segments that are generally more senior and likely to vote. This includes not only the aging of the population but also growing shares of Latinos and Asians in the future who will be native-born and the lengthening residence of the foreign-born.

According to the composition-based projection, white voters can be expected to decline from 70.4 percent of the electorate in 2000 to 50.8 percent in 2030 and will fall to the 50 percent majority line in 2031 (table 7.3). Latinos, in contrast, are expected to increase their share of the electorate from 14.5 percent in 2000 to 29.0 percent in 2030, but will not reach 50 percent majority status until 2073. Meanwhile, the share of African American voters will

Table 7.3   Alternative Projections of Future Ethnic Shares of the California Electorate

	2000	2010	2020	2030	Year Reaching 50 Percent
Fixed voting rates, changing population mix					
White	70.4%	63.5%	56.9%	50.8%	2031
Latino	14.5	19.1	24.2	29.0	2073
Asian	7.4	9.7	11.4	13.1	—
Black	7.8	7.7	7.4	7.0	—
Total	100	100	100	100	—
Accelerated voting rates, changing population mix					
White	70.4	58.8	52.1	46.3	2024
Latino	14.5	25.1	30.6	35.3	2061
Asian	7.4	9.0	10.5	12.0	—
Black	7.8	7.1	6.8	6.4	—
Total	100	100	100	100	—

Source: Calculations by the author, with assistance from Seong Hee Min.
Notes: The fixed composition–based projection applies per capita voting rates to projected population from the California Demographic Futures project, detailing that population by ethnicity, age, nativity, and duration in the United States. The accelerated alternative assumes what would happen if two changes were introduced: the voting rates of all subgroups of Latino foreign-born double, and the voting rates of all subgroups of Latino native-born equal those of native-born whites of the same age group. Per capita voting rates are derived from the CPS November voting supplements of 2000 and 2004.

hold steady between 7 to 8 percent, reflecting their stable population share (varying only from 6.5 percent to 6.6 percent) much more closely than the erratic projections based on the extrapolation method. At the same time, the Asian share is projected to nearly double, from 7.4 percent to 13.1 percent, and thus will nearly match their share of the total population in 2030. Overall, these projections appear consistent with what some others have projected.[43]

How realistic is the assumption that past rates of voting will hold constant in the future? A recent wave of Latino mobilization has been spurred by debates in the U.S. Congress over immigration reform, highlighted by more than one million people marching in the streets of Los Angeles on May 1, 2006. Events of this magnitude could accelerate the rates of naturalization, registration, and voting turnout beyond the fixed rates we have assumed.[44] It is impossible to say how much effect this might have, but it warrants testing an alternative projection based on some dramatic new assumptions. What if all categories of Latino foreign-born were to *double* their rates of voting, and what if all Latino native-born were to increase their voting to be *equal to those of white native-born* residents of the same age? What impact would these assumptions have on the acceleration of Latino voting strength (and on decreases in the voting strength of whites and others)?

The results of these accelerated assumptions are presented in the lower panel of table 7.3. There we show that the white share of all voters will drop more quickly, falling to the 50 percent line in 2024 rather than 2031, as expected under the fixed rate assumptions. And Latinos' voting share will rise even faster than before, reaching the 50 percent line in 2061 instead of 2073. Thus, the acceleration scenario speeds up the transfer of political power by about a decade, but that transfer point is still two decades off.

No matter what projection of future voting is to be believed, clearly the imbalance of population and voting is not going to be eliminated anytime soon. California will need to manage this problem for decades to come. And the rest of the nation will be encountering the imbalance with greater urgency in coming years, because the numbers of Latinos and Asians in many states will continue to outpace the growth of whites and blacks. As I have shown, this is more than a philosophical and ethical problem of equal representation. Indeed, there are strong differences in preference between voters of the white majority and other groups. Whites' greater pessimism about the future, their dislike of population changes, and their distaste for the immigrant burden they perceive are all factors that depress their willingness to invest in California's future. Clearly, there are major advantages for older white voters in cultivating the rising generation—advantages for expanding the workforce, for growing the base of middle-class taxpayers, and for securing the value of their homes. But those advantages are not yet widely perceived, and in the meantime some elements within the large base of white voters could pose an obstacle to planning a better future.

The Dynamics of White Majority Influence

If future investment—often requiring new taxation—is so clearly needed, it surely should attract voter support. The question is: how much, or how long, will the average preference among the white voting majority hold back the fiscal policies preferred by members of the other population groups that form the new majority? Here, for simplicity, we treat the white majority as a single voting bloc. In fact, it is a composite of many groups—liberals, conservatives, Republicans, Democrats, independents, environmentalists, antigrowth activists, business interests, soccer moms, and more. Nonetheless, the average white voter's opinions are just that—an average of all these segments. Similarly, the average black, Latino, or Asian voter also represents an average of many segments within each of those broad groups. We cannot pretend to break down the electorate in such detail. In keeping with the demographic transition, we merely track the four broad racial-ethnic groupings that make up most of the nation's population.

For the foreseeable future, the outcome of elections will depend on the relative size of the different voting blocs, the strength of their convictions, and the relative disparity between their voting preferences. As long as the number of white voters outweighs the others, they will have greater leverage over the total outcome. As argued earlier, the outgoing majority of white voters are likely, on average, to have views that do not support the future. How easily can those views be outweighed by the incoming majority? How long will it take for the growing size of the incoming majority to begin to offset the white advantage?

The interplay of relative voting strength and degree of support determines the total outcome on a majority-vote ballot measure. If whites vote only 40 percent in favor of an issue—resembling the white support of 38.6 percent reported here for higher spending and taxes—the remaining voters need to vote at extremely high levels of support to achieve passage at 50 percent by the total electorate. The degree of offset required would decline if the white vote were closer to 50 percent. Nonetheless, the required offset will decline over time as whites slowly become a smaller share of the electorate. In 2000, 73.8 percent of voters who were not white would have needed to vote in the affirmative to offset white support of only 40 percent. By 2010, we anticipate that 67.4 percent support among nonwhites would be sufficient to offset 40 percent support among whites (and 63.3 percent by 2020 and 60.4 percent by 2030).[45]

It goes without saying that supermajority requirements for passage of a measure would increase the white voting leverage even further. For example, in 2010, if white voters support a measure at the rate of 40 percent, other voters could achieve a total outcome of 50 percent by supporting the measure at 67.4 percent. However, *to achieve a 55 percent total outcome*, other voters would need to support the measure at the rate of 81.1 percent. Thus, increasing the threshold for passage by only 5.0 percentage points imposes the hurdle of an additional 13.7 percentage points on other voters in order to overcome the white voting leverage. In this way we can see how the imposition of supermajority requirements prolongs the influence of the outgoing voter majority and delays the electoral leadership of the new majority of the future.

Rather than expect to achieve electoral success in such a polarized racial context, the more likely path to success is to formulate ballot measures that attract a higher percentage of support by whites. The fact of the matter is that the white majority counts enormously in the state's political decisions. In twenty years it may be possible for other voters to offset then-diminished white voting strength, but for the foreseeable future strong voting support is required from a large portion of the white electorate; most likely drawn from liberal and moderate segments, such support could also appeal to the enlightened self-interests of conservatives. The surest path to gaining support for better investments in the future is to gain broader support within the white electorate. Disseminating better information on the benefits of the demographic transition is a necessary key step.

Conclusions on the Demographic Voting Imbalance

Underrepresentation of growing population groups poses a challenge to governance by the people and a potential threat to future well-being. The growing reliance on institutions of direct democracy—policymaking by statewide elections—rather than elected political representation undermines principles of equal representation when a large fraction of residents cannot or do not vote. More generally, a key structural feature of the demographic transition is the dominance by the previous majority through their seniority advantages. No matter that in California the minority groups have grown to be a majority of the population; even there, the white voters' continued dominance necessitates that it be whites who take ownership of leading the demographic transition to successful resolution.

Latino representation among voters is nowhere near proportional to their share of total population or even their share of adult citizens. Although there may have been substantial growth in the number of Latino elected representatives, the lagging representation among voters reduces Latinos' influence on gubernatorial and statewide ballot measures. White voters in California, despite whites' declining population share (roughly 45 percent in 2006), constitute 65 to 70 percent of the electorate. Accordingly, given the great leverage of their voting strength, their opinion dominates California, even though their preferences differ substantially from those of Latinos, African Americans, and Asians and even though whites are a minority of the population.

My concern in looking at the consequences of this imbalance is less about political power for its own sake and more about the potential neglect of the future. The practical import of the voting imbalance is that it privileges the political preferences of the long-established white population, which, to a greater degree than the Latino or Asian subgroups, expresses less stake in the future. White voters tend to be much older and are less likely to be raising children at home. Many of them already have homes and worry only about property taxes. In California the older voters remember the past, appear to vote in reaction to its loss, and are more pessimistic about the future, whereas young and immigrant voters express a more optimistic orientation to the future. Many white voters object to the arrival of immigrants and the ethnic changes they create, and as a result a substantial number are disinvesting in education for the next generation, as well as withdrawing support from other tax-supported investments.

Under our democratic system, voters are expected to express their perceived self-interest, but the future welfare of California as a whole is caught in this mismatch of voting power and future outlook. How to remedy this problem is a challenge that should command our attention. It is a natural consequence of the demographic transition because of the structural differences in temporal perspective. Accelerated voter registration initiatives can help restore more representative balance to the electorate, but the evidence cited in this chapter shows that increasing voter registration is not enough. Also required is greatly expanded voter education among both the old and new majorities about how self-interests relate to the future. Disseminating better information on the benefits of the demographic transition is a necessary key step.

There is a more responsible path, one based on a new recognition of interdependency and mutual self-interest that spans the incoming groups and the old majority. We need a renewed commitment to finding that path where the self-interests of many different groups converge. We now turn to that challenge.

Chapter 8

An Evolving Social Contract
with Many Strands

THE 2004 PRESIDENTIAL election revealed a nation deeply divided on political grounds. The supposed "blue" and "red" states in actuality may have been mostly a sea of purple, varying only a couple of percentage points in favor of one party or the other. But within those states there were surely stark differences of opinion. And now immigration has exploded onto the national stage as a newly divisive issue. The preceding chapter disclosed that the outlooks of conservatives and liberals on this issue are sharply opposed. Immigration is different from other contested issues, however, in that, paradoxically, it could create the basis for building a new consensus. One theme being tested in Congress, "securing our borders," presents immigration as a unifying threat from outside the United States. A different unifying theme is suggested here: promoting intergenerational cooperation and harnessing immigrant energies to help solve some of the problems of an aging society.

The new conflict over immigration could help us escape the confines of old polarizing debates. In fact, immigration is not an isolated problem, and the solutions developed to address it are integrally connected to the functioning of the whole of society. Our reactions to the issue of immigration shed light on our presumptions about citizenship, benefits, and responsibilities. So much has changed in America from the time of the last great wave of immigration early in the twentieth century. The social context for reception is vastly different now because our views on individualism and shared protections or benefits have evolved a great deal. In essence, the renewal of mass immigration provides an opportunity to reassess just how much our expectations have shifted over the last century. The challenge of the continuing demographic transition invites us to imagine how the social contract might evolve in the coming decades to better accommodate these changes.

American citizens must wonder whether the country is in an endless spiral of polarization. How much worse will these divisions grow? Yet the raw material for achieving new consensus in America may be right at our feet, if we care to look for it. A new consensus is less likely to promote new values than to draw on old themes that have successfully bonded our society in the past, perhaps repackaging them in a new combination. Whatever the solution, it will need to be attuned to the new demands of the twenty-first century rather than the old problems of decades past. Simply asserting the good sense of selected earlier solutions that were developed for earlier problems is not a recipe for success. Many liberal Democrats, for instance, might call for a return to New Deal principles, a policy that would be anathema to conservative Republicans, who would emphasize greater individual freedoms in pursuit of the American Dream by calling for a smaller government similar to what preceded the New Deal. Cutting taxes, cutting benefits, and cutting wages—even promoting or denying access to citizenship—are proclaimed simultaneously as solutions and as problems. In sum, seemingly any proposed basis for unity is viewed as a threat by one outspoken or powerful segment of society or another. If the terms of the immigration debate do not fundamentally change, divisiveness and polarization will grow, and the issues will not be settled by a majority vote, even to the detriment of our common fate.

The demographic transition creates compelling new challenges for the twenty-first century that call for a rethinking of both problems and solutions, but the early results from California—our leading state in the demographic transition—are not encouraging. California is deeply divided in the midst of its transition from majority-white to majority-minority. As detailed in the previous chapter, the state's residents are torn by expectations of high levels of public services (especially for the young) and desires for lower taxes (especially by older voters). On the one hand, we have evidence of a great turnaround in the state's fortunes, much of it due to upward mobility among settled immigrants that has been greater than expected. Yet immigrants are still more likely to be seen as a liability than an asset, especially by older white citizens, who in the future may be most in need of the support of immigrant residents. The voters are plainly expressing their individual self-interests, and despite occasionally generous or altruistic concessions, they may not be giving sufficient regard to what would work well for the whole of society—or for their own interests—over the long haul.

What is missing in California and the United States today is an organized sense of unified purpose—a broadly accepted, common social understanding that establishes a positive vision of the future and appeals to both the struggling new generation and the more advantaged voter majority. What is missing is a widely accepted *social contract*, which I regard less as a statement of political philosophy than as an expression of shared understanding of a unified purpose. Indeed, the supreme challenge we face today is arriving at a new agreement about a widely recognized basis for the cooperation we need to guide public policy. Agreement about a social contract especially requires the willing participation of the voters and taxpayers who must approve its provisions and pay for any needed improvements. To resolve the current impasse and arrive at a new future that the great majority would consider better than the alternative, we are seeking something new, and that solution may well require both compromise and new understanding from every group.

In this chapter, I place perceived self-interest and immigration in the context of the evolving social contract in the United States. This review is necessarily broad, because it is important to recognize several competing claims by proponents of different versions of the social contract. In the pages that follow, readers of all political persuasions will find their favored views illuminated in a context that may shed new light. The explanations offered here are not a critique of the pluses and minuses of each view; instead, I emphasize that different views are more responsive to some problems than others. As problems change in society, so must the favored social contract. And much has changed from the early twentieth century to the present and into the near future.

What Is a Social Contract?

"The social contract" is a term drawn from political philosophy but now widely used to signify a popularly assumed compact of individual rights and responsibilities, often mediated by government. Political theorists of social contract theory base their philosophical claims on the timeless relationships between individuals and the state.[1] The perspective taken here, however, embraces an inclusive definition that is socially grounded and contingent on historical events and conditions. Changes in this implicit contract over the past century in the United States have been dramatic, and further changes are surely in store. Those changes will be driven by new recognitions of urgent social problems or broad-based social expectations that shift in response to new threats and accustomed living conditions. An understanding of this evolution may hold some clues useful to those who are seeking to formulate a new recipe for growing a workable consensus.

It deserves emphasis that the notion of a "contract" is only a metaphor; no one is actually bound to the social contract, yet it does imply a general agreement that requires "buy-in" or tacit acceptance. The nature of the social contract is rarely specified, as one would expect of any other kind of contract, and this amorphousness is what allows so many competing notions about it to coexist. One key to reaching consensus, therefore, is to embrace all the various claims for certain priorities by forging a new, inclusive definition of the social contract. Although many may claim to know what the best social contract for America is, no citizen's individual claim can be legitimate if it fails to show respect for the competing claims of fellow Americans.

A Flexible Definition

It is a myth that Americans once subscribed to a single, universally accepted social contract. Nor has the social contract ever been composed of a single premise, despite the claims of various proponents. Indeed, the political scientist Rogers Smith has offered a "multiple-traditions thesis": he holds that Americans may share a common political culture, but that it consists of a mix of competing traditions that express themselves in different combinations at different times.[2] Accordingly, it may be more useful to assume that the prevailing social contract is composed of *multiple strands*, each of which receives relative emphasis at different times but has greater and prolonged support from particular subgroups. Some strands are long-standing and rooted in the earlier political culture of America. Other strands emerged in the twentieth century either in response to a dire need created by historical circumstance or as a product of the positive expectations generated in favorable times. Newer strands may be clear expressions of other, long-standing major strands in the social contract. Other strands, however, may be newly forged under the pressure of new problems and opportunities. Whatever its origins, each strand lives on within the political culture, but the weight given it as part of the social contract shifts with the times. An overarching conclusion drawn here is that the social contract has expanded over the decades through an accumulation of expectations and claims. Americans appear very reluctant to surrender any of their prior beliefs in the social contract, although the weight of opinion may prioritize some newer themes. It is the ambiguity present in this mix that creates confusion about what is the social contract.[3]

My goal is to acknowledge many of these existing strands so that we can better understand the whole. From that appreciation we should be better able to sketch how the social contract might adapt to the new demands generated by the demographic transition. In particular, today's core issues require new attention to one strand of the social contract that has been relatively neglected until recently: intergenerational bonds (which are fully explored in the next chapter). But first it is necessary to understand the competing strands and draw vital lessons about their respective contributions—how they gained strength and why support for some of them weakened.

One overarching definition of the social contract serves our purposes well because it highlights the essential structure required of any strand that contributes to the social contract. This contemporary, generalized definition of a social contract was first expressed by the sociologist Beth Rubin, who sees the social contract as the "*underlying shared social understandings that structure cooperation within a world of self-interested people possessing unequal resources.*"[4] This general definition is both flexible and concisely focused. Take note of its four components: (1) shared social understandings, (2) structure cooperation, (3) self-interested people, and (4) unequal resources. Government-based definitions of the social contract often place primary emphasis on the second and fourth components, structure cooperation and unequal resources. Yet those definitions depend heavily on implicit agreements about the first and third components, shared social understandings and self-interested people. In our contemporary world, until these latter components are adequately addressed, there is little hope of restoring consensus about a desired social contract. Indeed, self-interest and social understandings are the vital elements that support different premises of the social contract; without them, the other elements crumble.

An Evolving, Multifaceted Social Contract

The social contract is woven from multiple strands that have accumulated over time, each originally initiated from a different social understanding that was widely shared. The modern era of the social contract is often regarded as commencing with the New Deal, which was a response to the Great Depression of the 1930s.[5] However, important themes in today's social contract were already well established at that time. My argument is that the social contract's evolution reflects three themes. The first theme is that the fundamental basis for the contract is provided by only three major strands, each of which has deep-seated, long-lasting support: cultural cohesion and the American creed, the American Dream of unrestrained upward mobility, and belief in collective protections and services. Americans subscribe to all three of these strands, but at various times in history one or another has been relatively more strongly endorsed by a majority of the people. A second theme in the contract's evolution is the emergence of specific minor strands over the years in response to specific historical contingencies. Each of these has arisen from a shared social understanding initiated by a perceived problem of widespread importance and supported by fundamental beliefs drawn from one or more of the major strands in the social contract. A third theme in the evolution is the accumulation of these strands over time. None of the strands has expired or been supplanted by successors, even though some are mutually exclusive and have been championed by different proponents. In essence, the expectations continue to expand for the social contract of the American people. Today at least a dozen major and minor strands can be identified that contribute in different ways to the social contract in the United States. Few of these are directly equivalent to one another. Only a few express the quid pro quo usually associated with a contract, yet all express beliefs about the benefits of shared life in the United States, and all have been the basis for political mobilization.

It may be useful to think of the social contract as having evolved through five eras since 1900 (immigration was a prominent factor in only the first and last):

1. Rugged individualism and immigrant incorporation (pre-1930)
2. The New Deal and World War II (1930 to 1950)
3. Middle-class entitlement (1950 to 1975)
4. Limiting government (1975 to 2010)
5. The new immigration and an aging society (2010 to ?)

These eras overlap with one another, both because the same individuals have lived through multiple eras, carrying beliefs from one to the next, and because strands of the contract that were developed in one era are carried over in later eras. Nonetheless, particular strands received notable emphasis in each of these eras, addressing particular perceived problems of the day. Ultimately, the problems have changed, and different strands have emerged to guide new problem solutions.

All of this is essential background for understanding the new era just beginning. How does this new era differ from the era of limited government and middle-class entitlement that preceded it? And how is it similar to the era a century earlier, when immigration was last so prominent? Indeed, much has changed since that time, and all the intervening expectations are woven into our new understanding of the social contract. But the excesses of prior eras also become part of the context for the new social contract being formed. What follows is a proposal for a very broad sketch of this social evolution. Surely this deserves to be much more detailed than is possible here, as historians know best, but an appreciation for the dynamics of the evolution of the social contract will help us assess how it might progress in the future. Following the Rubin definition, the account that follows emphasizes the changing basis of shared social understanding that has shifted support for different strands of the contract. Also to be noted is how the legacy of earlier strands carries over to later eras. Recognizing this dynamic mix also increases the likelihood of building the consensus needed for the future.

An attempt to summarize these multiple strands prior to their explanation is presented in table 8.1. The three major strands are listed across the top. The underlying premise for each strand is given, as is its most important early expression. The minor strands are then listed beneath the major strand(s) with which they are associated. These are presented in a rough chronological order, with the more recent strands appearing at the bottom of the table. Although it could be argued that intergenerational support is one of the oldest strands—indeed, it is one common to most societies throughout history—it is listed at the bottom because of its importance to the future. We now turn to an account of how it all changed.

Immigration and the Changing Basis of Shared Social Understanding

The conservative revolution that placed the Republican Party in control of Washington, D.C., for most of the past three decades was founded on an abhorrence of "big government." What is so baffling to liberals and other ob-

Table 8.1   Multiple Strands in the Evolving Social Contract in the United States

	Major Strands		
Minor Strands	Cultural Cohesion and American Creed	American Dream of Unrestrained Upward Mobility	Collective Protections and Services
	All who share in America's opportunities should conform to a common linguistic, civic, and consumer culture; all who conform deserve equal rights. Early expressions: Americanization; suffrage movement	Upward mobility should be unrestrained by class restrictions or government action and is based solely on the hard work of personal striving. Early expressions: rugged individualism; social Darwinism	Government has a duty to protect citizens from poverty and economic disadvantage; society members depend on each other in the struggle against threats. Early expressions: Great Depression; New Deal; World War II
Accord of labor and capital			Labor should share in economic prosperity, and both labor and capital can profit by cooperation.
Military service rewards	Young adults who serve their country in wartime deserve reward for their sacrifice.		Young adults who serve their country in wartime deserve reward for their sacrifice.
Relief for victims			Special assistance should be granted to deserving victims of natural disasters or of current or past injustices.

Ample public services			The middle class and the poor deserve ample, high-quality public services.
Equality of subgroups	Equal opportunity and civil rights must apply across races, genders, religions, and other differentiations.		Equal opportunity and civil rights must apply across races, genders, religions, and other differentiations.
Entitlement of the middle class		The middle class should expect ever-increasing prosperity and services.	The middle class should expect ever-increasing prosperity and services.
Limited government		Minimal government intrusion on economic freedom; government should not be a burden on the middle class via taxes or regulations.	
Intergenerational public support (for children and the elderly)	Society requires the working-age population to invest in children (future workers) and support the elderly (life rewards).	Society requires the working-age population to invest in children (future workers) and support the elderly (life rewards).	Society requires the working-age population to invest in children (future workers) and support the elderly (life rewards).

Source: Author's compilation.

servers is why the leaders of the conservative movement show so little appreciation for the major innovations of social protection that emerged from the
New Deal and were carried forward in the Great Society of the 1960s. Fundamentally, the shared social understandings that once supported those government programs have changed, and until the reasons for that shift can be
understood there is little hope for building a new consensus that can bridge
the more moderate Republican and Democrat factions.

A History of Newcomers, Shared Struggle, and Prosperity

Viewing these changes through the lens of immigration provides a broader
perspective and can be illuminating. So much changed between the time of
the last great wave, which peaked in 1907 with the immigration of 1.3 million new residents, and 2005, the latest high point in the recent wave: 1.1
million legal permanent residents were added in the United States that year,
along with an estimated 500,000 or more illegal immigrants.[6] Back in 1907,
immigrants could expect scant support from agencies at any level of government. Once they met the rules for admission, workers and their families were
left to their own devices and had to rely on their own rugged individualism.
Taxation was minimal, as were public services, except for roadways, sanitary
systems, the postal system, and rudimentary public schooling. Health and
safety regulations were poorly developed, as was publicized by Jacob Riis in
the case of tenement housing and by Lewis Hines for workplaces.[7] Slowly the
Progressive reform movement began to institutionalize standards that were
more in keeping with the norms of native-born Americans. Nonetheless, very
little was asked of immigrants other than hard work and conformity to the
precepts of American citizenship.

Cultural Cohesion and the American Creed   Indeed, a central assumption of
the social contract during the first half of the twentieth century was the premise of *cultural cohesion.*   Waves of immigrants had been incorporated into
American society through social practices that pressured newcomers to shed
their foreign appearances and allegiances. Later, an active policy of "Americanization" strove to reduce ethnic differences and encourage immigrants to
blend in with the dominant culture.[8] This program of cultural conformity
was accompanied by encouragement to become politically incorporated into
the American citizenry. The *"American creed"* is a set of core political beliefs
that stress the values of equality and political self-determination; the term was

first popularized in Gunnar Myrdal's 1944 study of African Americans' exclusion from full participation in American civic life.[9] The historian Gary Gerstle draws the distinction between America's civic nationalism—which emphasizes equal rights and incorporation into our democracy—and a less spoken racial nationalism that favors white residents over others.[10] Thus, African Americans' cultural allegiance and eager participation in both voting and military service could not keep them from being treated as less equal citizens until the civil rights movement began to attack the contradictions. This racial hurdle was more readily overcome by newcomers from Europe, who were more fully incorporated into the civic nation than were native-born residents of color. Peter Salins, the provost and vice chancellor for academic affairs for the state university system of New York, has described an "assimilation contract" that had three canons—work hard, learn English, and believe in the American Idea, which he defines as promoting civic unity through liberal democratic and egalitarian principles. This bargain was sealed by an offer (even encouragement) to take up citizenship.[11]

Following the curtailment of immigration after the 1920s and the declining presence of new immigrants through the middle decades of the century, and after the collectivizing experience of World War II, maintaining cultural cohesion was widely assumed to not be a pressing matter. The major exceptions were both on political dimensions. The "red scare" denied Communists access to the American creed, and severe political censorship of Communist sympathizers in the 1940s and 1950s was imposed by the House Committee on Un-American Activities, and most famously by Senator Joseph R. McCarthy. The other exception was the continuing tension of race relations before the civil rights movement was finally successful in gaining equal rights for African Americans and others.

The American Dream and Unrestrained Upward Mobility   A second major strand in the social contract pertained to economic prosperity. The *American Dream* was the long-standing belief that by virtue of hard work in a land of opportunity, unlimited upward mobility was possible. Unlike European countries, where class structures were rigid and land had long been subdivided and was tightly held, in nineteenth-century America opportunities were much more open. In spite of the abusive laissez-faire excesses of the late nineteenth century, many Americans were able to buy land, and some could climb to the top. Emblematic was the rags-to-riches story of Horatio Alger and the mythical rise of many industrial giants who started as stockroom boys.

The American Dream was associated with the related concepts of rugged individualism and social Darwinism, the latter of which extolled the virtues of competitive struggle and lent the American Dream a moral imperative seemingly grounded in natural law.[12] Capitalism and notions of survival of the fittest were compatible concepts, and the two were intertwined in conservative attacks against government regulations. Even if the conscious philosophy of social Darwinism had largely disappeared by the time of World War I, its underlying moral precepts were folded into the continuing belief in unfettered struggle to obtain the American Dream. The American Dream remains an important strand of the social contract today, and its proponents argue that government should place no barriers in the paths of ambitious men or women who strive for maximum success.

Collective Protections and Services   Against the background of the early twentieth century and the two prevailing major strands in the social contract, we can better appreciate how the world wars and especially the Great Depression became defining events that generated new premises and a new era for the social contract. Indeed, so powerful were the effects of this prolonged period that the strand that emerged in the social contract at this time has attained major status. Indeed, as we will see, this new major strand has spawned a number of minor strands that continue to draw the support of both liberals and conservatives to this day.

The Great Depression dramatically challenged the American Dream's emphasis on rugged individualism, and it surely ended any lingering sentiments about survival of the fittest. "Social Darwinism may have made sense when those in economic distress could be cast as the losers in a stiff competition of life. It made less sense when everyone knew someone who was unemployed and impoverished, when many or most people seemed to be losers in the process."[13] Indeed, one conclusion from Peter Lindert's cross-national historical research is that nations that are likely to support the growth of a welfare state are those where a majority of voters feel vulnerable, that is, they fear that the middle and bottom ranks of society could trade places.[14]

The New Deal was a response to the Great Depression, a unique time in American history. Certainly there were some precedents, but public spending on social programs escalated sharply in both the United States and Europe after 1930.[15] No doubt the disaster of the Great Depression was a traumatizing experience that shaped collective consciousness and precipitated unprecedented government action.[16] At one point in 1933, 24 percent of workers were unemployed, but these job losses penetrated both the working and middle classes, spreading the fear that everyone's job was at risk.[17] Moreover, property foreclosures reached dangerous levels, uprooting families from homes and farms and leaving banks holding assets that could not be sold. In this context, the federal government's introduction of social insurance, jobs and antipoverty programs, and mortgage insurance protections could be seen not only as aiding the economy but also as responding to the social insecurities felt so broadly throughout American society. Thus, President Franklin D. Roosevelt called his new set of *collective protections* in the social contract "the New Deal." Often overlooked was the strategic assistance the New Deal gave to the nation's immigrant population. In the words of a leading historian: "Perhaps the New Deal's greatest achievement was its accommodation of the maturing immigrant communities that had milled uneasily on the margins of American society for a generation or more before the 1930s."[18]

This economic program of collective protection and support was closely followed by the galvanizing experience of World War II, which not only involved the soldiers in the armed forces but also enlisted every resident in America in the war effort. "The Good War," as it has been called, was a unifying experience, a struggle against external forces of evil that could only be won through single-minded mutual support.[19] This may have been the last time in American history when there was such widespread agreement about our collective purpose. Indeed, the disagreements about political direction that were debated in the mid-1930s quickly disappeared when an external threat to American political values was launched from Nazi Germany.[20]

The Great Depression so closely followed by the World War II experience generated conditions ideal for supporting unprecedented public programs by the federal government. Sustained over a decade and a half, the shared experience shaped a deeply felt social understanding about common purpose, collective struggle, and social protections for the benefit of both the poor and the middle class. With the end of the depression and the war, this era of the social contract and its outlook did not come to an end overnight. Attitudes lingered, kept alive by a generation whose values were forged in this experience and fostered by continued struggle against external threats, principally communism (the Korean War and the cold war). The question to be answered over subsequent decades was whether this newfound belief in collective social support was a momentary response or whether it reflected a permanent shift in the national political character. In particular, would the desire for unfettered, individual striving embodied in the American Dream once again supplant the desire for collective protections? Although the emphasis of the 1930s and 1940s on collective support in the social contract provided a foundation that would last for decades, it was slowly weakened, and at an accelerating pace after 1980.

Growing Entitlement Through the 1950s and 1960s

Following the war, the country entered an era of enormous prosperity that was fed by both economic growth and public investment. This era was sustained for so long that its assumptions still have influence today, and primary among them is a feeling of middle-class entitlement. Added on to all the prior premises in the social contract were newly learned expectations about government's provision of services and a rising standard of living. Immigrants were largely invisible through this entire period of a broadening social contract, although second- and third-generation descendants enjoyed the rising prosperity of the mainstream. Prior to the full-blown emergence of entitlement, a number of minor new strands emerged in the social contract, all of which were specific expressions of the major strands.

Rewards for Military Service   The returning members of the armed forces posed new issues following World War II. A strong shared understanding was that military service should be rewarded so that the former soldiers could fully participate in the good life of America that they had protected. This new strand in the social contract was supported by two major strands: cultural cohesion and the American creed, and collective protections and services. Veterans' benefits were not without precursors. These benefits had been provided after the First World War, and the early version of a social policy of disability benefits and old-age pensions established after the Civil War accounted for as much as one-quarter of all federal expenditures at the end of the nineteenth century.[21]

After World War II, however, there was a quantum shift in the scope of support for rewarding military service, built on the newfound strength of its supporting major strands. The newly established veterans programs reached well beyond medical and old-age supports and instead targeted veterans who were young and healthy. The GI Bill promoted college education, and the Veterans Administration sponsored a new home loan program that lowered down payments to as low as 5 percent of the purchase price. Through these reward programs, millions of young adults were catapulted into a higher socioeconomic status by government action that allowed them to bypass the presumptions of unfettered private progress in the American Dream strand of the social contract. In addition, although it should not have been necessary, military service also underscored the citizenship rights of the former soldiers, paving the way for their acceptance as full members of society. This benefit speeded the full assimilation of those whose parents had participated in the mass immigration early in the twentieth century, and it also prepared the way for the civil rights movement among African Americans in the 1950s.

Relief for Victims   The larger federal government spawned by decades of depression and war began to offer important peacetime protections as well. Slowly, federal programs grew that offered relief for victims of natural disasters. Rutherford Platt describes three periods in the evolution of federal disaster assistance.[22] Prior to 1950, only negligible or ad hoc assistance was offered in the greatest natural disasters, such as the San Francisco fire and earthquake of 1906, the great Mississippi flood of 1927, and the New England hurricane of 1938. Following World War II, however, citizens began to expect more from their government. Passage of the Disaster Relief Act of 1950 signaled the beginnings of a new era of limited federal assistance to communities and (after 1969) individuals. The steady stream of legislation that followed was inspired by the civil defense orientation of the cold war era (what we today would call homeland security). The eventual watershed legislation was the Stafford Act of 1988, which unleashed abundant federal disaster relief assistance for any counties receiving a presidential declaration of disaster status. The federal role was supposed to be supplemental and deferential to state authority, but declarations rapidly escalated through the 1990s. Thus, in just four decades, expectations for emergency relief had rapidly mounted and become entrenched.

How entrenched was the resistance to rolling back this relief strand in the social contract became especially evident when the George W. Bush administration initiated efforts to curtail the role of the Federal Emergency Management Agency (FEMA). The 2005 catastrophe of Hurricane Katrina in Louisiana and Mississippi shined a spotlight on the federal government's weakened capacities and led to an outcry that reasserted social and political priorities. The premise of federal relief for victims, even if relatively recent in origin, is a minor but now permanent strand in the social contract that has grown to be considered practically a birthright among Americans, including conservative southerners who were part of Bush's principal political base.

Accord Between Labor and Big Business   Yet another strand of the social contract that emerged in the entitlement period is the accord between labor and big business. Indeed, some even refer to this as *the* social contract, perhaps because an actual contract was produced through negotiations with organized labor. The roots of this minor strand lie in the major strand of collective protections, specifically in the 1936 National Labor Relations Act, which offered federal protection for the right to organize unions and required employers to bargain in good faith. However, postwar prosperity created a new, more favorable basis for making these bargains. Mass production lowered the cost of goods, and rising consumer incomes created growing demand both domestically and abroad. In this era a new strand of the social contract took hold that emphasized the collective bargaining gains of organized labor with respect to big business. Beth Rubin describes how labor and capital could share in the economic prosperity through explicit agreements: "The coordination of employers' and employees' interests was the goal of the labor-capital accord. At least three major aspects of collective bargaining agreements created those shared interests: . . . wages were often tied to increases in productivity . . . cost-of-living adjustments [were automatic] . . . [and] seniority rewarded workers for being stable, reliable, and cooperative."[23] Frances Fox Piven and Richard A. Cloward term this accord "the industrial era social compact," and they lament its later dismantling in the United States after what they describe as a power struggle won by capital, aided by industrial restructuring, immigration, and political attacks on unions.[24] The fading of America's post–World War II advantage in economic productivity (think General Motors and Toyota) was surely part of this change as well.

Expectations of Ample Public Services Each new provision of services ratcheted up the expectations of what was desired in the social contract. A relative unanimity of objectives was based in the new shared experiences of the American people, which contrasted so sharply to those of the 1930s and 1940s. During the 1950s and 1960s, sustained increases in real income—on the order of 40 percent per decade—spawned even more rapid growth in the public sector. Government expenditures rose 51 percent in the 1950s and 57 percent in the 1960s, in constant dollars, and state and local governments had ample funding for massive public investments in roads and schools, backed by federal assistance programs as well as local taxpayers' support.[25] Although public-sector programs (and hence tax burdens) were growing faster than incomes, their expansion was readily absorbed by the average family's rapid income growth. These government programs returned real benefits to the middle class. New superhighways, originally proposed for moving troops, became the pathways of a more mobile suburban lifestyle. And massive investment in better education systems, including higher education opportunities, greatly increased the average educational preparation of young adults. This progress was sustained over so many years that the expectation that ample public services could be assumed as a right of all Americans came to form another continuing strand in the social contract.

Middle-Class Entitlement The persistently rising standard of living through the 1950s and 1960s began to create a fundamental change in the social understanding that supported the social contract. The new understanding shifted away from protection against the risk of unemployment and poverty and now reasserted an earlier, pre-Depression strand in the social contract: the American Dream. Yet there was a new expectation attached to this strand.

The middle class had grown to be a formidable majority in the postwar years. By one statistical account, the proportion of the nation living at a middle-class standard of living or better expanded from 12 percent in 1940 to 65 percent by 1970.[26] In this time, homeownership—often equated with the American Dream by the housing industry and held as a symbol of the dream by consumers—surged from less than half of the nation's households in 1940 to nearly two-thirds by 1970 (rising from 44 percent to 63 percent).[27] That rate of progress was fueled by the government programs just discussed, and many citizens began to take for granted the physical infrastructure and services also provided by the public sector. The length of the expansion in well-being gave rise to an expectation that it should be continuous, and this new social understanding was so widely shared that it was tantamount to a new strand in the social contract.

Although the strand of middle-class entitlement might appear to be merely the product of other preexisting strands in the social contract, in fact it was new and different. This new strand merged the premises of two major strands by combining collective protections against downfall with the individual upward aspirations of the American Dream. Heavily subsidized, this strand of entitlement created the most advantaged generation in history by adding something new to the expectation of an opportunity to work hard for individual riches and the expectation of collective protection against poverty and unemployment: the new expectation of mass comforts as well. This new premise of the social contract emphasized the entitlement of the middle class to achieve a privileged consumer life style, including homeownership, ease of car ownership, safe suburban communities, and good schools, as documented so ably by Robert Samuelson.[28] With memories of the Depression and the war years fading, and with the experience of rapid technological progress and burgeoning government programs, the idea that each generation should enjoy *increasing* prosperity and advantages became a belief so widespread that it was socially institutionalized as an entitlement and became a new strand in the social contract.

The Beginnings of Fragmentation and Discord

In the latter half of the twentieth century, many strands of the social contract had accumulated and become increasingly interwoven. For a time, through the late 1960s, it was possible to accommodate multiple, competing strands at the same time. Both the labor-capital accord strand of the social contract and the middle-class entitlement strand coexisted with the earlier collective protection strand, as well as with the American Dream and rewards for military service strands. Moreover, employers, workers, and residents all benefited from government investments in infrastructure and ample public services, fueled by rising taxes amid rich economic growth. In a time when many, including President Kennedy, believed that "a rising tide lifts all boats,"[29] the poor, the working class, the middle class, and employers could all profit. Multiple strands of the social contract coexisted without contradiction.

However, the moment of crisis soon arrived for the nation's consensus about its priorities in the social contract. In the years from 1965 to 1975, several parts of the postwar consensus came apart at once, exposing deeply held assumptions that had not been debated as part of the social contract. In brief, the fractures that jolted the nation in the late 1960s marked the end of the entitlement era and pushed the collective protections premises of the 1930s and 1940s even further into the past. And yet, paradoxically, the emerging era of limited government still accommodated the generations that had lived through the earlier eras and would not surrender their benefits. Some forty years later, we have yet to recover from this breakdown and discover a new basis for widespread agreement. The following overview—offered directly and without critical comment—may lead to new perspective on our current divisions.

Equal Opportunity   The civil rights movement waged in the 1950s was initially focused on voting rights and equal opportunity for blacks in the South, but it spread in the 1960s and 1970s to battles over desegregation in the North. The fundamental value of equal opportunity for all groups in the nation's social contract drew upon precepts in the major strand of cultural cohesion and the American creed. Yet the new battle for civil rights and equal opportunity also challenged other beliefs lurking within that strand that supported a racial definition of culture and citizenship. From this protracted struggle a new, more specifically defined strand emerged in the social contract. The equal opportunity strand not only was rooted in cultural cohesion and the American creed but also drew upon the major strand of collective protections.

The new strand reached its broadest consensus during the Birmingham, Alabama, campaign led by Dr. Martin Luther King Jr.; in his "I Have a Dream" speech of August 28, 1963, delivered on the steps of the Lincoln Memorial, he asked only for the Negro people to be treated like all other Americans. Indeed, the rights to vote, to schooling, to work, and to ride on the bus without discrimination were accepted as among the most basic human rights by most Americans. The television-newsreel depiction of well-dressed blacks being physically assaulted, despite their passive disobedience, brought home the brutality of Jim Crow segregation and subjugation in the South. Complete sympathy for the struggle for equal rights was won among the northern white middle class, and among many southerners as well, and a series of landmark federal legislative acts were passed in rapid succession.[30] Not until the social implications of these values were brought home through the implementation of programs did consensus falter. Although widely embraced in principle, broad dissension arose when equal opportunity policies were put on the ground in northern states. The implementation of specific government policies to restructure the status quo, such as segregated schools and housing, unleashed turmoil and backlash among working- and middle-class whites, not just in less progressive small towns but even in New York City and the San Francisco region.[31]

The equality movement subsequently spread to include women's rights and later the rights of gays and others. For all the attention given to these neglected groups, less weight was given to the interests of a large majority. Soon the political pollsters were identifying a new "social issue" in politics that defined a new majority of the population. Under the heading "Demography Is Destiny," Richard Scammon and Ben Wattenberg wrote: "If young, poor, and black are what most voters aren't, let us consider the electorate for what it largely is. . . . In short: middle-aged, middle-class whites." The social issue to which this majority responded was said to be composed of several factors: fear of the crime wave, worries about race, revulsion toward the appearance of and disrespect shown by young adults of the counterculture, distaste for various expressions of the new sexuality, and objection to the lack of respect shown for hardworking, taxpaying members of the mainstream society.[32] Thus, the dissension and unrest among the majority population group created fertile ground for political leaders to drive wedges into the democratic majority of voters. It did not take long for Richard Nixon to develop his "southern strategy" to capture voters who had been surfaced by George Wallace in 1968, both in the South and in working-class areas of the North.[33] Unable to protect what Douglas Massey calls the Achilles' heel of liberalism from divisive attack, the electoral competition caused the fundamental equality strand in the social contract to pull against other essential strands and undermined political support for Democrats' broader social policy agenda.[34]

Cultural Cohesion and the American Creed Resurface   In the tumultuous period of the 1960s and 1970s, a long-standing basis for shared agreement became reactivated: cultural cohesion and the American creed. What resurfaced this premise in the social contract was not the resurgence of immigration, but rather the emergence of two movements made up of native-born Americans. Parallel to the civil rights movement, black nationalists challenged the value of the American state in which other African Americans were seeking legitimacy. A new militancy arose that rejected the nonviolent tactics of Dr. King and threatened armed action. Some believe that this movement of black separatism propagated a new belief in cultural pluralism that was then adopted by white ethnics, spawning the eventual movement to multiculturalism.[35] Often overlooked, because it was not ethnically based, was the self-styled "counterculture" of the late 1960s. Composed of hippies, war protesters, and dropouts from society, mostly from the white middle class, the counterculture movement may have been more threatening, both because it drew from a much larger population base and because it seemed to betray its middle-class white roots. Counterculture members also attracted a good deal more publicity through their images and actions. This group adopted physical symbols to emphasize their cultural differences from the mainstream, including long hair and clothing their mothers considered uncivilized, and they staged equally symbolic actions, such as the burning of bras and draft cards. Mobilized most actively around resistance to the Vietnam War, the counterculture movement challenged not only the legitimacy of the war effort but also the supremacy of the dominant culture.

Confronted with this display in television and print media, if not in person, many in the majority recoiled in revulsion (see the earlier discussion of the "social issue"), and the cultural fragmentation thus introduced has reverberated ever since. All of these movements—equality, ethnic identity, and counterculture—created a separation from the middle-class majority that could be politically exploited. In many ways these divisions still dominate our political landscape. When the legacy of Vietnam and Watergate was added, a lasting fracture in the nation's sense of collective purpose was compounded by a disillusionment and loss of trust in government.[36]

Government Seen as a Taker, Not a Provider

Closely following the opening of that divide in culture and allegiance, economic collapse in the 1970s generated a new widely shared social understanding that soon erupted in a fiscal discontent that challenged previous premises in the social contract. In discussions of the dismal future in chapter 4, I emphasized the pervasive effect of the abrupt halt in income growth enjoyed by Americans. With that downturn—which Frank Levy has called "the quiet depression"—the prior willingness to support public spending began to wither in the 1970s. Nonetheless, government expenditures per capita continued to rise by 16 percent.[37] Subsequently, in the quarter-century from 1973 to 1996, family income increased a total of only 6.9 percent, while government expenditures rose 51.9 percent.[38] In this context, a new era emerged in the social contract, one fraught with ambivalence: efforts were made to limit government so that middle-class individuals could struggle for individual gains.

The Fiscal Revolt   The taxpayer revolt revealed a substantial limitation in prior strands of the nation's social contract, namely, that voters believed in supporting public services that would be used by others only if they were enjoying ample economic gains themselves. With the stagnating economic progress of the middle class, support eroded for funding the growing costs of public services and collective protections, especially those aimed at the poor rather than the middle class. New political leaders emerged who exploited this sentiment and stoked the resentment of the middle class by mobilizing voters around opposition to taxes. The contradiction is that Americans did not surrender their belief in a right to ample public services, even if the means to pay for them had been sharply cut back. (Recall from chapter 7 that even a majority of conservative California voters resist cutbacks in services.)

If ever there was a recipe for loss of optimism in government and American society, surely this was it: an unpopular war, cultural dissension, and political scandal, followed by faltering income growth and heavier tax burdens. Once the middle class began to struggle for income gains in the 1970s, the past assumptions supporting an agreed-on social contract came under voter attack, first in California—where surging home values spawned a property tax revolt that led to passage of the infamous Proposition 13 in 1978—and then nationwide and in the United Kingdom under the so-called Reagan and Thatcher Revolutions. The middle class could no longer easily support benefits for the poor, or even for their own middle-class neighbors. In sharp contradiction to the social contract accepted during the New Deal and World War II years and more recently in the Great Society era, government became viewed as no longer a protector and provider but a taker.

Downsizing Government and the Contract with America   The conservative movement to limit the size of government first reached prominence on the national stage in the 1964 presidential campaign of Barry Goldwater; after the mid-1970s, the movement steadily picked up steam, fueled by the taxpayer revolt and then the Reagan Revolution of the 1980s. The limited government premise finds its strongest support when it is coupled with the struggle of the middle class to sustain its prosperity and broader entitlements. The core themes of Newt Gingrich's "Contract with America," introduced at a press conference on September 27, 1994, succinctly express the premises of the new strand in the social contract emphasizing a downsized government whose objective is to reduce collective protections and remove drags on middle-class prosperity.

The Contract with America was rooted in three core principles, as set out at the 1994 press conference:

> "*Accountability.* The government is too big and spends too much, and Congress and unelected bureaucrats have become so entrenched to be unresponsive to the public they are supposed to serve. The GOP contract restores accountability to government.
>
> "*Responsibility.* Bigger government and more federal programs usurp personal responsibility from families and individuals. The GOP contract restores a proper balance between government and personal responsibility.
>
> "*Opportunity.* The American Dream is out of the reach of too many families because of burdensome government regulations and harsh tax laws. The GOP contract restores the American Dream."

The view reflected in these statements is that the middle class can no longer afford government, at least not the type of activist and protective government established in the era of the New Deal and expanded by legislation passed in the 1960s. The "Contract with America" sought consensus based on shared dissatisfactions and uncertainties more than shared political philosophies or even shared interests.[39] It urged government to help people less (the poor) and make them more self-reliant, as in the pursuit of the American Dream prior to the New Deal. If government would be more accountable to the middle-class majority and spend less on unneeded services, the middle class would fare better. The Contract was silent on the matter of public services for the middle class, relief for victims, and other premises of the social contract that might still have been broadly held.

The Emergence of the New Demographic Threat

My argument has been that each strand in the social contract has emerged in response to particular historical conditions and that the legacy of these strands is cumulative. Today the demographic transition now threatens the American sense of community purpose in new ways, and at the same time it poses new opportunities. How might the social contract adapt to this new condition? The challenge of immigration has combined with a new population diversity, about which we have learned the voters are not entirely pleased. The resulting trend toward greater fragmentation and discord does not augur well for the ability of the state of California or the nation to invest in its future the way we once did.

Only now, at the turn of the twenty-first century, has immigration returned as a factor in the social contract, with responses to immigration becoming a new divisive force since 1990 in California, and more recently in the United States. As a result of the resumption of mass immigration, a new challenge to cultural cohesion has emerged. Scholars such as Samuel Huntington and a host of editorial opinion writers are expressing deep fears about the threat of growing immigration to the American identity. Meanwhile, since California's Proposition 187 in 1994, voters in several states have placed initiatives on the ballot that would restrict illegal immigrants from using taxpayer-funded services. These voters are drawn disproportionately from the long-established population that feels itself shrinking and does not wish to support the newcomers with its tax monies.

A different and even more compellingly urgent aspect of the demographic transition looms on our doorstep. The aging of the giant baby boom generation poses an unprecedented challenge. For the first time in history, we will be asked to accommodate a large and abrupt increase in the ratio of retired to working adults. In this same time frame, the demographic transition will bring a resurgent number of foreign-born residents. How can the social contract respond to these new historical pressures? The unraveling of the social contract in the midtwentieth century may be irreversible, although some of its strands can be rewoven in new combinations. But most importantly, how can a new social contract be constructed that is appropriate for the new century because it is especially attuned to the new problems? The solution to these problems will mark the beginning of a new era in the social contract, one founded on responses to the new immigration and the challenges of an aging society.

The relationship of immigration to the social contract has been turned on its head since the early twentieth century, and the differences between now and then could hardly be more stark. Prior to 1930, immigrants were expected to assimilate to the core culture, but little was held out in the way of collective protections or support beyond a program of Americanization and schooling. Immigrants were given nothing more than an opportunity to pursue the American Dream through their own hard work. Even though immigrants often were incorporated politically more rapidly than today, they were expected to be self-reliant and not dependent on the public treasury.[40] Today, ironically, when our modern welfare society provides so many more taxpayer-funded services for the benefit of immigrant newcomers, there is a division of opinion among intellectual leaders and advocates (if not the general public) about whether immigrants should assimilate. Cultural differences are surely to be celebrated, but they also can become political wedges that force divisions in the social contract.

In the new age of immigration, when new expectations have accumulated in the social contract, immigrants are far more dependent on taxpayer generosity, and yet how might they garner stronger support among those taxpayers? Many taxpayers certainly appear eager for excuses to deny immigrants access to the major collective protection and services provision of the social contract.[41] The choice by immigrant advocates to *not* emphasize the major strand of cultural cohesion and the American creed assumes that other strands of the social contract—principally, the equality of subgroups and ample public services—will be sufficient to compel public support for immigrants. This assumption overlooks the undermining of notions of shared community by recent invocations of the equality of subgroups, and so this strand can hardly be counted on to justify membership by noncitizens. Not to favor the strand of cultural cohesion and the American creed also would seem to be a risky bet at a time when the limited government strand is still gathering strength and support for collective protections and services is in full retreat. Indeed, the one collective purpose being debated with regard to immigration is the newfound interest in protecting U.S. borders. Although many invoke the major American Dream strand in the social contract when they point out that immigrants just want to come here to work, that appears to be nullified without support from the major strand of cultural cohesion and the American creed. In any event, the voters are split on whether immigrants are a benefit or burden. Perhaps there is another strand of the social contract that can be invoked in support of immigrants? How might that be interwoven with preexisting strands?

Conclusion: How Will the Social Contract Adapt to Our New Problems?

The midtwentieth-century consensus on the social contract, a civic understanding that Gary Gerstle terms the Rooseveltian nation, has now largely unraveled in the era of middle-class entitlement and limited government. At the root of this transformation in the social contract is the faltering economic progress of the middle class. In times of gradual slippage, as opposed to full-blown disaster, every person scratches independently for his or her own piece of the pie. In the face of fragmented civic community, this response is encouraged all the more.

Old class divisions between the middle class and the poor are not what threatens consensus about the social contract. Instead, national attention has turned to reflection on individual differences and subgroup values. As revealed in the presidential election of 2004, political and cultural divisions are separating the "red" states of the heartland and the "blue" states along the coasts. Although many states are within a few percentage points of tipping the other way, the residents *within* the states may be more deeply divided from one another. During the 1980s and 1990s, the politically charged culture wars intensified and are now often described as a polarization of ideological worldviews based on the social issues of abortion, gun control, gay rights, religion, and parenting philosophy (permissiveness).[42] Moreover, as we discovered in the preceding chapter, a sharp polarization in relative tolerance toward immigration is expressed by conservatives and liberals.

Let's leave these differences aside. There is little to be gained in debates between groups with such entrenched positions. Instead, there may be another basis for growing a common understanding. Neither class nor values gives us a basis for agreement on the problem to be solved. Instead, the new challenge we all face is life in a nation undergoing demographic transition. And the solution to many of the problems we face is a commonality based on age. A great many people are growing older and will require support, and a great many other people are going to need help shouldering the workload. This problem is different from before. It also provides a fresh opportunity to restructure the social contract to gain broad-based support in the new century.

Chapter 9

Rediscovering the Intergenerational Social Contract for the Twenty-First Century

TO SOME OBSERVERS, it would appear that the social contract in America is hopelessly shattered. The current equation for despair is deep cultural divisions combined with political disillusionment and multiplied by economic insecurity. In this view, it is surely every man, woman, and child for himself or herself. Yet is that ever true? Adults and children are certainly interconnected, from one generation to the next. None of the previously discussed strands of the social contract have emphasized this fact. In all the debates over helping the poor versus helping the middle class to achieve the good life, many people have lost sight of a fundamental truth: government expenditures are not aimed at helping specific classes so much as certain *age groups*, principally children (largely through state governments, in the form of education) and the elderly (largely through the federal government, through Social Security and Medicare).

Our solutions for the twenty-first century may lie in a previously neglected strand of the social contract. In the past, what has been assumed to be mere background and not under debate are the intergenerational bonds of support between the working generation and both children and the retired generation. In recent years, however, public attention has begun to turn to this neglected strand of the social contract because of the looming crisis in Social Security and other old-age support for the giant baby boom generation. This strand of intergenerational support may be particularly instrumental for broader purposes as well, because the generations span many divides. Generations bridge racial and ethnic groups, link native-born and immigrant populations, and span between the present and the future. Thus, the intergenerational strand of the social contract is not limited to caring for the problems of an aging society. Instead, and more broadly, we should recognize the promise it holds for healing divisions and building a new sense of shared purpose about the future.

Today intergenerational relations have taken on paramount urgency. These relations are more strained than at any time in memory, not simply because the age structure will soon be top-heavy with the elderly, whose needs we must accommodate, but also because of the racial divide that separates the older and younger generations. This racial divide appeared first in California but is emerging in much of the rest of the nation. This is a major challenge that must be confronted if we are to strengthen not only the intergenerational strand of the social contract but also the whole of society.

The future, it is said, creeps in on tiny feet: any failure of the intergenerational contract to promote the welfare of children would be a severe blow to the future. They are the ones who will pay the taxes for today's workers when they retire. Today's children will fill those workers' shoes when they retire from the economy, and they will be the ones from whom retired homeowners hope to receive a good price for their homes when they want to sell and move to smaller quarters. Without investment in the younger generation— no matter their race—today's workers will be damaging their own interests. Embracing such "self-interest rightly understood" has been an American virtue since the days of early nationhood, when Alexis de Tocqueville first noted it.[1] Indeed, a new understanding must be shared in the United States with regard to the mutual self-interest of different groups and our interdependency as we move forward into the future.

Asymmetries Between Age Groups

In the timeless relationship, the young and the elderly are dependents supported by those of working age. This relationship is well understood in every family, and yet families in the contemporary United States do not care for

Figure 9.1   Spending and Taxes in California, by Age, 2000

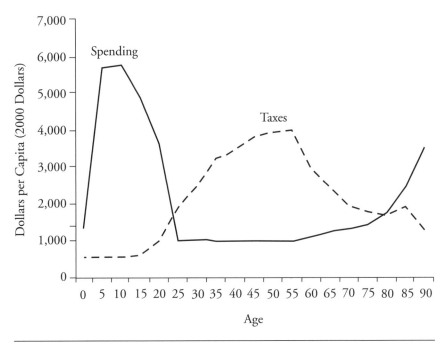

Source: Lee, Miller, and Edwards (2003). Supplemental material provided by Ryan Edwards.

their own members without public assistance. Family members of different ages rely on specific services, while working-age adults contribute to the public treasury that supports those services.

Figure 9.1 displays the asymmetry in taxation and service beneficiaries as observed in 2000 in California.[2] Per capita public expenditures soar among children, fall to one-fifth that level among middle-aged adults, and then rise again among the elderly. The very high state expenditures on children and young adults are due to the age-concentrated costs of public education, which consume 51 percent of annual state revenues in California.[3] The moderately high expenditures on the elderly stem from public pensions and Medi-Cal expenses, which together amount to perhaps 15 percent of the annual state budget.[4] (The much greater federal government contribution to the elderly is addressed in a later section on the federal budget.)

Conversely, taxation is nil for children (save via sales tax) and also low for the elderly, but it soars in middle age (figure 9.1). Only 22 percent of annual state revenues in California comes from business, borrowing, or other sources. The bulk of the revenue is derived from personal income taxes (48 percent) and sales taxes (30 percent), both of which can be attributed to individual taxpayers. These shoppers and earners are predominantly the broad middle-age groups of adults, age twenty-five to sixty-four. The pattern portrayed in figure 9.1 starkly represents the issue: the principal taxpayers are not the same people as the service beneficiaries. The unkind term that some disgruntled taxpayers—often those over fifty, without any children at home—employ to describe the beneficiaries is "tax eaters."

The age imbalances in taxes and spending are intertwined with the costs and benefits of immigration to California and the United States. In a nutshell, more of the fiscal benefits of immigration go to the federal level, while more of the service costs fall to state and local governments. Also, immigrants tend to be more expensive when newly arrived and to return greater benefits later. Accordingly, we need to cost immigration out over a full life cycle. Alternatively, we also should cost out the fiscal impacts over the life cycle of immigrants' children. The authoritative study conducted in 1997 by the National Research Council reported detailed simulations over three generations by the noted economic demographer Ronald Lee. Those studies found substantial lifetime contributions by immigrants, net of services received, and even higher contributions from their children, but they confirmed that most of the net benefit goes to the federal level.[5] The NRC study found that the impacts of immigration depend not only on the relative numbers of immigrants but also on their age at arrival—whether before or after the expense of schooling, in the high-taxpaying middle-aged period, or in retirement years. Also, the impacts are considerably less positive for immigrants with less than a high school education and more positive for those educated beyond high school. Given the negative impacts in the short term on local communities and state governments, it is understandable if taxpayers raise questions about the place of immigrants in the social contract. However, among both immigrants and the native-born, the expenses of children and the elderly are not borne wholly within the family. A large portion is covered through public education, Social Security, and publicly supported health care.

Only through a social contract of *intergenerational support* can this age asymmetry of tax payments and benefits be sustained. Indeed, in this light we comprehend an entirely different strand of the social contract "interpreted as being a social policy contract based in intergenerational transfers of resources through the mediums of taxation and social expenditure."[6] The gerontologist

Vern Bengston explains this "contract" in a manner consistent with the approach we have adopted: "What is the *contract across generations and age groups?* Put most simply, it is a set of shared expectations and obligations—what sociologists term *norms*—regarding the aging of individuals and the succession of generations."[7] The contract extends to the support of the elderly through pensions, Social Security, and health care, providing a *reward* to society's retired workers and parents. However, at the same time the contract includes education and other support services for children—in effect an *investment* in those who represent the future workers, parents, and taxpayers of society.

There is nothing automatic about this contract. David Hayes-Bautista, Werner O. Schink, and Jorge Chapa caution that it is not always certain whether "the intergenerational compact is to be honored. . . . First, [society's] workers must be economically productive enough to meet the needs of the older and younger generations. Second, those workers must have the desire to forgo part of what they produce to meet the needs of a society's dependents."[8] Indeed, beginning with the stagnation of income growth in the 1970s, when the middle class began to struggle for their perceived entitlement, taxpayers began to grow stingier about supporting dependent members of society. Hayes-Bautista and his colleagues hint darkly that if the current generation does not invest in the upcoming Latino generation, not only will Latinos be unprepared to shoulder the burden of helping the elderly, but they may even decide that they owe those seniors no support.

The taxpayers, meanwhile, harbor their own doubts: if we dig deeper into our pockets, they seem to ask, what is the likelihood that recipients of benefits will make good use of our investment? And they surely would add: how do we know our investment will even pay off with benefits for ourselves? If agreement is to be struck on a new social contract, negotiations will require evidence of productivity, as well as concessions on all sides.

Such a revolt of the future generation has not been suggested very widely. In fact, thus far, there has been very little discussion of the costs of not investing in the new generation. Instead, for the past two decades the elderly have been treated much more lavishly, while children have been relatively neglected in the intergenerational strand of the social contract. Of course, the elderly, not children, can vote and directly sway public policy, but most adults can anticipate the day when they too will join the ranks of the elderly. Thus, the elderly are treated as a highly favored, universal interest group:

Older Americans do not maintain their government benefits merely because they are able to impose their will on an unwilling public, but because the vast majority of Americans, of all ages, share that agenda. . . . If this is a generation war, it is a one-sided conflict, with nearly everyone on the side of the elderly. But why is there such universal support for their programs? The answer lies in the unique nature of the elderly as an interest group in society. *America is divided into two groups: Those who are old, and those who are becoming so.* That fact has not made for great political conflict over programs for the elderly.[9]

A curious finding is that middle-aged adults often express even stronger support for elderly interests than do the elderly themselves. One in-depth study conducted by John Logan and Glenna Spitze in the region around Albany, New York, reported, for example, that 78.1 percent of people age forty to forty-nine felt that too little is spent on assistance to the elderly, compared to 58.9 percent of those age seventy to seventy-nine. Similarly, the study found that 36.6 percent of those age forty to forty-nine, but only 15.5 percent of those age seventy to seventy-nine, strongly agreed with the statement that "anyone over sixty-five should be entitled to health care at an affordable cost."[10] Logan and Spitze conclude that "on a broad range of policy and family issues, people's attitudes do not reflect their current generational self-interest . . . [and instead] older people's attitudes seem to give greater weight to the needs of younger generations, and vice versa. Relations across age groups apparently have an altruistic character."[11] Despite this happy note, this study did not examine age groups younger than forty, and so we do not know if the altruism these researchers observed extended to young adults and children.

Intergenerational Fairness

The premise of an intergenerational obligation in the social contract did not become highly visible and a subject of concern until the 1980s, when the issue of intergenerational equity emerged in scholarly debates.[12] It is one thing to support program assistance for the average older person; it is quite another to prioritize that assistance when the numbers of older people are growing rapidly. The implications of population projections for an aging society began to creep into public discussion as it became clear that the United States would have a much larger population of seniors after 2020 and that this growth would be accompanied by much slower growth in the working-age population.

The Weight of the Elderly and the Fiscal Crisis

In Chapter 3, we saw that the ratio of persons age sixty-five and older is projected to soar in the United States, rising from just under 250 elderly in 2010 for every 1,000 persons age twenty-five to sixty-four to 410 per 1,000 in 2030, and rising higher thereafter. These concerns about the growing weight of elderly dependents are widely known and have inspired discussion of various reform proposals for Social Security, such as those put forth by the Bush administration in 2005. What is less recognized, however, is that the growing liabilities for Social Security payments are outweighed by growing obligations for health care expenditures. And both of those obligations are exceeded by the even larger growing expenditure required for interest payments on the accumulating national debt. Especially striking is the projected growth in health care expenditures. Not only are the elderly living longer, but the annual per capita cost of health care also is rising markedly. Multiply larger numbers of elderly by higher costs, guarantee coverage by the federal government, and the result is that a larger portion of the federal budget must be consumed. These current costs are borne by today's taxpayers, and any unmet costs for which money is borrowed must be repaid by the children who will be tomorrow's taxpayers.

Official confirmation of the magnitude of intergenerational crisis has been newly provided in budget simulations prepared by the Government Accountability Office of the federal government. From 2006 to 2020, if all current tax laws are retained, expenditures for Social Security entitlements are expected to grow from 23.0 percent to 30.7 percent of federal revenue, and expenditures for Medicare will balloon from 13.7 percent to 23.9 percent of federal revenue.[13] After 2020, the growth in both of these financial obligations is expected to escalate more sharply, but even in just the next fourteen years these two budget components alone will consume an extra 18 percent of anticipated revenue in the federal budget (see figure 9.2). Given current tax laws and other needs of government, a large and growing budget deficit will be incurred. Thus, the GAO projects that the annual debt payments on the borrowing needed to cover that deficit will double from 9.3 percent of annual revenue in 2006 to 18.8 percent by 2020, and will spiral out of control thereafter.[14] Taken together, these three items alone—Social Security, Medicare, and interest payments on debt—will increase their share of the federal government's total anticipated revenue from 45.9 percent in 2006 to 73.3 per-

Figure 9.2   Federal Budget Allocation as a Percentage of Projected Federal Revenue

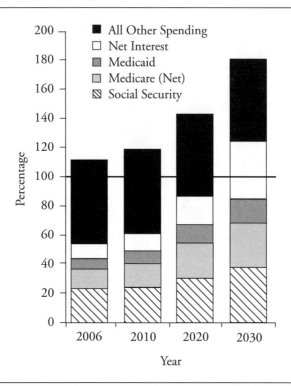

Source: GAO, August 2006 analysis—"More Realistic Simulation."

cent by 2020. Within just a decade, federal spending will have overshot anticipated annual revenue by more than 40 percent. Accordingly, without even heavier borrowing in the future, there will be very little left over, the GAO reports, for the bulk of government: "The category 'all other spending' includes much of what many think of as 'government'—'discretionary' spending on such activities as national defense, homeland security, veterans health benefits, our national parks, highways and mass transit, foreign aid, plus 'mandatory spending' on the smaller entitlement programs."[15]

The outlook generated by this scenario is so extreme that it cannot actually occur, even if it is generated by the most realistic current assumptions. As the GAO observes, these simulations lead to an overarching conclusion: current fiscal policy is unsustainable over the long term. Absent reform of federal retirement and health programs for the elderly—including Social Security, Medicare, and Medicaid—federal budgetary flexibility will become increasingly constrained. Assuming no changes to projected benefits or revenues, spending on these entitlements will drive increasingly large, persistent, and ultimately unsustainable federal deficits and debt as the baby boom generation retires.[16]

The challenge is to keep the fiscal gap from growing out of hand. The latest GAO simulation shows that, to hold the debt ratio at its 2006 level, an extra 8 percent share of the gross domestic product must be allocated to correcting this problem every year for the next seventy-five years. This amounts to a present value of $61 trillion, or $485,000 for each full-time worker.[17] The fiscal gap can be closed by either reducing spending or raising taxes, or by any combination of the two that produces this figure. Given that most of the spending is locked in by entitlements and that both Republican and Democratic administrations have shown little ability to cut discretionary spending, it seems likely that most of the fiscal gap will be covered by eventual tax increases. However, there will also be extreme pressure on the federal government to lessen its promised entitlements, such as by delaying the age of eligibility.

Independent economists affirm the crisis at hand and paint a dire portrait. Laurence J. Kotlikoff, Jagdeesh Gokhale, and others have developed a method they call generational accounting—a comprehensive assessment of revenues, expenditures, assets, and liabilities totaled across all levels of government.[18] The insight gained from this method is that the lifetime tax rate for future generations—our children—must be 78 percent higher than it is at present if we are to cover the debts and liabilities being left unfunded today: "The big whammy—the amount being left for future Americans to pay—equals the amount of government bills less the contributions of current generations to paying those bills, [and] *the less that current generations pay of them, the greater is the burden that will be left for those coming in the future.*"[19]

This imposition of burden on the future has not occurred through malicious intent. The baby boomers cannot help it if they were born into such an oversized generation. And the costs of health care are escalating in part because of improved technology and in part because of our desire to protect life at all costs. Who is to say that the quest for better health and longer lives should be curtailed? Moreover, today's senior generation, the parents of the baby boomers, may have just had the good fortune to be born at the right time: having come of age in the decades of booming prosperity and having faced favorable conditions at every life stage, they have been termed the "Good Times" cohort.[20] Similarly, some have designated those born between the late 1920s and early 1940s as a subsidized or "welfare generation" that has been especially advantaged, first by the government programs aimed at the young after World War II through the 1960s, and then by the shift to elderly interests post-1980. Others have recognized an "aging of the welfare state,"[21] or at least a "graying of the federal budget."[22]

It is difficult to identify precisely which generations benefit the most from the tax laws and benefit streams that prevail as they pass through their life stages. Not only does each generation have a unique experience, but both their contributions and their benefits are stretched out over many decades. Nonetheless, economic demographers have achieved useful insights. Considering Social Security and Medicare together, generations born before 1960 will all receive more benefits than they paid in taxes. The largest winners are those who were born between 1900 and 1920 and who arrived at age sixty-five between 1965 and 1985. For these fortunate individuals, lifetime benefits have exceeded lifetime payments by an amount equivalent to more than 7 percent of their lifetime income. Surplus benefits for the baby boom generation will decline to roughly 3 percent of lifetime income, and for those born after 1975 benefits will fall short of payments, declining to a projected 3 percent eventual shortfall for children born in 2005.[23] Cutting taxes will not correct this shortfall of benefits relative to taxes. Experimenting with the lifetime effects of different formulations, Antoine Bommier, Ronald Lee, Timothy Miller, and Stephane Zuber conclude: "Our analysis suggests that all current generations would gain from policies that preserve benefit levels by raising taxes, as against the reverse, and that is also true for their children and grandchildren."[24]

The Advantage of the Elderly

In brief, generational fortunes have reversed. The inequity is that today's elderly have established a very well supported lifestyle that massive numbers of baby boomers will soon try to emulate. Yet all the deferred debt required to maintain that lifestyle will be passed on to the next generation, which will have to pay higher taxes even though they may be less prepared economically and educationally to assume that burden than the earlier generation.

At one time the elderly were disproportionately poor and deserving of government assistance. When poverty was rediscovered in America in the early 1960s, the elderly at that time were survivors of the Great Depression. Aged thirty-five and older in 1930, they took the hardest economic losses, and by 1950, when the postwar boom was under way, most of them, at age fifty-five and older, were too old to benefit from the boom. Instead, the generation just twenty to thirty years younger avoided the ill effects of the Depression and was poised to exploit all the postwar opportunities, including the educational funding provided by the GI Bill and federally guaranteed mortgages at low interest rates. By the 1980s it was already clear that the elderly were no longer the disadvantaged group they had been in 1960. Where once the elderly poverty rate was twice as high as that for young adults, it plunged from 33 percent in 1960 to 12 percent in 1980, and subsequently fell to 7 percent in 2000, well below the rate for young adults.[25] Meanwhile, the elderly advantage in homeownership rates had expanded from being twenty-two percentage points higher than the rate for the young in 1980 to thirty-three points higher in 2000.[26]

Not only are the new elderly relatively prosperous, but they also have benefited from government support justified by more programs under the social contract than any other generation. When this group reached elder status after 1980, they had benefited both from all the programs put in place for their disadvantaged elderly predecessors and from all the accumulated benefits of the postwar programs aimed at young adults. Thus, this "Good Times" or "subsidized" generation was uniquely advantaged by government programs of collective protection.

This has led to an unusual age profile to consumption in the United States, one skewed toward the older ages. Researchers led by the economic demographer Ronald Lee have sought to measure more precisely the consumption benefits pertaining to each age group and accumulated over the lifetime. Whereas in most societies the mean age of wage earners well exceeds the mean age of consumers, implying a transfer of support from older to younger generations, in the United States the mean age of earners lies *below* the mean age of beneficiaries, implying an upward transfer to the older generation. Close examination of the per capita age profile of consumption shows substantial and continuous increases from age twenty to the end of life, unlike in other societies where consumption is flat through the life cycle and even declines in old age. In the United States, privately funded consumption does turn downward after age fifty-five, but publicly supported consumption, consisting largely of health care, rises markedly in this older age group and carries total consumption to unprecedented levels for each individual on average.[27]

It is a fair guess that most of the elderly have little knowledge of how their generation is likely to compare to those that will follow. Nor do they fully recognize how much of their current entitlements have been prepaid by their own tax contributions. While reaping rich benefits, conservative members of the older generation, paradoxically, have also participated in the taxpayer revolt and supported the limited government strand of the social contract. These self-interested choices exploit the opportunities presented by fortunate timing in history but lead to the growing generational inequities discussed here, a situation that could be seen as *intergenerational plunder*. Matthew Price observes that "'plunder' would be more apt [a description], since resources are being seized in the absence of their rightful owners, or without their ability to respond."[28] Surely this is unintentional, because it is so spread out over the decades that the plunder is almost invisible, and if no one complains, how is the older generation to even know what it has done?

Racial Intergenerational Justice

The intergenerational injustice is compounded by race, especially in California. As we saw in chapter 3, only 28.6 percent of the younger generation is anticipated to be non-Hispanic white in 2010, a far different proportion from the 60.0 percent who are white in the older generation. Indeed, David Hayes-Bautista and his colleagues foresaw this compounding of race and generation some twenty years ago when they called for a new concept that they termed the interethnic compact: "With the emergence of an age-ethnic stratified population, the intergenerational compact will quickly take on the flavor of an implicit interethnic compact. The political implications of this transformation are serious indeed, for a failure to seal that compact will impair the future of the intergenerational compact."[29] Indeed, those fears have been borne out to a large degree.

Scholars of public finance have found that racial diversity has an unfortunate relation to political decisions about public spending. In one of the most comprehensive cross-national reviews, Peter Lindert concludes: "Ethnic homogeneity strongly promotes every kind of social transfer program through government. Stated the other way around, ethnic fractionalization is a strong negative influence on the political will to raise taxes for social spending and related public investments."[30] Focusing solely on the United States, James Poterba reviews a sizable literature and tests a number of propositions relating age group diversity and support for education. He finds that states with a heavier share of the population in elderly age groups provide significantly lower educational spending per child. Moreover, this reduction is accentuated when the elderly and the school children are drawn from different racial groups.[31] Combined with the growing racial divide, this finding does not augur well for the future of California or the United States.

In the face of the demographic transition, is it possible that some are engaged in a rearguard action to obstruct the change? Indeed, Peter Schrag, the longtime California political journalist, observes that the apparent dysfunction in the state's political and governmental systems could be construed as an effort by the majority voters to "protect themselves against that majority of minorities . . . [and to] hold the new California at bay."[32] As noted in a preceding chapter, the white minority of the population retains a two-thirds voting majority in California. Compared to voters in other groups, they are more pessimistic about the future and have a greater dislike for population changes. And white support for paying taxes for more services is much lower, especially if they consider immigrants a burden, which many of them do. Voters who hold this view are especially unlikely to support the school bonds needed by all the children in the state. One hopes that this democratic expression of self-interest is not shortsighted and self-defeating.

Injustice Perpetrated on the Future

Expressions of self-interest in the present risk injury to the future whenever costs and benefits are spread unevenly between the present and the future. The longer the lag between present decision and future outcomes, the lower the likelihood that self-interests are well considered. As an example, decisions about educating California's future labor force are especially troublesome. The outcomes of today's schooling decisions will not be fully borne out in the workforce for one or two decades, and then any discovered errors in outcome will not be easily correctable, at least not for the "lost" generation of new workers. Yet the political preferences of today's majority threaten the economic viability of the future majority and, through them, the future of the state.

Much of the inequity is unintentional and stems merely from the desire to be fiscally prudent today, but we need to assess the implications over time in the clearest way possible. In simple terms, the strategies chosen for supporting public service needs in California shift a substantial share of responsibility from the present to the future. Bonds are debt instruments that shift financial obligations to the shoulders of future taxpayers. Through bonds, funds for schools and infrastructure construction are provided in the present in exchange for future public expenditures to cover a series of annual payments that will retire the debt. If the workforce benefits from these education investments also accrue in the future, it could make sense to defer those payments, so that benefits and costs are matched in time.

In California, however, shortfalls in current operating expenses have also been funded through future debt incurred under governors Davis and Schwarzenegger,[33] amounting to $20 billion in new bonded indebtedness just since 2000.[34] Although investments returning future dividends can justify financing by future payments, that can hardly apply to current operating expenses, which should be covered by current revenue. Lifestyles in the present are being financed by taxpayers of the future. This is equivalent to taking a mortgage on your house to pay for a wonderful vacation you already enjoyed last summer. The time frames of benefit and cost are not synchronized. No individual would think this wise. Yet in the context of public finance, we are eager to pass the buck. In fact, the example of mortgaging *your* house may not apply. Today's situation more closely resembles mortgaging *your neighbor's* house to pay for your own vacation. That surely should be unethical and disallowed within an agreed social contract.

At one time the system for future investment seemed to be working smoothly. In the era of leadership by Governor Pat Brown, during the 1950s and 1960s, California built the best freeway system in the nation and invested in the largest and highest-quality system of higher education.[35] Today it is widely believed that the current generation has enjoyed the fruits of those prior investments without continuing to make the commitments required for the future. Subsequent decades have not witnessed a commensurate stream of public investments. Instead, Californians have been living off the past; now the cupboard is growing bare, and the state needs to play catchup.[36] Following passage of Proposition 13 in 1978, and continuing through the dismal era of the 1990s, California skipped a generation in public investment. Any new commitments will now be covered in the future, not by today's taxpayers. The racial justice issue, it could be said, is that the generation skipping its payments is largely white, while the generation being asked to cover the deferred obligations and play catchup is Latino, Asian, and African American. This fact may not sit well once it is recognized.

Bridging Demographic Fault Lines to Rebuild the Social Contract

The nation is just beginning to confront its generational divide, prompted by the impending retirement of the large cohort of baby boomers. Their retirement will reduce the skilled workforce and the number of well-endowed taxpayers at the same time as it adds numerous claimants of publicly supported retirement benefits. This effect will be amplified by the transfer of current expenses to the future through the growing government debt, and the future rich rewards promised to our elderly also must be paid by the new generation of workers. In California, most starkly, this divide coincides with a racial division between an older white electorate and the younger, nonwhite generation that will carry the burden postponed to their shoulders. It is clear to all who have examined it that this situation cannot be sustained and that the inequity will not be long borne once it is widely recognized. Yet the burden and the cost of solutions are only compounded by our delay in discovering what needs to be done today.

The Growing Weakness of Earlier Strands in the Social Contract

Each of the strands in the social contract is based on a different premise responding to current problems and potentialities. As those historical conditions change, so does the support for the strand that responded to them. Some adherents of a particular strand never lose the faith, but the median voter sways with the times, and the youngest adults are more prone to adopt new sets of priorities than are the old-timers. Indeed, it is the outcome of struggles for new recruits that defines whether a political movement still has vital appeal or whether it has outlived its usefulness and is populated only by former adherents. In this light, we begin to understand the crucial political importance of the intergenerational crisis that has so disadvantaged young people. They are the most likely candidates to rally for a change. How well do the established strands of the social contract speak to their interests?

In the previous chapter, I described the growing fragmentation of common purpose that followed a weakening of cultural cohesion and a backlash against the equality of subgroups strand. This was politically exploited through Scammon and Wattenburg's "social issue," which identified a winning voter majority.[37] Thirty years later, much has changed. To begin with, young adults since 1980 have become far less fearful of the "social issue" than were the middle-aged voters identified by Scammon and Wattenburg. The generational divide in social values is no longer marked at age thirty and may well be sixty today, now that the baby boomers have advanced to that age.[38] Although certain regions of the country contain a disproportionate number of social conservatives, even many southerners have grown their hair long, and so the symbols of difference are no longer as shocking. In general, Americans are much more accustomed to cultural differences than they once were, and the loss of cultural cohesion probably galvanizes the young much less than the old.

Instead, today the growing weight of the elderly is creating a new political reality. For the most part, attention has been directed only to the voting power of the elderly, but recently the political dialogue has begun to focus on the burden that the growing numbers of elderly will soon impose on the working-age population. This burden is a product of both larger numbers and the growing entitlements accorded to seniors. In most families it is well recognized that the young adults are not as well off as previous generations. On this issue, given the clear-cut reversal of generational fortunes, it is clear that the younger generation may be ripe for political mobilization.

The foregoing may describe the political self-interest of the younger generation, but this group still represents a minority of voters, and it is not clear that their struggles have yet been perceived as important to society at large. In principle, every society has the interest of its young at heart, for they represent the future. It is the young who will carry on the valued traditions, who will raise the next generation, who will run the economy, and who will support the elderly. There is no debate that the young are vital to the common good or that the preservation and growth of any society is heavily dependent on nurturing of the young.

The growing crisis in America is that the reigning strands of the social contract have neglected this essential duty and undermined this vital interdependency. Emphasis on limited government prevents the collection and allocation of societal resources in support of the young. At the same time, what meager tax resources are available have been redirected to the needs of the voting majority, the advantaged generation that is striving to maintain its middle-class entitlement and now has claimed the ever-growing rewards of seniors. The unfortunate result is that the legacy of a major premise in the social contract—collective protection and services—has been reserved more for the support of the older generation than for the young. This risks undermining the future development of the next generation, which will support the seniors.

How aware are seniors of this outcome? I think they are not informed and would be shocked if they learned the score. As Isabel Sawhill, one senior citizen who *is* very well informed, puts it: "We're the grown-ups who should be taking care of America for future generations. Instead, we're bequeathing a fiscal mess of biblical proportions."[39] Sawhill also points out that many elderly are beginning to confront the generational problem: "A recent AARP Bulletin, belying the stereotype of the greedy senior, put two naked toddlers on its cover and superimposed on their backs the grim headline '$156,000 in debt.'" Even though most of our elected leaders may not be publicizing the gravity of our situation, seniors are beginning to wake up to the mess.

The new realization to be confronted is that both the nation and the state of California face a grave threat to their future. If the older generation consumes all the resources, with relatively little reinvested in the young, our society and economy will not function as well as we are accustomed to. We must rethink how the social contract should be restructured to cope with the impending generational crisis of society. The impending retirement of the giant baby boom generation is the precipitating event that will bring this crisis home.

Rebuilding the Social Contract Through Mutual Self-Interest

The challenge we face is restoring faith in public decisionmaking and building a new consensus for a collective social contract that can serve the needs of all generations. Surely the needs are great, but to be effective, *it is essential that the new social contract be grounded in the self-interests of today's voting majority.* None of these voters are children, and few of them are Latinos, immigrants, or even the grown children of immigrants. The latter groups may represent the future, but they do not represent the current electorate. We need to rethink the nature of a social contract, expressing it more broadly without central reliance on government and emphasizing a broader appeal that embraces the white, two-thirds electoral majority as well as those most in need.

The general definition of the social contract that we have adopted holds the key to possible solutions. Recall that the definition emphasizes the "underlying shared social understandings that structure cooperation within a world of self-interested people possessing unequal resources."[40] This shared understanding requires us to examine the reasons for supporting social cooperation and the shared purposes to which that cooperation should be applied.

Mutual self-interest, or Tocqueville's "self-interest rightly understood," must be recognized as a vital component of a viable social contract. A social contract is intended to mediate between the self-interest of an individual and the interests of the broader society. The objective is to align an individual's self-interest with the interests of others in society, creating a *sense of community interdependence and shared destiny*. When people believe that they share a destiny with others in their community, they are more likely to support policies that favor the community as a whole rather than just their own narrow self-interest.

A new, demographically based social contract can lay out the road map needed for a lifetime of prosperity for all the residents of the nation. Under this new social understanding, we must reemphasize the intergenerational support strand of the social contract. Looking ahead, we see that the middle-aged taxpayers of today will become the dependent seniors of tomorrow. And when they reach that senior position, the neglected children of today will become the middle-aged taxpayers on whom the seniors will lean. In fact, the young should become the reliable taxpayers, the essential workforce replacements, and the valued home buyers. *It is this intergenerational sharing across decades that constitutes the new basis for a shared social understanding that can support cooperation.* By emphasizing mutual self-interest, we will once again be able to marshal broad support for building unity, shared destiny, and a common purpose.

Conclusion on Revamping the Social Contract

What will be the prevailing social contract in the next decade? If recent trends are extended, it might be a contract that emphasizes minimal government, the entitlement of the middle class, and continued support for the elderly. However, analyses by the Government Accountability Office, by Kotlikoff and his colleagues, or by Ron Lee and his associates indicate that such a scenario is not in the least sustainable. In fact, our historical review of different strands in the social contract suggests that the particular expressions of strands often do not remain unchallenged for more than three decades. The supporting conditions change, and new urgent problems arise. By 2010 the new ideas of the 1970s and 1980s will be growing old and tired, and members of the younger generation, who will be valued political recruits, will be growing disaffected. If those old ideas prove incapable of responding to the current needs of the day, they are likely to be supplanted by new strands that are more effective.

The underlying dynamic to be appreciated is demographic change. In important ways, demography is destiny and will inevitably set the agenda. The aging of the giant baby boom generation is inexorable, as it was for their parents and as it will be for their children. Because of its large size, the impact of the baby boom generation on retirement institutions cannot be treated lightly: responding to their needs and meeting their entitlements will probably overrun the bounds of limited government. We can continue to borrow from the needs of children and the next generation only so much before the backlash will be felt. This mounting generational injustice is made more acute by its compounding with race. The growing diversity of the younger population, infused by immigrants, is a prominent factor, nowhere more so than in California. Should the older generation continue its disproportionate appropriation of fiscal resources, the result may be a deep resentment and angry backlash, leading to either (sooner) a gradual redistribution between generations or (later) a radical and abrupt correction.

We must immediately begin to address the needs of this younger generation, not only for its own sake, or to avoid conflict, but because of self-interest rightly understood by the older generation. If we invest in the younger generation now, there is a substantial added payoff promised to the older generation, as well as to the state of California and the whole of the nation. That payoff will come in the form of future skilled workers to replace the retirees, new middle-class taxpayers to support retirement benefits and other services, and future home buyers who can afford to pay a good price to seniors. This payoff will be a response to a collective need, and investing for that payoff is a collective responsibility.

Skeptical citizens should ask: how will we know this can work? With their confidence dampened by the old dismal view of the future, many are prone to doubt that any good can come of the investment taken from their pocket. Promising a shared destiny is no great incentive if all that means is that everyone will go down with the ship. Instead, what is needed now is some reasonable hope that not only can the ship stay afloat, but also, if everyone pulls together, we can achieve the kind of progress most Americans want. In chapters 5 and 6, I presented the evidence that the California future has already turned much brighter and that immigrant upward mobility is much stronger than generally assumed. Nonetheless, the majority voters, as described in chapter 7, still have the power to undercut that future unless they see their interests aligned with those of the incoming population majority.

In the present chapter, I have argued that the two groups' interests should be aligned, and I have suggested how the social contract can be rebuilt through an emphasis on the mutual self-interest of intergenerational cooperation. For that argument to be fully persuasive, however, we need evidence that the promised payoff for the older generation will indeed occur. We must now examine that evidence. In the next chapter, we turn to the question of how likely it is that immigrant children will fare well in school and grow into skilled workers, as well as into middle-class taxpayers. We then address the question of how likely it is that these immigrant children will ever become homeowners, and whether they can be expected to offer very much when purchasing their homes. As we shall see in the next two chapters, there is indeed a much more hopeful future that can be attained, but it will require greater attention to investing in our children, the precious homegrown assets who will replace the retiring baby boomers.

PART III

MUTUAL SELF-INTEREST FOR A HOPEFUL FUTURE

Chapter 10

Growing the New Skilled
Workforce and Middle-Class
Taxpayer Base

DEMOGRAPHIC CHANGE and the economy appear headed on a collision course in California and the United States unless the powerful demographic currents can be turned to advantage. The crux of the problem is that forecasts of employment growth indicate rising demand for more highly educated workers, but demographic trends are working in the opposite direction: the average educational attainment of the workforce is being reduced. Only by elevating the educational level of the newest generation entering the workforce can the collision between demographic change and the economy be avoided. The rising new generation could pose a hazard for California's future in particular, but it also contains great opportunities that should not be squandered.

This depiction of a threat is the most common story about education and the future. It is based in substantial truth and widely accepted. However, it verges on a story of despair and emphasizes the pessimistic view of the glass as half-empty. Our examination of the evidence behind this threat will show that it is real, but we need to also address another outlook. There is a story of hope to be told. As threatening as the collision may be, there are some very positive trends on which we should be building. Yes, the glass is half-empty, but it is also half-full, and growing fuller. If we care to embrace the hopeful future and take the necessary steps toward serious problem-solving, we can all come out ahead. The positive signs are there for those who look.

The efficacy of the intergenerational social contract outlined in the preceding chapter relies on a clear demonstration of mutual self-interest. At heart is a renewed emphasis on investment in the education of the next generation, no matter what their ethnic background, and a trust that this investment will pay off. A substantial outpouring of research studies since the late 1990s have reached a similar conclusion: success in meeting the educational challenge of preparing the new generation is the single most important task for the future. In this chapter, I draw upon these studies—both national and California-focused—for the collective wisdom they offer. Supplemented by the findings on immigrant upward mobility and the dynamics of population transition, the story that emerges has a commanding urgency, both in the benefits to be gained and the hazards to be avoided. Once again, California provides the best example of the urgency of the decisions that must be made.

The unusually low educational attainment levels of Latinos have been the source of greatest concern. There are wide disparities in educational attainment in California, as elsewhere in the United States. Among residents of prime working age, 36.7 percent of non-Hispanic whites have completed a BA or more advanced degree, compared to 18.0 percent of African Americans, 8.1 percent of Latinos, and 44.9 percent of Asian Americans (table 10.1). Thus, the growth in Latinos and Asians presents two opposite forces on the overall college-graduate share of the population. However, as we have seen, Latinos are a much larger factor in California's overall growth, and so their exceptionally low educational attainment has a great impact. In fact, immigrant Latinos have much lower education levels than those who are native-born and have been attending U.S. schools for their entire lives. Nonetheless, the educational attainment of native-born Latinos falls below that of African Americans and all other groups. This deficiency, which must be remediated, requires collaboration between education leaders, taxpayers, and Latino youth and parents.

The strategic importance of Latino youth for the United States as a whole is highlighted in the major new study by the National Research Council:

Table 10.1   Disparities of Educational Attainment Among Adults Age Twenty-Five to Sixty-Four, by Race and Nativity, California, 2000

	Less Than High School	BA Degree or Higher
Non-Hispanic white	7.5%	36.7%
Non-Hispanic black	15.6	18.0
Latino: Total	51.8	8.1
Native-born	24.2	13.7
Immigrants	66.0	5.3
Asian and Pacific Islander: Total	15.5	44.9
Native-born	6.1	51.2
Immigrants	17.2	43.8
Total	21.8	28.1

Source: Census 2000, PUMS 5 percent file for California.

Rising numbers of Hispanic young people will slow the nation's overall population aging and can partially offset the growing burden of dependency produced by an aging majority. But their success in doing so depends on the level of their earnings, which in turn depends on their education and acquisition of job-related skills.[1]

What makes these crisis issues are the abrupt impacts looming from the retirement of the baby boom generation. Not only are large numbers expected to exit the workforce in a very short time period, but this group also is much better educated than previous rounds of retirees. In fact, members of this generation are better educated than other groups in the workforce today, and so their departure will leave a particular gap in the skilled workforce. The baby boom retirements will be hitting every state in the nation, and just as California's skilled workforce is being sharply depleted, the nationwide competition for replacements will be intense. It will not be easy to borrow replacement workers from other locations. Every state will need to develop its own talent.

Already we can see in California that the skilled workforce is becoming more homegrown than it once was, and this leaning will tip precariously in the coming decade when the retirement-induced shortages begin to hit. California's employers will need to rely much more heavily on state and local investments in education than they have in the past. The practical problem is that a worker cannot be trained overnight. Given the development time needed to pass through middle school, high school, and college, we must recognize that the coming shortages are upon us now.

Fortunately for California, it holds some advantages in this competition, if it plays its cards right. The state's population is younger than in most other states, owing to large waves of recent immigrants and its growing young Latino population. Accordingly, the baby boomer retirements will not hit California as hard as many other states will be hit. In addition, evidence presented here reveals that homegrown workers are more likely to stay in California than are those who were recruited from other states. The upshot is that California should be better able to retain a skilled workforce developed from its own resources. In addition, the low average educational attainment of Latino residents, although a present problem, creates the opportunity for substantial upgrading that could offset other losses. This chapter examines the upgrading that is required and the potential benefits if taxpayers make the required investments. At bottom, more than a workforce is being prepared. The new workers also constitute future consumers and taxpayers and, indeed, the new middle class. It cannot be overstated how much is at stake, but the solutions take time and they can no longer be put off.

Baby Boomer Retirements and the Workforce Challenge

California and the nation are on the threshold of some of the most rapid social and economic changes in many decades. Already deeply engaged in a dramatic social transition, the pace of change will reach a crescendo when the giant baby boom generation plunges into retirement. Policymakers at the state and federal levels have begun to pay better attention to these predictions of change because they are based on a simple and inexorable arithmetic and because now the predicted future is drawing very near. In 2005 there were 9.7 million baby boomers in California between the ages of forty and fifty-nine, accounting for 51.0 percent of the prime working-age population.[2] By 2020 they will be fifty-five to seventy-four—squarely situated for mass retirement from the workforce. They will be replaced by younger, possibly less-educated workers. Will these replacements prove adequate?

How Big Are the Shoes?

The most acute changes will probably unfold just ten years from now when it proves difficult to fill the shoes of so many retirees. The example that follows is about California, but every state faces similar losses from the retirement of the baby boomers. Specifically, three million workers from the baby boom generation will exit the California workforce between 2010 and 2020.[3] (Similar losses will continue between 2020 and 2030.) This workforce loss will stem from all sources, including death and out-migration from the state as well as simple retirement.[4] The departees will be replaced by young adults who are newly entering the labor force. Over four million young workers are expected to join the labor force between 2010 and 2020. Although this number is larger than the number of retirees, it is very deficient compared to previous decades. As discussed later, the characteristics of the workers in this young generation are very different from those of the workers they are replacing. In addition, the impact of the sheer number of workers is significant. Together with losses in other age groups, the workforce departures of the baby boomers will depress labor force growth far below the rates for recent decades.

The anticipated annual losses of the baby boomers from the workforce will be most acute in the years between 2015 and 2020 and will drive down annual growth of the labor force to barely 0.6 percent per year. As discussed in chapter 3, labor force growth is expected to slow by even more in the United States as a whole—to 0.4 percent per year—and it could fall to negative rates in some slower-growing states. These growth rates amount to roughly half the already low rates of labor force growth currently experienced in both California and the United States (see figure 3.3). It is likely that some regions of the United States will feel the labor force shortage long before California does, at which time employers and economic development agencies will mount broad campaigns to recruit workers from more workforce-rich states like California. That effort, of course, will exacerbate the pressure on California and other states to supply their own workforce needs.

Future Job Skill Requirements

As if the retirement-driven slowdown in overall labor force growth were not a large enough problem, it coincides with a period of expected increase in skill requirements. This is part and parcel of the shift toward a creative, high-tech, and information-based economy. Over the course of recent decades the California economy has steadily shifted toward industries that require higher education, and within those sectors, reliance on workers with BAs or more advanced degrees has only intensified. For example, the fastest-growing area of the economy is the broad services sector, in which many of the workers are highly educated: in 2002, 25.0 percent of workers in this sector held a BA degree, and 15.9 percent held a more advanced degree. Moreover, skill requirements in this sector have been increasing gradually over time.[5]

Forecasts of economic growth in California call for continued increases in college-educated employment. A study conducted by David Neumark for the Public Policy Institute of California built on other studies to prepare a broad-based view of future skill requirements. Between 2000 and 2020, the changing mix of industries in the state economy is expected to nudge upward the requirements for workers with BA or more advanced degrees, and this increase will be greater in California than in the United States as a whole.[6] If, in addition, the trends *within* industries continue to follow their recent trend toward employing more college graduates, the implication is that the share of the workforce with a BA degree or higher would need to expand by about one-third in both California and the United States (although it is not likely that this will fully transpire). Another recent study, following simpler procedures, reached a similar conclusion, reporting that although 22.3 percent of California workers in 2002 held a BA degree or higher, a higher share of the growth in workers through 2022 will require a BA—28.3 percent.[7] Based on these studies, a reasonable conclusion is that the California workforce needs to increase the overall share who are college graduates by about one-quarter by 2020.

In fact, virtually all commentators on the future California economy would be likely to concur with the conclusion reached by the Neumark study:

> Projections of California's economic future indicate that the workforce will have to be considerably more educated than it currently is. . . . Thus, it seems likely that the principal challenge posed by economic change in California over the next two decades is for increased investment in human capital, on which a modern, technologically advanced, and service-oriented economy increasingly depends.[8]

The challenge, of course, is that a new workforce cannot be prepared in a single year; it takes a decade or more of schooling, and young workers already launched into the workforce, many with families to support, cannot easily be sent back for retraining. Considerable foresight is required because of the very long pipeline in the educational production of new workers. Regrettably, such early visioning did not transpire a decade ago, or it was not widely heeded. At the time, California leaders understandably were preoccupied with overcoming the debilitating effects of the recession in the early 1990s. Now California must plan its new workforce in a very short time frame, motivated by an urgency unseen in the state since the postwar economic and city building boom of the 1940s.

The New Reliance on a Homegrown Workforce

Is there a shortcut to building a skilled workforce? Couldn't each state simply import workers from other states and nations? That solution would provide a much speedier response to growing needs, and it would avoid the fiscal burden of having to pay for the workers' education. Such a neat solution—if only it would work. One can imagine all fifty states striving to pirate workers from one another, battling over a fixed sum of college graduates. Alternatively, Congress could increase by manyfold the number of visas issued to high-skilled immigrants, but any substantial increase in immigration is not likely to be considered a popular alternative.

The strategy of importing workers is not a new one; in fact, that is largely how California built its workforce in the past, drawing mainly on migrants from other U.S. states. This is revealed by the very low ratio of workers who were born inside California, amounting in 1970 to only 31.0 percent of the California workforce. Among college-educated workers, the proportion was only 29.0 percent, meaning that fully 71.0 percent of college-educated workers had moved to California to take up residence later in their lives. These very low California-born figures do not account for workers who may have come to the state as young children with their parents and who attended primary and secondary schools here. Still others may have moved to California to attend college, then stayed on afterwards. Nonetheless, birth in California does prove to be a very useful recorded benchmark, one we must rely on for lack of other data on the age of arrival in California of workers from other states.[9]

We have somewhat greater knowledge, ironically, about residents born in other nations than about those born elsewhere in the United States, as highlighted in a recent study of changes in California's working-age population. In the last quarter-century, from 1980 and 2005, fully two-thirds of the working-age population growth in the state was provided by foreign-born residents.[10] Indeed, new immigrants accounted for about 60 percent of labor force growth nationwide between 2000 and 2004.[11] In the coming quarter-century, by contrast, barely one-third of the labor force growth in California will be covered by immigration. Instead, the bulk of the labor force needs are expected to be filled by the grown children of immigrants, most of them Latino. These new additions to the workforce will have been largely schooled in California.

In the past there has been a steady rise in the proportion of the workforce that was born in California, increasing from 29.0 percent in 1970 to 35.3 percent in 2000 among college-educated workers.[12] But the increase has been far greater among younger workers, who reflect more recent trends. Older workers reflect an earlier era, so that among college-educated workers ages fifty-five to sixty-four in 2000, only 26.1 percent were California-born (table 10.2). However, among young, college-educated workers, 39.8 percent were California-born, including 51.6 percent of Latinos in 2000. At the same time, only 14.3 percent of young Asian college-educated workers were California-born. In fact, the share of California-born workers has increased substantially over time in every racial-ethnic group except Asians. Despite the tremendous role of immigration in increasing the number of Asian workers, the skilled workforce as a whole has become increasingly homegrown.

There are good reasons to believe that California in the future will become even more reliant on homegrown workers than it was in 2000, and this will likely be true of most other states as well. The sharp slowdown in workforce growth that we have described, combined with the rising demand for skilled workers, will stiffen the competition that each state faces in attracting skilled workers. The high cost of housing in California and the state's possibly faltering quality of life may make California less of a magnet to outsiders than it was in the 1970s and 1980s. Already, as discussed in earlier chapters, we have evidence of California's reduced attraction since 1990 for both immigrants and domestic migrants from other states. And California's employers will face recruitment raids by employers based in other states experiencing even less labor force growth than California. Indeed, the Neumark study observes that "the extent to which in-migration is likely to occur depends in part on how the demand for workers of different educational levels evolves in the rest of the country."[13] Yet that study also foresees that demand for skilled workers

Table 10.2   California-Born Share of Labor Force with BA Degree or Higher, by Age and Ethnicity, California, 2000

	15 to 24	25 to 34	35 to 44	45 to 54	55 to 64	65 to 74	Total
Non-Hispanic white	52.8%	46.4%	42.7%	38.8%	30.3%	26.2%	40.5%
Non-Hispanic black	66.7	50.1	38.7	28.0	9.9	6.7	35.7
Latino	64.8	51.6	40.4	39.7	31.3	25.0	45.1
Non-Hispanic Asian	25.8	14.3	12.3	10.1	6.9	12.0	12.6
Total	48.4	39.8	36.2	33.6	26.1	23.7	35.3

Source: PUMS, 2000, California.

will be strong in the rest of the United States. The obvious conclusion is "therefore that the state's economy may have to rely, in large part, on boosting educational levels among the state's current residents."[14]

What has not been appreciated to date is the greater retention value of California's homegrown workforce. Workers raised in California have strategic importance because their attachment to remaining in the state is so much stronger. In contrast, footloose workers who are imported to California may not constitute as reliable a basis for building the state's future workforce. Consider these facts: of the college-educated residents living in California, one in nine (10.9 percent) subsequently moved out of the state in just five years' time.[15] This assessment is not based on newly minted college graduates but on all seasoned adults age thirty to thirty-four, the prime age for building a skilled workforce. The point deserving attention is the difference that California birth makes. Of those college graduates who were born in other states, fully 18.4 percent departed within five years. In contrast, the California-born residents were much less footloose: only 6.1 percent out-migrated (table 10.3). A similar pattern is observable for each racial-ethnic group: California-born college graduates were three times as likely to remain in California as those who were born in other states. Cumulated over successive five-year intervals, as much as half of the non-California-born skilled workforce could be lost by the time they turn forty.

The implications for economic development strategies in both California and other states seem clear. The expected shortage of skilled workers ensuing from the baby boomer retirements will generate a battle for skilled workers. California is already less able to rely on imported workers than was once pos-

Table 10.3   Rates at Which College-Educated Workers Migrated from California to Other States Between 1995 and 2000

	All Races	Non-Hispanic White	Non-Hispanic Black	Asian and Pacific Islander	Latino
Total	10.9	12.5	13.4	7.2	7.0
Born in other states	18.4	18.6	20.2	14.2	15.7
Born in other countries	8.2	10.6	20.9	7.1	7.0
California-born	6.1	6.7	4.0	4.3	4.1

Source: Census 2000, PUMS 5 percent file for California and the United States.
Notes: Migration period is 1995 to 2000; "college-educated" is BA degree or higher; the selected age cohort was thirty to thirty-four in 1995 and thirty-five to thirty-nine in 2000.

sible, and the trend should accelerate toward a higher degree of homegrown dependence in the workforce. Moreover, as we have noted, skilled workers recruited to California generally have more questionable attachments and cannot be retained in the state as readily. They are easy targets for out-of-state recruiters. For that reason, workers born out of state will provide a much less reliable basis for building the economy. Immigrants from other countries and states will bring highly valued vitality and innovation, but California-born workers will constitute the core of the skilled workforce in California.

Call it favoritism, if you will, but an added objective seems justified in this regard. It should go without saying that parents in California, who are also the taxpayers, would surely prefer that it be their children who take on the high-skilled and better-paid jobs being created in the state. From the public perspective, if their children are going to remain in the state, as seems fairly likely, it is better for all if they become high-earning taxpayers rather than be cast aside in favor of newcomers who arrive with better preparation. For all these reasons, the state needs to focus more on developing a skilled workforce that is homegrown.

Will the Workforce Decline in Quality?

A major question is whether or not California, or any state, can produce workers of sufficient quality to sustain a continued increase in its skilled workforce. Grave concern about this has been expressed in many quarters, and indeed, there are signs that the trend in rising workforce quality is threatening to level off or even decline. Yet contradictory evidence drawn from short-term indicators suggests that there has been a recent spurt in skill levels in some sectors of the population. It is not clear that this increase can be sustained, and in any event, the growing polarization in skill level between population groups is surely not desirable.

The Outlook for Slower Increases in the College-Educated Workforce

The preceding review found that economic forecasts call for a continued increase in the college-educated share of the workforce. As an approximate benchmark, we have ascertained that employment trends in California call for an increase between 2000 and 2020 of about one-quarter in the workforce share that hold a BA or more advanced degree. Between 1970 and 2000, the share with a BA degree or more increased from 14.8 percent to 28.1 percent, in the prime workforce ages of twenty-five to sixty-four, and the forecast would call for a further increase to 35.0 percent by 2020.

Many warning signs suggest that this increase will not materialize. The primary evidence is that the rate of increase slowed markedly in the United States between the 1990 and 2000 censuses, suggesting a leveling off that led even the Census Bureau to ask, "Have We Reached the Top?"[16] One has to ask if both the United States and California workforces are approaching a point where average skill levels might even decline. This trend is out of sync with the growing demand for higher-skilled workers, and it is also out of step with the economic incentives for higher education due to the growing premiums paid to college graduates versus high school graduates.[17]

A major basis for concern is the changing ethnic makeup of the working-age population. A widely cited study by Patrick J. Kelly drew upon Census Bureau projections of the population to demonstrate that the combination of faster-growing ethnic groups with much lower educational attainment will lead to a decline in the overall educational attainment of the workforce in the nation and most individual states. This conclusion is reached if it is assumed that existing gaps in educational attainment between racial and ethnic groups will persist in the future.[18] For the United States as a whole, the share of adults with a BA or more advanced degree would be expected to fall by 1.0 percentage point from 2000 to 2020. California would experience the second-greatest decline in the fifty states (after New Mexico), with its BA share falling by

2.6 percentage points. Kelly concludes that it is necessary to improve the educational attainment of the rapidly growing low-achieving groups if we are to forestall this outcome. The logic of the analysis has been widely endorsed, even if the analytical results might prove somewhat exaggerated.[19] They certainly underscore the impending collision and the need for action.

A different factor working to slow the increase in educational attainment may be even more potent. The high rate of achievement among the baby boom cohort about to retire could help to lower the BA share in the future. Both in California and the United States, the older cohorts are much better educated now than before, making it harder for young cohorts entering the workforce to push up the average. As recently as 1980 there was a wide gap between the BA shares of the California population ages fifty-five to sixty-four (14.8 percent) and those ages twenty-five to thirty-four (24.2 percent).[20] Thus, as the older group moved into retirement, they could be easily replaced by a younger generation that was much better educated, thereby causing a rise in the average educational level in the prime working ages. By 2000, however, all had changed. At that time the share of the older group with a BA degree or better had climbed to 28.0 percent, and the BA share of the population ages twenty-five to thirty-four was actually *lower*, at 26.6 percent. This reversal between young and old is expected to become more extreme in the coming decade. Hans Johnson's study for the Public Policy Institute of California emphasizes that the baby boomer cohorts are the best educated in history, exceeding the educational attainment of both preceding and following generations. Johnson explains this as partly due to male baby boomers' added incentive to get a student deferment by attending college during the Vietnam War years.[21] The census data show that in 2000 the BA share among California residents ages forty-five to fifty-four was 31.2 percent, three percentage points higher than for the cohort preceding them into retirement. When these workers begin to retire, the young replacements will need to have an even higher BA share in order to forestall decline in the average for the working-age population. Thus, the slowdown in the BA share driven by ethnic changes will be amplified by the baby boom retirement effect.

Differences between women and men also may depress the BA share in the future. Much of the rising BA share among working-age people in the past has been created by the catchup of young women, whose educational attainment was once well below that of men but whose college graduation rates have now begun to exceed those of men. Back in 1980, young men in California held substantially higher BA shares than women (27.5 percent versus 21.1 percent), but by 2000 women ages twenty-five to thirty-four had caught up to men and surpassed their BA shares (25.1 percent among men versus 28.2 percent among women). Strong progress in college completion was observed among women in every major racial-ethnic group, and in all groups save Asian Americans, women now surpass men's educational attainment. Without this rapid progress among women, the overall BA share among young adults would have declined from 1980 to 2000. Looking ahead, continued rapid increases for women may not be as likely, since women with the highest college aptitude and the most neglected opportunities have probably already been tapped. Moreover, since women are only half the population, future gains in overall college completion also require a revival of men's college participation, which has declined recently in every group except Asian Americans.

A final factor limiting future educational gains is the inadequate facility capacity in the state of California for producing as many college graduates as desired by the student body and the public. Rapid growth in the student-age population is often termed "tidal wave II," harkening back to an earlier wave of growth in the 1960s. Projections suggest an increase in enrollment at the undergraduate level of nearly half a million students within one decade.[22] Should physical facilities and staffing fail to keep pace with this 20 percent increase in enrollment, the anticipated increase will be stifled. Thus, the social and economic potential for educational upgrading is subject to physical capacity constraints.

Polarization and Recent Increases in Educational Attainment

For all the reasons cited here, we would expect the rising BA share in the California workforce to falter and even turn downward. In fact, the overall trend since 1980 has been surprisingly variable: after first rising for decades, the BA share turned downward through the early 1990s, but then rebounded upward again. In fact, the most recent trend defies most expectations. This inconsistency in the trend generates substantial uncertainty about the coming decade, making it especially difficult to foresee the future with confidence. The good news is that, with trends so changeable and poorly determined, perhaps they are more susceptible to the influence of policy direction.

From 1980 to 1990, the share of twenty-five- to thirty-four-year-olds attaining a BA degree declined in the United States for the first time in decades, but beginning about 1995 the share resumed its upward trend, and at an accelerated rate. This resurgence occurred in all major racial-ethnic groups except Latinos, although it did occur among native-born Latinos.[23] A Census Bureau study seeking to forecast the likely trajectory of educational attainment in the nation found considerable uncertainty about whether this upward turn in 2000 was anomalous or would be sustained, although the authors were inclined to the optimistic view.[24]

Unfortunately, the surprising rise in the BA share early in the twenty-first century has been accompanied by increased polarization. Latinos have not generally participated in the current upsurge in college graduation, and so a markedly widening gap is fracturing the workforce. The post-1995 trend in California is revealed in annual data collected from 1995 through 2005 (figure 10.1). Even though there is considerable fluctuation from year to year, owing to the small sample of the California population in the Current Population Survey, the trend line is clear-cut. The very low BA share among Latinos of working age showed very slight increase—barely 1.0 percentage point—over the ten-year period. In contrast, the BA share among non-Latinos, already higher than 32 percent in 1995, increased by an additional 8.9 percentage points by 2005. Combining the two portions of the working-age population, the overall BA share increased 5.1 percentage points in a decade, tracking at a pace of change that reflects the combined weight of the Latino and non-Latino populations. The increased BA share in just ten years was nearly as great as that recorded in the twenty years from 1980 to 2000.[25]

It is unknown how long this current upsurge might continue because it departs from recent history and defies all the forces that are expected to slow the rate of increase in the BA share. The only possible explanation supporting an upsurge in the BA share is the growing premium of higher earnings paid to college graduates relative to others. Whether that is sufficient to reshape the careers of both younger and older workers is unlikely, and indeed evidence indicates that not all demographic subgroups have received the news about a higher education premium.

More likely this period of resurgence will be brief and is doomed to end. We must underscore that the period through 2005 precedes the baby boomer retirements and their expected impact of reducing education levels between 2010 and 2030. Closer analysis also shows that the rate of increase in both California and the United States has been nearly twice as great among women as among men. The female trend has not yet reached the point of slowing

Figure 10.1   Growing Achievement Gap Between Twenty-Five- to Sixty-Four-Year-Old Hispanics and Non-Hispanics in Percentage with a BA Degree or Higher, 1995 to 2005

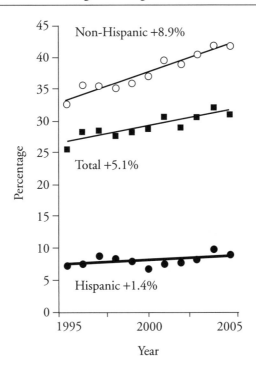

Source: Current Population Survey.

progress that we have expected, but once it does, that slowdown also will curb the upward rise in the population's BA share. Nonetheless, were the current trends to prevail as long as through 2020, the overall BA share at ages twenty-five to sixty-four would reach 39 percent, matching or exceeding the requirements forecast by employers.

That skill target would be achieved, however, at great social and economic risk, for even greater polarization would be yielded in California. Should the trends continue, a BA share of about 55 percent would be found among non-Latinos, compared to about 11 percent among Latinos. The gap between Latinos and others would have widened to forty-four percentage points, compared to the gap in 1995 of about twenty-five percentage points. Such extreme polarization is clearly undesirable. It would be much healthier for society and the economy to raise the BA share among Latinos. Not to mention that the unexplained rise in college graduation among non-Latinos is not reliable and should not be counted on to persist. Indeed, extrapolation of this trend poses a risky basis for continuing to raise the overall education level of the workforce. A sounder basis, one with social equity advantages as well, is to promote more equal educational access among Latinos whose economic potential has not yet been exploited. A "diversity scorecard" can help reorient institutions to better develop neglected human resources.[26]

Growing the New Middle-Class Taxpayer Base

When the baby boomers retire, they will generate heavy fiscal impacts that need to be absorbed. The retirees will continue to pay state and federal taxes, albeit at a somewhat reduced level, but the major impact will be their increased drain on the public treasury through entitlement programs that support the elderly. As explored in previous chapters, Social Security, Medicare, and other programs will consume increasingly large shares of federal and state budgets. Not to deny the seniors their due, but we have to ask: who will cover these bills? A future population of middle-aged and younger taxpayers who are well educated and prosperous, or taxpayers with lower incomes than today? If the latter, it may prove difficult to sustain the benefit levels of seniors in the future.

Growing the new base of middle-class taxpayers is closely related to building a skilled workforce. Both hinge on the crucial matter of educational attainment, and both require greater attention to developing the full potential of the Latino segment of the population. The added feature in the case of taxpayers is the relationship between education level and earnings. Higher-income taxpayers obviously can contribute more to the social support of seniors and others than can those who are not paid as well. Thus, the prospects for building a larger base of middle-class taxpayers rest squarely on a second question, following that of how many will be highly educated—namely, how much will a higher education contribute toward higher earnings and higher household income?

The Earnings Gain from Higher Education

The linkage between education and lifetime earnings has been described as "the big payoff." The Census Bureau assesses this link by assuming how much people will earn over their work lives if wage rates hold constant in the future. Work careers can then be summed up as people pass from age to age, with an accumulation of earnings identified separately for those of each education level. The findings for the United States as a whole are that the average college graduate with a bachelor's degree, working full-time year-round, can expect to earn $2.1 million between ages twenty-five and sixty-four.[27] This is greater than the earnings for workers with an associate's degree from a community college by 36.9 percent, and it is 74.5 percent greater than for those with only a high school degree. Of course, those with an advanced degree earn even more, $4.4 million on average for those with a professional degree such as an MBA or law degree. Not all people of a given education level earn the same amount. One important difference is that women at each educational level historically have earned about two-thirds to three-quarters as much as men, although the gap is smaller for more recent graduates.[28]

In the context of the demographic transition, the differences between racial-ethnic groups are especially relevant. White non-Hispanic workers earn roughly 20 percent more than other workers with the same educational degree, but the amount of increase in earnings associated with a higher education is roughly similar for all groups, as summarized in figure 10.2. All groups appear to gain a comparable advantage with an advanced degree, although the weaker benefit of a bachelor's degree for Latinos could prove somewhat discouraging to those thinking of advancing from an associate's degree.[29] In California the earnings of Latinos relative to those of others who hold a bachelor's degree has been estimated as 15 to 23 percent lower, a difference that reflects lower quality of education and possibly discriminatory factors.[30] One projection to 2020 suggests that if all adults in the state have the same educational attainment as white non-Hispanics, and if they receive the same earnings at each education level, the total personal income in the state will be $101.6 billion higher than otherwise expected. On the other hand, if present inequities continue while the racial-ethnic mix of the state proceeds to change, personal income per capita will fall by $2,475 in California—by far the greatest decline of any state.[31] Summed over 40 million residents, that is a lot of lost purchasing power.

As it stands today, shifting from a predominantly white to a Latino workforce would tend to build a population with relatively less education and, at each education level, less earnings. It should go without saying that there is a great benefit for California businesses in generating higher earn-

Figure 10.2   Lifetime Earnings by Education and Race-Ethnicity

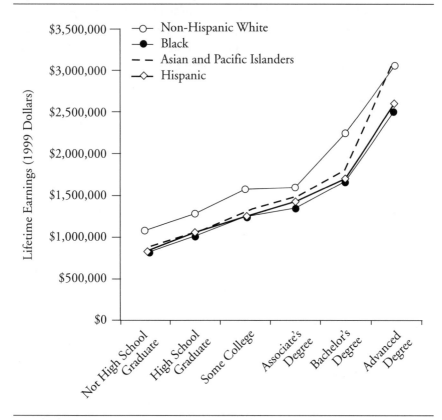

Source: Jennifer Cheeseman Day and Eric C. Newburger, "The Big Payoff: Educational Attainment and Synthetic Estimates of Work-Life Earnings," Current Population Reports, P23-210 (Washington: U.S. Census Bureau, 2002), table 3.
Note: Calculated from ages twenty-five through sixty-four, full-time year-round workers only, assuming the wage rates at each age and education level continue in the future.

ings among consumers. As described later in the chapter, there also are clear benefits for the public sector and fellow taxpayers because higher earnings can support higher tax contributions. To forestall declines in these economic capacities, all interests would prefer to see educational attainments increase among Latinos. It also would be desirable to enhance the quality of this education so that Latinos can command more equal pay based on their credentials.

Increased Tax Contributions from
More-Educated Residents

One of the first California studies to estimate the economic benefits of elevating Latino educational attainments was prepared by the California Research Bureau, a state agency. Elias Lopez and his associates estimated that the effect of educating Latinos at the levels of non-Latinos would advance the wages of the state's 4.4 million Latino workers from $88 billion to $116 billion (in 1998 dollars).[32] The net increase of $28 billion would spur increases in sales taxes and other public revenue, in particular yielding an increase in state income tax revenues of $1.7 billion. The addition of this much income to the state economy would have multiplier effects yielding many economic benefits. The authors emphasize a distributional impact that would also benefit the public sector: "Because of Latinos' higher wages and lower unemployment rates, fewer of them would require social services (e.g., welfare, food stamps, Medi-Cal)."[33]

A similar analysis conducted in the state of Texas also assessed the impact of closing socioeconomic differentials among racial-ethnic groups on incomes and tax revenues. The state demographer, Steve Murdock, and his associates project state tax collections that would be $18.2 billion (in 2000 dollars) higher in 2040 if Latinos could be advanced to the income levels of Anglos (white non-Hispanics).[34] Although the projection might seem fanciful, and it is not meant as an absolute prediction, the alternative scenario is less attractive. If income disparities remain in place rather than closing, the authors find, state revenues per household would decline by about 10 percent.

The benefits of investing in higher education in California were recently addressed in a comprehensive fashion by a team of researchers at the University of California at Berkeley. Henry Brady, Michael Hout, and Jon Stiles have concluded that greater educational attainment leads to higher earnings and "will produce a windfall for state coffers due to increased revenue from income taxes and decreased spending on social services and incarceration."[35] Other studies have also emphasized this two-part benefit from increased tax revenues, on the one hand, and decreased service dependence and law enforcement on the other.[36] The conclusion emphasized in the Berkeley study is that for every new dollar invested in raising college completion rates, the state will receive a net return on investment of three dollars. Although the obstacle is that the investment is required up front, it is estimated that the fiscal pay-back will be received by the time the college graduate reaches the age of thirty-five, and the total size of that impact could be dramatic. Summed across all members of a high school graduating class, the benefit of investing in increased college-going compared to current conditions amounts to nearly $3 billion in extra tax revenue projected over their lifetimes. Repeated across successive waves of graduating classes, this could add up to real money.

Plans for Elevating Latino Educational Attainment

In theory, it would be nice if Latinos graduated from college at the rates that white non-Hispanics do, but how realistic is that hope? Even if the funding makes sense in theory, is this quest too impractical to risk our scarce tax dollars? These are fair questions that many skeptics are sure to raise, and they deserve serious consideration because there are risks on both sides. On the one hand, budgets are extremely tight in the public sector, and no one wants to waste precious resources by pouring them down a so-called rat hole. Yet, at the same time, if we do nothing different, the inexorable process of demographic transition will lead to a near-certain decline in both incomes and public revenue. Either of these feared outcomes reflects an outlook of despair. The decision to invest in a better future takes control of that fate and makes prudent sense, but this future of hope can be achieved only if there is a plan for using those funds effectively.

Fortunately, a number of leading experts in the education field have put their minds to work on this challenge. Even though raising the educational achievement levels of Latinos is an issue of national significance, the burden of meeting this challenge will fall on only a handful of states where the great majority of Latino youth reside: California and Texas, followed by New York, Florida, and Illinois. Federal assistance may be warranted, but the bulk of the funding and leadership must emerge from each of these states, and solutions will need to be worked out at the state and local levels.

One national study commissioned by the Hispanic Scholarship Fund assessed the feasibility of doubling the rate of Latino college graduation within ten years. This goal was initially set by the Hispanic Scholarship Fund in 1996, with a target date of 2006. As of 2005, the national percentage of Latinos ages twenty-five to thirty-four who hold a BA degree remained stuck at 11.3 percent, well below the 18 percent goal. The RAND Corporation laid out a strategy for doubling the BA share among Latinos in the United States.

Operating and capital costs would need to increase by $6.5 billion, but that would be exceeded by an estimated two-to-one benefit-to-cost ratio for the public sector, and by a four-to-one ratio if private benefits are added. However, RAND noted that additional support programs tailored to the needs of Latino students would be crucial to the success of the plan. These would include programs focused on keeping students in college as well as preventing high school dropout, with interventions coordinated across all levels of education. Such additional support costs are difficult to estimate, but RAND concluded that "even if the highest cost were assumed, the public would still reap more revenues than it would expend on meeting the goal."[37]

Similarly, the California Research Bureau called for a coordinated strategy to elevate Latinos' socioeconomic status, one that would link not only all levels of education but also employers, redevelopment agencies, health care providers, and pensions and retirement systems.[38] This kind of comprehensive strategy is warranted because of what the National Research Council study of the Hispanic future judged the accumulated disadvantages that pose a barrier to educational opportunities.[39] The pathways to success begin with active parental involvement at home, but expert counseling is needed at each stage from preschool onward. For example, a study by the Tomas Rivera Policy Institute highlighted the lack of "college knowledge" among Latino parents about such things as the necessary gateway courses for the college-bound or even the availability of financial aid that would make college possible for their children.[40] Failure to anticipate and plan positively within the family may derail many children well before they reach the age of eighteen.

A feasible path to elevating enrollment must also identify sources of funding to make the needed investments. It does not matter if the investments pay off on paper over the long run—states need to find the funds in the present budget. Those funds need to be planned as part of a comprehensive strategy to meet future needs in higher education; this is the sort of strategy or plan that California currently lacks. To address this problem, Nancy Shulock and her colleagues have proposed a "shared solutions" strategy in California.[41] The financing framework presented in their study recognizes that state appropriations cannot be increased enough within current fiscal restrictions (26 percent would be required). Instead of implementing that single solution, they suggest combining three additional solutions, including increased student fees, greater institutional efficiencies, and greater systemic efficiencies linking high schools and institutions of higher education. It might be noted that the emphasis on efficiencies is also helpful for gaining political support for any increase in state funds.

The Immigrant Assimilation Bonus

Left undiscussed in much of the education literature is the issue of immigration and immigrant assimilation. The data collected from educational institutions contain no information on those issues. The emphasis instead is on gender and race or Hispanic origin. The absence of information on length of residence in the United States creates a blind spot and weakens our understanding of future trends. In fact, the prospects for the educational upgrading of the Latino population are far more favorable than generally assumed because of what might be termed the *assimilation bonus*. Longer-settled residents are more likely to benefit from U.S. schooling than those who are recently arrived. This is true especially of young adults who arrived long ago as children, and even more so of those whose families arrived in the United States one or two generations earlier. Immigration scholars have amply demonstrated how much greater is the educational attainment of the children and grandchildren of Latino immigrants.[42]

Failure to account for the assimilation bonus that is likely to occur in the next decade has led to a much more discouraged outlook than can be justified. As discussed in preceding chapters, recent immigrant arrivals predominate in decades when immigration soars, but the average length of settlement is growing longer now that immigration has slowed its acceleration and the children of previous immigrants (the second generation) are coming of age. (This changing length of settlement was summarized for young Latinos living in California in figure 6.1.)

What exactly is the impact of length of settlement on the odds of finishing high school or earning a BA degree? Data compiled for Latinos in California provide a good indication of what can be expected (table 10.4). Among all the young Latinos in California ages twenty-five to thirty-four, only 55.4 percent have completed high school and 7.3 percent have earned a bachelor's degree. Those who are native-born have substantially higher rates of achievement, rising above 80 percent high school completion and reaching as high as 15.1 percent college completion.[43] Immigrants in this age group who have lived more than twenty years in the United States also fare much better than more recent arrivals because the longer-settled ones would have arrived as young children and thus attended school in this country. But in most depictions of

Table 10.4   Educational Attainment of California Latinos at Age
Twenty-Five to Thirty-Four, by Length of Settlement

	High School or Higher	BA Degree or Higher
Foreign-born		
Zero to nine years	37.1%	4.4%
Ten to nineteen years	39.1	3.4
Twenty years or more	61.6	8.0
Native-born		
Second-generation	83.5	15.1
Third-generation or more	82.4	11.5
All persons	55.4	7.3

Source: Current Population Survey, 1998, 2000, and 2002 pooled.

Latino educational achievement, all these different subsets of Latinos are mixed together, with their average achievement weighted by the respective sizes of the different subgroups.

The distorting influence of the large concentration of immigrant *newcomers* has been a theme throughout this book. Here in the education data, those newcomers are subsumed in the general category "Hispanic" and mixed with other Latinos who may have lived in the United States for more than twenty years, who were born in the United States, or whose parents were born here. Under conditions of rising immigration, more and more of the Hispanic category takes on the character of new immigrants. When immigration stabilizes, as it has in California, the longer-settled immigrants take on greater weight and begin to sway the averages for all Latinos. These dynamics are masked within most education data and prevent us from seeing the underlying trend that enables us to make a more reliable forecast.

In fact, there is a substantial bonus in higher educational attainment that is likely to derive from the growing length of settlement of adults and youth from immigrant families. This can be seen when we apply the population forecasts by generation and length of settlement that were developed by the California Demographic Futures project.[44] Data reported in table 6.1 describe the growing length of settlement among California Latinos ages twenty-five to thirty-four. In 2030 there will be roughly half as many recent immigrant arrivals and twice as many native-born. When combined with the data presented here on educational attainments, we can project how much the average educational attainment of Latinos will shift even if the achievement rates hold exactly constant in every category. The simple shift toward longer-settled residents will raise the high school completion share by one-fifth, from 55.4 percent to 68.1 percent, and will raise the bachelor's degree share by two-fifths, from 7.3 percent to 10.3 percent.

This assimilation bonus promises several benefits. For one, these increases from growing length of settlement, by themselves, are far less than may be desired, but they provide a significant boost to other efforts and can be built upon for even greater success. In fact, recognition of how greatly recent immigration has biased our perceptions of Latinos' prospects may make the new plans to increase Latino achievements seem more realistic. The low average attainment levels have exaggerated the impression that Latinos are not interested in school and have a low propensity to succeed. In fact, the evidence of sharp increases in educational achievement among those with deeper roots in the United States indicates a readiness for educational upward mobility. This readiness lays the basis for even stronger gains if stimulated by proactive educational policies. An overall implication, finally, is that the ranks of the Latino college-educated and, more broadly, of middle-class taxpayers are more primed for expansion than past trends would have us believe.

Conclusion: Is Education a Cost or a Benefit?

Far from a catastrophic collision with the future economy, the new demographic changes actually hold some promise of helping to solve future problems. But it depends on what policymakers choose to make of the human resources of California and of the nation as a whole. With or without the new immigrants and the growing Latino population, the baby boomers are still going to retire. The challenge is replacing them in number and quality, in both the workforce and the taxpayer base.

This chapter has reviewed the essential facts of our future situation, some of which are well known and others of which may have been overlooked. Indeed, the Latino population that carries such weight in our economic future has far lower educational attainment than other groups. If nothing else changes from the educational disparities we observe today, the growing reliance on this disadvantaged group will depress the future skill level of the workforce and lower the tax revenues contributed to meet a broad array of growing public needs.

Of the possible solutions to the challenge ahead, only one appears likely to be effective. But first, it is natural that policymakers would wish to try out the alternatives that seem the easiest. One favored approach is to make no changes and simply let the conditions of the early 2000s persist, including the increasingly wide disparities between Latinos and others. However, it is certain that some aspects of current conditions will not persist. The inexorable processes of the demographic transition ensure that all of us will grow older year by year. The baby boomers will definitely retire and leave a void in the workforce. Today's children will grow up, enter the workforce, and enter the ranks of taxpayers or service dependents. For its part, the economy will try to operate with the reduced skill levels available, and the public sector will attempt to raise tax revenue from a diminished middle class. So we have a contradiction: to allow conditions to persist, to make no changes, is to ensure a drastic and undesirable change.

A second approach is to raise the college education level of non-Latinos even higher in order to offset the low achievements of Latinos. That strategy, now under way, appears to be working in the short run, but it cannot be sustained once the losses begin from the retirements of the highly educated baby boomers. Moreover, encouraging such increased polarization among residents would only increase social costs and waste productive human resources. Further, when the increases in college graduates among non-Latinos began to taper off, as must be expected, we would be left with both an inadequate workforce and the accumulated social problems. A tactic of such extreme polarization has only short-term advantage and should not be judged acceptable as part of any solution that can sustain the future.

A third possible strategy is to continue importing workers from other states and nations; this has been a principal strategy used in California in the past, but as I have argued, it will not work in the future. Already California's workforce is becoming more homegrown, and once the baby boomer retirements begin in earnest, the competition for skilled workers will deny California and all other states their sources of outside recruits. Indeed, other states will attempt to raid workers from each other, especially from California, which has a younger population and a larger pool of potential workers. Fortunately, the data presented here show how much more committed are California's homegrown workers. College-educated workers born in other states are three times as likely to move out of state; indeed, as many as half depart before they reach the age of forty.

The homegrown workforce strategy, the fourth alternative, is the only reliable way to plan a workforce to cover future needs. Investing in today's children requires difficult budgeting decisions, but it returns a reward that experts estimate is two to four times the size of the investment. And we are likely to see those homegrown workers remaining as committed citizens of California. Given that the majority of the youth to be educated in California—indeed, the majority of the future labor force—are Latino, there is no other sensible alternative. As difficult as this task might seem, there is much evidence that offers hope: the unrecognized assimilation bonus of the next decade, the evidence of how Latinos convert their added education into higher earnings and taxpaying contributions, and the positive returns on investment that many have estimated. Ultimately, we must choose to pursue the workforce investment strategy because the alternatives are so undesirable for all residents, Latino and non-Latino alike. Homegrown investment is truly the foundation for choosing a hopeful future rather than continuing in despair.

Chapter 11

Sharing the American Dream: The Linked Interests of Older Home Sellers and Younger Home Buyers

OWNERSHIP OF one's home is so widely valued in this country that it is often termed the American Dream. Property ownership signifies attainment of a middle-class standard of living, and for immigrants it has a special meaning of landed settlement. Indeed, attainment of homeownership represents proof of the opportunities in America to get ahead by hard work, and thus homeownership is the most tangible symbol of a major strand in the social contract, as discussed in chapter 8.[1] Attainment of homeownership is not only a principal indicator of economic and social well-being but also the primary measure of housing achievement in the United States.[2] The recognized benefits of homeownership are substantial, including a more stable and secure housing environment for families, the ability to customize physical space to meet changing needs and tastes, and a property interest in the governance of neighborhoods and cities. For all these reasons, the federal and state governments provide tax breaks and other incentives to promote homeownership among residents.

Despite these merits, homeownership is a topic full of contradictions and paradoxes. An overriding feature of homeownership in many people's eyes is its high price of attainment and the investment it represents: it costs a lot of money, but it can make a lot of money. This turns the notion of affordability on its head. A paradox to be explained is that when housing becomes *less* affordable, people flock to it more, but when it becomes more affordable, they avoid its purchase. In addition, opinions about the affordability of homeownership are often totally reversed between those who have it and those who do not. On the one hand, we often hear public concern over the problem of worsening housing affordability. Such public hand-wringing is displayed by public officials, housing advocates, and renters who would like to buy their first home. After purchasing a home, however, people view the issue completely differently. For homeowners, rising house prices are a good thing from which they derive a direct financial benefit. This is no small matter, because ownership of a home is an investment that often represents the largest share of a family's wealth portfolio. Given that three-quarters or more of voters already own a home, voters' self-interest about rising prices often contradicts public concern about affordability problems.

Homeownership is about private gain, but it is also about public investment. Indeed, homeownership is the quintessential product of our mixed economy of public and private investment. On the one hand, each homeowner stands to gain privately from rising home prices, but homeownership is stimulated by the largest public subsidies in the income tax code, and home purchasers who deliver the profit to sellers are heavily backed by public education investments. In turn, as part of the social contract, homeowners contribute the property taxes needed to make local government run. Those tax monies support education, which in turn supports higher housing prices. More than just the premium paid by buyers for homes in better school districts, educational investments in children lead to higher-skilled adults who can pay higher prices for homes.

The contradiction most germane to the thesis of this book is that, even though buyers and sellers are supposed to be competing with opposite intent in the purchase negotiations, in reality they are locked in a long-term partnership. Home buyers need home sellers to help them buy their homes, and home sellers need home buyers to offer them a good price. Even though these two forms of help may be separated by ten or twenty years in time, mutual self-interest suggests that homeowners invest in future home buyers, fostering their education and career development so that they will be able to pay a higher price for homes when they are offered. This partnership is invisible at times, but when the masses of baby boomers begin to relinquish their high-priced homes, the linked interests of sellers and buyers will become fully evident.

The preceding chapter discussed the impact of the demographic transition on the workforce and the issues that are especially worrisome to business owners, workforce development agencies, and personnel managers. The average worker, by contrast, may be less concerned about being replaced on the job when he or she retires. The two-thirds of U.S. households that are home-owning, however, and especially the three-quarters of older people who are homeowners, may feel much more acute interest in the impact of the demographic transition on their home values. This chapter argues that the only way to foster rising prices and at the same time make homeownership more broadly accessible is to bring more of the younger generation into the middle class and enhance their economic capacity. Public investment in higher education is essential for stimulating their social and economic progress. Any major consequences of this progress for home prices would reinforce the previous chapter's conclusions about the workforce and the taxpaying advantages of better-educated citizens. Every homeowner should take note.

During the demographic transition, the new prospect of diminished skills in the future workforce and a reduced middle class could undermine the continued growth in house prices. Demographic change will work to lower, on average, the financial capacity of young, would-be homeowners at the same time as it is driving up the number of retirees who are would-be home sellers. The confrontation between these two forces of change darkens the horizon a decade ahead. Whereas the young will benefit from falling prices, the financial security of older citizens is clearly threatened. Particularly hard hit will be older homeowners who are seeking to trade down or otherwise cash in their housing investments to support their retirement.[3] Recognition of this threat to personal fortunes could create a shared interest between these older homeowners and the young aspiring home buyers of the new generation.

For the moment, the tremendous price boom of 2002 to 2005 has cast aside any worries about the impact of demographic change on house prices. True, a steady parade of news stories trumpets the risk that the boom in house prices is just a bubble ready to burst, and some housing markets have already begun their decline. Burst or not, prices surely will settle to a much more sedate pace of change. The question not asked during these bubble debates has been whether there will still be enough high-priced buyers five or ten years after the boom, especially if more of the buyers are Latino. And even less on the radar are still more ominous questions related to the inexorable process of aging: How long will it be before the giant baby boom generation reaches the point where it begins to flood the housing market with homes for sale, many of them in the high-priced category beyond the reach of the rising new generation? Could it be that we are poised for a *generational housing bubble* of epic proportions? Although it would be premature to specify the timing and magnitude of such a bubble, it is possible to begin to assess its outlines in this chapter.

How the fortunes of aging home sellers are linked with those of immigrant youth is a new question. Once posed, it will not go away, and as time passes its answer will become ever more urgent. When we finally see exactly how their fortunes are linked, it may be too late. As part of the analysis that follows, I estimate the degree to which the attainment of different levels of education can stimulate greater achievement of homeownership and facilitate the purchase of higher-priced homes. To achieve the requisite levels of education, our youth need to devote themselves to their studies more than a decade earlier than the time in their lives when we hope they will be making a house purchase. The adult generations need to help our youth prepare for all their adult roles, including home buying.

As an aid to foresight, I present a number of projections that display reasonable scenarios of home buying and selling. Both the would-be homeowners and the would-be home sellers will find much of interest here, especially given the sizable sums at stake. The projections are developed for California, the state where the demographic changes have proceeded furthest and where housing prices are among the highest.

Unequal Achievement of Homeownership

The homeownership rate in California lags well behind that of the United States as a whole. Although at one time California's homeownership rate approximated the nation's, the share of homeowning California households remained stagnant in the range of 54 to 57 percent from 1950 through 2000, while the nation's homeownership rate climbed from 55 to 66 percent. Indeed, lower rates of homeownership than California's are found only in three states—New York, Hawaii, and Nevada. What held down homeownership in California was the state's heavy reliance on a less-settled population fed by high migration, combined with rapid increases in home prices in the 1970s and 1980s that made homeownership less attainable for newcomers. Rapid racial and ethnic changes are now compounding those earlier forces that depressed homeownership.

The New Groups That Dominate Home Buying

Owning a home is a goal widely shared among immigrants as well as native-born residents. In fact, immigrants have begun to play a crucial role in the housing market of California and the United States, despite their generally lower homeownership rates. Already, from 1990 to 2000, the foreign-born have accounted for a sizable share of the net gains in the number of home-owners—20.7 percent in the United States and 73.9 percent in California.[4] Housing experts have declared that the growth in the number of immigrant home buyers forms an essential stabilizing force in the housing market as the giant baby boom generation passes its peak home-buying age.[5]

Real estate analysts have been commenting on the demographic revolution in California's housing market for several years. It is obvious from the names displayed in property transactions. Where once Smith was the number-one name among buyers (as recently as 1997), by 2002 that name had fallen to fourth most common.[6] Similarly, Johnson had been third and now was only ninth most common. Instead, of the ten most common surnames among home buyers in 2002, six were Spanish and two were Asian—Nguyen, a highly common Vietnamese name, and Lee, common among Chinese, Korean, and some English-stock Californians. Garcia, the top-ranked name, had risen from third over the last ten years, and Lopez had increased from tenth to fifth most common, Hernandez from twelfth to sixth, and Martinez from eleventh to seventh. By 2005 all of the top five names among home buyers in California were Hispanic, as were four of the top ten names nationwide (compared to two in 2000).[7] Clearly, Latinos have become much more prominent in the housing market. The future trajectory is likely to follow their growing share of the population.

A disquieting thought is that a market dominated by Latinos might not command prices as high as sellers would like. The evidence is that home buyers with Spanish surnames pay about three-quarters as high a price as do buyers whose last name is Smith or Johnson.[8] They are not paying lower prices for the same house; rather, the evidence is that Latinos are concentrated in lower-priced brackets. A saving element, from the standpoint of sellers, could be that Asian buyers pay higher prices—the Lees pay 28 percent higher amounts for their homes than the Smiths, while the Nguyens pay 11 percent higher. It is not clear that there will be enough Asian buyers to offset the declining numbers of Smiths or the rising numbers of Garcias. That concern is examined more closely in the next section.

Differences Between Racial-Ethnic Groups

Access to homeownership is unevenly distributed by race and ethnicity. In 2005 white non-Hispanic households in California had the highest rate of homeownership of any race group (66.7 percent), while the lowest was among African American households (40.2 percent).[9] Latinos have a slightly higher rate, 47.0 percent, while Asian and Pacific Islander households have a higher homeownership rate, albeit still below that of whites (56.9 percent). Also observed is that native-born Latinos and Asian Americans have moderately higher homeownership rates than is common among immigrants in the same racial-ethnic group (see table 11.1). This categorization is very rough, because it pools all age groups together, and it also lumps together new immigrant arrivals and longer-settled immigrants. In fact, people who are older or longer settled have had more time to acquire better housing circumstances.

Not all homes are of equal quality or desirability. The best measure for comparing the homes owned by different groups is the reported house value. Table 11.1 reports the median house values recorded in the 2005 American Community Survey (ACS).[10] These values are reported near the crest of the great housing price boom and provide a reasonable indicator of the relative gaps in house values between owners of different races or ethnicity. Compared to white, non-Hispanic homeowners, the median house value among black homeowners is only 79 percent as high and among Latinos only 75 percent, as high, but Asians' house values are actually 108 percent of whites'. Unlike homeownership rates, house values are only slightly lower among immigrants than among native-born members of the same racial-ethnic group (table 11.1). Nonetheless, it is notable that even though the values of the homes owned by Asians are higher than those of whites, at the same time their likelihood of buying a home is lower.

House values soared dramatically in the last five years, but more for some groups than others.[11] Among all homeowners in California, the median house value increased 113.7 percent from 2000 to 2005. The greatest increase was among African Americans and Latinos, at 147.4 percent and 149.1 percent, respectively. That increase reflects the much greater growth in demand and

Table 11.1   Disparities of Homeownership and House Value, by Race and Nativity in California

	Owners	Ratio to White	Median Value	Ratio to White	Number of Households
Non-Hispanic white	66.7%	—	$516,142	—	6,785,794
Non-Hispanic black	40.2	0.60	408,151	0.79	823,257
Latino: Total	47.0	0.71	388,016	0.75	3,350,996
Native-born	52.2	0.78	408,920	0.79	1,322,934
Immigrants	43.7	0.66	374,784	0.73	2,028,062
Non-Hispanic Asian: Total	56.9	0.85	555,173	1.08	1,504,517
Native-born	59.5	0.89	562,583	1.09	314,316
Immigrants	56.2	0.84	553,178	1.07	1,190,201
Total	58.3		477,546		12,750,694

Source: American Community Survey 2005 PUMS.
Note: Homeownership is expressed as a percentage of households.

competition at the bottom of the price distribution, where the homes of these racial-ethnic groups are often located. In fact, among white non-Hispanic homeowners, the median house value increased only 119.6 percent (and among Asians 121.7 percent). It might seem curious that every group experienced a greater gain than the average. The explanation is that the median in 2005 included proportionally more Latino homeowners than in 2000, and even though all groups made gains, the growing weight of Latinos held down the average increase. Between 2000 and 2005, Latino homeowners accounted for 40.4 percent of the total growth in the number of homeowners in California, and as a result they increased their share of current homeowners from 17.4 to 21.2 percent. Thus, even during the boom, in which Latinos have prospered more than most, their growing presence is placing downward pressure on house prices overall.

More than race and ethnicity is involved in shaping disparities of homeownership and house value. Older households have much higher attainments in these categories than younger members of the same racial-ethnic group. For example, among white, non-Hispanic households, the homeownership rate is only 35.2 percent at ages twenty-five to thirty-four, rising to 60.8 percent at thirty-five to forty-four, and continuing to rise until it reaches 81.1 percent at ages sixty-five to seventy-four.[12] Similarly, with respect to median house values, young adults typically begin their housing careers in lower-valued units and often do not move into the most expensive units they will attain until late middle age. General price appreciation in the housing market over recent decades has carried previous home buyers to much higher levels, even if they do not move to another unit. And homeowners who move are usually trading up to a larger or better-quality home. Thus, one reason why whites have generally higher homeownership rates and house values is that they are concentrated in older age brackets. Nonetheless, seniors who have reached the culmination of their housing career must find someone younger who can occupy their home at its current high price. Failure to locate such a qualified buyer will cause these sellers to lower the prices on their houses to brackets where a sufficient number of buyers can be found. Thus, in coming decades the house value at the end of a career may be somewhat less than supposed.

The Coming Crisis for Aging Home Sellers
House Values and Supply and Demand

House values are strange beasts. Not as whimsical as the stock market, housing values can still go up and down far more than is warranted by the price of their construction. House values are based on the scarcity of homes and the land they are built on. That scarcity depends on both supply and demand. First there is a relatively fixed supply of land in locations that are convenient to employment centers and attractive to live in. Available land is also tightly regulated by zoning and building codes so that new construction is slow to be permitted. As a result, any increase in demand is too slowly met by new supply, creating a surplus of house seekers who bid up prices in an escalating spiral. The initial increase could be triggered by an upturn in the local economy that spurs employment growth (the story in California in the 1980s), by a decline in mortgage interest rates (as in the 2002 to 2005 boom), or simply by a demographic shift that launches more households into the market (as with the entry of the baby boomers in the 1970s).

What has not been witnessed in the United States since the Great Depression is a supply-and-demand situation where these dynamics run in reverse—a downward spiral instead of the cycle of surplus home seekers driving up prices and encouraging more heated competition. Can the baby boom undo in the 2010s what it began to create in the 1970s? The evidence presented in the following sections outlines the risk ahead. Both supply and demand are likely to change in unfavorable ways—supply because large numbers of retired baby boomers could flood the market with houses for sale in the same time period, and demand because there may not be enough buyers who are qualified to pay the high prices being asked.

The Demographic Foundations of Housing Demand

Often the market's fundamental support is so steady that it becomes almost invisible and taken for granted. It can be such a normal background condition that it is difficult to imagine the factor's absence or what might be the market response. For most of the last three decades, the housing market has been driven by the upward mobility of the baby boom generation. The leading edge of the generation passed age thirty in 1976, triggering the first housing price boom and the first wave of gentrification in U.S. cities. This was followed by eighteen more years of oversized birth cohorts providing the raw increase in home seekers to fuel subsequent booms in the late 1980s and more recently the period 2002 to 2005. When the last members of the baby boom passed age thirty in 1994, the front ranks were pressing into their fifties. Even in 2006, the baby boomers filled the age groups from forty-two to sixty. This is an age range with very high homeownership rates and high house values. The steepest growth in demand is behind them—typically, that occurs around ages thirty to thirty-five—but the baby boomers are filling a lot of homes they own in California—3.1 million of the 6.5 million total owned homes in the state to be exact.[13] After thirty years of steady growth, the baby boomers are passing sixty, and we can begin to imagine a future day when the demand from this group will begin to shrink.

The demographic shift in California's adult population will inevitably lead to changes in the housing market, but the timing is unknown. Thus far, the shift has been gradual, unlike the cyclical surges in employment and interest rates, and so its effects have been scarcely noticed. As we look ahead, it is not difficult to imagine a very different outcome looming on the horizon. Although there is clearly a problem here, not enough is known to make even a crude guess on the exact timing of a shortfall of buyers relative to sellers.

As a first step, I have assembled data to indicate the average annual rate of buying and selling homes for people in different age and racial-ethnic groups. This is an improvement on the standard available data, which report current numbers of homeowners or net changes in that number between two points in time. With annual rates of buying and selling, we can approximate market activity more reasonably. For example, even if there is no increase in the homeownership rate, a fixed number of people could generate a lively amount of market demand if they simply sold their homes and bought others—essentially trading homes among themselves. When the buy rates exceed the sell rates, an excess of market demand would be indicated, whereas if the sell rates exceed the buy rates, the opposite would occur. Although the number of buyers has been relatively easy to determine in the past—surveys simply interview people who recently moved in—information on sellers has been more elusive because sellers move away and cannot be interviewed. My research group developed methods for estimating the number of sellers and buyers by characteristics in each time interval, designing these for use with two very different datasets and yielding similar results.[14] The California results selected for presentation are shown in figure 11.1.

The average annual rate of purchase (estimated from 1995 to 2000) peaks at 2.9 percent for people ages thirty-five to thirty-nine, thereafter declining in a steady manner.[15] This is consistent with what we know about young adults experiencing the greatest increases in homeownership rates and accounting for a disproportionate share of home sales. More unusual are the findings on "sell" rates or terminations of occupancy. Those thirty-five to thirty-nine year-olds also have high rates of selling, presumably because their active buying is often accompanied by sales of previous homes. Sell rates remain surprisingly constant at around 2.0 percent per year for 40 years, not rising until ages seventy to seventy-four and older.

Buy rates that exceed sell rates indicate net increases in homeownership for the age group, as witnessed particularly in the younger ages. The most noteworthy point about the annual rate of buying and selling is that buying exceeds selling until ages fifty-five to fifty-nine, only after which does selling begin to predominate.[16] The front ranks of the baby boomers have already begun to cross that point. The gap between buying and selling is small at first, but by ages seventy-five to seventy-nine, selling is three times more common than buying, a stage the baby boomers will reach by 2020.

Comparison of racial-ethnic groups indicates substantially lower rates of buying and selling by all groups other than whites (figure 11.2). Buy rates among whites remain appreciably higher than other groups from ages fifty through eighty, but the sell rates among whites are even more substantially el-

Figure 11.1   Average Annual Rates of Buying and Selling, per 100
People of Each Age, California

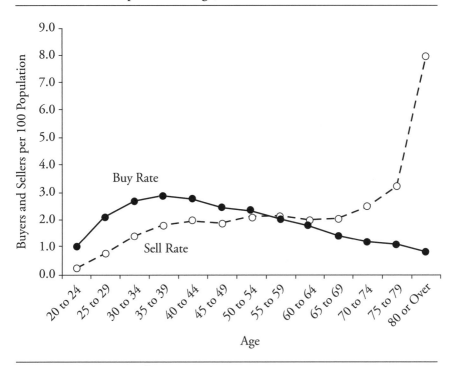

Source: PUMS 5%, 1990 and 2000.

evated through late middle-age and elderly years, approximately doubling the sell rates of Latinos. The implication is that the baby boom generation will soon be passing into an age span where white homeowners have especially high likelihood of selling their homes.

The net result of buying and selling by different groups can be projected for future years. Our data cannot speak to the effects of cyclical changes in income growth, employment or interest rates, but they indicate the underlying demographic basis for housing demand that would be activated by those short-term conditions. Thus the data reported here pertain to the long-term potential demand that supports house values. A snapshot of the underlying demand likely to exist in California in a single year, 2020, is provided in figure 11.3.[17] Steep losses of white homeowners in older ages are produced by the excess of sellers over buyers. In the single year of 2020 this amounts to a

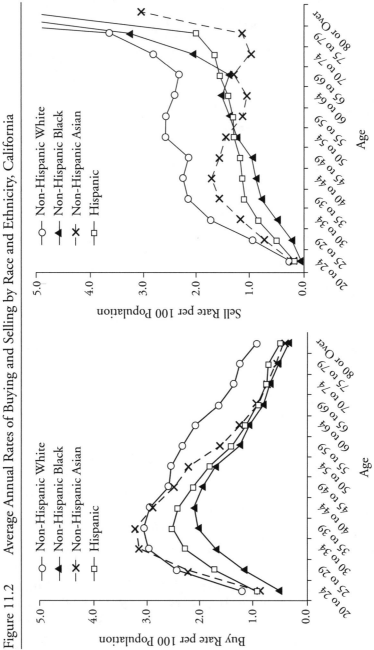

Figure 11.2   Average Annual Rates of Buying and Selling by Race and Ethnicity, California

Source: PUMS 5%, 1990 and 2000.

Figure 11.3   Projection of Excess of Buyers Over Sellers, by Age and
                Ethnicity, California in 2020

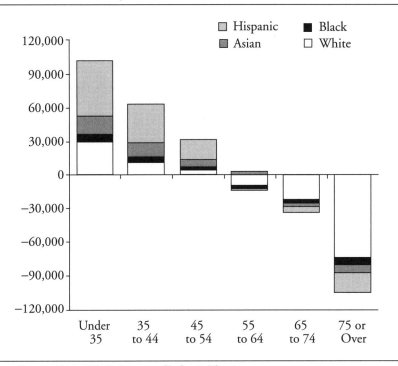

Source: Census 2000, PUMS 5 percent file for California.

net loss of 74,006 homeowners at ages seventy-five and above and an additional loss of 22,139 at ages sixty-five to seventy-four. African Americans, Asians, and Latinos among baby boomers contribute additional losses of homeowners as they pass further into their senior years.

The total number of buyers and sellers expected in 2020 more than breaks even due to the large gains of buyers over sellers at young ages, with Latinos accounting for at least half this gain. White and Asian homebuyers in these young ages are each expected to be less than half as numerous as Latinos. Thus the net shift in demand is away from older white homeowners who have ridden the recent boom to higher house values than others. Instead, the growth is now among the young and especially among Latinos who have lower purchasing potential on average, given current patterns. An additional factor that could undermine house values of existing homeowners in the future, given the relative balance between total numbers of buyers and sellers, is the unknown quantity of new construction that would be added to the competition for higher-priced buyers. During the deep California recession of the early 1990s, new construction of single-family homes for sale exceeded 70,000 units per year. Is that likely to be sustainable in future years if so many existing homes are being offered for sale?

Overall, much is uncertain about future housing markets and, although there will be mounting pressure for a market adjustment to match the new profile of demand, the exact timing of the downshift is unknown. Most likely the correction of the generational housing bubble would be triggered by a recessionary downturn. After the recession normally expected housing market recovery would not ensue because the underlying demand is so diminished relative to the burgeoning number of would-be sellers. The slump in home sales and house values would likely extend at least several years and grow deeper as even larger numbers of baby boomers continued to pass age 75 for another decade or more. Barring increases in the purchasing power of the younger generation, this scenario could well commence a few years before or after 2020, but much more is needed to be learned about these dynamics.

The New Hazard of a Senior-Dependent Homeownership Market

The housing market in California and the nation will be entering uncharted waters in the coming decade or two. Never before has the growth in homeowner demand been so senior-dependent. What this will mean is unclear, but it is likely to be very different from what we have known before. Surely, these older homeowners will not be driving prices upward as much as they did when they were younger. There have been false alarms in the past about impending price declines due to old age, the most famous of which was issued by the Harvard professors Gregory Mankiw and David Weil.[18] Mankiw is noted for his macroeconomic theories, not housing or demographic analysis, and he later was appointed the chairman of the Council of Economic Advisers in the George W. Bush administration. The two authors were misled by the fact that housing consumption reported in the 1970 and 1980 censuses peaked at age forty to forty-five and thereafter declined. When they wrote in 1989, the leading edge of the baby boom born in 1946 was poised to cross that line. Using their econometric techniques, Mankiw and Weil projected that house prices could collapse by 47 percent between 1990 and 2010, and that projection naturally drew a lot of attention in financial circles. John Pitkin wrote with the author about this misguided reasoning, which we termed the age cohort fallacy.[19] Common sense told observers that hardly anyone ever spends less on housing or moves to a cheaper unit as they grow older (especially not at fifty), but the Harvard scholars were captivated by data they had misread.

The fallacy of expected downward movement was created because elderly people at the time lived in cheaper housing. However, the elderly had *not* recently moved to those units: the great majority of older homeowners live in homes they purchased two or three decades earlier. In fact, those homes, when first purchased at younger ages, were already smaller and cheaper than those later occupied by the baby boomers. When actual cohorts were traced across decades, there was little evidence of downward shifting to lower-priced homes. In fact, if anything, the cohorts gravitated slowly to more expensive homes with more amenities, and even if they did not move, their homes appreciated because the neighborhoods they lived in became more valuable over time.[20] Subsequent events have borne out how misguided was the Mankiw and Weil false alarm about falling house values due to aging.

In the coming decade, we face a harsher reality of aging and house values. There is no need to project to the decade beyond 2020; the years after 2015 could begin the decline. Within ten years' time, a substantial number of elderly homeowners are likely to disappear from the homeownership market. These are high-risk years for mortality, household dissolution, migration out of state, or a move to retirement home living. How great the risk of lost homeowners will be is seen in the following figures. Of the half-million California homeowners age seventy-five and older in 1990, fully 71.4 percent had terminated their homeownership by 2000, when they would have been eighty-five and older.[21] Among those age sixty-five to seventy-four in 1990, losses were not as substantial, but their numbers were still reduced by 29.4 percent within a decade, when they would have been seventy-four to eighty-four. Overall, a very large number of seniors' homes were sold within a decade.

The clear implication of these data is that the housing demand of the baby boomers is likely to come to a wrenching halt after 2020, if not before. The frank concern is that the oldest and most advantaged homeowners will reach an age where they must sell but that they will find the market heavily dominated by would-be buyers who lack the means to pay the prices the baby boomers are asking. After decades of upward demand pressure, we could be entering an age of downward pressure on prices.

The Benefit of Higher Educational Achievements

One reason that homeownership and house values may be so much lower for Latinos than others could be their much lower educational attainment. Without higher education, potential home buyers will find it difficult to secure jobs that pay a sufficient income to afford homeownership. And even if such buyers are able to purchase a home, the lack of a well-paying job will relegate them to the market in lower-priced homes. Let's take a look at the actual data showing what difference an education makes. Considering the home-buying behavior of household heads with different educational attainments, we can compare immigrants and the native-born, examining Latinos and Asians as well as the white, non-Hispanic native-born.[22] For this purpose, it is useful to focus on a single age group, thirty-five- to forty-four-year-olds, a group that is among the most likely to supply home buyers for seniors who wish to sell.[23] Also, in order to see more clearly the effects of a U.S. education, we look only at immigrants who arrived in the United States before age ten. Because of the restriction to those currently age thirty-five to forty-four, these immigrants cannot be newcomers but only those who have resided at least twenty-five years in the United States.

Higher Homeownership

As a basic point of comparison, 75.3 percent of the white native-born household heads and spouses in California who hold a bachelor's degree or higher are the owners of the houses they occupy (figure 11.4, left). This is moderately higher than the homeownership rates of those with an associate's degree and well above the rates for those with only a high school degree and no college attendance (61.8 percent). In comparison to white residents, native-born Asians have an even higher likelihood of homeownership if they have a college degree and somewhat lower homeownership if they are not educated beyond high school. Asian immigrants, in contrast, have the highest homeownership, surpassing the homeownership rates of the white or Asian native-born at every educational level save the highest. This unusually high homeownership propensity of Asian households is widely recognized and has not been fully explained.[24] Native-born Latinos have homeownership rates that closely

Figure 11.4 Education Effects on Homeownership Rates at Age Thirty-five to Forty-four Among the Native-Born and Immigrants, Observed at Age Thirty-five to Forty-four, by Race-Ethnicity, California, 2000

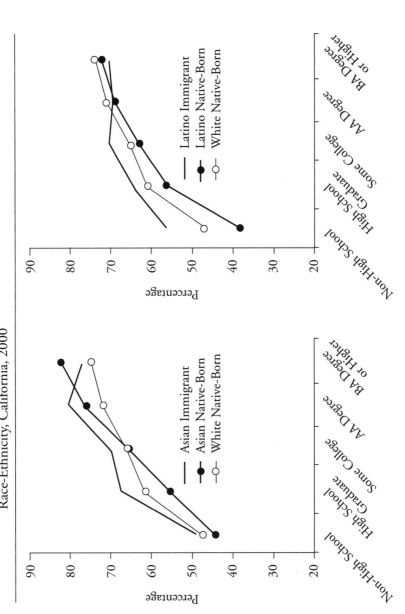

Source: 2000 PUMS.
Note: California: immigrants include only those who arrived in the United States before age ten, that is, those who were young enough to enroll in elementary school. 1999 dollars.

follow those of whites in higher education brackets (figure 11.4, right). Immigrant Latinos, however, exhibit homeownership rates that far exceed those of native-born Latinos in all save the two highest education brackets. In fact, among immigrants who lack a high school degree, there is a surprisingly high level of homeownership, nearly ten percentage points higher than among the white native-born and more than eighteen percentage points higher than among the Latino native-born.[25] College-educated Latinos do not exhibit the same degree of "overattainment," and in fact, it is somewhat puzzling that there is virtually no gain in homeownership between residents who attended some college and those with either an associate's or bachelor's degree.

To summarize the effects of education on homeownership attainment, the likelihood of homeownership rises substantially for those with a college degree, but it is higher than expected among lower-educated Latinos and among Asians in most education groups. Immigrants who, by the definition used here, arrived in the United States before age ten generally achieve higher rates of homeownership for the same amount of education than both their native-born coethnics and the white native-born. Bear in mind that the total effect of education on homeownership depends not only on the effects displayed in figure 11.4 but also on how many of these adults are concentrated in higher rather than lower education levels. Asians and whites, who, on average, have higher rates of college completion, thus exhibit higher overall homeownership rates than Latinos, many of whom have failed to advance beyond high school.

Higher House Values

Attainment of homeownership is a key threshold, but the full impact of population growth on the housing market is expressed through the price levels of the homes purchased. For this purpose, house value is measured by the median value reported by the home's occupants. Not the actual sales price, the reported house value is an estimate of what the home might sell for, and the median is the point at which half the homes sell for more and half for less. Although these estimates are subject to error, they have proved remarkably unbiased: some people overestimate their house values, while a roughly equal number underestimate them.[26] As a result, a comparison of the median values in different groups provides a reasonable indication of how much house prices vary across different criteria. Although the comparisons that follow (drawn from the rich data provided in the 2000 census) precede the great boom that approximately doubled housing values for all, they provide a good depiction of the relative differences between groups.

Much higher house values are reported by white native-born householders with a bachelor's degree ($329,000) than by those with only a high school degree ($186,000), with an especially large increase in house value of 46.0 percent between those with an associate's degree and those with a BA. As shown in figure 11.5, both immigrant and native-born Asians own generally more expensive homes than the white native-born with comparable education. Conversely, Latino immigrants and native-born own housing that is much less expensive than that of the white native-born with comparable education. Among high school graduates, the house values of Latino native-born are 13.6 percent lower than for white native-born, a difference that expands to 24.2 percent lower among bachelor's degree holders (figure 11.5).

In summary, for all groups, successively higher educational attainment is associated with higher house values (as it is with higher earnings). A bachelor's degree affords an especially large increase in house values. The house values of immigrants and native-born of the same educational level are very similar, unlike homeownership rates, which are higher for immigrants. Eagerness to buy a home is one thing; ability to purchase a more expensive home may be another. Asians generally occupy homes with higher values than do the white native-born, while Latinos occupy homes with substantially lower values relative to the education of the homeowners. This lower house value among Latinos is not surprising in view of the lower earnings they receive for comparable educational degrees, as found in the preceding chapter.

Conclusion

Home buying and selling is one of the ways in which the generations are most strongly linked. The impending retirement of the baby boomers from the job market has its parallel in the housing market, although many retirees will continue to occupy their homes until forced out by poor health. The buildup of housing wealth over a lifetime can be considerable, especially when house values double in five years, as they have since 2000 in California. The challenge is dealing with the imminent collision between house price trends and the aging of the baby boom generation, on the one hand, and changing demography in California and the nation, on the other. We face the prospect of a catastrophic generational housing bubble—a sustained, demographically based downturn in house values that could be a boon for struggling young

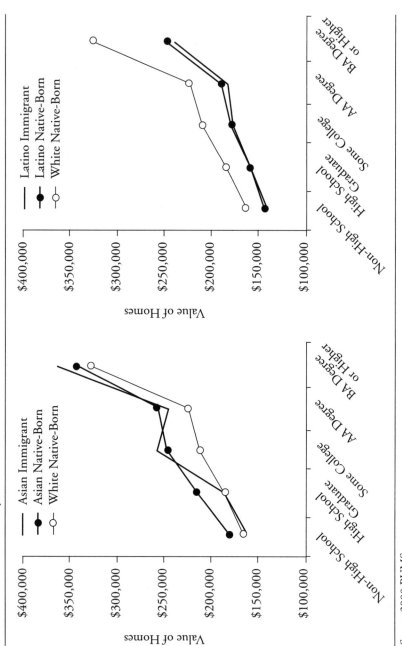

Figure 11.5   Education Effects on the Value of Owned Homes at Ages Thirty-Five to Forty-Four, Among the Native-Born and Immigrants, Observed at Ages Thirty-Five to Forty-Four, by Race-Ethnicity, California

Source: 2000 PUMS.
Note: California: immigrants include only those who arrived in the United States before age ten, that is, those who were young enough to enroll in elementary school. 1999 dollars.

adults and a wipeout for seniors. Mankiw and Weil may have failed in their forecast that baby boomers would depress the housing market thirty years earlier when they crossed age forty-five, but now it is reasonable to fear the impact around 2020 when the boomers begin to cross age seventy-five.

We know that the baby boomers' housing life cycle will come to an end, and it seems certain that the ethnic and immigrant changes in the demographic transition will limit the number of buyers who are non-Hispanic white. The housing market is surely going to transition to a more Latino-dominated mix. That group may be numerous enough to replace the white seniors. The only question is whether enough young households will have the wherewithal to pay seniors the prices they are asking for their homes. A shortfall of buyers in the upper price ranges will compress the entire price structure downward, creating a buyers' market that has not been seen for a very long time. At the end of the baby boomers' housing life cycle, we will move to an era whose features are unknown.

One solution explored here, continuing the theme of chapter 10, is reaping the benefits of higher education. Given the currently disadvantaged status of many in the younger generation, it is uncertain that they can step up to the role of home buyer. Fortunately, the evidence in preceding chapters has documented the remarkable upward mobility of the longer-settled immigrant population and their children. Whether they can climb high enough is unclear, but the race has already begun between immigrant upward mobility and the impending decline in demand from baby boomer retirements.

If we could plan a soft landing to avoid the dreaded generational housing bubble in the next two decades, it would require some acceleration of the progress being made by the younger generation. With a little better income, would-be home buyers could stretch to a higher bid for sellers' homes. Extremely low interest rates would certainly help as well, but that cannot be planned. The one action tool within our grasp is to promote the educational preparation of the next generation. That one investment can elevate the earnings potential of grown children and thereby enhance their home-buying potential. This is another reward that home sellers could reap for all their years of paying taxes. The American Dream is indeed a key piece of the social contract, but its success depends on the collective provision of services and a recognition of how much the generations depend on one another.

PART IV

A SHARED DESTINY AND A NEW SOCIAL CONTRACT

Chapter 12

Conclusion: Steps Toward
Building a More Hopeful Future

THE FUTURE of America remains to be decided. The outlook of despair inherited from the early transition period has now been joined by an alternative—an outlook of hope that builds on more recent immigrant trends and on a mutual self-interest that promises to help solve urgent problems of native-born citizens. The citizen-voters who are thinking men and women now have a new choice of futures that they can adopt in belief and action. In this concluding chapter, I review the choices and the respective policy implications.

The demographic transition in which we are engaged is full of stress and dismay. Many people, of course, are most attuned to the problems they perceive in the moment, not those likely to unfold in the future. Yet even those momentary problems are judged in the context of both the remembered past and an imagined future. A clear aim of this book has been to draw out those remembrances and imaginings, placing them on the table for closer examination and discussion. The intent has been to place these in a better perspective by showing both how different parts fit together and how the future differs from the past.

This book has covered a broad sweep in time, and not simply because a longer time frame enables us to trace causes and consequences. What is more important is that the longer view more closely marks the life stages of individuals from childhood to retirement and thus allows us to see their interdependencies and shared self-interests. Over the course of their lives, most individuals' roles and self-interests change markedly: they transition from being children cared for as dependents to young adults who are growing into vital workforce roles; then they pass further into late middle age as mature adults making their greatest contributions as wage earners and taxpayers. Following retirement, there is another role change: from net contributor to net beneficiary of public support. Our focus on the baby boom generation has served both to illustrate this passage through the life stages and to highlight the impacts when a great many individuals make similar transitions in a short time.

Immigrants are best understood as individuals who are also following life stages very similar to those of the native-born. Indeed, they are not Peter Pans, forever frozen in the life stage at which they arrived in America. But their lives assume an added dimension of transition to America, followed by their progressive adaptation to and merger into our society. An important aim of this book has been to make apparent this process of immigrant advancement and integration, as well as the interaction between immigrant progress and the aging of the baby boomers, and to suggest how this interaction can benefit all of America.

What allows us to see these life changes writ large across the decades is the demographic perspective. Projecting these changes forward in time gives us unique insight into the future of our society. Certainly demographics are widely recognized as important for describing differences between types of people in a given year. However, an even greater contribution of a demographic perspective may be the window it provides on the dynamics of change across the decades. Forming a vital underpinning to the arguments presented here, this approach highlights the common humanity and interdependence of seemingly different groups. Not only do all people pass through similar life stages, but there are intrinsic bonds that tie together the generations, and at different points in our lives we all change roles.

Simple extrapolations from a moment in time lie behind many arguments about the meaning of immigration for our future. Our conceptions of a future of despair were driven by trends perceived prior to 2000 in the United States and prior to 1990 in California. Before that time, the accelerating annual arrival of immigrants was causing many people to fear unlimited expansion in the foreign-born population. In addition, because immigration was only recently resurgent, most immigrants were recently arrived and had not yet achieved much upward mobility. In that context, it was easy to imagine a very bleak future—a nation coping with huge numbers of foreigners, all frozen in the status of newcomers.

Today we are beginning to understand a new future for America that builds on more recent trends and a deeper understanding. Immigration to the United States early in the twenty-first century has ceased its acceleration in numbers and could either stabilize at its current high level or decline somewhat. Drawing on the experience in California, where immigration ceased its acceleration a decade earlier, we can see that this stabilization will be accompanied by a greater predominance of longer-settled immigrants and more prevalent upward mobility. This creates a much more hopeful outlook for the immigrants and their impacts on society. In fact, when we combine this new immigrant outlook with that of our aging society, we discover a future with potentially even greater mutual benefit. To achieve that potential, however, we must overcome important obstacles to understanding and acceptance.

Resisting or Embracing the Ongoing Change

The current demographic transition, the third in a series that have swept the United States and other developed nations, is making a markedly different society. Given that most people would prefer not to have the world change from what they have known, save for the elimination of particular irritants or threats, the demographic transition is widely considered to pose an inherent problem. The immigration and ethnic changes accompanying the third transition in particular present social and political challenges. Several different aspects of change are intertwined in the transition, however, and some, such as aging, are not easily stopped. Indeed, efforts to express disapproval of some parts of the transition could lead to even worse outcomes than otherwise might be likely. Accordingly, all the dimensions of the transition must be considered as a whole. Given the strength of the forces at work, it would be wise to explore how they can be made to work on behalf of building a better society.

The Older Outlook of Despair

Strong opposition to the transition is rooted in a scenario for the future characterized by despair. We should grant that there are many reasons why some are pessimistic: the steady decline in the prominence of the white population is deflating to many of the people who are accustomed to being in the majority. Combining their apprehension on this score with a sense that foreign cultures are taking over and concern about the increasing economic struggles of the middle class, many citizens, not surprisingly, wish to put a stop to the transition. One policy motivated by such despair is to make admission much more restrictive for immigrants, including the reinforcement of the border (although the expense and efficacy of such efforts remain in doubt). Another despair-based policy is to discourage immigrant settlement by blocking access to services, even at the risk of penalizing U.S.-born children and current residents as well as immigrant newcomers. Yet another approach is to remove any policy preferences that aid ethnic minorities in employment, education, or other services (again targeting even U.S.-born citizens). All of these policies are being tested and might slow the immigrant or ethnic transition. Although their effectiveness remains in doubt, such measures at least temporarily mitigate despair in some quarters, even if they increase the despair in others.

Other dimensions of the transition are less easily addressed. In particular, the aging process is universally disliked, but this can be slowed very little. Inexorably the baby boomers are growing older, with their front ranks, including Presidents Bush and Clinton, now passing sixty. Most of these new elderly expect to retire sometime in the next twenty years, and they also expect to receive their entitled Social Security, Medicare, and other benefits. Another mounting source of despair is the growing budget deficit in the United States, the anticipated shortfall in the Social Security trust fund, and the projected burden of so many future elderly, along with the uncertainty of what to do about these issues. Raising the retirement age, trimming the level of entitlements, and raising taxes are policy options, and all of them could in fact prove necessary, but none of them sounds appealing to citizens or their elected leaders. The demographic transition is leading us into a terrible jam.

Newfound Hope Through Mutual Self-Interest
An underlying theme of this book has been to identify ways to turn the *problem* of the demographic transition into an *advantage*. This search for new opportunities for improvement is motivated by an inspired story of hope for the future. In fact, I have identified a mutual self-interest that ties together two very different generations, each of which has resources that the other needs at particular times. Today the voters and taxpayers, who are mostly middle-aged

and older, hold the power to invest in the younger, school-age generation, many of whom are ethnically different or of immigrant origin. In twenty years, these children will have matured and will be filling the skilled jobs in the workforce vacated by the retiring baby boomers. Of course, the baby boomers might not really care who replaces them in their jobs, even if that is crucial to business leaders and public officials. Other replacement needs, however, could have a direct impact on the baby boomers, and it is the mutual self-interest represented by these needs that could prove more persuasive.

The grown children who have been educated with taxpayer assistance will not simply be workers. They will also enter the ranks of taxpayers, and if they are well enough trained, they will command well-paying jobs that support healthy tax contributions. Those will be dearly needed if we are to support so many elderly with such a high level of retirement benefits. Rather than despair about the growing number of retirees or focus on cutting their benefits, an alternative stance emphasizes the hope of growing the base of required taxpayer support. Inspired by this hope, the generational view reveals that present taxpayer support of a strong educational system is not simply an expenditure but an investment in growing the capacity of future taxpayers.

There are even greater benefits that these newly created, high-skilled young workers could return to future retirees. It is they who will probably respond in the greatest numbers when so many baby boomers try to sell their homes. The relative shortage in the workforce has its direct parallel in the housing market. The elderly sell many more homes than they buy, and when the giant baby boom generation passes age seventy, a growing rush of sellers will be seeking to cash in their housing investments, whether to move to more comfortable retirement quarters or to draw on their equity for long-term care or retirement support. Should there be a surplus of sellers over buyers in high-priced brackets because the younger generation is not sufficiently educated to hold jobs that would enable them to buy homes in these brackets, downward pressure on prices will erode much of the equity stored in the home values of the elderly. This generational housing bubble could prove far deeper and more long-lasting than the simple downturn following the housing price boom of 2002 to 2005. Thus, the buyer and seller relationship will link the fortunes of different generations, and that linkage will echo a different relationship formed earlier when the older generation supported investment in the education of their future home buyers.

Homegrown Human Investment: A New Priority

What is newly apparent is that homegrown investment must be substantially increased in California and the whole of the United States. This is a significant change from the past, when a majority of the skilled workers needed in California were found by borrowing from other states and nations. That practice lingers on as an assumed solution to current and future problems. However, as reviewed in chapter 10, the state has already begun to rely more heavily on homegrown college graduates, and it will be far more important in the future than it was in the recent past that California workers, taxpayers, and home buyers be homegrown. Consider the competition ahead: the baby boomer retirements beginning very soon will drive down the growth rate of the U.S. workforce to barely one-half percent per year, less than one-third of the growth rate that prevailed at the beginning of the new century. This slowdown will threaten to stifle economic growth in less desirable locations, and it will make young replacement workers even more precious and sought after. Recruiting competition could become ferocious as businesses and economic development agencies strive to pirate away the best talent and as growing areas deplete the workforces of less-advantaged areas. The early signs of population decline and brain drain from parts of the Midwest and even upstate New York are but a hint of massive change soon to be unleashed.

What of immigration from abroad as a solution to the coming shortages in workers, taxpayers, and home buyers? Certainly immigration already accounts for a large share of the net increase in the U.S. workforce, but this source of replacement workers to serve our needs may be limited in its future expansion. For one reason, the growing political pressure in the U.S. Congress to reform immigration is more likely to lead to reductions in new arrivals than to increases. Although it is not expected that this pressure for reform will mount to the point of massive curtailment of immigration, as occurred last in the 1920s, political pressure is likely to be a moderating force over the next decade at least.

In addition, the traditional sources of immigration to the United States will not be generating as many migrants as before. The dramatic slowdown of fertility in Mexico was noted in chapter 3. The decline from 6.8 to 2.4 children per woman since 1970 will severely cut labor force growth in Mexico as more recent birth cohorts come of age. That will enhance the relative job prospects of new workers within Mexico and may limit the future flow to the United States. Rapid economic development and falling fertility in Asia could have a similar depressant effect on the number of would-be immigrants from those nations to the United States. Also, global economic restructuring is redirecting more economic investment abroad, and the recent trend of off-shoring production to lower-cost countries is exporting jobs, not importing workers. For all these reasons, the relative attractions of America in the future may not be what they were in the past.

Whatever the potential supply of immigrants, domestic social policy goals also argue against reliance on immigration to meet future needs. Even if the desired numbers of immigrants could be attracted, and at the right skill levels, there are strong grounds for emphasizing a homegrown strategy. There is long-standing and near-universal support in the United States for expanding the size of the middle class. A corollary of that goal is reducing poverty and the growing economic polarization that has been widening the gap between the fortunes of higher- and lower-income groups in the United States. A larger middle class would benefit both consumers and businesses and broaden the ranks of the voters and taxpayers at the heart of our democratic society. Importing high-skilled immigrants to meet key economic needs is an expedient short-range strategy, but over the long haul it is far preferable to educate the children already living in America to become our skilled workers of tomorrow. A very unpleasant scenario has already begun to arise (as discussed in chapter 10) from our neglect of a large portion of our existing human resources; as we import workers to meet our higher-end economic needs, we foster the creation of a permanent underclass. Such a deliberate strategy of polarization should be widely disowned by both citizen-voters and their elected representatives.

Surely the competition precipitated by the shrinking growth of the workforce could be the basis for despair, but such an outlook overlooks the opportunity contained in the problem. Thinking men and women will recognize a different path to a better future. The citizens of California and the other states will surely want to emphasize raising and investing in their own replacement workers and taxpayers. Not only will it become ever more difficult to attract migrants from other locales, but as was shown in chapter 10, workers who were raised in-state are three times as likely to stay in-state as those borrowed from elsewhere. Thus, homegrown resources are not easily recruited away, and the homegrown investment in workforce, taxpayers, and home buyers should pay extra dividends in the two decades ahead. Finally, as a major further benefit, this investment strategy is consistent with the social policy goals of reducing polarization and expanding access to the middle class. This forecast of greater reliance on homegrown workers, taxpayers, and home buyers provides even greater incentive to help create a hopeful scenario for the future.

Choosing Our Pathway to a More Hopeful Future

It is the citizen-voters of America who will lead us into the future. For reasons described in chapter 2, all but the most farsighted of our elected leaders are reluctant to take command of issues whose benefits lie beyond their term of office. They will only follow the lead of new demands generated by the citizenry. Citizens must first make sense, however, of all the options that are being churned up as the nation struggles to make its way through our current transition. They might be tempted to seize on a single option as the key to salvation, but regrettably, there is no single silver bullet solution. The pathway to a better future instead is paved with a series of specific adjustments, each of which can contribute only partially to the desired goals.

The many different options and adjustments reinforce one another in different packages, with some options pursuing the old vision of despair for the future and others pursuing a future of hope. The strategy of despair is tempting to adopt because it is easier to mobilize broad-based support for a strategy that is reacting to negative trends already felt. In contrast, the strategy of hope anticipates trends that have not yet unfolded, and so most citizens have not been goaded into this sort of action. Foresight is at a premium, and few citizens have yet heard the message of the coming future. This book has certainly aimed to make that future more real and understandable. Gaining cooperative understanding on any issue has clearly grown more difficult in recent years, for reasons explored in chapter 8. But the urgent problems looming before us now beg for our concerted attention to the shared understanding that has newly emerged.

A New Social Contract

The intergenerational social contract proposed in this book is a key guide to our cooperation in making a better future. The new understanding of interdependency creates an opportunity to span divisions in our society that separate not only age groups but racial-ethnic groups, immigrants, and the native-born. This new, shared social understanding also could help build bridges between groups of voters of different economic classes or political persuasions. Through this new social understanding, perhaps more of our citizens and leaders could also learn that the demographic changes of the great transition do not pose insurmountable problems but rather are changes that can be accommodated and even turned into part of the solution for making a better future.

The trust implied in a social contract is especially important when planning the future because future events and facts are unknown and cannot be proven. Instead, citizens must rely on a shared understanding of a believable and desirable future that can be created. To be effective, this shared vision of the future must address the particular needs and fears of different groups, yet at the same time it must focus on the common purpose and emphasize *mutual* self-interest. In essence, the shared future is a compromise that citizens can choose to accept or not, but as they assess the alternative visions of the future competing for dominance, they inevitably will make their choice. The dominant alternative today, of course, is the vision of a future of despair.

Recommended Steps for Building the Future of Hope

The future of hope has much appeal, and many forces are converging to make it seem more attainable, but what specific steps must we take to ensure that this vision of the future comes to fruition? Many different suggestions have been raised in this book, and perhaps it would be helpful to summarize the most important ones. This recommended package of policies and practices for building the more hopeful future is not a menu from which each person should choose a different item. As will be apparent, the complete set is needed because it balances various concerns in a manner that could marshal the broad base of support required for this shared endeavor. When we choose the future of hope, we begin today to build that future.

The first suggested step is to affirm just how far America has come in building a democratic society composed of many ethnic groups. Ours is a work in progress that is guided by high aspirations, and we should adopt the mission of making the United States, with California at the forefront, the world leader in achieving a just and effective resolution to the great demographic transition that is sweeping the developed world. Our great history of building a nation from many people can also be our proud future. Our society has not fully achieved its stated goals, but we have made enormous progress in the last half-century, as we shall in the next. Today many more countries are beginning to follow the path that the United States has pioneered, but most are struggling. In this great world effort, we are exemplary, even if we also are troubled. Let us strive to create *at home* the model democracy for the twenty-first century by building on our previous accomplishment.

Second, in pursuit of that mission we should evaluate and discuss all short-range decisions related to immigrants, children, and the elderly in light of their implications for America's progress and leadership through the long-range transition. Putting these decisions in perspective will help us judge better what is the right thing to do.

The third step on the path to the future of hope is to conduct an important moral discussion of intergenerational gratitude and responsibility. As part of this, we need to acknowledge the many contributions made in the past and present by our senior generation, including not just today's retirees but all those over age forty-five. Their efforts and seniority status both deserve our respect. In addition, so that we can all appreciate the respective contributions made to a common cause, this discussion should acknowledge the present and future contributions of the rising generation. Our communications media, educational institutions, and religious communities all have a role to play in leading this discussion of who we are and how much we owe.

A fourth step in building the hopeful future is to accelerate the rate of integration of immigrants into the mainstream of U.S. society and the U.S. economy. We need to assist their economic advancement and their full participation in our society, including early incorporation into our democratic political process. Becoming full partners in America entails naturalization to citizenship, voting, and participation in local political decisionmaking. This partnership also includes learning English to supplement the language of the homeland because English is the common language for civic discourse. In turn, we must appreciate that assimilation is a two-way street and that the newcomers also contribute to our common culture. Many of the newcomers encourage us, by their example, to reemphasize our respect for family values and hard work, and they offer us new ethnic traditions that enrich our cities and our daily lives in many ways.

A fifth step required if we are to achieve the hopeful future is stabilization of the flow of new immigrants. What has been so discomforting to many people is that the number of new arrivals is unmonitored and increasing without limits. The great majority of the public prefers that immigration be sustained, but their desire is to avoid future escalation or a loss of control. Even though there are good reasons to believe that the long-term trend in immigration is already leveling off, taking more deliberate control over future increases would probably instill greater confidence in the future.

A sixth necessary step is for citizen-voters and taxpayers to embrace the homegrown strategy and increase their investment in the education of the next generation. This will cost money, and the costs will be disproportionately incurred by the senior generation and native-born residents of America. Their contribution must be acknowledged, but it should also be acknowledged that the investment will be returned with future benefits, namely, the creation of new workers, taxpayers, and home buyers. Under the sway of a more pessimistic view of the future, many citizens have been shrinking from these investments, but their priorities may now be changing.

The seventh and final step reinforces the others. Citizen-voters and taxpayers deserve some signs of good-faith effort to not waste their financial contributions. This book may have provided evidence of immigrant upward mobility that is far greater than most have suspected, but even greater assurances are needed. Allocated greater funds with which to educate our children, the education profession must redouble its efforts to deliver quality education in a more efficient manner. Equally important in this endeavor are parents, who set values for their children, provide the home life essential for doing homework, and encourage their children to make their studies a priority. The effort ahead to increase workforce skills and grow a more equal society will take a full partnership of children, parents, educators, and taxpayers.

Who will execute all these necessary steps for choosing a future of hope? Indeed, there is no central authority that can carry out these recommendations. Many different agencies, institutions, and organizations can contribute in different ways. However, this is not primarily about government or organizations, but about the citizens of this country and their choice of the future they wish to occupy. It is citizens who must speak up and demand access to this new future of hope. Only they—not their elected leaders or the managers of today's organizations—have a vision long enough to include the future life in America of their children and grandchildren. The enormous debt being shoved onto the shoulders of the younger generations and the underinvestment in their common future are unconscionable. Leaders with short terms of office have avoided even telling the score to the American public. But the impending retirement of the baby boom generation has now forced the day of reckoning we have postponed for so long.

The citizens of America must finally choose the future they prefer. In response to their demands, grassroots voluntary organizations, churches, and other religious groups will draw together their constituents and help. Also contributing to the leadership will be major organizations that advocate for the interests of particular groups in society. The communications media that provide the public forum for many of our deliberations will undoubtedly also play a major role. A wealth of experts—scholars, educators, and commentators—are willing to contribute new fact finding and new interpretations that will aid the public's judgment. Public interest organizations and the political parties will surely want to weigh in with their own opinions on the two alternative courses for the future—a future of despair marked by retreat into isolated self-interest or a future of hope marked by common investment for the good of our mutual self-interest. Some will say there is a third alternative that is some combination of the two, and that could be possible. But the risk is that a compromise between hope and despair will yield only more of the same uninspired procrastination.

Rediscovery of hope in America is one of the great endeavors of our time. Without hope for the future, the nation will only continue its spiral of continuing fragmentation and polarization. Confronting our differences and transforming them into new opportunities may require some new thinking— especially about the mutual self-interest that spans the generations and links ethnic groups—but making this effort promises very practical and tangible rewards. As great as the struggle of the transition may be, it could renew and strengthen the civic bonds that have made America, formed of so many diverse people, so great a nation.

Appendix A

Supplementary Analysis of the Economic Turnaround

IT IS ESSENTIAL to appreciate the dynamics of the economic turnaround in several dimensions. The United States and California share similar economic turning points, but the graphical evidence presented here shows how much more exaggerated the California experience has been. For this purpose, we also need to compare conditions before 1990 with those that followed, because it is the contrast of conditions in different phases that has so affected the mood in the state. Four key barometers of economic well-being illustrate this experience: the unemployment and poverty rates, per capita income trends, and average home prices (see figure A.1).

California tracked the nation fairly closely until the sustained crash commenced in the 1990s. A wide gap opened at that point, but this was substantially closed in the eventual recovery period—with the exception of home prices, which soared skyward after 2002. The recession seemed much worse because of the boom that preceded it. For seven consecutive years, from 1984 through 1990, civilian employment in the state had boomed, averaging 459,000 additional jobs per year (a 3.7 percent average annual growth rate). In 1991 that growth abruptly ended. In just one year, employment fell by 362,450 jobs, and the losses continued for two additional years.[1] This marked

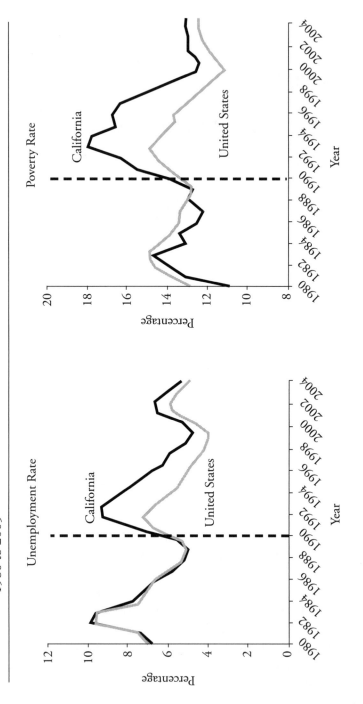

Figure A.1   Trends in Unemployment, Poverty, Income, and House Values, California and the United States, 1980 to 2005

Figure A.1   (*Continued*)

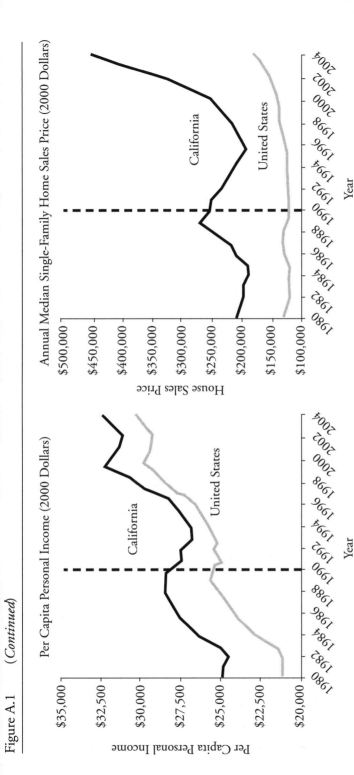

Source: U.S. Bureau of Labor Statistics; Current Population Survey; U.S. Bureau of Economic Analysis; National Association of Realtors; California Association of Realtors.

the most protracted recession in California since the Great Depression. A downturn in the national economy was made much worse in California by the downsizing of federal spending on the military and the aerospace industry, which had been concentrated in southern California. Ironically, this misfortune rose directly from the ending of the cold war, for which former California governor Ronald Reagan could take some credit.

Unlike the aftermath of prior recessions, the subsequent recovery of employment growth was slow to take hold, proceeding at only 1.2 percent per year from 1994 through 1996. Migration into California drastically slowed in this period, and the impact on the housing market was severe, from both falling prices and a downturn in new construction so sustained that it has been termed the "great California housing collapse."[2] Finally, in 1997 job growth began to return to levels resembling the robust growth of the 1980s. Although the end-of-decade dot-com crash had its greatest impact on the San Francisco region and led to slower employment growth from 2001 through 2003, in only one year, 2002, was there a net decline in employment, by 52,458. This was just a minor speed bump compared to the trauma of the early 1990s. And by 2005 employment growth was again yielding new opportunities like those of the booming 1980s.

The depth of hardship in California, followed by recovery, is indicated by the unemployment rate and can be compared to the nation's in figure A.1. From a base level of 6.9 percent in 1980, unemployment rates rose substantially during the recession of 1982 to 1983, reaching 10 percent, then fell for six straight years, ultimately settling at a level only three-quarters as high as the 1980 base year. Throughout this cycle, California tracked exactly with the nation. However, when unemployment began to rise again in 1990, surging in the recession years of 1991 to 1993 to another peak, California tracked well above the nation's unemployment rates. Thereafter from that peak, unemployment rates slowly declined for seven years to a level about equal to that of 1990, before again bumping upward in the recession of 2002. In recent years, California's unemployment rate still remains higher than the nation's, although much of the previous gap has been closed.

Income and house values have each tracked this economic cycle in their own way. Per capita personal income slipped downward in each recession and slumped protractedly in the early 1990s, but it has trended steadily upward over the decades, even when adjusted for inflation (see figure A.1). Expressed in constant dollars, per capita personal income has increased with each expansion, reaching a level 15 percent above the base year in 1990 and 30 percent higher in 2000 ($32,464). Thus, the average California resident is much better off economically than during the early 1990s, or in any other year since 1980. However, these benefits have not been spread uniformly.

Overshadowing the favorable gains in income, the poverty rate in California has not performed as well. In 1993 poverty reached a peak of 18.2 percent of the population, two-thirds higher than its level in the 1980 base year. Subsequently, it fell to 12.7 percent in 2000, but this best-in-decades poverty rate was still higher than in 1980. It seems contradictory that per capita income should have expanded to a level so much better than before, while poverty worsened. The widely accepted explanation is income polarization, as documented in a series of studies by Deborah Reed and her associates at the Public Policy Institute of California. The top segment of the income distribution, which has enjoyed considerable gains, accounts for a larger share of total income in the state, while the bottom fraction has languished and declined.[3] In fact, those at the bottom disproportionately live in immigrant families, many of them new arrivals.[4] Their success in exiting poverty will be essential to reducing the state's overall poverty level. With a growing immigrant population, there is real concern about whether California can sustain its favorable trend in income growth or whether this is just a momentary success before the growing weight of the immigrant population pulls the state downward into greater economic desperation. Fortunately, surprising new evidence, discussed in chapter 6, is very encouraging about these prospects.

Of greater concern to middle-class Californians, particularly the long-resident, predominantly white population, is the course of housing values. As discussed earlier in chapter 4, the sustained fall in median home sale prices was deflating to California homeowners' sense of economic well-being. The inflation-adjusted trend in figure A.1 indicates that when prices first peaked in 1989, they were a good 30 percent higher in real dollars than in 1980. Subsequently, house values declined for seven years to a level below that of the base year before finally recovering. Fueled by record low interest rates, as well as by the scarcity of housing for sale brought on by decade-long construction shortages, housing prices resumed an upward climb in 1997 that escalated even more sharply in 2003 and 2004. The price gains continued through all of 2005, reaching levels far above their previous peak in 1989. In 2004 the median home sales price in California, $450,990, was more than twice the national average of $185,200. Prices had also increased more than twice as fast that year (by 21.4 percent) as in the nation (9.3 percent).[5] Such extraordinary price gains set California apart from the nation as a whole, although a few metropolitan areas outside California experienced similar spikes in house prices. Many have worried about a real estate price bubble that could burst and send prices downward. However, as we explore in chapter 11, the real worry should be about a larger, generational housing bubble when all the baby boomers try to sell their homes to a less advantaged population.

Appendix B

Supplementary Analysis
of Voters' Opinions

VOTERS' OPINIONS depend on many different factors. My doctoral student Seong Hee Min and I conducted a series of statistical analyses of voters' opinions in order to weigh carefully the effects of different factors against one another. These all draw on the rich set of public opinion polls conducted by the Statewide Survey of the Public Policy Institute of California, under the direction of Mark Baldassare. We estimated linear probability regressions with the data so that we could measure the effects of each variable while holding all other variables constant. We applied this same technique to several opinion outcomes that had a binary (yes/no) nature, usually treated as one equals yes and zero equals no. Although a number of different forms of statistical regression are possible, this method held distinct advantages for our purposes.[1] We have transformed the outcome metric from zero or one to zero or one hundred, the sole difference being that coefficients are all one hundred times larger, that is, they are equivalent to percentages instead of proportions that are in decimals. The advantage this holds for interpretation is that an estimated coefficient of 7.0 implies that the given factor raises the probability of holding the designated opinion by seven percentage points.

Pessimism About Future Quality of Life

Pessimism about the quality of life in the future is measured as the percentage of likely voters who think that living conditions will grow worse in the future. The estimated effects of each factor on this pessimistic belief are shown in table B.1. The effect of each variable is expressed as the difference in opinion held by voters belonging to one category versus those belonging to another category that is made the statistical reference group. For example, voters of Asian heritage are 13.7 percent less likely than whites, who are the reference group, to express pessimism about future quality of life. As another example, voters who believe the public education system is getting worse are 20.6 percent more likely to be pessimistic about overall quality of life than are voters who do not think education is getting worse. In this way, the reader can assess the effect of each variable independent of the others. Not all of these effects are statistically significant, because normal sampling variation in a survey of this size creates random fluctuations. The degree of confidence we have that the estimate is truly different from zero, on either the positive or the negative side, is indicated by the number of asterisks that follow each coefficient. Estimates that have two or three asterisks are generally considered to be statistically significant, while those with only one are borderline.

Dislike of Population Growth

This analysis estimates the effects of different factors on the opinion that population growth is a bad thing. Results are reported in table B.2.

Dislike of Immigrants

This analysis addresses opinions about whether immigrants are more of a burden than a benefit. Two surveys that use the same question are presented in table B.3, one from 1998 and the other from 2004. Presented side by side, the findings from these surveys show the reader how much the explanatory factors may have changed over time, although we do not directly test the significance of those changes. The intercept in the model (also called constant) shows that is the average opinion response of voters in the reference category. In this analysis, the reference group is largely formed by native-born white men who are political moderates. (Income has little bearing in this case.) The fact that the intercept has declined from 45.2 to 37.0 indicates that the reference group's opinion that immigrants are a burden has declined over time.

(*Text continued on p. 274*)

Table B.1   Pessimism About Future Quality of Life: Factors Explaining the Probability That California Voters Believe Living Conditions Will Be Worse Rather Than Better or No Change in 2025

Factor	Percentage Point Increase or Decrease in Belief Due to Each Factor
Race	
Asian	−13.7**
Black	−16.9***
Hispanic	−3.9
White non-Hispanic (ref)	—
Other	−0.1
Age	
18 to 24	−16.0***
25 to 34	−4.5
35 to 44	−5.2
45 to 54 (ref)	—
55 to 64	−1.1
65 or over	0.4
Gender	
Male (ref)	
Female	−4.9**
Nativity	
Native-born (ref)	—
Foreign-born (citizen)	−4.4
Education	
Less than high school	11.2*
High school (ref)	—
Some college	4.4
BA degree or higher	5.8*
Income	
Less than $20,000 (ref)	—
$20,000 to $39,999	−8.6*
$40,000 to $59,999	−5.4
$60,000 to $79,999	−6.2
$80,000 or more	−5.0
Homeownership	
Owner	−6.9**
Renter (ref)	—

Table B.1   (*Continued*)

Factor	Percentage Point Increase or Decrease in Belief Due to Each Factor
Expected population growth	
Rapidly	16.4***
Other (ref)	—
Public education system	
Get worse	20.6***
Other (ref)	—
Air quality	
Get worse	18.3***
Other (ref)	—
Job opportunities and economic condition	
Get worse	16.2***
Other (ref)	—
Traffic conditions	
Get worse	9.5***
Other (ref)	—
Affordable housing	
Get worse	9.1***
Other (ref)	—
Confidence in state planning	
Low confidence	2.1
Other (ref)	—
Confidence in local planning	
Low confidence	8.4***
Other (ref)	—
Political leaning	
Liberal	1.0
Moderate (ref)	—
Conservative	−2.4
Intercept	4.8
Observations	1,462
R-squared	0.273

Source: PPIC Statewide Survey (August 2004): subsample of regular voters defined by those who indicated they always or usually vote.
***$p < 0.01$; **$p < 0.05$; *$p < 0.1$

Table B.2   Undesirable Population Growth: Factors Explaining the
Probability That California Voters Believe Population Growth Is
a Bad Thing Rather Than a Good Thing or of No Consequence

Factor	Percentage Point Increase or Decrease in Belief Due to Each Factor
Race	
Asian	−1.2
Black	−9.7**
Hispanic	−8.0**
White non-Hispanic (ref)	—
Other	−1.9
Age	
18 to 24	−10.7**
25 to 34	−9.3**
35 to 44	−1.8
45 to 54 (ref)	—
55 to 64	1.1
65 or over	−1.4
Gender	
Male (ref)	—
Female	5.5**
Nativity	
Native-born (ref)	—
Foreign-born (citizen)	−7.2*
Education	
Less than high school	2.6
High school (ref)	—
Some college	−4.5
BA degree or higher	−7.1*
Income	
Less than $20,000 (ref)	—
$20,000 to $39,999	4.7
$40,000 to $59,999	8.8*
$60,000 to $79,999	9.2*
$80,000 or more	2.6
Homeownership	
Owner	−2.3
Renter (ref)	—
Expected population growth	
Rapid	2.6
Other (ref)	—

Table B.2   (*Continued*)

Factor	Percentage Point Increase or Decrease in Belief Due to Each Factor
Public education system	
Get worse	2.8
Other (ref)	—
Air quality	
Get worse	3.2
Other (ref)	—
Job opportunities and economic conditions	
Get worse	7.7***
Other (ref)	—
Traffic conditions	
Get worse	5.9
Other (ref)	—
Affordable housing	
Get worse	6.6**
Other (ref)	—
Place to live	
Get worse	20.0***
Other (ref)	—
Confidence in state planning	
Low confidence	2.6
Other (ref)	—
Confidence in local planning	
Low confidence	4.0
Other (ref)	—
Political leaning	
Liberal	4.3
Moderate (ref)	—
Conservative	2.6
Intercept	34.7***
Observations	1,456
R-squared	0.139

Source: PPIC Statewide Survey (August 2004): subsample of regular voters defined by those who indicated they always or usually vote.

***$p < 0.01$; **$p < 0.05$; *$p < 0.1$

Table B.3   Undesirable Immigrants: Factors Explaining the Probability
That California Voters Believe Immigrants Pose More of a
Burden Than a Benefit or Make No Difference

	Percentage Point Increase or Decrease in Belief Due to Each Factor	
Factor	1998	2004
Intercept	45.2***	37.0***
Race		
Asian	−3.4	−21.5***
Black	1.3	6.4
Hispanic	−17.2***	−22.2***
White non-Hispanic (ref)	—	—
Other	−8.4	−9.0
Age		
18 to 24	−6.3	9.8
25 to 34	0.1	−4.2
35 to 44	0.9	−2.1
45 to 54 (ref)	—	—
55 to 64	1.1	6.0
65 or over	2.6	−6.8
Gender		
Male (ref)	—	—
Female	6.5**	3.1
Nativity		
Native-born (ref)	—	—
Foreign-born citizen	−16.9***	−6.8
Income		
Less than $20,000 (ref)	—	—
$20,000 to $39,999	−1.1	5.2
$40,000 to $59,999	−3.8	7.3
$60,000 to $79,999	−4.9	10.0*
$80,000 or more	−6.1	4.6
Political leaning		
Liberal	−4.6	−12.3***
Moderate (ref)	—	—
Conservative	9.1***	18.4***
Observations	1,246	1,157
R-squared	0.059	0.131

Source: PPIC Statewide Survey (April 1998 and February 2004): subsample of regular voters
defined by those who indicated they always or usually vote.
***$p < 0.01$; **$p < 0.05$; *$p < 0.1$

Support for Higher Taxes and Spending

Table B.4 follows a different format for the presentation of these detailed analyses. Model 1 includes only demographic and economic factors in the explanation of the percentage of voters who prefer higher taxes and spending. The addition of three political opinion variables in model 2 doubles the explanatory power of the model (R-square of 0.300 instead of 0.161). When those political opinions are added, they tend to absorb some of the prior effect that was ascribed to other variables in model 1. For example, the negative effect of homeownership is reduced nearly by half, probably because more homeowners held some of the negative political opinions that are now directly measured in model 2.

The Effect on Fiscal Preferences of the Perception That Immigrants Are a Burden

The statistical analysis constructed for this question has a single model, as presented in table B.5. The outcome measure here is positive support for the Proposition 55 school bonds, as expressed in an opinion poll taken three weeks before the election. Net of all other factors, we can judge the negative impact on willingness to support the bonds (–8.5 percent) of the perception that immigrants are a burden. What is noteworthy in this model is that the effect exists even after accounting for other powerful political opinions that are likely to discourage voter support. Voters who feel that a lot of tax money is wasted are 7.7 percent less willing to support the state school bonds, and conservative voters are 9.3 percent less likely than moderate voters (or 17.6 percent less likely than liberals) to support the bonds. We note also the very high intercept value of 74.8, representing the base level of support by the reference group before any of these negative effects are tallied. This suggests a fairly high level of support, but we also note that the R-square is very low, only 0.096. That indicates that the model has a low explanatory power: there is simply a lot of idiosyncrasy in voter opinion on this issue that cannot be explained.

Table B.4 Support for Higher Taxes and Spending: Factors Explaining the Probability That California Voters Want to Expand Support for Services Rather Than Lower Taxes and Spending or Don't Know Response

Factor	Percentage Point Increase or Decrease in Support Due to Each Factor	
	Model 1 (Based on Demographics and Economics)	Model 2 (Also Factoring in Political Opinions)
Political leaning		
Liberal		20.1***
Moderate (reference)		—
Conservative		−17.8***
Trust in government		
Trust		3.5
No trust (reference)		—
Waste taxes		
Waste taxes a lot		−16.6***
Other (reference)		—
Race		
Asian	12.0*	10.0
Black	20.6***	18.5***
Hispanic	18.3***	13.7***
White (reference)	—	—
Other	3.9	3.5
Age		
18 to 24	26.6***	18.3***
25 to 34	10.1**	8.6**
35 to 44	−4.7	−2.0
45 to 54 (reference)	—	—
55 to 64	−6.1	−2.2
65 or over	−13.4***	−5.1
Gender		
Female	11.7***	6.6**
Male (reference)	—	—

Table B.4   (*Continued*)

Factor	Percentage Point Increase or Decrease in Support Due to Each Factor	
	Model 1 (Based on Demographics and Economics)	Model 2 (Also Factoring in Political Opinions)
Children		
Present	4.2*	8.5**
Not present (reference)	—	—
Nativity		
Foreign-born citizen	9.5*	9.4*
Native-born (reference)	—	—
Education		
Less than high school	4.2	1.6
High school (reference)	—	—
Some college	−6.6	−7.2*
BA degree or higher	3.0	−4.2
Income		
Less than $20,000 (reference)	—	—
$20,000 to $39,999	3.0	4.9
$40,000 to $59,999	−3.2	−0.9
$60,000 to $79,999	−5.5	−4.4
$80,000 or more	−9.7*	−5.9
Homeownership		
Owner	−11.0***	−6.6
Renter (reference)	—	—
Constant	45.2***	51.5***
Observations	1,064	1,064
R-squared	0.161	0.300

Source: PPIC Statewide Survey (June 2003): subsample of regular voters defined by those who indicated they always or usually vote.
***p < 0.01; **p < 0.05; *p < 0.1

Table B.5   The Effect of Perceived Immigrant Burden on Willingness to Pay Taxes: Factors Explaining the Probability That California Voters Will Support the Proposition 55 Statewide School Bond Measure

Factor	Percentage Point Increase or Decrease in Support Due to Each Factor
Political leaning	
Liberal	8.3**
Moderate (reference)	—
Conservative	−9.3**
Waste taxes	
Waste taxes a lot	−7.7**
Other (reference)	—
Immigrants are burden	
Burden	−8.5***
Benefit or other (reference)	—
Race	
Asian	1.5
Black	1.3
Hispanic	7.7
White (reference)	—
Other	−14.7*
Age	
18 to 24	0.4
25 to 34	−6.6
35 to 44	−3.9
45 to 54 (reference)	—
55 to 64	−7.4
65 or over	−8.8*
Gender	
Female	8.6***
Male (reference)	—
Children	
Present	10.8***
Not present (reference)	—

Table B.5   (*Continued*)

Factor	Percentage Point Increase or Decrease in Support Due to Each Factor
Nativity	
Foreign-born citizen	−0.6
Native-born (reference)	—
Education	
Less than high school	−4.4
High school (reference)	—
Some college	−5.7
BA degree or higher	−0.6
Income	
Less than $20,000 (reference)	—
$20,000 to $39,999	−12.2**
$40,000 to $59,999	−11.9**
$60,000 to $79,999	−20.1***
$80,000 or more	−15.8***
Homeownership	
Owner	−5.7
Renter (reference)	—
Constant	74.8***
Observations	1,066
R-squared	0.096

Source: PPIC Statewide Survey (February 2004): subsample of regular voters defined by those who indicated they always or usually vote.
***$p < 0.01$; **$p < 0.05$; *$p < 0.1$

Notes

Chapter 1

1. See chapter 7 for details on how this projection was carried out and comparisons to other voting projections.

2. The homeownership rate of Latino immigrants in California soared from 16.3 percent in 1980, when they had recently arrived, to 51.9 percent in 2000, twenty years later. In the United States as a whole, Latinos made even greater gains, reaching 55.9 percent homeownership in 2000. Data are drawn from the public use microdata files of the 1980 and 2000 censuses. This underrecognized and astounding record of progress is described thoroughly in chapter 6.

3. Survey information on immigration from www.Gallup.com/poll (accessed July 17, 2005).

4. Analysis of data described in Mark Baldassare, "Statewide Survey: Californians and Their Government," (San Francisco: Public Policy Institute of California, February 2004).

5. In Texas the work of the state demographer, Steve Murdock, has gained considerable attention in the state legislature, as have Marta Tienda and Teresa Sullivan through their efforts in the domain of higher education. Steve H. Murdock et al., *The New Texas Challenge: Population Change and the Future of Texas* (College Station: Texas A&M University Press, 2003); Marta Tienda and Teresa Sullivan, "The Texas Higher Education Opportunity Project," available at: http://www.texastop10.princeton.edu.

6. Marta Tienda and Faith Mitchell, eds., *Multiple Origins, Uncertain Destinies: Hispanics and the American Future* (Washington, D.C.: National Academies Press, 2006), 14.

7. We discuss the detailed projections from the GAO in chapter 9. For a study endorsed by several Nobel Prize–winning economists, see Laurence J. Kotlikoff and Scott Burns, *The Coming Generational Storm: What You Need to*

Know About America's Economic Future (Cambridge, Mass.: MIT Press, 2005).

8. Haya El Nasser, "Analysis Finds Boom in Hispanics' Home Buying," *USA Today*, May 11, 2006, 1.

9. Ernest L. Boyer, *Scholarship Reconsidered: Priorities of the Professoriate* (Princeton, N.J.: Carnegie Foundation, 1990).

10. The perspective offered here may appear novel, because only recently have a few scholars begun to contemplate the unique configuration of changes we face. William Frey and Ross DeVol have observed that aging baby boomers and new immigrants are dominant factors in America's new demography: "America's Demography in the New Century: Aging Baby Boomers and New Immigrants as Major Players." Working paper 9. (Santa Monica: Milken Institute, 2000). In Europe, David Coleman has identified a sweeping population transition that includes low birth rates, an aging society, and ethnic change due to immigration. "Immigration and Ethnic Change in Low-Fertility Countries: A Third Demographic Transition," *Population and Development Review* 32(September 2006): 401–46. In terms of policy, the Harvard law professor and social theorist Mary Ann Glendon has suggested that immigration could be usefully coupled as a planned solution to the problems of an aging society. "Principled Immigration," *First Things* 164(June/July 2006): 23–26.

Chapter 2

1. Charles E. Lindblom and David K. Cohen, *Usable Knowledge: Social Science and Social Problem Solving* (New Haven, Conn.: Yale University Press, 1979).

2. Howard Gardner, *Changing Minds: The Art and Science of Changing Our Own and Other People's Minds* (Boston: Harvard Business School Press, 2004).

3. This example is taken from a series of surveys reported by Karl E. Case and Robert J. Shiller, "Is There a Bubble in the Housing Market?" *Brookings Papers on Economic Activity* 2(2003): 299–362.

4. Barry Glassner, *The Culture of Fear: Why Americans Are Afraid of the Wrong Things* (New York: Basic Books, 1999), xi.

5. The method of extrapolation is a constant annual rate of increase. Compounded across successive decades, the foreign-born share escalates upward, reaching 20.8 percent extrapolated from the 1990 vantage point, and 30.8 percent based on 2000.

6. Forecast prepared by Jeffrey Passel for the National Research Council, as reported in Marta Tienda and Faith Mitchell, eds., *Multiple Origins, Uncertain*

Destinies: Hispanics and the American Future (Washington: National Academies Press, 2006), 62. In addition, the latest projections of foreign-born prepared by the Census Bureau, which preceded the 2000 census and would surely be revised upward today, yielded a foreign-born share of 12.5 percent; Frederick W. Hollmann, Tammany J. Mulder, and Jeffrey E. Kallan, "Methodology and Assumptions for the Population Projections of the United States: 1999 to 2100," working paper 38 (Washington: U.S. Census Bureau, Population Division, 2000).

7.   In fact, an earlier version of projections prepared by the California Demographic Futures project had foreseen the slowdown in immigrant growth recorded in 2000. The reasoning is detailed in Dowell Myers, John Pitkin, and Julie Park, *California Demographic Futures: Projections to 2030, by Immigrant Generations, Nativity, and Time of Arrival in U.S.: Full Report* (Los Angeles: University of Southern California, School of Policy, Planning, and Development, Population Dynamics Research Group, February 2005), available at: http://www.usc.edu/schools/sppd/research/popdynamics/CDFFULLreport2005.pdf.

8.   Mark Baldassare, "Special Survey on Population" (San Francisco: Public Policy Institute of California, December 2005), as discussed in chapter 4. Admittedly, given that half the babies are born to foreign-born mothers, one could say that immigration is responsible for these as well.

9.   Jacob S. Siegal and David A. Swanson, eds., *The Methods and Materials of Demography* (San Diego: Academic Press, 2004).

10.   Jeffrey S. Passel and Roberto Suro, "Rise, Peak, and Decline: Trends in U.S. Immigration, 1992–2004" (Washington: Pew Hispanic Center, 2005).

11.   These are the "middle series" projections, normally regarded as the more likely scenario; Hollmann, Mulder, and Kallan, "Methodology and Assumptions for the Population Projections of the United States: 1999 to 2100," table E.

12.   The planning theorist James Throgmorton has championed the view that the rhetoric of storytelling is a principal means of generating support for collective initiatives, as highlighted by the title of one of his essays, "Planning as Persuasive Story Telling About the Future: Negotiating an Electric Power Rate Settlement in Illinois," *Journal of Planning Education and Research* 12(1992): 17–31.

13.   Peter Schwartz, *The Art of the Long View: Planning for the Future in an Uncertain World* (New York: Doubleday, 1996), 38.

14.   Recent philosophical thinking on pessimism has raised a similar idea, namely, that the difference between pessimists and optimists is in their treatment of

time; Joshua Foa Dienstag, *Pessimism: Philosophy, Ethic, Spirit* (Princeton, N.J.: Princeton University Press, 2006).

15. There is a rich tradition of reflection on the points in this section. For example, see Nathan Keyfitz, "The Social and Political Context of Population Forecasting," in *The Politics of Numbers*, edited by William Alonso and Paul Starr (New York: Russell Sage Foundation, 1987). See also Andrew Isserman, "Projection, Forecast, and Plan," *Journal of the American Planning Association* 50(1984): 208–10. For a broad review, see Dowell Myers and Alicia Kitsuse, "Constructing the Future in Planning: A Survey of Theories and Tools," *Journal of Planning Education and Research* 19(2000): 221–31. A very recent collection of thought that emphasizes scenarios and forecasts as part of plans is Lewis D. Hopkins and Marisa Zapata, eds., *Engaging Our Futures: Forecasts, Scenarios, Plans, and Projects* (Cambridge, Mass.: Lincoln Institute for Land Policy, 2007).

Chapter 3

1. D'Vera Cohn and Darryl Fears, "Hispanics Draw Even with Blacks in New Census: Latino Population Up 60% Since 1990," *Washington Post*, March 7, 2001, A1.

2. Andrew Sum, Neeta Fugg, and Ishwar Khatiwada, with Sheila Palma, "Foreign Immigration and the Labor Force of the U.S.: The Contributions of New Foreign Immigration to the Growth of the National Labor Force and Its Employed Population, 2000 to 2004," (Boston: Northeastern University, Center for Labor Market Studies, 2004).

3. "Immigration Trend Summary," Gallup Poll News Service, www.gallup.com, accessed July 15, 2005.

4. U.S. Census Bureau, "Oldest Baby Boomers Turn 60!" *Facts for Features* (special edition), CB06-FFSE.01, December 12, 2005.

5. Peter Schrag, *California: America's High-Stakes Experiment* (Berkeley: University of California Press, 2006).

6. The percentage of Americans living in rural areas is drawn from series A73-81 and the figures on electrification from series S108-119 in U.S. Census Bureau, *Historical Statistics of the United States*, bicentennial edition (Washington: U.S. Census Bureau, 1975).

7. The second transition was first identified by Lesthaeghe and van de Kaa in a Dutch publication in 1986. Publications in English soon followed: Dirk J. van

de Kaa, "Europe's Second Demographic Transition," *Population Bulletin* 42 (March 1987): 3–57, and Ron Lesthaeghe, "The Second Demographic Transition in Western Countries: An Interpretation," in *Gender and Family Change in Industrialized Countries*, edited by Karen Oppenheim Mason and An-Magritt Jensen (Oxford: Clarendon Press, 1995). A more recent summary can be found in David Coleman, "Facing the Twenty-first Century: New Developments, Continuing Problems," in *The New Demographic Regime: Population Challenges and Policy Responses*, edited by Miroslav Macura, Alphonse L. MacDonald, and Werner Haug (New York and Geneva: United Nations, 2005).

8. Van de Kaa ("Europe's Second Demographic Transition," table 1) cites much evidence from Dutch surveys, including the finding that the percentage of residents agreeing that a couple's voluntary childlessness is acceptable increased from 27 percent in 1966 to 60 percent in 1970 and 79 percent in 1980. Also, the percentage of residents agreeing that the labor force participation of married women with school-age children is acceptable rose from 17 percent in 1965 to 56 percent in 1970. Similar evidence in the case of the United States is reported by Reynolds Farley in "The 1960s: A Turning Point in How We View Race, Gender, and Sexuality," in his *The New American Reality: Who We Are, How We Got Here, Where We Are Going* (New York: Russell Sage Foundation, 1996).

9. Population Reference Bureau, "2005 World Population Data Sheet," updated figures available at: http://www.prb.org.

10. Mary M. Kent and Carl Haub, "Global Demographic Divide," *Population Bulletin* of the Population Reference Bureau (December 2005), available at: http://www.prb.org.

11. This formulation of a third great demographic transition was first presented in Dowell Myers, "California and the Third Great Demographic Transition: Immigrant Incorporation, Ethnic Change, and Population Aging, 1970 to 2030," paper presented to the conference "America's Americans: The Populations of the United States," British Library, London, May 8 and 9, 2006.

12. Kevin Kinsella and David R. Phillips, "Global Aging: The Challenge of Success," *Population Bulletin* of the Population Reference Bureau (March 2005), available at: http://www.prb.org.

13. The notion that increased immigration could compensate for low fertility was dramatized in a 2000 report from the UN Population Division, *Replacement Migration: Is It a Solution to Declining and Aging Populations?* ESA/P/WP.160 (New York: United Nations, 2000). However, that study found that extreme

increases in the numbers of immigrants would be required to forestall an over-all lagging of the working-age population. At any given moment in time, the benefits of immigration may not be apparent, and over time the impact may be very modest, as charged by immigration critics in the United States; see Steven A. Camarota, "Backgrounder: Immigration in an Aging Society: Workers, Birth Rates, and Social Security" (Washington, D.C.: Center for Immigration Studies, 2005). Recent careful demographic research by Wolfgang Lutz and Sergei Scherbov reports a number of simulations for the European Union through 2050. The authors find that immigration cannot forestall population aging. However, "there is a clear compensatory relationship between fertility and migration. A TFR (total fertility rate) of 1.0 and a migration gain of 1.2 million per year yields the same old-age dependency ratio in 2050 as a TFR of 2.2 and a migration gain of zero"; see Wolfgang Lutz and Sergei Scherbov, "Future Demographic Change in Europe: The Contribution of Migration," in *Europe and Its Immigrants in the Twenty-first Century: A New Deal or a Continuing Dialogue of the Deaf?* edited by Demetrios G. Papademetriou (Washington, D.C.: Migration Policy Institute, 2006), 220.

14.   David Coleman also has recently proposed a third demographic transition—which he demonstrates with population projections for European nations—but his interest is fixed on the ethnic transition as a population of "foreign-origin" (including both the foreign-born and their descendants) begins to replace old-stock residents; see David Coleman, "Immigration and Ethnic Change in Low-Fertility Countries: A Third Demographic Transition," *Population and Development Review* 32 (September 2006): 401–46.

15.   The notion of racial identity has changed over time: some ethnic groups we now consider white, such as the Irish, were once treated as if they were a separate race. On this and the racial effects of recent immigration, see Frank D. Bean, Jennifer Lee, Jeanne Batalova, and Mark Leach, "Immigration and Fading Color Lines in America," in *The American People: Census 2000*, edited by Reynolds Farley and John Haaga (New York: Russell Sage Foundation, 2005).

16.   United Nations, "Final Document of the Forum," quoted in Miroslav Macura, Alphonse L. MacDonald, and Werner Haug, eds., *The New Demographic Regime: Population Challenges and Policy Responses* (New York and Geneva: United Nations, 2005), 290–91.

17.   Population data from 2000 and before are taken from the decennial census. Projections were prepared by the U.S. Census Bureau (interim projections released April 2005).

18. Mary Elizabeth Hughes and Angela O. Rand, "The Lives and Times of the Baby Boomers," in Farley and Haaga, *The American People*.

19. Karen Yourish and Laura Stanton, "A Graying Population," *Washington Post*, March 9, 2005.

20. Mitra Toossi, "A Century of Change: The U.S. Labor Force, 1950–2050," *Monthly Labor Review* (May 2002): 15–28.

21. For details, see Liana C. Sayer, Philip N. Cohen, and Lynne M. Casper, "Women, Men, and Work," in Farley and Haaga, *The American People*. For a critical assessment of remaining inequality, see David A. Cotter, Joan M. Hermsen, and Reeve Vanneman, "Gender Inequality at Work," also in Farley and Haaga, *The American People*.

22. Toossi, "A Century of Change," 27.

23. The BLS projections show a rise in participation rates at age sixty-five and older—representing nonretirement—that reaches 21.0 percent participation for men in 2020, compared to 16.4 percent in 1990. Among women age sixty-five and older, participation rates are expected to rise from 8.7 percent in 1990 to 12.7 percent in 2020; see Toossi, "A Century of Change," 22.

24. Peter A. Morrison, "A Demographic Perspective on Our Nation's Future: A Documented Briefing" (Santa Monica, Calif.: RAND Corporation, 2001).

25. Historical data are taken from the Current Population Survey (CPS). Projections from 2005 through 2030 borrow labor force participation trends from the BLS national study (see Toossi, "A Century of Change," 22) and assume that California's participation rates will change proportionally to the nation's. These rates are then applied to the Census Bureau 2004 series of population projections for the nation and California, a more up-to-date series than was available for Toossi's study.

26. On the challenges of intermarriage and multiracial identity for projections of racial and ethnic groups, see Barry Edmonston and Jeffrey S. Passel, "How Immigration and Intermarriage Affect the Racial and Ethnic Composition of the U.S. Population," in Frank D. Bean and Stephanie Bell-Rose, eds., *Immigration and Opportunity* (New York: Russell Sage Foundation, 1999). Data reported here are derived from the decennial censuses of 1970, 1980, 1990, and 2000. Projections for 2010, 2020, and 2030 are taken from two sources: for the United States, interim projections issued by the Census Bureau in 2005; for California, projections issued in 2004 by the Demographic Research Unit of the California Department of Finance.

27. Many have written on the politics and scientific concerns behind the changing

menu of racial categories offered in the Census Bureau's decennial census or current surveys. For example, see Clara E. Rodriguez, *Changing Race: Latinos, the Census, and the History of Ethnicity in the United States* (New York: New York University Press, 2000), and Charles Hirschman, Richard Alba, and Reynolds Farley, "The Meaning and Measurement of Race in the U.S. Census: Glimpses into the Future," *Demography* 37(3, August 2000): 381–93.

28. Historical data for California are taken from California Department of Finance, Demographic Research Unit, "Race-Ethnic Population with Age and Sex Detail, 1970–1989 [and 1990–1999]" (December 1998 [and May 2004]).

29. Historical data for the United States are taken from Campbell Gibson and June Kay, "Historical Census Statistics on Population Totals by Race, 1970 to 1990, and by Hispanic Origin, 1970 to 1990, for Large Cities and Other Urban Places in the United States," working paper 76 (Washington: U.S. Census Bureau, Population Division, 2005). The 2000 data are drawn from the decennial data of Census 2000.

30. Latinos are expected to reach 50 percent of the total in 2040. Projection data for California cited in the text and for figure 3.5 are taken from California Department of Finance, Demographic Research Unit, "Race-Ethnic Population with Age and Sex Detail, 2000–2050" (May 2004).

31. Data are not shown for Florida because the trend line of that state is virtually indistinguishable from that for the United States as a whole. Also, it should be noted that current population estimates reported by the Census Bureau for 2005 reveal even lower white shares of each state's population than shown in figure 3.5. That is not necessarily an indication of an accelerating downward trend but is at least partially due to a redefinition of the white population to exclude people of multiple racial origins. The data reported in the figure maintain a more consistent definition across the decades. For this purpose, I use the most recent (but dated—1996) series of projections prepared by the Census Bureau to show race and Hispanic origin for states. Paul R. Campbell, "Population Projections for States by Age, Sex, Race, and Hispanic Origin: 1995 to 2025," report PPL-47 (Washington: Census Bureau, Population Division, 1996).

32. U.S. Census Bureau, "U.S. Interim Projections by Age, Sex, Race, and Hispanic Origin" (2004), available at http://www.census.gov/ipc/www/usinterimproj/.

33. Rogelio Saenz, "Latinos and the Changing Face of America," in Farley and Haaga, *The American People*.

34. For excellent summaries of immigration in the United States, see Philip Martin and Elizabeth Midgley, "Immigration to the United States," *Population Bulletin*

of the Population Reference Bureau (54, no. 2, 1999); Mary M. Kritz and Douglas T. Gurak, "Immigration and a Changing America," in Farley and Haaga, *The American People.*

35. Department of Homeland Security, Office of Immigration Statistics, *Yearbook of Immigration Statistics: 2004,* table 1 (Washington: U.S. Government Printing Office, 2005).

36. New immigrant arrivals settled in cities, later moving to suburbs as they climbed the economic ladder, but the exodus was delayed by the Great Depression and World War II. As foreseen by the legendary land economist Homer Hoyt, the diminished flow of replacements led to the spread of abandoned areas and "gray areas" throughout many inner cities that had formerly been immigrant gateways. Ultimately, programs of urban renewal and other efforts were undertaken to repair the urban condition. See Dowell Myers, "Immigration: Fundamental Force in the American City," *Housing Facts and Findings* (Fannie Mae Foundation) (Winter 1999): 3–5.

37. "Perhaps the New Deal's greatest achievement was its accommodation of the maturing immigrant communities that had milled uneasily on the margins of American society for a generation or more before the 1930s"; David M. Kennedy, *Freedom from Fear: The American People in Depression and War, 1929-1945* (New York: Oxford University Press, 1999), 378.

38. Richard D. Alba, *Italian Americans: Into the Twilight of Ethnicity* (Englewood Cliffs, N.J.: Prentice-Hall, 1985).

39. These data are derived from several sources: Campbell Gibson and Emily Lennon, "Historical Census Statistics on the Foreign-Born Population of the United States, 1850–1990," Population Division working paper 29 (Washington: U.S. Census Bureau, 1999); U.S. Census Bureau, Population Division, Census 2000 public use microdata sample (2000); Population Projections Program, "Projections of the Resident Population by Race, Hispanic Origin, and Nativity: Middle Series, 1999 to 2100," NP-T5 (final projections consistent with the 1990 census) (Washington: U.S. Census Bureau, Population Division); California Demographic Futures project, projections by John Pitkin, version 5.0.

40. Using a special tabulation of the public use microdata sample from the 1970 census reveals that, in 1970, 34.3 percent of the foreign-born were age sixty or older, compared to only 12.9 percent of the native-born.

41. The California Demographic Futures projections were developed under the methodological leadership of John Pitkin, a principal in the firm of Analysis

and Forecasting, Inc. A conventional cohort component method based on age, sex, and race of population was extended to incorporate dimensions of nativity, generation, and decade of arrival in the United States. For this purpose, schedules of gross migration rates into and out of California, as well as fertility and mortality rates, needed to be developed for each of these more detailed population subgroups. Although most of the future foreign-born and their children are already here and aging in place, substantial uncertainty surrounds the number of future new arrivals. The CDF assumes that the immigration levels to the United States in future years will remain at roughly the same level as the last few years. Of course, this assumption would have to be revised if substantial changes were made to immigration policy. For more details, see Dowell Myers, John Pitkin, and Julie Park, *California Demographic Futures: Projections to 2030, by Immigrant Generations, Nativity, and Time of Arrival in U.S.: Full Report* (Los Angeles: University of Southern California, School of Policy, Planning, and Development, Population Dynamics Research Group, February 2005), available at: http://www.usc.edu/schools/sppd/research/popdynamics/ CDFFULLreport2005.pdf.

42.   The USC data are referenced and utilized, for example, in Ellen Hanak and Mark Baldassare, eds., *California 2025: Taking on the Future* (San Francisco: Public Policy Institute of California, 2005), and Center for Continuing Study of the California Economy, "The Impact of Immigration on the California Economy," a report commissioned of the California Regional Economies Project (September 2005), available at: http://www.labor.ca.gov/panel/ impactimmcaecon.pdf.

43.   Very few population projections in the nation contain any information on the foreign-born. The Census Bureau's last effort in 1998 is now outdated. And neither the California Department of Finance nor Steve Murdock's team in Texas nor any other group has prepared foreign-born projections for a specific state. Surely the annual flow of new arrivals in future years is uncertain, and this might also be politically contentious for government agencies. Nonetheless, the bulk of the foreign-born population is already in residence and can be aged forward with standard demographic techniques. It bears mentioning that the standard techniques for the projections used by demographers were developed largely in the period from 1940 through 1970, a time when immigration was of much less consequence. Given the growing importance of this population segment, the absence of such information is now more notable.

44.   Note that the Census Bureau projections extend only to nativity, not to second-

generation status or decade of arrival for the foreign-born; Population Projections Program, "Projections of the Resident Population by Race, Hispanic Origin, and Nativity: Middle Series, 1999 to 2100," NP-T5 (final projections consistent with the 1990 census) (Washington: U.S. Census Bureau, Population Division, 2000).

45. The recent National Research Council study of Hispanics and the American future reported a projection (prepared by Jeffrey Passel) for the foreign-born share of the total U.S. population that equaled 16.2 percent in 2030; see Marta Tienda and Faith Mitchell, eds., *Multiple Origins, Uncertain Destinies: Hispanics and the American Future* (Washington, D.C.: National Academies Press, 2006), 62.

46. Nolan Malone, Kaari F. Baluja, Joseph M. Costanzo, and Cynthia J. Davis, "The Foreign-Born Population: 2000," Census 2000 brief, C2KBR-34 (Washington: U.S. Census Bureau, 2003), table 1.

47. Future numbers of immigrant arrivals are highly uncertain because they are subject to abrupt shifts in policy, the economy, or war. Nonetheless, forecasters find it most likely that immigration will not rise much beyond the levels observed around 2000 and that a fairly constant or even declining level will be sustained over the next two decades. This is the assumption adopted in the Census Bureau projections described earlier, and it is also adopted in the California Demographic Futures projections, as noted previously. Similarly, the National Research Council study on Hispanics and the America future reports an expected net immigration of Hispanics to cease its increase, varying from 8.1 million for the 1990s to 7.3 million for the 2010s; Tienda and Mitchell, *Multiple Origins, Uncertain Destinies*, 24. This slowdown is based in part on the falling birthrates in Mexico, as discussed earlier in the chapter. If abrupt changes in policy or the economy do occur, the future number of arrivals could even be much lower. See also the discussion in chapter 2.

48. According to the Immigration and Nationality Act, an immigrant is any alien (noncitizen) living in the United States who was not admitted under a temporary visa. See the definitions offered by the Department of Homeland Security, Office of Immigration Statistics, available at: http://www.uscis.gov/graphics/shared/statistics/standards/index.htm. Thus, there are legal immigrants, termed "permanent resident aliens" (often called "green card" holders), and illegal immigrants, whose entry was not authorized. Also counted among the foreign-born are temporary residents, such as those entering on a student visa. (It bears noting that as many as half of these illegal or unauthorized immigrants did not

cross the border illegally but are visa overstayers who once held legal status as visitors.)

49. The available data are flawed in various ways. One flaw is that these numbers are probably undercounted, especially among foreign-born residents who are temporary residents, and there is heaping of responses on years ending in zero because some respondents round off their year of arrival as, for example, 1980, instead of 1979 or 1981. Others have questioned the meaning of the term "arrival" when immigrants may be crossing the border in a circular pattern of repeated visits. Nonetheless, these Census Bureau data are still found to provide a useful representation of the arrival of new immigrants over time; see Dowell Myers, "Accuracy of Data Collected by the Census Question on Immigrants' Year of Arrival," working paper PDRG04-01 (Los Angeles: University of Southern California, School of Policy, Planning, and Development, Population Dynamics Research Group, 2004).

50. The data on annual authorized immigrants are adjusted to remove over two million immigrants who had previously arrived illegally and were later allowed to adjust their immigration status to authorized immigrants, largely recorded from 1989 to 1992 under provisions of the Immigration Reform and Control Act of 1986.

51. Jeffrey S. Passel, "Unauthorized Migrants: Numbers and Characteristics," background briefing prepared for the Task Force on Immigration and America's Future, Pew Hispanic Center, Washington, June 2005.

52. Estimates of this share vary; Passel ("Unauthorized Migrants," 12) finds that 45 percent of unauthorized residents lived in California in 1990. Of those who were later legalized under provisions of the Immigration Reform and Control Act, fully 53 percent were living in California.

53. California's share of unauthorized residents is from ibid. The share of new unauthorized immigrants was calculated by the author based on California's share of the difference between CPS estimates of new immigrants and those officially reported by the federal government for 2000 to 2003.

54. Ibid.

Chapter 4

1. Benjamin M. Friedman, "Meltdown: A Case Study—What America a Century Ago Can Teach Us About the Moral Consequences of Economic Decline," *Atlantic Monthly* (July–August 2005): 68 (emphasis added).

2. Peter Schrag, *Paradise Lost: California's Experience, America's Future* (Berkeley: University of California Press, 2004), 7 (emphasis added).

3. Ibid., 9–11, where the centrality of this observation to Schrag's thesis is most succinctly stated.

4. Public trust began to falter in the mid-1960s before the war in Vietnam became widely unpopular, probably because of the civil rights struggles, urban riots, and other disruptions; Arthur H. Miller, "Political Issues and Trust in Government: 1964–1970," *American Political Science Review* (September 1974): 951–70. Protests over Vietnam then served to deepen divisions, and the subsequent Watergate scandal hardened distrust into public cynicism. On this "explosion of alienation," see Stanley B. Greenberg, *Middle-Class Dreams: The Politics and Power of the New American Majority* (New Haven, Conn.: Yale University Press, 1996), 117–10, and associated appendices.

5. In constant dollars, the median family income rose 43 percent in the 1950s and 41 percent in the 1960s; Frank Levy, *The New Dollars and Dreams: American Incomes and Economic Change* (New York: Russell Sage Foundation, 1998), tables 3.1 and 3.2.

6. For richly informative depictions of life in the 1950s, see Mary Elizabeth Hughes and Angela O. Rand, "The Lives and Times of the Baby Boomers," in *The American People: Census 2000*, edited by Reynolds Farley and John Haaga (New York: Russell Sage Foundation, 2005).

7. Reynolds Farley, *The New American Reality: Who We Are, How We Got Here, Where We Are Going* (New York: Russell Sage Foundation, 1996), 64–66.

8. Ironically, we now recognize in hindsight that the 1950s were not a reliable standard of normalcy. Not only were the income gains that decade highly unusual, but the supposedly typical family life of the 1950s is now considered an aberration. The most direct indicator of this is that the fertility rates in the 1950s that precipitated the baby boom generation were well above those of most decades in the previous fifty years. In a real sense the burgeoning birthrate represented a social reaction to the ravages of the Great Depression and the restrictions of the war years, events that also were not normal in the context of U.S. history. Robert L. Heuser, *Fertility Tables for Birth Cohorts by Color: United States, 1917–73* (Rockville, Md.: U.S. National Center for Health Statistics).

9. Levy, *The New Dollars and Dreams*, table 3.3.

10. Ibid., tables 3.1 and 3.2.

11. Ibid., 62, table 4.3.

12. Ibid., table 3.3.

13. The ratio of government expenditures to personal income has been described as "the price of government." David Osbourne and Peter Hutchinson argue that this ratio has fluctuated above and below its long-run average of about 35 percent in the United States. They show that the ratio peaked in the early 1980s before taxpayer resistance drove it down again; David Osbourne and Peter Hutchinson, *The Price of Government* (New York: Basic Books, 2004), figure 2.5.

14. Robert J. Samuelson, *The Good Life and Its Discontents: The American Dream in the Age of Entitlement, 1945–1995* (New York: Random House/Times Books, 1995).

15. See Jeffrey Madrick, *The End of Affluence: The Causes and Consequences of America's Economic Dilemma* (New York: Random House, 1995); Greenberg, *Middle-Class Dreams*; Samuelson, *The Good Life and Its Discontents*. The earliest book of this theme may be Katherine S. Newman, *Falling from Grace: Downward Mobility in the Age of Affluence* (Berkeley: University of California Press, 1988).

16. Samuelson, *The Good Life and Its Discontents*, 6 (emphasis added).

17. Carey McWilliams, *California: The Great Exception* (New York: Current Books, 1949).

18. For the fullest recognition of the discouraging effects of these concentrated calamities, see Kevin Starr, *Coast of Dreams: California on the Edge, 1990–2003* (New York: Knopf, 2004). See also Mike Davis, *Ecology of Fear: Los Angeles and the Imagination of Disaster* (New York: Vintage Books, 1998) and Schrag, *Paradise Lost*.

19. On the essential task of remembering and commemorating the past as a necessary step to removing it as an obstacle to embracing a new future, see Howell Baum, "Forget to Plan," *Journal of Planning Education and Research* 19(1999): 2–14.

20. California's teams dominated baseball, basketball, and football. Led by Magic Johnson, the Los Angeles Lakers, with their "showtime" offense, had become America's basketball team, winning championships four times in the 1980s, while the San Francisco 49ers, led by Joe Montana, were three-time Super Bowl champions of the National Football League. Major league baseball was also dominated by California teams in the late 1980s; in the 1988 and 1989 World Series, both teams were from California. Californians may have grown to ex-

pect a championship every year, but then during the 1990s only one California team won a championship in all three sports combined.

21. Davis, *Ecology of Fear*, 8.

22. The Loma Prieta quake in the San Francisco area was followed by the 7.5 magnitude Landers quake (June 28, 1992) in a relatively unpopulated area and the 6.7 magnitude Northridge quake (January 17, 1994), causing fifty-seven deaths and over $20 billion in damage in the Los Angeles area ($42 billion if lost business expenses are included). The Northridge quake was said to be the costliest natural disaster in U.S. history (prior to Hurricane Katrina): it was declared by the Federal Emergency Management Agency (FEMA) to have exceeded the combined costs of the Loma Prieta earthquake, Hurricane Andrew, and Hurricane Hugo (Davis, *Ecology of Fear*, 7). Other, smaller quakes had more localized effects (for example, the Sierra Madre quake of 1992 outside Los Angeles) but drew media attention and sustained awareness of the looming danger from earthquakes.

23. Captain Donald R. Parker, Oakland Office of Fire Services, "The Oakland–Berkeley Hills Fire: An Overview," available at: www.sfmuseum.org/oakfire/overview.html (accessed May 28, 2005).

24. Mike Davis describes homeowners' fears "that an invisible army of careless, embittered strangers was lurking in the brush" (*Ecology of Fear*, 131). He also quotes a *Los Angeles Times* editorial: "What the arsonists did to us in the last two weeks they can do to us next week, or the one after that. . . . We are no longer fighting 'it'; we are fighting 'them'" (132).

25. The steep changes were duly recorded by the CPS. Nationwide, unemployment rose from 5.6 percent to 6.9 percent between 1990 and 1993, while poverty rates rose from 13.5 percent to 15.1 percent. The impact was far worse in California. Unemployment rates in the state shot from 5.8 percent in 1990 to 9.5 percent in 1993 and would not return to the 1990 level until 1999. Meanwhile, poverty rates increased from 13.9 percent in 1990 to 18.2 percent in 1993, and also would not subside to the 1990 level until 1999.

26. Mark Baldassare, *When Government Fails: The Orange County Bankruptcy* (Berkeley: University of California Press, 1998).

27. House price trends are based on data supplied by the California Association of Realtors, "2005 California Housing Market Annual Historical Data Summary," and adjusted to constant 2000 dollars with the consumer price index. Further detail is provided in figure 4.1.

28. Hans Johnson and Richard Lovelady, "Migration Between California and

Other States: 1985–1994," a joint research project of the California Research Bureau of the California State Library and the Demographic Research Unit of the California Department of Finance (1995).

29. David O. Sears, "Urban Rioting in Los Angeles: A Comparison of 1965 with 1992," in *The Los Angeles Riots: Lessons for the Urban Future*, edited by Mark Baldassare (Boulder, Colo.: Westview, 1994).

30. Hans Johnson, *Undocumented Immigration to California: 1980 to 1993* (San Francisco: Public Policy Institute of California, 1996). These figures on net annual increase are an average of independent estimates and adjusted by Johnson for a moderate increase in the census undercount (series D in table 6.3).

31. Philip Martin, "Proposition 187 in California," *International Migration Review* 29(1, 1995): 255–63.

32. Mark Baldassare, "Special Survey on Population" (San Francisco: Public Policy Institute of California, December 2005), 1–3.

33. Demographic Research Unit, "Report E-6: County Population Estimates and Components of Change by County: July 1, 2000–2004" (Sacramento: California Department of Finance, February 2005).

34. As discussed in chapter 3, the figures on illegal immigration are very uncertain because arrivals are undocumented. However, discussion there and in chapter 5 explains the falloff of unauthorized immigration to California. Given Jeffrey Passel's estimate of 700,000 annual unauthorized immigrants to the United States, and given California's much reduced share of those new arrivals, which I place in the vicinity of 13 to 15 percent of the national arrivals, we can arrive at a rough estimate of how many are coming to California each year.

35. Survey information on immigration retrieved July 17, 2005, from www.gallup.com/poll/.

36. The share preferring an increase in immigration rose from single digits prior to 1999 to 16 percent of adults in 2005. Relatively more Hispanics (21 percent) that year desired increased immigration than blacks (18 percent) or non-Hispanic whites (14 percent).

37. Charles R. Chandler and Yung-mei Tsai, "Social Factors Influencing Immigration Attitudes: An Analysis of Data from the General Social Survey," *Social Science Journal* 38(2001): 177–88; M. V. Hood and Irwin L. Morris, " 'Brother, Can You Spare a Dime?' Racial-Ethnic Context and the Anglo Vote on Proposition 187," *Social Science Quarterly* 81(1, March 2000): 194–206; Farley, *The New American Reality*.

38. Indeed, recent research shows that citizens with more cosmopolitan orienta-

tions are more likely to prefer larger numbers of immigrants; see Jeannie Haubert and Elizabeth Fussell, "Explaining Pro-Immigrant Sentiment in the U.S.: Social Class, Cosmopolitanism, and Perceptions of Immigrants," *International Migration Review* 40(Fall 2006): 489–507.

39. Thomas J. Espenshade and Katherine Hempstead, "Contemporary American Attitudes Toward U.S. Immigration," *International Migration Review* 30(2, 1996): 535–70.

40. Steven A. Camarota, "Economy Slowed, but Immigration Didn't: The Foreign-Born Population, 2000–2004," backgrounder (Washington: Center for Immigration Studies, November 2004).

41. The two polls asked an identically worded question and were conducted by the Public Policy Institute of California: "PPIC Statewide Survey: Special Survey on the California State Budget" (January 2006), and "PPIC Statewide Survey: Special Survey on Education" (April 2006).

42. After the April poll data were collected, a major demonstration about immigration reform was held in Los Angeles in May 2006 and drew half a million people.

43. Exchange of July 25, 1993, quoted in Peter Brimelow, *Alien Nation: Common Sense About America's Immigration Disaster* (New York: HarperCollins, 1996), xvii.

44. Recall how many African Americans, Asian Americans, and even Latinos supported the Proposition 187 restrictions on immigrant services in California.

45. Farley, *The New American Reality*, 33.

46. Projections are from U.S. Census Bureau, "U.S. Interim Projections by Age, Sex, Race and Hispanic Origin," available at: www.census.gov/lpc/www/usinterim proj (released March 18, 2004).

47. Gregory Rodriguez, "Pouty White People: Why So Downbeat on the Future? Well, Start with Racial Changes," *Los Angeles Times*, September 26, 2004, M1.

48. Brimelow, *Alien Nation*, xxi.

49. See Gary Okihiro, *Margins and Mainstreams: Asians in American History and Culture* (Seattle: University of Washington Press, 1994).

50. The booing incidents were more than passing news stories; they have worked their way into accounts of political culture by Kevin Starr and Hayes-Bautista, among others. Each round of World Cup competition—held every four years—raises the issue anew, not just with regard to Mexicans but also among Koreans and other foreign-born residents from soccer-crazy countries. Immigration critics draw a connection between reliance on foreign language and

support of foreign teams over U.S. teams: "Here we clearly see a direct correlation between a Latino being more comfortable with English and having a vested interested in the fate of the USA. If that doesn't encapsulate the issue of assimilation, I don't know what does"; John Ziegler, "World Cup Shows Their True Colors," *Los Angeles Times*, June 24, 2005, B15.

51.   Peter D. Salins, *Assimilation American Style* (New York: Basic Books, 1997).

52.   Samuel Huntington, *Who Are We? The Challenges to America's National Identity* (New York: Simon & Schuster, 2004), 221.

53.   Huntington, *Who Are We?*, 229, quoting Mark Falcoff.

54.   Fully 57 percent of whites think that California will be a worse place to live in two decades, compared to 34 percent of Asians, 39 percent of Latinos, and 49 percent of African Americans; Mark Baldassare, "Special Survey on Californians and the Future" (San Francisco: Public Policy Institute of California, August 2004).

Chapter 5

1.   After California teams won nine major championships in the 1980s, under stars such as Magic Johnson and Joe Montana, during the 1990s California experienced only a single championship in any of the three major professional sports. However, in the first half-decade of the 2000s, four championships again were won in the state: the Los Angeles Lakers over the Indiana Pacers (2000, basketball), the Los Angeles Lakers over the Philadelphia 76ers (2001), the Los Angeles Lakers over the New Jersey Nets (2002), and the Anaheim Angels over the San Francisco Giants (2002, baseball). In addition, although the Los Angeles region continues as the nation's largest without a professional football team, in the college ranks the University of Southern California Trojans returned to national prominence after experiencing their own doldrums in the 1990s, with three Heisman Trophy winners and (nearly) three straight national championships from 2003 to 2005.

2.   Stuart Gabriel, Joe Mattey, and William Wascher, "Compensating Differentials and Evolution in the Quality-of-Life Among U.S. States," *Regional Science and Urban Economics* 33(5, September 2003): 619–49.

3.   California Air Resources Board monitoring data show that the average number of days per year that exceeded the federal one-hour ozone pollution limits in the Los Angeles region was 138 in 1989 to 1991, but only 36 in 1999 to 2001; data available at: http://www.arb.ca.gov/aqd/aqdpage.htm (accessed August 10,

2005). This decline began in the 1970s but was especially sharp in the 1990s owing to stricter fuel emission standards for new vehicles.

4. Mark Baldassare, "Special Survey on Californians and the Future: PPIC Statewide Survey" (San Francisco: Public Policy Institute of California, August 2004), 9.

5. Douglas S. Massey, Joaquin Arango, Graeme Hugo, Ali Kouaouci, Adela Pellegrino, and J. Edward Taylor, *Return to Aztlan: The Social Process of International Migration from Western Mexico* (Berkeley, Calif.: University of California Press, 1998), and Roger Waldinger, "Network, Bureaucracy, and Exclusion: Recruitment and Selection in an Immigrant Metropolis," in Frank D. Bean and Stephanie Bell-Rose, eds., *Immigration and Opportunity: Race, Ethnicity, and Employment in the United States* (New York: Russell Sage Foundation, 1999).

6. Stacy Harwood and Dowell Myers, "The Dynamics of Immigration and Local Governance in Santa Ana: Neighborhood Activism, Overcrowding, and Land-Use Policy," *Policy Studies Journal* 30 (1, 2002): 70–91.

7. Ivan Light, *Deflecting Immigration* (New York: Russell Sage Foundation, 2006).

8. Jeffrey S. Passel, "Unauthorized Migrants: Numbers and Characteristics," background briefing prepared for the Task Force on Immigration and America's Future (Washington: Pew Hispanic Center, June 14, 2005).

9. Douglas S. Massey, Jorge Durand, and Nolan J. Malone, *Beyond Smoke and Mirrors: Mexican Immigration in an Era of Economic Integration* (New York: Russell Sage Foundation, 2002).

10. Ivan Light, *Deflecting Immigration*. Light credits the USC demographer David Heer with first suggesting the saturated opportunities explanation.

11. On the Los Angeles trends of the 1990s compared to those of the 1980s, see Dowell Myers, Julie Park, and Sungho Ryu, "Dynamics of Immigrant Settlement in Los Angeles: Upward Mobility, Arrival, and Exodus," final report to the Haynes Foundation, working paper PDRG05-05 (Los Angeles: University of Southern California, Population Dynamics Research Group, August 25, 2005), available at: http://www.usc.edu/schools/sppd/research/popdynamics/Myers_Dowell_HaynesFinalReport_083105.pdf.

12. Víctor Zúñiga and Rubén Hernández-León, eds., *New Destinations: Mexican Immigration in the United States* (New York: Russell Sage Foundation, 2005), and William H. Frey, "Census 2000 Reveals New Native-Born and Foreign-Born Shifts Across U.S.," Research Report No. 02-520 (Ann Arbor, Mich.: Population Studies Center, University of Michigan, 2002).

13. Iowa State University, *The Impact of Immigration on Small to Midsize Iowa*

Communities: A Citizen's Guide for Change (Ames, Iowa: Iowa State University, June 2001).

14. New evidence on the importance of displacement from Los Angeles as a feeder to dispersal has recently been offered by James Elliott, "Network Saturation and Internal Migration of U.S. Immigrants to and from Leading Gateway Cities," paper presented to the annual meeting of the Population Association of America, Los Angeles, March 31, 2006.

15. Jeffrey S. Passel and Wendy Zimmerman, *Are Immigrants Leaving California?* (Washington, D.C.: Urban Institute, April 2001).

16. There are alternative ways to define the second generation, from requiring two immigrant parents, at one extreme, to requiring only one immigrant parent and one native-born parent, at the other. In the scientific approach used by demographers and taken here, the definition focuses on the birth records of the mother: the second generation shown in the figure 5.3 includes only residents whose mothers were immigrants.

17. Dowell Myers, John Pitkin, and Julie Park, "California's Immigrants Turn the Corner," Urban Initiative Policy Brief (Los Angeles: University of Southern California, May 2004), exhibit 3.

Chapter 6

1. "Quote of the Day" attributed to Dowell Myers, *New York Times*, January 30, 1997, A16. This comment was contained in a same-day article by Carey Goldberg, "Hispanic Households Struggle Amid Broad Decline in Income," A1.

2. The generality of this settlement pattern is shown by the substantial negative correlation (–0.28) between the relative size of the foreign-born population in an area and the share of those foreign-born who are newly arrived (calculated for metropolitan areas with at least 500,000 population). This calculation and comparisons across metropolitan areas reported in the text are drawn from the 2000 census data reported in GCT-P10: "Place of Birth, Year of Entry, and Citizenship Status of the Foreign-Born," (Washington: Census Bureau, 2003).

3. 1990 census, Summary File 3 data, reported in DP-2: "Social Characteristics, 1990," (Washington: Census Bureau, 1993).

4. Marta Tienda and Faith Mitchell, "Introduction: E Pluribus Plures or E Pluribus Unum?" in *Hispanics and the Future of America*, edited by Marta Tienda and Faith Mitchell (Washington, D.C.: National Academies Press, 2006), 3.

5. Samuel Huntington, "The Hispanic Challenge," *Foreign Policy* (March–April 2004). The essay was extracted from his book *Who Are We? The Challenges to America's National Identity* (New York: Simon & Schuster, 2004).

6. Richard Alba, John Logan, Amy Lutz, and Brian Stults, "Only English by the Third Generation? Loss and Preservation of the Mother Tongue Among the Grandchildren of Contemporary Immigrants," *Demography* 39(3, August 2002): 467–84.

7. Alejandro Portes and Richard Schauffler, "Language and the Second Generation: Bilingualism Yesterday and Today," *International Migration Review* 28(4, Winter 1994): 640–61.

8. State of California, Department of Finance, Demographic Research Unit, *Race-Ethnic Population with Age and Sex Detail, 2000–2050* (Sacramento, May 2004). This projection is subject to some uncertainty, but it is widely accepted in California as reasonably accurate. These projections are the standard used for planning purposes by state agencies and others.

9. Cited in David E. Hayes-Bautista, *La Nueva California: Latinos in the Golden State* (Berkeley, Calif.: University of California Press, 2004).

10. Huntington, *Who Are We?* 229, quoting Mark Falcoff.

11. Some might wish to question the certainty of the projections offered here. The California Demographic Futures population projections by generation might fail to foresee a dramatic resurgence in new Latino immigrants coming to California. However, our reasoning for rejecting that assumption was plainly stated in chapter 5. Less certain is the language use of the coming second generation compared to today's second generation. It is plausible that Spanish use will retain a stronger grip on native-born Latinos in the future because of the influence of the newcomers replenishing local communities. Both Huntington and some leading immigration experts have highlighted the effects of replenishment; see Mary C. Waters and Tomas R. Jimenez, "Assessing Immigrant Assimilation: New Empirical and Theoretical Challenges," *Annual Review of Sociology* 31(2005): 105–25.) However, continuous replenishment has been a factor in Latino communities for the last three decades, and its effects on language preference should already be evident. If anything, with a stabilization of immigration levels in California, we should expect replenishment to slow its increase or even be reduced in the future. Certainly we know that newcomers will have much lower weight in Latino communities in the future than in the past. In any event, these uncertainties are fairly minor in comparison to Huntington's omission of the changing generational mix in the Latino

population. That is by far the greatest source of error leading to his misconclusion.

12. Marta Tienda and Faith Mitchell, eds., *Multiple Origins, Uncertain Destinies: Hispanics and the American Future* (Washington, D.C.: National Academies Press, 2006), 5.

13. These indicators are representative of three domains within the broad topic area of assimilation, namely economic integration, residential integration, and civic incorporation, but they do not reflect a fourth domain, acculturation. For a comprehensive review of the general evidence on the various forms of assimilation, including an assessment of the evolving scholarly thought, see Richard D. Alba and Victor Nee, *Remaking the American Mainstream: Assimilation and Contemporary Immigration* (Cambridge, Mass.: Harvard University Press, 2003).

14. Four of the indicators—high school diploma, above poverty, homeownership, and citizenship—were collected in the March 2005 Current Population Survey, while voting participation was recorded in the November 2004 CPS conducted after the presidential election; English proficiency (speaking well or very well) was derived from the 2000 census, using the public use microdata sample (PUMS). Because the census does not ask about parents' place of birth, we are not able to distinguish between the second and third generations among the native-born.

15. In a subsequent section, I trace cohorts of immigrants as they settle longer over the decades; those results verify the broad findings of this first comparison.

16. Georges Vernez, Allan Abrahamse, and Denise D. Quigley, *How Immigrants Fare in U.S. Education* (Santa Monica, Calif.: Rand Corporation, 1996).

17. Barry R. Chiswick, "Speaking, Reading, and Earnings Among Low-Skilled Immigrants," *Journal of Labor Economics* 9(2, April 1991): 149–70.

18. William A. V. Clark, *Immigrants and the American Dream: Remaking the Middle Class* (New York: Guilford Press, 2003).

19. Louis DeSipio, "Building America, One Person at a Time: Naturalization and Political Behavior of the Naturalized in Contemporary American Politics," in *E Pluribus Unum? Immigrant, Civic Life and Political Incorporation*, edited by Gary Gerstle and John Mollenkopf (New York: Russell Sage Foundation, 2001); Taeku Lee, S. Karthick Ramakrishnan, and Ricardo Ramirez, eds., *Transforming Politics, Transforming America: The Political and Civic Incorporation of Immigrants in the United States* (Charlottesville: University Press of Virginia, 2006).

20. U.S. Census Bureau, Current Population Survey (November 2004), detailed table 1, available at: http://www.census.gov/population/www/socdemo/voting/cps2004.html (updated May 25, 2005).

21. As, for example, in Steven A. Camarota, "Importing Poverty: Immigration's Impact on the Size and Growth of the Poor Population in the United States," paper 15 (Washington, D.C.: Center for Immigration Studies, 1999).

22. The poverty rates in this section are taken from Dowell Myers, John Pitkin, and Julie Park, "California's Immigrants Turn the Corner," Urban Initiative Policy Brief (Los Angeles: University of Southern California, May 2004), exhibit 5.

23. Although Latino poverty rates are generally higher, and are of particular concern, they also reflect the overall trend, with poverty first rising from 21.7 percent of the Latino foreign-born in 1970 to 25.0 percent in 1990, then dipping to 24.2 percent in 2000.

24. Of course, the poverty rate does rise and fall with economic recession and expansion, yet the poverty trend measured from decade to decade in successive censuses avoids any bias of changing economic cycles. By good fortune, the censuses of 1970, 1980, 1990, and 2000 all were conducted at the same favorable point in the economic cycle—near the peak of a period of economic expansion. For details, see Dowell Myers, "Cohorts and Socioeconomic Progress," in *The American People: Census 2000*, edited by Reynolds Farley and John Haaga (New York: Russell Sage Foundation, 2005), 143, 160–62.

25. Nor is measurement error a likely explanation. The census measured poverty in identical fashion in the two decades. The one possible discrepancy is that superior efforts at data collection led to a reduced census undercount in 2000. The extra population captured in Census 2000 was drawn from hard-to-count segments of society, that is, those most likely to be living in higher-than-average poverty. Accordingly, were it not for the improvements in undercount, the poverty rate might have fallen even more than we have measured.

26. For more detailed explanation, and with evidence for the United States as a whole, see Myers, "Cohorts and Socioeconomic Progress."

27. For details on Asian as well as Latino immigrants, see Myers, "Cohorts and Socioeconomic Progress"; Myers et al., "California's Immigrants Turn the Corner"; and Dowell Myers and Julie Park, "Poverty Among Immigrant Cohorts: Improvement or Persistence over Time," paper presented at the annual meeting of the Population Associate of America, Washington, D.C., 1997.

28. The method does not trace the same individuals across time. Rather, it observes the same cohorts of people at multiple points in time, identifying them by their

ethnicity and their reported year of arrival in the United States. Thus, we are measuring changes in the average poverty for each subgroup as we repeatedly observe the group each decade. For details on this cohort method, see Myers, "Cohorts and Socioeconomic Progress."

29. The projections of poverty for immigrants were included in a report by Dowell Myers and John Pitkin, *Demographic Futures for California* (Los Angeles: University of Southern California, Population Dynamics Research Group, School of Policy, Planning, and Development, 2001), posted in January 2001 to the project website, www.usc.edu/schools/sppd/research/popdynamics. The poverty projections were the feature of Patrick McDonnell, "Immigration to State Slows, Study Finds," *Los Angeles Times*, January 23, 2001, A1.

30. Progress was slightly overprojected for the longest-settled immigrants, largely because this model did not incorporate age effects. After passing age forty, cohorts generally experience much less improvement in poverty, and after age fifty, poverty may even rise. Thus, this particular projection model was most effective in capturing the experience of more recent arrivals, who were largely young adults. Nonetheless, the discrepancies were fairly small for even the longest-settled arrival cohorts.

31. William A. V. Clark, *Immigrants and the American Dream.*

32. These data were taken from the public use microdata files of each decennial census, following methods described in Myers, "Cohorts and Socioeconomic Progress."

33. Dowell Myers and Cathy Yang Liu, "The Emerging Dominance of Immigrants in the U.S. Housing Market, 1970–2000," *Urban Policy and Research* 23(3, 2005): 347–65.

34. Myers, "Cohorts and Socioeconomic Progress"; Dowell Myers and Seong Woo Lee, "Immigrant Trajectories into Homeownership: A Temporal Analysis of Residential Assimilation," *International Migration Review* 32(Fall 1998): 593–625.

35. Census 2000, Summary File 3, table P22 (Washington: Census Bureau, 2003). Pertains to all ethnicities.

36. A detailed analysis of this dynamic is offered in Myers, "Cohorts and Socioeconomic Progress," which describes a method for decomposing the total trend in the foreign-born rate into three factors: changes in the relative size of different arrival cohorts, the rate of upward increase within the cohorts, and changes in the initial starting level of the newest immigrant arrivals.

37. It also helps that the homeownership rate of new arrivals in 2000 was a little higher than in the prior decade.

Chapter 7

1. William A. V. Clark and Peter A. Morrison, "Demographic Foundations of Empowerment in Multiminority Cities," *Demography* 32(2, May 1995): 183–201; Jack Citrin and Benjamin Highton, *How Race, Ethnicity, and Immigration Shape the California Electorate* (San Francisco: Public Policy Institute of California, 2002).

2. Raphael Sonenshein, *Politics in Black and White: Race and Power in Los Angeles* (Princeton, N.J.: Princeton University Press, 1994); John Logan and John Mollenkopf, *People and Politics in America's Big Cities* (New York: Drum Major Institute for Public Policy, 2004).

3. Raised in Compton and initially trained on local city courts by their father, Richard, Venus and Serena Williams combined for five ladies' singles championships at Wimbledon between 2000 and 2005.

4. The Compton racial transition is described in Dowell Myers and Lee Menifee, "Population Analysis," in *The Practice of Local Government Planning*, edited by Charles Hoch, Linda Dalton, and Frank So (Washington, D.C.: International City Management Association, 2000), 67–68. For a detailed, on-the-ground account, see Albert M. Camarillo, "Black and Brown in Compton: Demographic Change, Suburban Decline, and Intergroup Relations in a South Central Los Angeles Community, 1950 to 2000," in *Not Just Black and White: Historical and Contemporary Perspectives on Immigration, Race, and Ethnicity in the United States*, edited by Nancy Foner and George M. Fredrickson (New York: Russell Sage Foundation, 2004).

5. Myers and Menifee, "Population Analysis," detail this ethnic transition by age group, showing how the older population lagged well behind the change initiated by parents and children.

6. For details, see Camarillo, "Black and Brown in Compton."

7. Council and mayoral rosters from 1961 to 2005 were supplied by Verneil McDaniel, City of Compton, in a message to Cathy Yang Liu, May 19, 2005.

8. Data are from Census 2000, Summary File 4, table PCT 44.

9. John G. Matsusaka, *For the Many or the Few: The Initiative, Public Policy, and American Democracy* (Chicago: University of Chicago Press, 2004).

10. Bruce Cain, Jack Citrin, and Cara Wong, *Ethnic Context, Race Relations, and California Politics* (San Francisco: Public Policy Institute of California 2000), 3.

11. Exit poll determinations of the race of voters are inexact, depending as they do on whether the interviewer makes a visual observation (with problematic results in cases of persons of mixed ancestry) and also on the differential refusal rates when interviewers are recruiting interviewees from among those exiting

the polls. The data reported are drawn from exit polls conducted by the *Los Angeles Times* (March 5, 2004, A20) and by the *Los Angeles Times* and Edison Media Research/Mitofsky International (*California Opinion Index* [San Francisco: Field Research Corporation, January 2005], table 3).

12.   Among the most scientific of general social and economic surveys, the CPS has the advantage of including questions about age and citizenship, as well as about race and voting participation. (The survey avoids questions about voting choices or political party.) Thus, we can draw a relatively more precise profile of who the voters are, and we can also compare California and the nation. Pooling three survey years together (1998, 2000, and 2002) and averaging results to represent the year 2000, we obtain a sufficiently large sample for analysis in California. A key drawback, but one prevalent in all surveys of voting, is that respondents tend to overreport their voting participation. Thus, the following discussion of "voters" is based on self-reported voters, not on actual observations of those casting ballots. For details of the survey, see Jennifer Cheeseman Day and Kelly Holder, "Voting and Registration in the Election of November 2002," *Current Population Reports,* P20-552 (Washington: U.S. Census Bureau (July 2004).

13.   "Regular voters" are defined as those who said they voted in the fall elections; we pooled results from one presidential year and two off years, thus creating a composite profile of "regular voters."

14.   Citrin and Highton, *How Race, Ethnicity, and Immigration Shape the California Electorate,* 16.

15.   Pei-te Lien, Christian Collet, Janelle Wong, and S. Karthick Ramakrishnan, "Asian Pacific–American Public Opinion and Political Participation," *PS: Political Science and Politics* 34(3, September 2001): 625–30.

16.   Fernando J. Guerra and Dwaine Marvick, "Ethnic Officeholders and Party Activists in Los Angeles County," Working paper, Institute for Social Science Research (Los Angeles: University of California, Los Angeles, 1986).

17.   Richard J. Timpone, "Structure, Behavior, and Voter Turnout in the United States," *American Political Science Review* 92(March 1998): 145–58.

18.   S. Karthick Ramakrishnan, *Democracy in Immigrant America: Changing Demographics and Political Participation* (Stanford, Calif.: Stanford University Press, 2005), 56–58. In addition, those residing longer at the same address may be self-selected for willingness to participate politically because it is homeowners rather than renters who are most likely to stay a long time in the same home and homeowners have large investment stakes. In addition, longtime residents have implicitly elected to express their "voice" to shape their local environment

rather than "exit"; see Albert O. Hirschman, *Exit, Voice, and Loyalty: Responses to Decline in Firms, Organizations, and States* (Cambridge, Mass.: Harvard University Press, 1970).

19. Over half of the gap between white and Latino voting rates in California is accounted for by Latinos' lower rate of citizenship. Lack of citizenship is also a major factor in the low voting rates of California's Asian residents, although underregistration is an even greater impediment in their case. Indeed, other California researchers have noted that the underregistration of Asians is striking, especially in view of the otherwise supportive factors of higher education and income; see Citrin and Highton, *How Race, Ethnicity, and Immigration Shape the California Electorate*, 27–32.

20. The data come from the Statewide Survey, a rich series of almost-monthly polls carried out by the Public Policy Institute of California (PPIC) under the direction of Mark Baldassare.

21. Mark Baldassare, "Statewide Survey: Special Survey on Californians and the Future" (San Francisco: Public Policy Institute of California, August 2004), 10. Note that the survey asks two questions about future quality of life, one about California in general, as addressed in an earlier chapter, and the other about "your part of California." Given that many of the other detailed questions also pertain to "your part," we analyze those results in this chapter.

22. Unfortunately, the survey data do not include a specific question on length of residence, and so we must rely on circumstantial evidence.

23. Details on the underlying statistical analysis may be found in appendix B, especially table B.1.

24. Mark Baldassare, *A California State of Mind: The Conflicted Voter in a Changing World* (Berkeley: University of California Press, 2002).

25. The survey opinions on trust in state government analyzed for this section are taken from the June 2003 PPIC Statewide Survey.

26. Mark Baldassare, "Special Survey on Californians and the Future."

27. Surveys in May 2001 and November 2005 found that 55 percent and 53 percent of residents, respectively, believed that immigration was the biggest population growth factor; Mark Baldassare, "Statewide Survey: Special Survey on Population" (San Francisco: Public Policy Institute of California, December 2005), 11.

28. See the discussion in chapter 3 on immigration's role in the "dismal future." Also observe how measurements of contributions and burdens have been a prominent part of scientific inquiries, such as the major investigation organized by the National Academy of Science and published in *The New Americans: Eco-*

nomic, Demographic, and Fiscal Effects of Immigration, edited by James P. Smith and Barry Edmonston (Washington, D.C.: National Academies Press, 1997).

29. Although it would be ideal to capture the public mood in 1988 and 1994 as well as in 2004, surveys of California voters with comparable questions are not available to facilitate analysis for those years.

30. Mark Baldassare, "Statewide Survey: Californians and Their Government" (San Francisco: Public Policy Institute of California, February 2004); Mark Baldassare, untitled Statewide Survey (San Francisco: Public Policy Institute of California, April 1998).

31. This analysis was performed with 2004 data alone because the 1998 data did not include education as a question; results are not shown in appendix B.

32. These figures are from the raw survey data and are not statistically adjusted. When they are adjusted for other factors and include voters of all races, we find that the gap doubled in size from 13.7 percent to 30.7 percent, or seventeen percentage points, an increase nearly as great as reported in the raw data.

33. This estimate is reported in the California Budget Project, *Budget Watch* (March 2006), 3. For comparison, total general fund spending in California is expected to be about $97 billion in 2006–2007. Nearly 60 percent of this budget was spent on children and youth.

34. Mark Baldassare, "Statewide Survey: Special Survey on the California State Budget" (San Francisco: Public Policy Institute of California, June 2003).

35. Mark Baldassare, June 2003 survey, 3.

36. Mark Baldassare, "Statewide Survey: Special Survey on the California State Budget" (San Francisco: Public Policy Institute of California, January 2006), 2.

37. See, for example, John Mark Hansen, "Individuals, Institutions, and Public Preferences over Public Finance," *American Political Science Review* 92(3, September 1998): 513–31.

38. Jonathan Baron and Ed McCaffery, "Starving the Beast: The Psychology of Budget Deficits," paper presented to the conference "Fiscal Challenges: An Interdisciplinary Approach to Budget Policy," University of Southern California Gould School of Law, February 2006.

39. The full series of analyses are reported in table B.4. An explanation that takes only demographic and economic factors into account is compared to one that adds factors representing political opinions.

40. Peter Schrag has written at length about this theme, most recently in *California: America's High-Stakes Experiment* (Berkeley, Calif.: University of California Press, 2006).

41. The survey question reads: "The March ballot also includes Proposition 55, the Kindergarten to University Public Education Facilities Bond Act of 2004. This $12.3 billion bond issue will provide funding for necessary education facilities to relieve overcrowding and to repair older schools. The projected fiscal impact includes a state cost of about $24.7 billion to pay off the costs of the bonds, with annual payments of about $823 million. If the election were held today, would you vote yes or no on Proposition 55?"

42. Exit poll data in California are consolidated in *California Opinion Index* (2005), table 3.

43. The political scientists Jack Citrin and Benjamin Highton (*How Race, Ethnicity, and Immigration Shape the California Electorate*, 67–77) used a similar compositional strategy in applying 2000 voting rates to future population changes. Under their status quo assumption, holding rates constant, they found that whites will constitute a 50 percent majority of the electorate around 2046. However, when they introduced an assumption that citizenship will increase among Latinos and Asians by 50 percent, the projected white share of voters then fell to 50 percent by 2030, virtually the same as our fixed-rates projection. Their calculations also suggest that the Latino year of reaching majority status will be around 2083, a decade longer than our projection with the latest date.

44. A national survey of Latinos in June 2006 reported that two-thirds of both native-born and foreign-born Latinos believed that the congressional debates over immigration reform were stimulating a long-lasting mobilization of Latino voters; Roberto Suro and Gabriel Escobar, "2006 National Survey of Latinos: The Immigration Debate" (Washington, D.C.: Pew Hispanic Center, 2006).

45. These estimates are based on the projected white share of the electorate, according to the preferred compositional method using constant rates, as reported in table 7.3.

Chapter 8

1. The philosophical tradition of social contract theory in political science is drawn from Locke and Rousseau and extended by Rawls. That literature treats the social contract as a timeless moral relationship of political philosophy. This theory overlaps with another body of thought about the political character of national identity and democracy in America that is rooted in Tocqueville and has been carried forward in the twentieth century by many others. Beginning with Myrdal, criticism has mounted that these ideals of democracy were only about the struggles of white men. Women and children played no role, and indeed did not have equal rights, and other racial groups, like African Americans

and Native Americans, were systematically dismissed. Scholarship since 1970 has concentrated on rethinking the political theory of national identity and the social contract to make it more inclusive.

2. Rogers M. Smith, "Beyond Tocqueville, Myrdal, and Hartz: The Multiple Traditions in America," *American Political Science Review* 87(3, September 1993): 549–66.

3. This formulation bears a clear parallel to Smith's multiple-traditions thesis, although it is not an outgrowth of that theory. The commonalities are an emphasis on multiple, interacting strands and the enduring political culture that hosts competing themes.

4. Beth A. Rubin, *Shifts in the Social Contract: Understanding Change in American Society* (Thousand Oaks, Calif.: Pine Forge Press/Sage Publications, 1996), 4.

5. Certainly notions of the social contract date back to Hobbes, Locke, and Rousseau, or even earlier, and the origins of the welfare state can be traced to the eighteenth century, but it is useful to mark the beginning of the modern era of the social contract from the dramatic escalation in collective expectations after 1930.

6. Office of Immigration Statistics, *Yearbook of Immigration Statistics: 2005* (Washington: Department of Homeland Security, 2006); Jeffrey Passel, "The Size and Characteristics of the Unauthorized Migrant Population in the U.S." (Washington, D.C.: Pew Hispanic Center, 2006).

7. Jacob A. Riis, *How the Other Half Lives: Studies Among the Tenements of New York* (New York: Charles Scribner's Sons, 1890); Jacob Riis, *The Making of an American* (New York: Macmillan, 1901); Russell Freedman, *Kids at Work: Lewis Hines and Crusade Against Child Labor* (New York: Clarion Books, 1994).

8. Gary Gerstle, "Liberty, Coercion, and the Making of Americans," *Journal of American History* 84: 524–58; David Tyack, "School for Citizens: The Politics of Civic Education from 1790 to 1990," in *E Pluribus Unum? Contemporary and Historical Perspectives on Immigrant Political Incorporation*, edited by Gary Gerstle and John Mollenkopf (New York: Russell Sage Foundation, 2001), esp. 344–50.

9. Gunnar Myrdal, *An American Dilemma: The Negro Problem and American Democracy* (New York: Harper & Row, 1962).

10. This contrast of civic and racial nationalism is made most clearly by Gary Gerstle, *American Crucible: Race and Nation in the Twentieth Century* (Princeton, N.J.: Princeton University Press, 2001).

11. Peter Salins, *Assimilation, American Style* (New York: Basic Books, 1997), 6.

12. Richard Hofstadter, *Social Darwinism in American Thought*, rev. ed. (Boston: Beacon Press, 1955).

13. Matthew C. Price, *Justice Between Generations: The Growing Power of the Elderly in America* (Westport, Conn.: Praeger, 1997), 23.

14. Peter H. Lindert, *Growing Public: Social Spending and Economic Growth Since the Eighteenth Century*, vol. 1 (Cambridge: Cambridge University Press, 2004), 27, 176–90.

15. Ibid.

16. Arthur G. Neal, *National Trauma and Collective Memory: Extraordinary Events in the American Experience* (Armonk, N.Y.: M. E. Sharpe, 2005), ch. 3.

17. David M. Kennedy, *Freedom from Fear: The American People in Depression and War, 1929–1945* (New York: Oxford University Press, 1999), 163–67.

18. Ibid., 378; see also Gerstle, *American Crucible*.

19. Studs Terkel, *The Good War: An Oral History of World War Two* (New York: Pantheon, 1986); Tom Brokaw, *The Greatest Generation* (New York: Random House, 1998).

20. This argument that America experienced a "powerful ideological revival" is made most pointedly by Philip Gleason, "Sea Change in the Civic Culture in the 1960s," in Gerstle and Mollenkopf, *E Pluribus Unum?*

21. Theda Skocpol, *Protecting Soldiers and Mothers: The Political Origins of Social Policy in the United States* (Cambridge, Mass.: Harvard University Press, 1995).

22. Rutherford H. Platt, *Disasters and Democracy: The Politics of Extreme Natural Events* (Washington, D.C.: Island Press, 1999), esp. ch. 1. "An implicit social compact was gradually forged between government and citizenry in which the former assumed a large share of disaster losses arising from the bad luck or bad judgment of the latter" (11).

23. Rubin, *Shifts in the Social Contract*, 30–31.

24. Frances Fox Piven and Richard A. Cloward, *The Breaking of the American Social Compact* (New York: New Press, 1997).

25. Frank Levy, *The New Dollars and Dreams: American Incomes and Economic Change* (New York: Russell Sage Foundation, 1998).

26. Reynolds Farley, *The New American Reality: Who We Are, How We Got Here, Where We Are Going* (New York: Russell Sage Foundation, 1996), 64–66.

27. Frank Hobbs and Nicole Stoops, *Demographic Trends in the Twentieth Century*, CENSR-4 (Washington: U.S. Census Bureau, 2002), figure 4.6.

28. Robert J. Samuelson, *The Good Life and Its Discontents: The American Dream in the Age of Entitlement, 1945–1995* (New York: Random House, 1995).

29. John F. Kennedy, remarks delivered in Pueblo, Colorado, August 17, 1962, reprinted in *Public Papers of the Presidents: 1962* (Washington: Office of the Federal Register, 1963), 626.

30. The Civil Rights Act of 1964, signed by President Lyndon B. Johnson, was the high-water mark of bold planning for the equality of subgroups. This was followed by the landmark Voting Rights Act of 1965, and it had been preceded by the Economic Opportunity Act of 1964, which launched many of the Great Society programs.

31. Former New York Governor Mario Cuomo got his political start mediating a dispute over public housing that was being "scattered" into the middle-class community of Forest Hills within New York City; see Mario Cuomo, *Forest Hills Diary: The Crisis of Low-Income Housing* (New York: Random House, 1974). The controversies over school busing were much more widespread. On the busing backlash in the Canarsie section of New York City, see Jonathan Rieder, *Canarsie: The Jews and Italians of Brooklyn Against Liberalism* (Cambridge, Mass.: Harvard University Press, 1985). For an assessment of the conflict in the generally liberal San Francisco Bay Area, see Lillian B. Rubin, *Busing and Backlash: White Against White in an Urban School District* (Berkeley: University of California Press, 1980).

32. Richard M. Scammon and Ben J. Wattenberg, *The Real Majority* (New York: Coward-McCann, 1970), 59, 40–43.

33. Thomas Edsall and Mary Edsall, *Chain Reaction: The Impact of Race, Rights, and Taxes on American Politics* (New York: Norton, 1992).

34. Douglas S. Massey, *Return of the "L" Word: A Liberal Vision for the New Century* (Princeton, N.J.: Princeton University Press, 2005), 22–25.

35. See Gleason, "Sea Change in the Civic Culture in the 1960s."

36. Arthur H. Miller, "Political Issues and Trust in Government: 1964–1970," *American Political Science Review* (September 1974): 951–70; Arthur G. Neal, *National Trauma and Collective Memory*; E. J. Dionne, *Why Americans Hate Politics: The Death of the Democratic Process* (New York: Simon & Schuster, 1992).

37. Levy, *The New Dollars and Dreams*, table 4.3.

38. Ibid., table 3.3.

39. Stanley B. Greenberg, a Democratic pollster and analyst, offers an insightful assessment of middle-class dissatisfactions, along with a critique of how the Republican "Contract with America" tapped those resentments, in "A New Con-

tract?" chapter 11 in his *Middle-Class Dreams: The Politics and Power of the New American Majority* (New Haven, Conn.: Yale University Press, 1996).

40. Marta Tienda, "Demography and the Social Contract," *Demography* (2002), 587–616. Tienda reports that extending voting privileges even to noncitizens was prevalent before the twentieth century, something that would be unheard of today. See also Evelyn Savidge Sterne, "Beyond the Boss: Immigration and American Political Culture from 1880 to 1940," in Gerstle and Mollenkopf, *E Pluribus Unum?*

41. This is most obvious in ballot initiatives to block illegal immigrants from public services, but it is expressed more generally with regard to all immigrants. See Frank D. Bean, Robert G. Cushing, Charles Haynes, and Jennifer V. W. Van Hook, "Immigration and the Social Contract," *Social Science Quarterly* 78(2, 1997): 249–68.

42. See James Davison Hunter, *Culture Wars: The Struggle to Define America* (New York: Basic Books, 1992); Edsall and Edsall, *Chain Reaction*; and George Lakoff, *Don't Think of an Elephant!: Know Your Values and Frame the Debate* (White River Junction, Vt.: Chelsea Green Publishing, 2004).

Chapter 9

1. Alexis de Tocqueville, "How the Americans Combat Individualism by the Principle of Self-Interest Rightly Understood," in *Democracy in America*, vol. 2 (1840), sect. 2, ch. 8.

2. Ronald Lee, Timothy Miller, and Ryan Douglas Edwards, *The Growth and Aging of California's Population: Demographic and Fiscal Projections, Characteristics, and Service Needs* (Berkeley: California Policy Research Center, 2003); supplemental material provided by Ryan Edwards.

3. The expenditure is expressed as a share of the state's general fund, as reported in the enacted budget for 2006–7, available at: www.ebudget.ca.gov/pdf/Enacted/BudgetSummary/BSS/BSS.html, accessed October 28, 2006.

4. This figure is difficult to disentangle from the budget with precision.

5. James P. Smith and Barry Edmonston, eds., *The New Americans: Economic, Demographic, and Fiscal Effects of Immigration* (Washington, D.C.: National Academies Press, 1997). Chapter 6 reports the short-term costs, while chapter 7 simulates the net benefits to be derived over the long term.

6. Alan Walker, "Intergenerational Relations and Welfare Restructuring: The Social Construction of an Intergenerational Problem," in *The Changing Contract*

Across Generations, edited by Vern L. Bengston and W. Andrew Achenbaum (New York: Aldine de Gruyter, 1993), 144.

7. Vern L. Bengston, "Is the 'Contract Across Generations' Changing? Effects of Population Aging on Obligations and Expectations Across Age Groups," in Bengston and Achenbaum, *The Changing Contract Across Generations*, 4–5.

8. David E. Hayes-Bautista, Werner O. Schink, and Jorge Chapa, *The Burden of Support: Young Latinos in an Aging Society* (Stanford, Calif.: Stanford University Press, 1988), 51.

9. Matthew C. Price, *Justice Between Generations: The Growing Power of the Elderly in America* (Westport, Conn.: Praeger, 1997), 83 (emphasis added).

10. John R. Logan and Glenna D. Spitze, "Self-Interest and Altruism in Intergenerational Relations," *Demography* 32(August 1995): 359. The finding that support for the elderly declines with age was confirmed by more detailed analysis controlling for education, marital status, political leaning, and other factors.

11. Ibid., 362.

12. The 1984 presidential address of Samuel Preston before the Population Association of America was among the first to call attention to the divergent trends for America's two groups of dependents, children and the elderly; Samuel H. Preston, "Children and the Elderly: Divergent Paths for America's Dependents," *Demography* 21(4, November 1984): 435–57.

13. "Long-Term Fiscal Simulation Data," August 2006 GAO analysis, available at: http://www.gao.gov/special.pubs/longterm/data.html (accessed September 24, 2006). These figures are for the simulation scenario described as "Discretionary Spending Grows with GDP and All Expiring Tax Provisions are Extended." The GAO terms this scenario "more realistic" because its assumptions about the future conform to recent trends and policy preferences, even though the GAO also emphasizes that the trends are unsustainable. For explanation see Government Accountability Office, "The Nation's Long-Term Fiscal Outlook: September 2006 Update: The Bottom Line: Today's Fiscal Policy Remains Unsustainable," GAO-06-1077R (Washington: GAO, 2006).

14. By 2030 interest payments will consume 39.2 percent of federal revenue, and by 2040, 77.8 percent.

15. GAO, "The Nation's Long-Term Fiscal Outlook: September 2006 Update," 2.

16. Government Accountability Office, "The Nation's Long-Term Fiscal Challenge," available at: http://www.gao.gov/special.pubs/longterm/challenge.html (accessed November 12, 2005).

17. GAO, "The Nation's Long-Term Fiscal Outlook: September 2006 Update," 5.

18. See Laurence J. Kotlikoff and Jagdeesh Gokhale, "Passing the Generational Buck," *The Public Interest* (Winter 1994): 73–81; and Laurence J. Kotlikoff and Scott Burns, *The Coming Generational Storm: What You Need to Know About America's Economic Future* (Cambridge, Mass.: MIT Press, 2005).

19. Kotlikoff and Burns, *The Coming Generational Storm*, 49 (emphasis in the original).

20. Carl L. Harter, "The 'Good Times' Cohort of the 1930s: Sometimes Less Means More (and More Means Less)," *PRB Report* 3(3, 1977): 1–4; see also the discussion in Dowell Myers, "Cohorts and Socioeconomic Progress," in *The American People: Census 2000*, edited by Reynolds Farley and John Haaga (New York: Russell Sage Foundation, 2005).

21. David W. Thomson, "A Lifetime of Privilege? Aging and Generations at Century's End," in Bengston and Achenbaum, *The Changing Contract Across Generations*, 221.

22. Susmita Pati, Ron Keren, Evaline A. Alessandrini, and Donald F. Schwarz, "Generational Differences in U.S. Public Spending, 1980–2000," *Health Affairs* 23(5, 2004): 131–41, 132.

23. These figures are all expressed in net present values. See Antoine Bommier, Ronald Lee, Timothy Miller, and Stephane Zuber, "Who Wins and Who Loses? Public Transfer Accounts for U.S. Generations Born 1850 to 2090," working paper 10969 (Cambridge, Mass.: National Bureau of Economic Research, December 2004).

24. Ibid., 12.

25. Myers, "Cohorts and Socioeconomic Progress," figure 2.

26. Ibid., figure 2.

27. Ronald Lee, Sang-Hyop Lee, and Andrew Mason, "Charting the Economic Life Cycle," working paper 12379 (Cambridge, Mass.: National Bureau of Economic Research, July 2006).

28. Price, *Justice Between Generations*, 109.

29. Hayes-Bautista et al., *The Burden of Support*, 55.

30. Peter H. Lindert, *Growing Public: Social Spending and Economic Growth Since the Eighteenth Century*, vol. 1 (Cambridge: Cambridge University Press, 2004), 27.

31. James A. Poterba, "Demographic Structure and the Political Economy of Public Education," *Journal of Policy Analysis and Management* 16(1, 1997): 48–66.

32. Peter Schrag, *California: America's High-Stakes Experiment* (Berkeley: University of California Press, 2006), 156.

33. Evan Halper, "State Pushes Problems into Future," *Los Angeles Times*, August 1, 2004, A1.

34. This estimate is reported in California Budget Project, *Budget Watch* (March 2006), 3. For comparison, total general fund spending in California is expected to be about $97 billion in 2006–2007. Nearly 60 percent of this budget was spent on children and youth.

35. For a comparison of today's challenges with "California's Golden Age," see Elisa Barbour and Paul G. Lewis, *California Comes of Age: Governing Institutions, Planning, and Public Investments* (San Francisco: Public Policy Institute of California, 2005).

36. A $43 billion bond issue requiring 6 percent of the state budget for debt service was planned for the fall 2006 election.

37. Richard M. Scammon and Ben J. Wattenberg, *The Real Majority* (New York: Coward-McCann, 1970).

38. A good summary of how much social values have changed since 1970, including the differences between generations, is provided in Reynolds Farley, *The New American Reality: Who We Are, How We Got Here, Where We Are Going* (New York: Russell Sage Foundation, 1996), esp. 33, 44–47.

39. Isabel V. Sawhill, "Debt Is Cheating Our Children's Future," *Kansas City Star*, April 23, 2006.

40. Beth A. Rubin, *Shifts in the Social Contract: Understanding Change in American Society* (Thousand Oaks, Calif.: Pine Forge Press, 1996), 4.

Chapter 10

1. Marta Tienda and Faith Mitchell, eds., *Multiple Origins, Uncertain Destinies: Hispanics and the American Future* (Washington, D.C.: National Academies Press, 2006), 7.

2. U.S. Census Bureau, "Table 2: Annual Estimates of the Population by Sex and Age for California: April 1, 2000 to July 1, 2005," SC-EST2005-02-06 (Washington: U.S. Census Bureau, Population Division, August 2006).

3. Labor force trends are drawn from the projection model introduced in chapter 3. This is indexed to the U.S. model reported in Mitra Toossi's "A Century of Change: The U.S. Labor Force, 1950–2050" (*Monthly Labor Review* [May 2002]: 15–28), as adjusted for the differential labor force participation rates observed in California and population projections by the Census Bureau.

4. Death and out-migration are accounted for in the Census Bureau's population projections. Retirement is measured by the declining percentage of residents in the state who are active in the labor force as they grow older. For example, the 2000 CPS reports that 88.8 percent of California men were either employed or

actively looking for work when they were forty-five to fifty-four, but that this rate was considerably lower at ages fifty-five to sixty-four (71.6 percent), especially among men sixty-five and older (18.8 percent). Among women, there is a similar difference, with labor force participation rates at ages forty-five to fifty-four equaling 73.5 percent, falling to 54.4 percent at ages fifty-five to sixty-four, and to 11 percent at ages sixty-five and older.

5. These figures are taken from David Neumark, "California's Economic Future and Infrastructure Challenges," in *California 2025: Taking on the Future*, edited by Ellen Hanak and Mark Baldassare (San Francisco: Public Policy Institute of California, 2005), table 3.3. See also table 3.4, which breaks down the service sector into four major subcategories. In the largest of these sectors, professional and related services, educational requirements are highest.

6. Ibid., table 3.6.

7. Robert Fountain and Marcia Cosgrove, with Petra Abraham Laptalo, *Keeping California's Edge: The Growing Demand for Highly Educated Workers* (Sacramento: Sacramento State University, Applied Research Center, 2006), table 1.6.

8. Neumark, "California's Economic Future and Infrastructure Challenges," 82.

9. The Census Bureau records the date of arrival and age of foreign-born immigrants to the nation. Unfortunately, no comparable data are collected about movers within the United States. All that can be ascertained is place of birth and place of residence five years before.

10. Dowell Myers, John Pitkin, and Julie Park, *California Demographic Futures: Projections to 2030, by Nativity, Immigrant Generations, and Time of Arrival in the U.S.: Full Report* (Los Angeles: University of Southern California, School of Policy, Planning, and Development, Population Dynamics Research Group, 2005), exhibit 11.

11. Andrew Sum, Neeta Fogg, and Ishwar Khatiwada, with Sheila Palma, "Foreign Immigration and the Labor Force of the U.S.: The Contributions of New Foreign Immigration to the Growth of the Nation's Labor Force and Its Employed Population, 2000 to 2004," project report (Boston: Northeastern University, Center for Labor Market Studies, July 2004), table 8. These authors also calculate that this immigrant labor force absorbed all of the employment growth in this time period, owing to the lower employment rates among the non-immigrant workforce (16).

12. These data are drawn from the public use microdata sample (PUMS) files of the decennial census.

13. Neumark, "California's Economic Future and Infrastructure Challenges," 78.

14. Ibid., 78–79.

15. The analysis measures migration between 1995 and 2000, including adults who were age thirty to thirty-four in 1995 and thirty-five to thirty-nine in 2000. The source of information is Census 2000 PUMS files. Only residents of California and other states are included; out-migrants to other countries are not measurable, and so the rate of departure from California may be somewhat underestimated, particularly for residents who were born in other countries and may have returned.

16. Jennifer Cheeseman Day and Kurt J. Bauman, "Have We Reached the Top? Educational Attainment Projections of the U.S. Population," working paper 43 (Washington: U.S. Census Bureau, Population Division, 2000).

17. A review of the literature on educational premiums and evidence of their growth in California and the nation is provided in Deborah Reed, *California's Rising Income Inequality: Causes and Concerns* (San Francisco: Public Policy Institute of California, 1999).

18. Patrick J. Kelly, *As America Becomes More Diverse: The Impact of State Higher Education Inequality* (Boulder, Colo.: National Center for Higher Education Management Systems [NCHEMS], November 2005). Supplementary state profiles formatted in a manner similar to the national data are also available at: http://www.higheredinfo.org/raceethnicity/.

19. Based on Kelly's report, the National Center for Public Policy and Higher Education issued a number of policy alerts. The premise of an emphasis on gaps is well deserved, and the growth of educational attainment is surely suppressed by the faster-than-average increase of less-educated groups. Nonetheless, Kelly's analysis may be somewhat exaggerated because it holds constant the educational attainment levels of each ethnic group at the level observed in 2000. In fact, attainment levels rose for each group in the decades leading up to 2000, as shown from 1980 to 2000 in Kelly's report (*As America Becomes More Diverse*, figure 14). It is not clear that any of this within-group increase is factored into his projections for 2020. Thus, the expected slowdown due to ethnic change may not be as extreme as Kelly projects.

20. The data cited here on the percentage of age groups holding a BA degree or higher are taken from the public use microdata files of the censuses in 1980 and 2000.

21. Hans P. Johnson, "California's Population in 2025," in Hanak and Baldassare, *California 2025*, 25.

22. This growth is the combined enrollment in the three major public higher education systems in California—the University of California, the California State University, and the community colleges. Enrollment will increase from 2,322,400 in 2005–2006 to 2,788,600 in 2015–2016. These projections are extended further into the future than other available sources, and they also take explicit account of growing enrollment rates, as reported in Nancy Shulock, Colleen Moore, and Mary Gill, *Shared Solutions: A Framework for Discussing California Higher Education Finance*, policy issue report (Sacramento: California State University, Institute for Higher Education Leadership and Policy, 2005), table 5.

23. Dowell Myers, "Cohorts and Socioeconomic Progress," in *The American People: Census 2000*, edited by Reynolds Farley and John Haaga (New York: Russell Sage Foundation, 2005), 154–57.

24. Day and Bauman, "Have We Reached the Top?"

25. The BA share at ages twenty-five to sixty-four in the 1980 census was 21.4 percent, while that in the 2000 census was 28.1 percent, an increase of 6.7 percentage points. These measurements are believed to be consistent over time, despite changes in the census questionnaire, following methods reported in Myers, "Cohorts and Socioeconomic Progress."

26. Estela Mara Bensimon, "The Diversity Scorecard: A Learning Approach to Institutional Change," *Change* (January–February 2004): 44–52.

27. Jennifer Cheeseman Day and Eric C. Newburger, "The Big Payoff: Educational Attainment and Synthetic Estimates of Work-Life Earnings," Current Population Reports, P23-210 (Washington: U.S. Census Bureau, 2002), figure 3.

28. Ibid., figures 5 and 6.

29. Latinos with a bachelor's degree have earnings that are 59.7 percent higher than those of Latinos with only a high school degree (less of a gain than was true among all workers), and only 18.1 percent higher than the earnings of those with an associate's degree. The latter group has a greater advantage over the high school graduates than is common among all workers (35.2 percent more earnings compared to a 27.5 percent gain among all workers). It is not known why earnings among Latinos with an associate's degree are so high or why earnings among those with a bachelor's degree are so relatively low in these national data, but this narrow wage difference represents a smaller premium for advancing to a bachelor's degree and might discourage some young adults from advancing to a higher education.

30. California Budget Project, "Boom, Bust, and Beyond: The State of Working

California," special report (Sacramento: California Budget Project, 2004), 8; Elias Lopez, Enrique Ramirez, and Refugio I. Rochin, *Latinos and Economic Development in California*, CRB-99-008 (Sacramento: California Research Bureau of the California State Library, 1999), 16.

31. Kelly, *As America Becomes More Diverse*, figure 28; supplementary state profile for California available at: http://www.higheredinfo.org/raceethnicity/. The projection does not take account of a potential devaluation in the earnings return from education that would follow if well-educated workers were in greater supply. Such an adjustment might be expected in theory but is impossible to gauge in its magnitude.

32. Lopez, Ramirez, and Rochin, *Latinos and Economic Development in California*, 30–32, 42–44.

33. Ibid., 43.

34. Steve H. Murdock et al., *The New Texas Challenge: Population Change and the Future of Texas* (College Station: Texas A&M Press, 2003), 67–71. Although Texas has the second-largest Latino population in the nation, that population is nevertheless much smaller than California's, and so the total dollar value of tax revenues is smaller.

35. Henry Brady, Michael Hout, and Jon Stiles, *Return on Investment: Educational Choices and Demographic Change in California's Future*, executive summary (Berkeley: University of California Survey Research Center, 2005), 3.

36. For example, see the RAND study by Georges Vernez and Lee Mizell, "Goal: To Double the Rate of Hispanics Earning a Bachelor's Degree," report prepared for the Hispanic Scholarship Fund (Santa Monica, Calif.: RAND Corporation, 2000).

37. Ibid., x.

38. Elias Lopez, Ginny Puddefoot, and Patricia Gándara, eds., *A Coordinated Approach to Raising the Socioeconomic Status of Latinos in California*, CRB-00-003 (Sacramento: California Research Bureau of the California State Library, 2000).

39. Barbara Schneider, Sylvia Martinez, and Ann Owens, "Barriers to Educational Opportunities for Hispanics in the United States," in *Hispanics and the Future of America*, edited by Marta Tienda and Faith Mitchell (Washington, D.C.: National Academies Press, 2006).

40. Maria Estela Zarate and Harry P. Pachon, "Perceptions of College Financial Aid Among California Latino Youth," policy brief (Los Angeles: Tomas Rivera Policy Institute, 2006).

41. Shulock, Moore, and Gill, *Shared Solutions*.

42. For example, see James Smith, "Assimilation Across the Latino Generations," *American Economic Review Papers and Proceedings* 93(2003): 315–19; Frank D. Bean and Gillian Stevens, *America's Newcomers and the Dynamics of Diversity* (New York: Russell Sage Foundation, 2003); Myers, "Cohorts and Socioeconomic Progress"; Deborah Reed, Laura E. Hill, Christopher Jepsen, and Hans P. Johnson, *Educational Progress Across Immigrant Generations in California* (San Francisco: Public Policy Institute of California, 2005).

43. Immigration experts have frequently found that college completion rates are lower for third-generation Latinos than for second-generation Latinos. The explanations are uncertain—one is that the children of immigrants may be more strongly motivated than third- and higher-generation Latinos, whose outlook may have become discouraged. A more recent explanation ventured by several observers centers on the presumption that the adults of long-standing Latino heritage who are the most assimilated and highest-achieving, especially those whose parents intermarried, might fail to identify themselves as Latino, and thus these college graduates would be "lost" from the Latino category; see Brian Duncan, V. Joseph Hotz, and Stephen J. Trejo, "Hispanics in the U.S. Labor Market," in Tienda and Mitchell, *Hispanics and the Future of America*, 267.

44. Myers, Pitkin, and Park, *California Demographic Futures*.

Chapter 11

1. John Pitkin, Dowell Myers, Patrick A. Simmons, and Isaac Megbolugbe, *Immigration and Housing in the United States: Trends and Prospects* (Washington: Fannie Mae Foundation, 1997); Dowell Myers and Seong Woo Lee, "Immigrant Trajectories into Homeownership: A Temporal Analysis of Residential Assimilation," *International Migration Review* 32(1998): 593–625; Richard D. Alba and John Logan, "Assimilation and Stratification in the Homeownership Patterns of Racial and Ethnic Groups," *International Migration Review* 26(1992): 1314–41; William A. V. Clark, *Immigrants and the American Dream: Remaking the Middle Class* (New York: Guilford Press, 2003).

2. Peter H. Rossi and Eleanor Weber, "The Social Benefits of Homeownership: Empirical Evidence from National Surveys," *Housing Policy Debate* 7(1, 1996): 1–36; William Rohe, Shannon Van Zandt, and George McCarthy, "Homeownership and Access to Opportunity," *Housing Studies* 17(1, 2002): 51–61; Richard K. Green and Michelle J. White, "Measuring the Benefits of Homeowning: Effects on Children," *Journal of Urban Economics* 41(1997): 441–61.

3. Many householders will cash in their investment without needing to sell and move. There are a great many financial instruments that make it possible to extract equity from homes while continuing to reside there, including home equity loans and reverse annuity mortgages; for more details, see Gillette Edmunds and Jim Keene, *Retire on the House* (New York: John Wiley, 2006). Maintaining or increasing the value of the home is crucial to these wealth extraction tools.

4. Dowell Myers and Cathy Yang Liu, "The Emerging Dominance of Immigrants in the U.S. Housing Market, 1970–2000," *Urban Policy and Research* 23(3, 2005): 347–65.

5. Pitkin et al., *Immigration and Housing in the United States*; George Masnick, "The New Demographics of Housing," *Housing Policy Debate* 13(2002): 275–321; National Association of Realtors, "Housing Opportunities in the Foreign-Born Market," special report (Washington, D.C.: National Association of Realtors, 2002); "The New Housing Market—And How to Make the Most of It," *Wall Street Journal*, June 14, 2004.

6. Surname data on homebuyers are drawn from DataQuick Real Estate News, news release available at: http://www.dqnews.com/WXNames0802.shtm (accessed March 13, 2006).

7. Haya El Nasser, "Analysis Finds Boom in Hispanics' Home Buying," *USA Today*, May 11, 2006, 1.

8. For example, in data made available for 1998, the Smiths paid a median price of $165,000 for their homes, while the Garcias paid $123,000, the Hernandezes $117,000, and the Martinezes $120,000. Meanwhile, the Lees paid $210,500; data posted by the DataQuick service at http://www.dqnews.com/WXNames0802.shtm (accessed March 13, 2006).

9. These data are drawn from the 2005 American Community Survey, a very large survey designed by the Census Bureau to replace the collection of detailed characteristics previously asked on the census form every ten years.

10. See note 9.

11. A general picture of house price trends in the United States and California is provided in figure A.1. The figures discussed here are computed by a comparison of the 2005 data in table 11.1 with similar data compiled from the 2000 census (data not shown).

12. Data are drawn from Census 2000, Summary File 4, table HCT3 (Washington: Census Bureau, 2004).

13. Data are drawn from Census 2000, Summary File 4, table HCT3 (Washington: Census Bureau, 2004).

14. My principal assistant in this research has been Sung Ho Ryu, a doctoral student in urban planning. The American Housing Survey (AHS) tracks a panel of houses and their occupants and fields interviews every two years. We compiled a series of interviews for each house in the sample and coded the instances when it appeared the prior occupant had vacated. The rate of departure could be calculated based on the occupant's characteristics in the prior interview. In a separate approach not based on a panel of houses, we used census data to estimate departures in two ways. First, recent buyers who were previously homeowners were said to also be sellers. (Repeat buyers were estimated based on ratios separately tabulated from the AHS.) The second way was especially useful at older ages: we measured the shrinkage of the cohort of homeowners between 1990 and 2000, say from ages fifty-five to sixty-four and from ages sixty-five to seventy-four. Those terminations could be due to migration out of state, departure to rental units or nursing homes, or death. We summed the incidents of selling or other termination and then divided that figure by the average number of people in the cohort over the decade. Although the results are remarkably similar, the census method is more effective at capturing terminations of occupancy near the end of life. And unlike the AHS, it also enabled us to identify the state of California.

15. It is important to note that this is a per capita model. The rates are expressed per 100 population, not per household. This is necessary to take account of the substantial changes in household size that occur through marriage, divorce, and widowhood. It bears mentioning that these rates for California residents are lower than in the nation as a whole. They also peak at a slightly older age in California. The buying rates reach 3.6 per 100 population among residents ages thirty to thirty-four in the United States.

16. The findings from the AHS analysis described in note 14 are almost identical on this: sell rates remain constant for forty years at around 2 percent, and buy rates cross over in the fifties.

17. The projection is carried out by applying the rates of buying and selling shown in figure 11.2 to population projections of the number of California residents in each age and racial-ethnic group in 2020. Projections prepared by the California Department of Finance in 2004 are selected for this purpose.

18. N. Gregory Mankiw and David Weil, "The Baby Boom, the Baby Bust, and the Housing Market," *Regional Science and Urban Economics* 19(1989): 235–58.

19. John Pitkin and Dowell Myers, "The Specification of Demographic Effects on Housing Demand" *Journal of Housing Economics* 3 (1994): 240–50.

20. Dowell Myers and John Pitkin, "Evaluation of Price Indices by a Cohort Method," *Journal of Housing Research* 6(1995): 497–518.

21. Data are drawn from the 1990 census, summary file 3, table H013, and the 2000 census, summary file 4, table HCT3.

22. The Census Bureau terms the head of household "the householder" and allows only one per household. However, in married couples, both husband and wife can be considered equally the household head, and for purposes of assessing the housing that spouses occupy together, it makes sense to count both spouses in the analysis.

23. A custom tabulation from the American Housing Survey shows that, of homes sold by elderly homeowners between 2001 and 2003, 29.4 percent were purchased by buyers under age thirty-five, and 24.9 percent were purchased by buyers ages thirty-five to forty-four. Buyers in the older age group generally purchase higher-priced homes than the younger buyers, and so they could be considered better prospects to pay a favorable price to elderly sellers.

24. Asians' high homeownership rate is partly attributed to unusually high educational attainment (controlled for here) or their patterns of saving and wealth-sharing within families. The highest homeownership rate is found among Chinese of Taiwanese origin; see Gary Painter, Lihong Yang, and Zhou Yu, "Heterogeneity in Asian American Homeownership: The Impact of Household Endowments and Immigrant Status," *Urban Studies* 40(3, 2003): 505–30, and Zhou Yu, "A Different Path to Homeownership: The Case of Taiwanese Immigrants in Los Angeles," *Housing Studies* 21(4, 2006): 555–84.

25. This surprising degree of homeownership attainment among Latinos, despite their low education, was highlighted by Dowell Myers and Seong Woo Lee, "Immigrant Trajectories into Homeownership: A Temporal Analysis of Residential Assimilation," *International Migration Review* 32(1998): 593–625.

26. The reliability of these self-reports of house value may seem surprising, but it has been repeatedly verified in tests that compare the reported value to estimates by independent appraisers or by subsequent sales prices.

Appendix A

1. Employment growth figures are from the historical data files of the Employment Development Department of the State of California, available at California LaborMarketInfo: http://www.labormarketinfo.edd.ca.gov/.

2. Dowell Myers and Julie Park, "The Great Housing Collapse in California," *Housing Facts and Findings* (Fannie Mae Foundation, 2002).

3. Deborah Reed, "Recent Trends in Income and Poverty," *California Counts: Population Trends and Profiles* (Public Policy Institute of California) 5(3, February 2004).

4. Reed, Deborah, *California's Rising Income Inequality: Causes and Concerns* (San Francisco: Public Policy Institute of California, 1999). S. Karthick Ramakrishnan and Hans P. Johnson, "Second-Generation Immigrants in California," *California Counts: Population Trends and Profiles* (Public Policy Institute of California) 6(4, May 2005).

5. California Association of Realtors, "2005 California Housing Market: Annual Historical Data Summary," available at: www.car.org.

Appendix B

1. Given the binary nature of the dependent variable, a more statistically efficient design would be to utilize logistic regression. For that purpose, the survey result is transformed to the log of the odds of a positive response, where the latter is the ratio of yes to no rather than yes relative to the total. Although logistic and linear probability regressions yield similar statistical conclusions, logistic regression is preferred in cases where the outcome variable has a mean that lies near the extremes, either zero or one. Given that the mean responses for our outcome variables lie in the midrange, between 0.30 and 0.70, this concern is less warranted. Moreover, the coefficients of the linear probability model are directly interpretable as percentage increases in voting support. Accordingly, we utilize the linear probability specification to facilitate better comprehension by the readers.

References

Alba, Richard D. 1985. *Italian Americans: Into the Twilight of Ethnicity.* Englewood Cliffs, N.J.: Prentice-Hall.

Alba, Richard D., and John Logan. 1992. "Assimilation and Stratification in the Homeownership Patterns of Racial and Ethnic Groups." *International Migration Review* 26: 1314–41.

Alba, Richard, John Logan, Amy Lutz, and Brian Stults. 2002. "Only English by the Third Generation? Loss and Preservation of the Mother Tongue Among the Grandchildren of Contemporary Immigrants." *Demography* 39(3): 467–84.

Alba, Richard D., and Victor Nee. 2003. *Remaking the American Mainstream: Assimilation and Contemporary Immigration.* Cambridge, Mass.: Harvard University Press.

Baldassare, Mark. 1998a. Statewide survey (no title). San Francisco: Public Policy Institute of California (April).

———. 1998b. *When Government Fails: The Orange County Bankruptcy.* Berkeley: University of California Press.

———. 2002. *A California State of Mind: The Conflicted Voter in a Changing World.* Berkeley: University of California Press.

———. 2003. "Statewide Survey: Special Survey on the California State Budget." San Francisco: Public Policy Institute of California (2003).

———. 2004a. "Special Survey on Californians and the Future: PPIC Statewide Survey." San Francisco: Public Policy Institute of California (August).

———. 2004b. "Statewide Survey: Californians and Their Government." San Francisco: Public Policy Institute of California (February).

———. 2005. "Special Survey on Population." San Francisco: Public Policy Institute of California (December).

———. 2006a. "PPIC Statewide Survey: Special Survey on Education." San Francisco: Public Policy Institute of California (January).

————. 2006b. "PPIC Statewide Survey: Special Survey on the California State Budget." San Francisco: Public Policy Institute of California (February).

Barbour, Elisa, and Paul G. Lewis. 2005. *California Comes of Age: Governing Institutions, Planning, and Public Investments.* San Francisco: Public Policy Institute of California.

Baron, Jonathan, and Ed McCaffery. 2006. "Starving the Beast: The Psychology of Budget Deficits." Paper presented to the conference "Fiscal Challenges: An Interdisciplinary Approach to Budget Policy." University of Southern California Gould School of Law.

Baum, Howell. 1999. "Forget to Plan." *Journal of Planning Education and Research* 19: 2–14.

Bean, Frank D., and Gillian Stevens. 2003. *America's Newcomers and the Dynamics of Diversity.* New York: Russell Sage Foundation.

Bean, Frank D., Jennifer Lee, Jeanne Batalova, and Mark Leach. 2005. "Immigration and Fading Color Lines in America." In *The American People: Census 2000,* edited by Reynolds Farley and John Haaga. New York: Russell Sage Foundation.

Bean, Frank D., Robert G. Cushing, Charles Haynes, and Jennifer V. W. Van Hook. 1997. "Immigration and the Social Contract." *Social Science Quarterly* 78(2): 249–68.

Bengston, Vern L. 1993. "Is the 'Contract Across Generations' Changing? Effects of Population Aging on Obligations and Expectations Across Age Groups." In *The Changing Contract Across Generations,* edited by Vern L. Bengston and W. Andrew Achenbaum. New York: Aldine de Gruyter.

Bensimon, Estela Mara. 2004. "The Diversity Scorecard: A Learning Approach to Institutional Change." *Change* (January–February): 44–52.

Bommier, Antoine, Ronald Lee, Timothy Miller, and Stephane Zuber. 2004. "Who Wins and Who Loses? Public Transfer Accounts for U.S. Generations Born 1850 to 2090." NBER working paper 10969. Cambridge, Mass.: National Bureau of Economic Research (December).

Boyer, Ernest L. 1990. *Scholarship Reconsidered: Priorities of the Professoriate.* Princeton, N.J.: Carnegie Foundation.

Brady, Henry, Michael Hout, and Jon Stiles. 2005. *Return on Investment: Educational Choices and Demographic Change in California's Future.* Berkeley: University of California, Survey Research Center.

Brimelow, Peter. 1996. *Alien Nation: Common Sense About America's Immigration Disaster.* New York: HarperCollins.

Brokaw, Tom. 1998. *The Greatest Generation.* New York: Random House.

Cain, Bruce, Jack Citrin, and Cara Wong. 2000. *Ethnic Context, Race Relations, and California Politics.* San Francisco: Public Policy Institute of California.

California Association of Realtors. 2005. *2005 California Housing Market Annual Historical Data Summary.* Los Angeles: California Association of Realtors; available at www.car.org.

California Budget Project. 2004. "Boom, Bust, and Beyond: The State of Working California." Special report. Sacramento: California Budget Project.

———. 2006. *Budget Watch.* Sacramento: California Budget Project (March).

Camarillo, Albert M. 2004. "Black and Brown in Compton: Demographic Change, Suburban Decline, and Intergroup Relations in a South Central Los Angeles Community, 1950 to 2000." In *Not Just Black and White: Historical and Contemporary Perspectives on Immigration, Race, and Ethnicity in the United States,* edited by Nancy Foner and George M. Fredrickson. New York: Russell Sage Foundation.

Camarota, Steven A. 1999. "Importing Poverty: Immigration's Impact on the Size and Growth of the Poor Population in the United States." Paper 15. Washington, D.C.: Center for Immigration Studies.

———. 2004. "Economy Slowed, but Immigration Didn't: The Foreign-Born Population, 2000–2004." Backgrounder. Washington, D.C.: Center for Immigration Studies (November).

———. 2005. "Immigration in an Aging Society: Workers, Birth Rates, and Social Security." Backgrounder. Washington, D.C.: Center for Immigration Studies.

Campbell, Paul R. 1996. "Population Projections for States, by Age, Sex, Race, and Hispanic Origin: 1995 to 2025." Report PPL-47. Washington: U.S. Census Bureau, Population Division.

Case, Karl E., and Robert J. Shiller. 2003. "Is There a Bubble in the Housing Market?" *Brookings Papers on Economic Activity,* no. 2: 299–362.

Center for Continuing Study of the California Economy. 2005. "The Impact of Immigration on the California Economy." Report of the California Regional Economies Project. Available at: http://www.labor.ca.gov/panel/ impactimmcaecon.pdf.

Chandler, Charles R., and Yung-mei Tsai. 2001. "Social Factors Influencing Immigration Attitudes: An Analysis of Data from the General Social Survey." *Social Science Journal* 38: 177–88

Chiswick, Barry R. 1991. "Speaking, Reading, and Earnings Among Low-Skilled Immigrants." *Journal of Labor Economics* 9(2): 149–70.

Citrin, Jack, and Benjamin Highton. 2002. *How Race, Ethnicity, and Immigration Shape the California Electorate.* San Francisco: Public Policy Institute of California.

Clark, William A. V. 2003. *Immigrants and the American Dream: Remaking the Middle Class.* New York: Guilford Press.

Clark, William A. V., and Peter A. Morrison. 1995. "Demographic Foundations of Empowerment in Multiminority Cities." *Demography* 32(2): 183–201.

Coleman, David. 2005. "Facing the Twenty-first Century: New Developments, Continuing Problems." In *The New Demographic Regime: Population Challenges and Policy Responses,* edited by Miroslav Macura, Alphonse L. MacDonald, and Werner Haug. New York and Geneva: United Nations.

———. 2006. "Immigration and Ethnic Change in Low-Fertility Countries: A Third Demographic Transition." *Population and Development Review* 32(September): 401–46.

Cotter, David A., Joan M. Hermsen, and Reeve Vanneman. 2005. "Gender Inequality at Work." In *The American People: Census 2000,* edited by Reynolds Farley and John Haaga. New York: Russell Sage Foundation.

Cuomo, Mario. 1974. *Forest Hills Diary: The Crisis of Low-Income Housing.* New York: Random House.

Davis, Mike. 1998. *Ecology of Fear: Los Angeles and the Imagination of Disaster.* New York: Vintage Books.

Day, Jennifer Cheeseman, and Kurt J. Bauman. 2000. "Have We Reached the Top? Educational Attainment Projections of the U.S. Population." Working paper 43. Washington: U.S. Census Bureau, Population Division.

Day, Jennifer Cheeseman, and Kelly Holder. 2004. "Voting and Registration in the Election of November 2002." Current Population Report P20-552. Washington: U.S. Census Bureau (July).

Day, Jennifer Cheeseman, and Eric C. Newburger. 2002. "The Big Payoff: Educational Attainment and Synthetic Estimates of Work-Life Earnings." Current Population Report P23-210. Washington: U.S. Census Bureau.

Department of Homeland Security, Office of Immigration Statistics. 2005. Table 1. *Yearbook of Immigration Statistics: 2004.* Washington: U.S. Government Printing Office.

DeSipio, Louis. 2001. "Building America, One Person at a Time: Naturalization and Political Behavior of the Naturalized in Contemporary American Politics." In *E Pluribus Unum? Immigrant, Civic Life and Political Incorporation,* edited by Gary Gerstle and John Mollenkopf. New York: Russell Sage Foundation.

Dienstag, Joshua Foa. 2006. *Pessimism: Philosophy, Ethic, Spirit.* Princeton: Princeton University Press.

Dionne, E. J. 1992. *Why Americans Hate Politics: The Death of the Democratic Process.* New York: Simon & Schuster.

Duncan, Brian, V. Joseph Hotz, and Stephen J. Trejo. 2006. "Hispanics in the U.S. Labor Market." In *Hispanics and the Future of America*, edited by Marta Tienda and Faith Mitchell. Washington, D.C.: National Academies Press.

Edmonston, Barry, and Jeffrey S. Passel. 1999. "How Immigration and Intermarriage Affect the Racial and Ethnic Composition of the U.S. Population." In *Immigration and Opportunity*, edited by Frank D. Bean and Stephanie Bell-Rose. New York: Russell Sage Foundation.

Edmunds, Gillette, and Jim Keene. 2006. *Retire on the House.* New York: John Wiley.

Edsall, Thomas, and Mary Edsall. 1992. *Chain Reaction: The Impact of Race, Rights, and Taxes on American Politics.* New York: Norton.

Elliott, James. 2006. "Network Saturation and Internal Migration of U.S. Immigrants to and from Leading Gateway Cities." Paper presented to the annual meeting of the Population Association of America, Los Angeles (March 31).

Espenshade, Thomas J., and Katherine Hempstead. 1996. "Contemporary American Attitudes Toward U.S. Immigration." *International Migration Review* 30(2): 535–70.

Farley, Reynolds. 1996a. *The New American Reality: Who We Are, How We Got Here, Where We Are Going.* New York: Russell Sage Foundation.

———. 1996b. "The 1960s: A Turning Point in How We View Race, Gender, and Sexuality." In *The New American Reality: Who We Are, How We Got Here, Where We Are Going.* New York: Russell Sage Foundation.

Fountain, Robert, Marcia Cosgrove, and Petra Abraham Laptalo. 2006. *Keeping California's Edge: The Growing Demand for Highly Educated Workers.* Sacramento: Sacramento State University, Applied Research Center.

Freedman, Russell. 1994. *Kids at Work: Lewis Hines and the Crusade Against Child Labor.* New York: Clarion Books.

Frey, William H. 2002. "Census 2000 Reveals New Native-Born and Foreign-Born Shifts Across U.S." Research report no. 02-520. Ann Arbor: University of Michigan, Population Studies Center.

Frey, William H., and Ross C. DeVol. 2000. "America's Demography in the New Century: Aging Baby Boomers and New Immigrants as Major Players." Working paper 9. Santa Monica: Milken Institute.

Friedman, Benjamin M. 2005. "Meltdown: A Case Study—What America a Century Ago Can Teach Us About the Moral Consequences of Economic Decline." *Atlantic Monthly*, July–August.

Gabriel, Stuart, Joe Mattey, and William Wascher. 2003. "Compensating Differentials and Evolution in the Quality-of-Life Among U.S. States." *Regional Science and Urban Economics* 33(5): 619–49.

Gardner, Howard. 2004. *Changing Minds: The Art and Science of Changing Our Own and Other People's Minds.* Boston: Harvard Business School Press.

Gerstle, Gary. 2001a. *American Crucible: Race and Nation in the Twentieth Century.* Princeton: Princeton University Press.

———. 2001b. "Liberty, Coercion, and the Making of Americans." *Journal of American History* 84: 524–58.

Gibson, Campbell, and June Kay. 2005. "Historical Census Statistics on Population Totals by Race, 1970 to 1990, and by Hispanic Origin, 1970 to 1990, for Large Cities and Other Urban Places in the United States." Population Division working paper 76. Washington: U.S. Census Bureau, Population Division.

Gibson, Campbell, and Emily Lennon. 1999. "Historical Census Statistics on the Foreign-Born Population of the United States, 1850–1990." Population Division working paper 29. Washington: U.S. Census Bureau, Population Division.

Glassner, Barry. 1999. *The Culture of Fear: Why Americans Are Afraid of the Wrong Things.* New York: Basic Books.

Gleason, Philip. 2001. "Sea Change in the Civic Culture in the 1960s." In *E Pluribus Unum? Contemporary and Historical Perspectives on Immigrant Political Incorporation,* edited by Gary Gerstle and John Mollenkopf. New York: Russell Sage Foundation.

Glendon, Mary Ann. 2006. "Principled Immigration." *First Things* 164(June/July): 23–26.

Government Accountability Office. 2006. "The Nation's Long-Term Fiscal Outlook, September 2006 Update: The Bottom Line—Today's Fiscal Policy Remains Unsustainable." Publication number GAO-06-1077R. Washington: Government Accountability Office.

Green, Richard K., and Michelle J. White. 1997. "Measuring the Benefits of Home-owning: Effects on Children." *Journal of Urban Economics* 41: 441–61.

Greenberg, Stanley B. 1996a. "A New Contract?" In *Middle-Class Dreams: The Politics and Power of the New American Majority.* New Haven: Yale University Press.

———. 1996b. *Middle-Class Dreams: The Politics and Power of the New American Majority.* New Haven: Yale University Press.

Guerra, Fernando J., and Dwaine Marvick. 1986. "Ethnic Officeholders and Party Activists in Los Angeles County." Working paper, Institute for Social Science Research. Los Angeles: University of California, Los Angeles.

Hanak, Ellen, and Mark Baldassare, eds. 2005. *California 2025: Taking on the Future.* San Francisco: Public Policy Institute of California.

Hansen, John Mark. 1998. "Individuals, Institutions, and Public Preferences over Public Finance." *American Political Science Review* 92(3): 513–31.

Harter, Carl L. 1977. "The 'Good Times' Cohort of the 1930s: Sometimes Less Means More (and More Means Less)." *PRB Report* 3(3): 1–4.

Harwood, Stacy, and Dowell Myers. 2002. "The Dynamics of Immigration and Local Governance in Santa Ana: Neighborhood Activism, Overcrowding, and Land-Use Policy." *Policy Studies Journal* 30(1): 70–91.

Haubert, Jeannie, and Elizabeth Fussell. 2006. "Explaining Pro-Immigrant Sentiment in the U.S.: Social Class, Cosmopolitanism, and Perceptions of Immigrants." *International Migration Review* 40(Fall): 489–507.

Hayes-Bautista, David E. 2004. *La Nueva California: Latinos in the Golden State.* Berkeley: University of California Press.

Hayes-Bautista, David E., Werner O. Schink, and Jorge Chapa. 1988. *The Burden of Support: Young Latinos in an Aging Society.* Palo Alto: Stanford University Press.

Heuser, Robert L. 1976. *Fertility Tables for Birth Cohorts by Color: United States, 1917–73.* Rockville, Md.: U.S. National Center for Health Statistics.

Hirschman, Albert O. 1970. *Exit, Voice, and Loyalty: Responses to Decline in Firms, Organizations, and States.* Cambridge, Mass.: Harvard University Press.

Hirschman, Charles, Richard Alba, and Reynolds Farley. 2000. "The Meaning and Measurement of Race in the U.S. Census: Glimpses into the Future." *Demography* 37(3): 381–93.

Hobbs, Frank, and Nicole Stoops. 2002. *Demographic Trends in the Twentieth Century.* Publication CENSR-4. Washington: U.S. Census Bureau.

Hofstadter, Richard. 1955. *Social Darwinism in American Thought.* Rev. ed. Boston: Beacon Press.

Hollmann, Frederick W., Tammany J. Mulder, and Jeffrey E. Kallan 2000. "Methodology and Assumptions for the Population Projections of the United States: 1999 to 2100." Population Division working paper 38. Washington: U.S. Census Bureau, Population Division.

Hood, M. V., and Irwin L. Morris. 2000. "'Brother, Can You Spare a Dime?' Racial-Ethnic Context and the Anglo Vote on Proposition 187." *Social Science Quarterly* 81(1): 194–206.

Hopkins, Lewis D., and Marisa Zapata, eds. 2007. *Engaging Our Futures: Forecasts, Scenarios, Plans, and Projects.* Cambridge, Mass.: Lincoln Institute for Land Policy.

Hughes, Mary Elizabeth, and Angela O. Rand. "The Lives and Times of the Baby

Boomers." In *The American People: Census 2000*, edited by Reynolds Farley and John Haaga. New York: Russell Sage Foundation.

Hunter, James Davison. 1992. *Culture Wars: The Struggle to Define America.* New York: Basic Books.

Huntington, Samuel. 2004a. *Who Are We? The Challenges to America's National Identity.* New York: Simon & Schuster.

———. 2004b. "The Hispanic Challenge." *Foreign Policy*, March–April.

Iowa State University. 2001. *The Impact of Immigration on Small to Midsize Iowa Communities: A Citizen's Guide for Change.* Ames: Iowa State University.

Isserman, Andrew. 1984. "Projection, Forecast, and Plan." *Journal of the American Planning Association* 50(1984): 208–10.

Johnson, Hans. 1996. *Undocumented Immigration to California: 1980 to 1993.* San Francisco: Public Policy Institute of California.

———. 2005. "California's Population in 2025." In *California 2025: Taking on the Future*, edited by Ellen Hanak and Mark Baldassare. San Francisco: Public Policy Institute of California.

Johnson, Hans, and Richard Lovelady. 1995. "Migration Between California and Other States: 1985–1994." Sacramento: California Department of Finance, Demographic Research Unit, and California State Library, California Research Bureau.

Kelly, Patrick J. 2005. *As America Becomes More Diverse: The Impact of State Higher Education Inequality.* Boulder, Colo.: National Center for Higher Education Management Systems.

Kennedy, David M. 1999. *Freedom from Fear: The American People in Depression and War, 1929-1945.* New York: Oxford University Press.

Kennedy, John F. 1963. Speech delivered in Pueblo, Colorado, August 17, 1962. In *Public Papers of the Presidents: 1962.* Washington: Office of the Federal Register.

Kent, Mary M., and Carl Haub. 2004. "Global Demographic Divide." *Population Bulletin* (December). Washington, D.C.: Population Reference Bureau, available at: http://www.prb.org.

Keyfitz, Nathan. 1987. "The Social and Political Context of Population Forecasting." in *The Politics of Numbers*, edited by William Alonso and Paul Starr. New York: Russell Sage Foundation.

Kinsella, Kevin, and David R. Phillips. 2005. "Global Aging: The Challenge of Success." *Population Bulletin* (March). Washington, D.C.: Population Reference Bureau, available at: http://www.prb.org.

Kotlikoff, Laurence J., and Scott Burns. 2005. *The Coming Generational Storm: What*

You Need to Know About America's Economic Future. Cambridge, Mass.: MIT Press.

Kotlikoff, Laurence J., and Jagdeesh Gokhale. 1994. "Passing the Generational Buck." *The Public Interest*, Winter 1994, 73–81.

Kritz, Mary M., and Douglas T. Gurak. 2005. "Immigration and a Changing America." In *The American People: Census 2000*, edited by Reynolds Farley and John Haaga. New York: Russell Sage Foundation.

Lakoff, George. 2004. *Don't Think of an Elephant! Know Your Values and Frame the Debate.* White River Junction, Vt.: Chelsea Green Publishing.

Lee, Ronald, Sang-Hyop Lee, and Andrew Mason. 2006. "Charting the Economic Life Cycle." NBER working paper 12379. Cambridge, Mass.: National Bureau of Economic Research (July).

Lee, Ronald, Timothy Miller, and Ryan Douglas Edwards. 2003. *The Growth and Aging of California's Population: Demographic and Fiscal Projections, Characteristics, and Service Needs.* Berkeley: California Policy Research Center.

Lee, Taeku, S. Karthick Ramakrishnan, and Ricardo Ramirez, eds. 2006. *Transforming Politics, Transforming America: The Political and Civic Incorporation of Immigrants in the United States.* Charlottesville: University Press of Virginia.

Lesthaeghe, Ron. 1995. "The Second Demographic Transition in Western Countries: An Interpretation." In *Gender and Family Change in Industrialized Countries*, edited by Karen Oppenheim Mason and An-Magritt Jensen. Oxford: Clarendon Press.

Levy, Frank. 1998. *The New Dollars and Dreams: American Incomes and Economic Change.* New York: Russell Sage Foundation.

Lien, Pei-te, Christian Collet, Janelle Wong, and S. Karthick Ramakrishnan. 2001. "Asian Pacific–American Public Opinion and Political Participation." *PS: Political Science and Politics* 34(3): 625–30.

Light, Ivan. 2006. *Deflecting Immigration.* New York: Russell Sage Foundation.

Lindblom, Charles E., and David K. Cohen. 1979. *Usable Knowledge: Social Science and Social Problem Solving.* New Haven: Yale University Press.

Lindert, Peter H. 2004. *Growing Public: Social Spending and Economic Growth Since the Eighteenth Century.* Volume 1. Cambridge: Cambridge University Press.

Logan, John, and John Mollenkopf. 2004. *People and Politics in America's Big Cities.* New York: Drum Major Institute for Public Policy.

Logan, John R., and Glenna D. Spitze. 1995. "Self-Interest and Altruism in Intergenerational Relations." *Demography* 32(August): 359.

Lopez, Elias, Ginny Puddefoot, and Patricia Gándara, eds. 2000. *A Coordinated Ap-*

proach to Raising the Socioeconomic Status of Latinos in California. Publication CRB-00-003. Sacramento: California State Library, California Research Bureau.

Lopez, Elias, Enrique Ramirez, and Refugio I. Rochin. 1999. *Latinos and Economic Development in California.* Publication CRB-99-008. Sacramento: California State Library, California Research Bureau.

Los Angeles Times and Edison Media Research/Mitofsky International. 2005. *California Opinion Index.* San Francisco: Field Research Corporation (January), table 3.

Lutz, Wolfgang, and Sergei Scherbov. 2006. "Future Demographic Change in Europe: The Contribution of Migration." In *Europe and Its Immigrants in the Twenty-first Century: A New Deal or a Continuing Dialogue of the Deaf?,* edited by Demetrios G. Papademetriou. Washington, D.C.: Migration Policy Institute.

Macura, Miroslav, Alphonse L. MacDonald, and Werner Haug, eds. 2005. *The New Demographic Regime: Population Challenges and Policy Responses.* New York and Geneva: United Nations.

Madrick, Jeffrey. 1995. *The End of Affluence: The Causes and Consequences of America's Economic Dilemma.* New York: Random House.

Malone, Nolan, Kaari F. Baluja, Joseph M. Costanzo, and Cynthia J. Davis. 2003. "The Foreign-Born Population: 2000." Census 2000 brief, C2KBR-34. Washington: U.S. Census Bureau.

Mankiw, N. Gregory, and David Weil. 1989. "The Baby Boom, the Baby Bust, and the Housing Market." *Regional Science and Urban Economics* 19: 235–58.

Martin, Philip. 1995. "Proposition 187 in California." *International Migration Review* 29(1): 255–63.

Martin, Philip, and Elizabeth Midgley. 1999. "Immigration to the United States." *Population Bulletin,* volume 54. Washington, D.C.: Population Reference Bureau.

Masnick, George. 2002. "The New Demographics of Housing." *Housing Policy Debate* 13: 275–321.

Massey, Douglas S. 2005. *Return of the "L" Word: A Liberal Vision for the New Century.* Princeton: Princeton University Press.

Massey, Douglas S., Joaquin Arango, Graeme Hugo, Ali Kouaouci, Adela Pellegrino, and J. Edward Taylor. 1998. *Return to Aztlan: The Social Process of International Migration from Western Mexico.* Berkeley: University of California Press.

Massey, Douglas S., Jorge Durand, and Nolan J. Malone. 2002. *Beyond Smoke and Mirrors: Mexican Immigration in an Era of Economic Integration.* New York: Russell Sage Foundation.

Matsusaka, John G. 2004. *For the Many or the Few: The Initiative, Public Policy, and American Democracy.* Chicago: University of Chicago Press.

McWilliams, Carey. 1949. *California: The Great Exception.* New York: Current Books.

Miller, Arthur H. 1974. "Political Issues and Trust in Government: 1964–1970." *American Political Science Review* (September): 951–70.

Morrison, Peter A. 2001. "A Demographic Perspective on Our Nation's Future: A Documented Briefing." Santa Monica, Calif.: RAND Corporation.

Murdock, Steve H., et al. 2003. *The New Texas Challenge: Population Change and the Future of Texas.* College Station: Texas A&M University Press.

Myers, Dowell. 1999. "Immigration: Fundamental Force in the American City." *Housing Facts and Findings* (Winter): 3–5.

———. 2004. "Accuracy of Data Collected by the Census Question on Immigrants' Year of Arrival." Working paper PDRG04-01. Los Angeles: University of Southern California, School of Policy, Planning, and Development, Population Dynamics Research Group.

———. 2005. "Cohorts and Socioeconomic Progress." In *The American People: Census 2000*, edited by Reynolds Farley and John Haaga. New York: Russell Sage Foundation.

———. 2006. "California and the Third Great Demographic Transition: Immigrant Incorporation, Ethnic Change, and Population Aging, 1970 to 2030." Paper presented to the conference "America's Americans: The Populations of the United States." British Library, London (May 8 and 9).

Myers, Dowell, and Alicia Kitsuse. 2000. "Constructing the Future in Planning: A Survey of Theories and Tools." *Journal of Planning Education and Research* 19: 221–31.

Myers, Dowell, and Seong Woo Lee. 1998. "Immigrant Trajectories into Homeownership: A Temporal Analysis of Residential Assimilation." *International Migration Review* 32(Fall): 593–625.

Myers, Dowell, and Cathy Yang Liu. 2005. "The Emerging Dominance of Immigrants in the U.S. Housing Market, 1970–2000." *Urban Policy and Research* 23(3): 347–65.

Myers, Dowell, and Julie Park. 1997. "Poverty Among Immigrant Cohorts: Improvement or Persistence over Time." Paper presented at the annual meeting of the Population Associate of America. Washington, D.C.

———. 2002. "The Great Housing Collapse in California." *Housing Facts and Findings*. Washington, D.C.: Fannie Mae Foundation.

Myers, Dowell, Julie Park, and Sungho Ryu. 2005. "Dynamics of Immigrant Settlement in Los Angeles: Upward Mobility, Arrival, and Exodus." Final report to the Haynes Foundation, working paper PDRG05-05. Los Angeles: University of Southern California, Population Dynamics Research Group (August 25), available at: http://www.usc.edu/schools/sppd/research/ popdynamics/Myers_Dowell_HaynesFinalReport_083105.pdf.

Myers, Dowell, and John Pitkin. 1995. "Evaluation of Price Indices by a Cohort Method." *Journal of Housing Research* 6: 497–518.

———. 2001. *Demographic Futures for California.* Los Angeles: University of Southern California, School of Policy, Planning, and Development, Population Dynamics Research Group, available at: www.usc.edu/schools/sppd/research/popdynamics.

Myers, Dowell, John Pitkin, and Julie Park. 2004. "California's Immigrants Turn the Corner." Urban Initiative Policy Brief. Los Angeles: University of Southern California.

———. 2005. *California Demographic Futures: Projections to 2030, by Immigrant Generations, Nativity, and Time of Arrival in U.S.: Full Report.* Los Angeles: University of Southern California, School of Policy, Planning, and Development, Population Dynamics Research Group (February), available at: http://www.usc.edu/schools/sppd/research/popdynamics/pdf/CDFFULLreport2005.pdf.

Myers, Dowell, and Lee Menifee. 2000. "Population Analysis." In *The Practice of Local Government Planning,* edited by Charles Hoch, Linda Dalton, and Frank So. Washington, D.C.: International City Management Association.

Myrdal, Gunnar. 1962. *An American Dilemma: The Negro Problem and American Democracy.* New York: Harper & Row.

National Association of Realtors. 2002. "Housing Opportunities in the Foreign-Born Market." Special report. Washington, D.C.: National Association of Realtors.

Neal, Arthur G. 2005. *National Trauma and Collective Memory: Extraordinary Events in the American Experience.* Armonk, N.Y.: M. E. Sharpe.

Neumark, David. 2005. "California's Economic Future and Infrastructure Challenges." In *California 2025: Taking on the Future,* edited by Ellen Hanak and Mark Baldassare. San Francisco: Public Policy Institute of California.

Newman, Katherine S. 1988. *Falling from Grace: Downward Mobility in the Age of Affluence.* Berkeley: University of California Press.

Okihiro, Gary. *Margins and Mainstreams: Asians in American History and Culture.* 1994. Seattle: University of Washington Press.

Osbourne, David, and Peter Hutchinson. 2004. *The Price of Government.* New York: Basic Books.

Painter, Gary, Lihong Yang, and Zhou Yu. 2003. "Heterogeneity in Asian American

Homeownership: The Impact of Household Endowments and Immigrant Status." *Urban Studies* 40(3): 505–30.

Passel, Jeffrey S. 2005. "Unauthorized Migrants: Numbers and Characteristics." Background briefing prepared for the Task Force on Immigration and America's Future. Washington, D.C.: Pew Hispanic Center, Task Force on Immigration and America's Future (June 14).

Passel, Jeffrey S., and Roberto Suro. 2005. "Rise, Peak, and Decline: Trends in U.S. Immigration, 1992–2004." Washington, D.C.: Pew Hispanic Center.

Passel, Jeffrey S., and Wendy Zimmerman. 2001. *Are Immigrants Leaving California?* Washington, D.C.: Urban Institute (April).

Passel, Jeffrey. 2006. "The Size and Characteristics of the Unauthorized Migrant Population in the U.S." Washington, D.C.: Pew Hispanic Center.

Pati, Susmita, Ron Keren, Evaline A. Alessandrini, and Donald F. Schwarz. 2004. "Generational Differences in U.S. Public Spending, 1980–2000." *Health Affairs* 23(5): 131–41.

Pitkin, John, and Dowell Myers. 1994. "The Specification of Demographic Effects on Housing Demand: Avoiding the Age-Cohort Fallacy." *Journal of Housing Economics* 3: 240–50.

Pitkin, John, Dowell Myers, Patrick A. Simmons, and Isaac Megbolugbe. 1997. *Immigration and Housing in the United States: Trends and Prospects.* Washington, D.C.: Fannie Mae Foundation.

Piven, Frances Fox, and Richard A. Cloward. 1997. *The Breaking of the American Social Compact.* New York: New Press.

Platt, Rutherford H. 1999. *Disasters and Democracy: The Politics of Extreme Natural Events.* Washington, D.C.: Island Press.

Population Reference Bureau. 2005. "2005 World Population Data Sheet." Washington, D.C.: Population Reference Bureau; updated figures available at: http://www.prb.org.

Poterba, James A. 1997. "Demographic Structure and the Political Economy of Public Education." *Journal of Policy Analysis and Management* 16(1): 48–66.

Portes, Alejandro, and Richard Schauffler. 1994. "Language and the Second Generation: Bilingualism Yesterday and Today." *International Migration Review* 28(4): 640–61.

Poterba, James A. 1997. "Demographic Structure and the Political Economy of Public Education." *Journal of Policy Analysis and Management* 16(1): 48–66.

Preston, Samuel H. 1984. "Children and the Elderly: Divergent Paths for America's Dependents." *Demography* 21(4): 435–57.

Price, Matthew C. 1997. *Justice Between Generations: The Growing Power of the Elderly in America.* Westport, Conn.: Praeger.

Ramakrishnan, S. Karthick. 2005. *Democracy in Immigrant America: Changing Demographics and Political Participation.* Palo Alto: Stanford University Press.

Ramakrishnan, S. Karthick, and Hans P. Johnson. 2005. "Second-Generation Immigrants in California." In *California Counts: Population Trends and Profiles.* San Francisco: Public Policy Institute of California.

Reed, Deborah. 1999. *California's Rising Income Inequality: Causes and Concerns.* San Francisco: Public Policy Institute of California.

———. 2004. "Recent Trends in Income and Poverty." *California Counts: Population Trends and Profiles.* San Francisco: Public Policy Institute of California.

Reed, Deborah, Laura E. Hill, Christopher Jepsen, and Hans P. Johnson. 2005. *Educational Progress Across Immigrant Generations in California.* San Francisco: Public Policy Institute of California.

Rieder, Jonathan. 1985. *Canarsie: The Jews and Italians of Brooklyn Against Liberalism.* Cambridge, Mass.: Harvard University Press, 1985.

Riis, Jacob A. 1890. *How the Other Half Lives: Studies Among the Tenements of New York.* New York: Charles Scribner's Sons.

———. 1901. *The Making of an American.* New York: Macmillan.

Rodriguez, Clara E. 2000. *Changing Race: Latinos, the Census, and the History of Ethnicity in the United States.* New York: New York University Press.

Rohe, William, Shannon Van Zandt, and George McCarthy. 2002. "Homeownership and Access to Opportunity." *Housing Studies* 17(1): 51–61;

Rossi, Peter H., and Eleanor Weber. 1996. "The Social Benefits of Homeownership: Empirical Evidence from National Surveys," *Housing Policy Debate* 7(1): 1–36.

Rubin, Beth A. 1996. *Shifts in the Social Contract: Understanding Change in American Society.* Thousand Oaks, Calif.: Pine Forge Press/Sage Publications.

Rubin, Lillian B. 1980. *Busing and Backlash: White Against White in an Urban School District.* Berkeley: University of California Press.

Saenz, Rogelio. 2005. "Latinos and the Changing Face of America." In *The American People: Census 2000*, edited by Reynolds Farley and John Haaga. New York: Russell Sage Foundation.

Salins, Peter. 1997. *Assimilation, American Style.* New York: Basic Books.

Samuelson, Robert J. 1995. *The Good Life and Its Discontents: The American Dream in the Age of Entitlement, 1945–1995.* New York: Random House/Times Books.

Sayer, Liana C., Philip N. Cohen, and Lynne M. Casper. 2005. "Women, Men, and Work." In *The American People: Census 2000*, edited by Reynolds Farley and John Haaga. New York: Russell Sage Foundation.

Scammon, Richard M., and Ben J. Wattenberg. 1970. *The Real Majority.* New York: Coward-McCann.

Schneider, Barbara, Sylvia Martinez, and Ann Owens. 2006. "Barriers to Educational Opportunities for Hispanics in the United States." In *Hispanics and the Future of America*, edited by Marta Tienda and Faith Mitchell. Washington, D.C.: National Academies Press.

Schrag, Peter. 2004. *Paradise Lost: California's Experience, America's Future.* Berkeley: University of California Press.

———. 2006. *California: America's High-Stakes Experiment.* Berkeley: University of California Press.

Schwartz, Peter. 1996. *The Art of the Long View: Planning for the Future in an Uncertain World.* New York: Doubleday.

Sears, David O. 1994. "Urban Rioting in Los Angeles: A Comparison of 1965 with 1992." In *The Los Angeles Riots: Lessons for the Urban Future*, edited by Mark Baldassare. Boulder, Colo.: Westview.

Shulock, Nancy, Colleen Moore, and Mary Gill. 2005. *Shared Solutions: A Framework for Discussing California Higher Education Finance.* Policy issue report. Sacramento: California State University, Institute for Higher Education Leadership and Policy.

Siegal, Jacob S., and David A. Swanson, eds. 2004. *The Methods and Materials of Demography.* San Diego: Academic Press.

Skocpol, Theda. 1995. *Protecting Soldiers and Mothers: The Political Origins of Social Policy in the United States.* Cambridge, Mass.: Harvard University Press.

Smith, James P. 2003. "Assimilation Across the Latino Generations." *American Economic Review Papers and Proceedings* 93: 315–19.

Smith, James P., and Barry Edmonston, eds. 1997. *The New Americans: Economic, Demographic, and Fiscal Effects of Immigration.* Washington, D.C.: National Academies Press.

Smith, Rogers M. 1993. "Beyond Tocqueville, Myrdal, and Hartz: The Multiple Traditions in America." *American Political Science Review* 87(3): 549–66.

Sonenshein, Raphael. 1994. *Politics in Black and White: Race and Power in Los Angeles.* Princeton: Princeton University Press.

Starr, Kevin. 2004. *Coast of Dreams: California on the Edge, 1990–2003.* New York: Alfred A. Knopf.

State of California, California Department of Finance, Demographic Research Unit. 1998. "Race-Ethnic Population with Age and Sex Detail, 1970–1989 [and 1990–1999]." Sacramento: California Department of Finance, Demographic Research Unit (December).

———. 2004. "Race-Ethnic Population with Age and Sex Detail, 2000–2050." Sacramento: California Department of Finance, Demographic Research Unit (May).

———. 2005. "Report E-6: County Population Estimates and Components of Change by County: July 1, 2000–2004." Sacramento: California Department of Finance, Demographic Research Unit (February).

Sterne, Evelyn Savidge. 2001. "Beyond the Boss: Immigration and American Political Culture from 1880 to 1940." In *E Pluribus Unum? Contemporary and Historical Perspectives on Immigrant Political Incorporation*, edited by Gary Gerstle and John Mollenkopf. New York: Russell Sage Foundation.

Sum, Andrew, Neeta Fogg, Ishwar Khatiwada, and Sheila Palma. 2004. "Foreign Immigration and the Labor Force of the U.S.: The Contributions of New Foreign Immigration to the Growth of the Nation's Labor Force and Its Employed Population, 2000 to 2004." Project report. Boston: Northeastern University, Center for Labor Market Studies (July).

Suro, Roberto, and Gabriel Escobar. 2006. "2006 National Survey of Latinos: The Immigration Debate." Washington, D.C.: Pew Hispanic Center.

Terkel, Studs. 1986. *The Good War: An Oral History of World War Two.* New York: Pantheon.

Thomson, David W. 1993. "A Lifetime of Privilege? Aging and Generations at Century's End." In *The Changing Contract Across Generations*, edited by Vern L. Bengston and W. Andrew Achenbaum. New York: Aldine de Gruyter.

Throgmorton, James. 1992. "Planning as Persuasive Story Telling About the Future: Negotiating an Electric Power Rate Settlement in Illinois." *Journal of Planning Education and Research* 12: 17–31.

Tienda, Marta. 2002. "Demography and the Social Contract." *Demography.* 587–616.

Tienda, Marta, and Faith Mitchell. 2006. "E Pluribus Plures or E Pluribus Unum?" Introduction. *Hispanics and the Future of America*, edited by Marta Tienda and Faith Mitchell. Washington, D.C.: National Academies Press.

———, eds. 2006. *Multiple Origins, Uncertain Destinies: Hispanics and the American Future.* Washington, D.C.: National Academies Press.

Timpone, Richard J. 1998. "Structure, Behavior, and Voter Turnout in the United States." *American Political Science Review* 92(March): 145–58.

Tocqueville, Alexis de. 1840. "How the Americans Combat Individualism by the Principle of Self-Interest Rightly Understood." *Democracy in America.* Volume 2, section 2, chapter 8.

Toossi, Mitra. 2002. "A Century of Change: The U.S. Labor Force, 1950–2050." *Monthly Labor Review* (May): 15–28.

Tyack, David. 2001. "School for Citizens: The Politics of Civic Education from 1790 to 1990." In *E Pluribus Unum? Contemporary and Historical Perspectives on Immigrant Political Incorporation,* edited by Gary Gerstle and John Mollenkopf. New York: Russell Sage Foundation.

United Nations Population Division. 2000. *Replacement Migration: Is It a Solution to Declining and Aging Populations?* Publication no. ESA/P/WP.160 New York: United Nations.

U.S. Census Bureau. 1975. *Historical Statistics of the United States.* Bicentennial edition. Washington: U.S. Census Bureau.

———. 1993. Census 1990. "Social Characteristics, 1990." Summary file 3 data, reported in DP-2. Washington: U.S. Census Bureau.

———. 2000. Census 2000. Public Use Microdata Sample File. Washington, D.C.: U.S. Census Bureau, Population Division.

———. 2004. "U.S. Interim Projections by Age, Sex, Race and Hispanic Origin." Released March 18. Available at: www.census.gov/lpc/www/usinterimproj.

———. 2005. "Oldest Baby Boomers Turn 60!" *Facts for Features* (special edition). Publication no. CB06-FFSE.01. Washington: U.S. Census Bureau (December 12).

———. "Projections of the Resident Population by Race, Hispanic Origin, and Nativity: Middle Series, 1999 to 2100." Publication NP-T5. Washington: U.S. Census Bureau, Population Division.

U.S. Department of Homeland Security, Office of Immigration Statistics. 2006. *Yearbook of Immigration Statistics: 2005.* Washington: Department of Homeland Security.

van de Kaa, Dirk J. 1987. "Europe's Second Demographic Transition." *Population Bulletin* 42 (March 1987): 3–57.

Vernez, Georges, Allan Abrahamse, and Denise D. Quigley. 1996. *How Immigrants Fare in U.S. Education.* Santa Monica, Calif.: RAND Corporation.

Vernez, Georges, and Lee Mizell. 2000. "Goal: To Double the Rate of Hispanics

Earning a Bachelor's Degree." Report prepared for the Hispanic Scholarship Fund. Santa Monica, Calif.: RAND Corporation.

Waldinger, Roger. 1999. "Network, Bureaucracy, and Exclusion: Recruitment and Selection in an Immigrant Metropolis." In *Immigration and Opportunity: Race, Ethnicity, and Employment in the United States*, edited by Frank D. Bean and Stephanie Bell-Rose. New York: Russell Sage Foundation.

Walker, Alan. 1993. "Intergenerational Relations and Welfare Restructuring: The Social Construction of an Intergenerational Problem." In *The Changing Contract Across Generations*, edited by Vern L. Bengston and W. Andrew Achenbaum. New York: Aldine de Gruyter.

Waters, Mary C., and Tomas R. Jimenez. 2005. "Assessing Immigrant Assimilation: New Empirical and Theoretical Challenges." *Annual Review of Sociology* 31: 105–25.

Yu, Zhou. 2006. "A Different Path to Homeownership: The Case of Taiwanese Immigrants in Los Angeles." *Housing Studies* 21(4): 555–84.

Zarate, Maria Estela, and Harry P. Pachon. 2006. "Perceptions of College Financial Aid Among California Latino Youth." Policy brief. Los Angeles: Tomas Rivera Policy Institute.

Zúñiga, Víctor, and Rubén Hernández-León, eds. 2005. *New Destinations: Mexican Immigration in the United States*. New York: Russell Sage Foundation

Index

Boldface numbers refer to figures and tables.